HUNTERS IN TRANSITION

HUNTERS IN TRANSITION

MESOLITHIC SOCIETIES OF
TEMPERATE EURASIA AND THEIR
TRANSITION TO FARMING

EDITED BY MAREK ZVELEBIL

Department of Archaeology and Prehistory, University of Sheffield

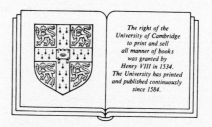

The right of the
University of Cambridge
to print and sell
all manner of books
was granted by
Henry VIII in 1534.
The University has printed
and published continuously
since 1584.

CAMBRIDGE UNIVERSITY PRESS

CAMBRIDGE

LONDON   NEW YORK   NEW ROCHELLE

MELBOURNE   SYDNEY

Published by the Press Syndicate of the University of Cambridge
The Pitt Building, Trumpington Street, Cambridge CB2 1RP
32 East 57th Street, New York, NY 10022, USA
10 Stamford Road, Oakleigh, Melbourne 3166, Australia

First published 1986

Printed in Great Britain at the University Press, Cambridge

British Library cataloguing in publication data

Hunters in transition:
mesolithic societies of temperate Eurasia
and their transition to farming. –
(New directions in archaeology)
1. Agriculture, Primitive – Eurasia
2. Mesolithic period – Eurasia
I. Zvelebil, Marek II. Series
630'.95   GN407.4

Library of Congress cataloguing in publication data

Main entry under title:
Hunters in transition.
(New directions in archaeology)
Includes index.
1. Mesolithic period––Europe––Addresses, essays,
lectures. 2. Mesolithic period––Asia––Addresses,
essays, lectures. 3. Agriculture––Origin––Addresses,
essays, lectures. 4. Neolithic period––Europe––Ad-
dresses, essays, lectures. 5. Neolithic period––Asia––
Addresses, essays, lectures. 6. Europe––Antiquities––
Addresses, essays, lectures. 7. Asia––Antiquities––Ad-
dresses, essays, lectures. I. Zvelebil, Marek.
II. Series.
GN774.2.AlH86 1986   631'.09'01   85-30867

ISBN 0521 26868 0

AN

CONTENTS

CONTRIBUTORS

Takeru Akazawa, The University Museum, The University of Tokyo,
    Hongo 7-3-1, Bunkyo-Ku, Tokyo, Japan.
Paul M. Dolukhanov, Institute of Archaeology, Dvortsovaya nab. 18,
    191041 Leningrad, USSR.
Clive Gamble, Department of Archaeology, University of
    Southampton, Southampton, UK.
J. K. Kozłowski, Institute of Archaeology, Jagellonian University,
    ul. Golebia 11, 31-007 Krakow, Poland.
Stefan K. Kozłowski, pl. Komuny Paryskiej 4 m 32, 01-627 Warzsawa,
    Poland.
James Lewthwaite, School of Archaeological Sciences, University of
    Bradford, Bradford BD7 1DP, UK.
G. N. Matyushin, Institute of Archaeology of the Soviet Academy of
    Sciences, Ulyanova Street 19, Moskva V 39, USSR.
Peter Rowley-Conwy, 147 Victoria Road, Cambridge, UK.
Slavomil Vencl, Institute of Archaeology, Czechoslovak Academy of
    Sciences, Letenskà 4, 11801 Praha 1, Czechoslovakia.
Marek Zvelebil, Department of Archaeology and Prehistory, University
    of Sheffield, Sheffield S10 2TN, UK.

ACKNOWLEDGEMENTS

Many people help in the preparation of an edited volume such as this and to them all I owe my deepest thanks. I am especially grateful to the contributors of this volume for making this venture possible, despite the barriers of language, distance and occasional delays in communication; and to Robin Derricourt, Kate Owen and Peter Richards of Cambridge University Press, who offered advice and encouragement at every stage of the book's preparation. Very special thanks go to Peter Rowley-Conwy, Jim Lewthwaite, Glynis Jones and Paul Halstead for much helpful advice and for many illuminating discussions held with carefree abandon at any time of day or night; to Debbie and Peter Rowley-Conwy for putting me up and for putting up with me on my frequent trips to Cambridge; to Robin Torrence and Robin Dennell for reading and commenting on earlier drafts of my own contributions; and to Jim Lewthwaite for preparing the index. I am grateful to the editors of *Punch* for permission to reproduce the cartoon in the frontispiece. And, above all, I thank my wife Robin, for all the time, patience and support given in the typing, proofreading and editing the text of this volume. Without her help, the volume would not be anywhere near completion, and I still would not know the difference between an uphill struggle and a piece of cake.

Marek Zvelebil
Sheffield
July 1985

THIS BOOK IS DEDICATED TO
GRAHAME CLARK
EMERITUS DISNEY PROFESSOR OF
ARCHAEOLOGY AT CAMBRIDGE,
WHO IN HIS THOUGHTS AND WRITINGS
STALKS THROUGH ITS PAGES,
THE GAMEKEEPER OF THE MESOLITHIC

Introduction: the scope of the present volume

Marek Zvelebil

The conceptual scope

The range of approaches, models and perspectives, currently relating to the mesolithic period and to the agricultural transition leaves some significant conceptual and geographical gaps which provided the initial motive for the writing of this volume.

The origins of agriculture in the western part of the Old World have always been viewed from the Near-Eastern perspective: a view that is not surprising in the light of historical developments. It has meant, however, that the temperate zone, situated on the fringes of the nuclear Near East has tended to be regarded as a recipient of economic and technological innovations, rather than as an independent actor in the process of postglacial adaptation. Although attempts have been made to rectify this situation in respect of later periods (Renfrew 1973), the temperate Mesolithic has so far been unable to get rid of the handicap associated with its origins. Even though the initial contempt for the period as one of cultural degeneration of little scientific interest was gradually replaced by the realisation that the Mesolithic 'was an essential prelude to fundamental advances in the development of culture' (Clark 1980, p. 7), a prelude it remained — a European overture before a Middle-Eastern symphony. The present volume adopts an explicitly temperate mesolithic perspective. Even though the views on the significance of the postglacial hunter-gatherer adaptations differ with individual contributors (i.e.

Chapters 2 to 4), hunter-gatherers in the temperate zone, and their response to the opportunities offered by domestication, form the central theme of the book. This approach is based on two essential propositions: (1) the temperate zone shares a range of conditions and offers a range of choices for the development of postglacial adaptations which differ from the possibilities offered by the 'nuclear areas' of the Middle East, and (2) the range of adaptations developed by the hunter-gatherers of the temperate zone parallel those based on the cultigens and domesticates of the nuclear Near East. This means that hunter-gatherer communities of the temperate zone were coping with problems similar to those encountered by the Near-Eastern populations and that domestication forms one among a number of pathways towards socio-economic intensification (see also Harris 1977; Testart 1982).

The temperate zone, as understood in this volume, encompasses those regions of Eurasia where broadleaved forests and temperate grasslands predominate or predominated during the Holocene. This includes the mixed deciduous/coniferous forests at its northern fringes and the Central-Asian steppes at its southern fringes, but it does not include the temperate, subtropical habitats of the Near East and China (Fig. 1).

The above definition is clearly a simplification and involves some arbitrary decisions. However the dominance of

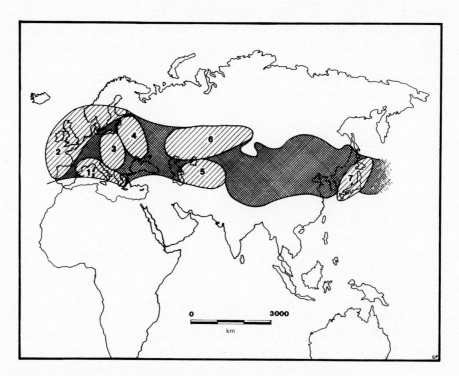

Fig. 1. The extent of the temperate zone and regions investigated in the volume. 1, the Mediterranean (Chapter 5); 2, Atlantic Europe (Chapter 6); 3, Central Europe (Chapter 7); 4, Eastern Europe (Chapter 8); 5, Central Asia (Chapter 9); 6, southern Urals and western Siberia (Chapter 10); 7, Japan (Chapter 11).

the temperate forest and grassland habitats is a good indicator of temperate conditions in their ecological and ecosystemic sense (Dylis and Sukhachev 1964; Holdridge 1967). The nuclear areas of the Near and Far East have been excluded for reasons of historical and cultural development — as the initial centres of domestication — as well as due to their natural conditions. Even though they could be seen as a part of the temperate zone, these areas (1) contain a range of subtropical species (Garrard 1984), (2) are not subject to seasonal fluctuations in the same way as the temperate regions in the more northerly latitudes, and (3) contain, above all a range of potential domesticates and cultigens not available in the more temperate regions further north. Within the scope of this definition, the temperate zone extends roughly between the fortieth and sixtieth degree of latitude in Europe and the thirty-fifth and fifty-fifth degree of latitude in Asia.

That the temperate zone is rich in food for hunter-gatherers has been emphasised by a number of authors (Clarke 1976; Paludan-Müller 1978; Testart 1982; Rowley-Conwy 1983) and in fact most contributors to this volume discuss the high productivity of temperate environments. Most of the productivity figures quoted, however, refer to the general biomass productivity, rather than productivity of particular habitats or of potential food resources. The range, structure, and seasonal variability of food resources are also less well understood. Bearing these gaps in mind, temperate *forest* areas can be distinguished by: (1) marked seasonal variability of resources, caused by variation in temperature, rather than precipitation; (2) low general diversity of animal species, but high

diversity of middle-sized ones; (3) high productivity of coastal and riparian zones; and (4) the presence of plants with storage organs within a mature ecosystem (roots, tubers, nuts). Temperate *grasslands* can be characterised as simple ecosystems of low diversity where seasonal variation is caused by fluctuations in both temperature and precipitation. The food-web structure is characterised by the high density of middle-sized and large herbivores and by high productivity of aquatic resources in riparian environments.

The treatment of hunter-gatherer adaptations within the temperate zone has not been free from geographical prejudice. While several areas, such as northern and western Europe, have been favoured with extensive research and a good publication record, others, such as Eastern Europe or Central Asia, have remained poorly represented in Anglo-American literature, despite the fact that considerable research has been carried out in these areas during the last 20 years. This is partly due to language constraints, partly to the unjustified assumption that nothing of interest can come out of non-British and non-American schools of thought, and partly to a regional parochialism which pervaded prehistoric archaeology until the 1960s. In presenting a more comprehensive coverage of the temperate zone in this volume, an attempt is made to redress this situation and to reduce the geographical elitism which prevailed in the study of postglacial hunter-gatherers until recently.

Despite the fact that the late mesolithic and early neolithic periods are related in many ways, despite the indications that the transition from the former to the latter was much more gradual than previously thought, and despite the fact that one cannot understand the transition without understanding the state of hunter-gatherer adaptations that preceded it, the mesolithic and neolithic periods outside the nuclear Near East have far too often been treated separately in separate publications, with the transition to farming, for the most part, belonging to the Neolithic. As a result, the introduction of farming has often been viewed out of its local mesolithic context and has been attributed to the mechanical forces of migration. In the present volume, an attempt is made to complete the transition to farming within the same covers and to analyse the introduction of farming in light of the conditions which prevailed within the individual regions (Chapters 5 to 11).

The Mesolithic both profited by, and suffered from, its association with the more recent hunter-gatherer adaptations. On the positive side, the work on the recent hunters and gatherers was useful in establishing the broad range of variation and some basic relationships in the organisation of hunter-gatherer soceities (Bettinger 1980; Winterhalder and Smith 1981; Lee and De Vore 1968). On the other hand, the recent work on past hunter-gatherers focused on hunting and gathering as a mode of production, regardless of its historical and chronological context. Such work does not address the specific conditions developing during the early Holocene and culminating in the spread of farming. In contrast, early postglacial hunter-gatherers within their historical perspective form the central theme of this volume.

The organisation of the volume

The volume is divided into two sections. The general section (Chapters 1 to 4) assesses the significance of the mesolithic period and provides a culture-historical background to the chapters dealing with the Mesolithic–Neolithic interface on a regional basis. We have three views represented here. Rowley-Conwy, in Chapter 2, makes a case for the Mesolithic as a period of broad variation in socio-economic organisation, with some intensification taking place for environmental reasons. Gamble, in Chapter 3, presents a rather different case. The watershed for the cultural innovation and conceptual advance is set back to the early Upper Palaeolithic, thus made to coincide with the advent of the modern man, *Homo sapiens sapiens*. The subsequent developments in the Mesolithic are interpreted as elaborations of the existing patterns, rather than qualitative changes. Vencl (Chapter 4) considers the role of hunter-gatherer populations in the transition to farming from the Central-European viewpoint, rather than from the European fringes. Mesolithic populations are seen as having contributed little or nothing to the subsequent cultural development of Europe, with most of the credit going to the immigrant farmers. His view, however, goes beyond the mere assertion that farmers blitzed Europe. He presents a carefully reasoned case in favour of farming colonisation, calling into question some of the basic assumptions of anti-diffusionists.

These three contributions provide a general introduction to the contributions in Part Two, which address the specific conditions of the development of mesolithic societies and the introduction of farming in selected regions of the temperate zone (Fig. 1). Lewthwaite, in Chapter 5, considers the case of the Mediterranean, especially its more temperate, north-western fringes. In Chapter 6, Zvelebil and Rowley-Conwy apply their model of the agricultural transition to the coastal zone of Atlantic Europe. S. K. Kozłowski and J. Kozłowski devote Chapter 7 to the Central-European evidence for the latest hunting–gathering, and the earliest farming, communities. In Chapter 8, Dolukhanov considers the evidence for the development of the postglacial hunter-gatherers in western Russia, while Chapter 9, by the same author, is devoted to the late glacial and early postglacial period in Central Asia.

Research into the early postglacial period in western Siberia is only beginning. Nevertheless, Matyushin, in Chapter 10, considers the evidence from the southern Urals and northern fringes of the Central-Asian steppes, an area that was in many respects crucial as the Eurasian cradle of nomadic pastoralism. At the eastern end of the Eurasian temperate zone, the case of Jomon Japan is reviewed by Akazawa in Chapter 11. Finally, in Chapter 12, an overview deals with the description and the meaning of those patterns that can be discerned across the regions. The regional chapters as well as the overview address the issues which are perceived as central to the problem of the Mesolithic–Neolithic transition: (1) the degree of sameness/difference with the Palaeolithic, (2) the development of sedentary, logistic hunter-gatherers, (3) the role of hunting–gathering populations in the transition to farming, and (4) the persistence of hunting–gathering adaptations in later prehistory.

References

Bettinger, R. L. (1980) 'Explanatory/predictive models of hunter-gatherer adaptation', in M. Schiffer, ed., *Advances in Archaeological Method and Theory*, pp. 189–255, Academic Press, New York.

Clark, J. G. D. (1980) *Mesolithic Prelude*, Edinburgh University Press, Edinburgh.

Clarke, D. (1976) 'Mesolithic Europe: the economic basis', in G. de G. Sieveking, I. H. Longworth and K. E. Wilson, eds., *Problems in Economic and Social Anthropology*, pp. 449–81, Duckworth, London.

Dylis, N. and Sukhachev, V. (1964) *The Fundamentals of Forest Biogeocoenology*, Nauka, Moscow.

Garrard, A. N. (1984) 'The selection of south-west Asian animal domesticates', in J. Clutton-Brock and C. Grigson, eds., *Early Herders and Their Flocks: Animals and Archaeology* 3. International series 202, British Archaeological Reports, Oxford.

Harris, D. R. (1977) 'Alternative pathways towards agriculture', in C. Reed, ed., *Origins of Agriculture*, pp. 179–223, Mouton, The Hague.

Holdridge, L. R. (1967) *Life Zone Ecology*, Tropical Science Center, Costa Rica.

Lee, R. and DeVore, I. (eds.) (1968) *Man the Hunter*, Aldine, Chicago.

Paludan-Müller, C. (1978) 'High Atlantic food gathering in north-western Zealand, ecological conditions and spatial represen-tation', in K. Kristiansen and C. Paludan-Müller, eds., *New Directions in Scandinavian Archaeology*, pp. 120–57, Danish Museum, Copenhagen.

Renfrew, A. C. (1973) *Before Civilisation*, Jonathan Cape, London.

Rowley-Conwy, P. (1983) 'Sedentary hunters: the Ertebølle example', in G. Bailey, ed., *Hunter-Gatherer Economy in Prehistory*, pp. 111–26, Cambridge University Press, Cambridge.

Testart, A. (1982) *Les Chasseurs-Cueilleurs ou L'Origine des Inégalités*, Société d'Ethnographie, Paris.

Winterhalder, B. and Smith, E. A. (eds.) (1981) *Hunter-Gatherer Foraging Strategies*, Chicago University Press, Chicago.

PART ONE

The mesolithic context of the transition to farming

Chapter 1

Mesolithic prelude and neolithic revolution

Marek Zvelebil

Mesolithic as a concept

For at least 60 years the postglacial hunter-gatherer cultures in Europe have been referred to as the Mesolithic, yet the meaning of the term has been a subject of debate since its inception. The concept was first introduced by Westropp in 1872 and then again by Brown in 1893, but it did not gain a measure of acceptance until the 1920s and 1930s (Macalister 1921; Burkitt 1925; Clark 1932, 1936). Originally intended to replace the previously postulated hiatus between the Old Stone Age and the New, this Cinderella of the Three Age system was born as a term of convenience, never fully gaining the status of a concrete stage in the evolution of mankind. Even as a stop-gap, the idea was not accepted by everyone: the apparent impoverishment of the period challenged the prevailing Victorian notions about social evolution, both Spencerian (de Mortillet 1883; Dawkins 1894; MacCurdy 1924; Osborn 1918) and Marxist (Childe 1925, 1935; Marrists in the Soviet Union). When Childe (1947) finally recognised the existence of the mesolithic period in the second edition of *The Dawn of European Civilisation*, he felt obliged to emphasise the chronological as opposed to the substantive nature of the period, while in the Soviet Union, the Mesolithic was not fully recognised until recently (Gurina 1966; Matyushin 1976).

The shift from evolutionary to historical and anthropological perspectives in the 1920s and 1930s brought to light the relative nature of the epochs within the Three Age System and effectively demolished the notion of absolute stages in the development of mankind. For the Mesolithic, this meant that the period retained its low status as a chronological stop-gap, although, with the removal of the unilinear evolutionary framework, it came to be more readily recognised. This ambivalent situation was well captured in the careful definition of the Mesolithic by Grahame Clark in 1936:

> In employing this term nothing more is implied than that the Mesolithic flourished in the main between the Palaeolithic and Neolithic civilisations in point of time; it may be emphasised that it is not intended to suggest an evolutionary stage between the two (*ibid*. 1936, p. xiv).

Despite the early work by Grahame Clark (1932, 1934, 1936) describing the cultures of the period and subsequently their economic and ecological context (*ibid*. 1946, 1948*a, b*, 1952, 1954), the Mesolithic was slow to attract attention as a period of importance. The retention of prejudices towards recent hunter-gatherers, itself a consequence of the European colonial expansion, and the poverty of archaeological evidence, strongly reinforced the view that the Mesolithic was a period of degeneration and decline (see Rowley-Conwy, Chapter 2; Clark 1978, 1980; Dennell 1985). As Clark (1978, p. 3) noted, 'It seemed happily symbolic that the new age should be represented by microliths, whose diminutive size neatly suggested their historical insignificance'.

During more recent years, the status of postglacial hunter-gatherer cultures received more recognition. Several developments combined to produce this change in attitude: (1) the discovery and excavation of mesolithic sites, most notably Star Carr (Clark 1954), with rich organic material which complemented the lithic industries, (2) the full realisation of the range and variety of recent hunter-gatherer adaptations, and (3) the replacement of the notion of cultural progress – an heir to the unilinear evolutionary views – by a more flexible concept of adaptation as a measure of cultural competence. Thus even technologically and socially simple cultures could now be perceived as 'successful' and effective within their niche.

With the volume of research increasing, however, the characteristics which were used to define the Mesolithic as a separate period began to dissipate. Thus the older chronological boundary of the period, the supposedly rapid break between the Pleistocene and the Postglacial, is now more likely to have been a gradual transition, lasting some 4000 years (Dennell 1983). Correspondingly, the change from the Upper Palaeolithic to the Mesolithic has been noted as more gradual than previously thought, with some 'mesolithic' attributes, such as microliths, occurring in the Magdalenian and other late palaeolithic cultures of the Ice Age, while other traditions, such as the Epigravettian, persisted in some areas into postglacial times with their palaeolithic features intact. At the more recent end of the period, polished tools and ceramics, traditionally regarded as a hallmark of the Neolithic, were

discovered in otherwise 'mesolithic' contexts, that is in association with microlithic assemblages and wild fauna. Finally, husbandry practices, which amounted to some form of domestication, are now thought to have been carried out in contexts regarded as mesolithic on geographical and artefactual grounds in that they were postglacial but pre-Neolithic. There is a large amount of variability, therefore, among early postglacial cultures and only some fit the original view of the Mesolithic as defined chronologically. Others are more palaeolithic in their character, or they exhibit one or the other principal 'neolithic' features: pottery or domestication.

Pigeon-holing variability is a hard job, and one likely to result in confusion. This is exactly what happened to the Mesolithic. Some authors have recently questioned the validity of the whole concept, showing the inclination to discard it as outdated and redundant (i.e. Dennell 1983; Gamble, Chapter 3); others attempted to endow it with a meaning other than chronological. These two opposing trends have resulted in the currently unsatisfactory situation, marked by several competing definitions for the Mesolithic, based on the presence/absence of controversial markers of the mesolithic and the neolithic periods (Tables 1 and 2).

Mellars (1981) tried to initiate a debate on the subject, which, regrettably has not been taken up. However, his attempt to define the Mesolithic on strictly chronological grounds as a period beginning at 10 000 BP must be rejected as being meaningless in terms of the cultural variation or behavioural patterns which characterise the early postglacial period. The problem appears to rest in finding a set of attributes which would occur within, but not outside, chronologically discrete boundaries. Attempts at finding such attributes, however, would inevitably result in barking up the tree of Victorian evolutionary idealism. Whatever the views on the definition of the Mesolithic, the cultural variability during the postglacial cannot be forced into a shopping-list definition of a period defined on a presence/absence basis.

If the concept of the Mesolithic is to be retained at all, as I believe it should, it should be a deliberately broad, yet socio-economically meaningful, definition. In the present volume, different authors use different definitions (see Tables 1 and 2) in recognition of the fact that we have yet to find a generally acceptable meaning for the Mesolithic. I would, however, propose the following notions as contributing to a useful definition of the concept: (1) the Mesolithic describes a historical development based on reconstruction from archaeological data; a particular condition in the evolution of human culture, which did not occur prior to the evolution of *Homo sapiens sapiens* and which is also different from ethnographically known hunter-gatherers; (2) in ecological terms, the Mesolithic represents cultural adaptations to temperate conditions within a hunting-gathering mode of subsistence[1] in the northern regions of the Old World; and (3) although farming originated in the Mesolithic, the Mesolithic does not form a chronological stage between the Palaeolithic and the Neolithic. In many regions of boreal and temperate Eurasia its

Table 1. *Different definitions of the Mesolithic*

=====

J. G. D. Clark (1932, p. xiv): A term of chronological significance denoting cultures that flourished between the Palaeolithic and Neolithic in point of time.

J. G. D. Clark (1962, p. 100): Cultural adaptations by the resident hunter-gatherer societies to the environmental changes of the early post-pleistocene period.

Binford (1968, p. 317): Mesolithic characterised by (1) major shift in the centres of population growth in Western Europe, (2) major change in the form of stone tools, (3) greater geographical variety in cultural remains, (4) marked increase in the exploitation of aquatic resources and wild fowl, (5) a shift towards small game hunting, (6) cultural degeneration when compared with the Upper Palaeolithic.

Mellars (1981, p. 15): Strict chronological definition, with the start of the Mesolithic set at 10 000 BP.

Newell (1984, p. 71): 'The Mesolithic period is the chronicle of the adaptation of the late glacial population of Western Europe to the rapid ecological change which marked the pleistocene/holocene border.'

Dolukhanov (1979; Chapters 8 and 9, this volume; and East European scholars in general): Non-ceramic cultures equal Mesolithic, ceramic cultures equal Neolithic, regardless of economy.

Kozłowski, S. K. and Kozłowski, J. (1978; Chapter 7, this volume): Mesolithic is defined
(a) chronologically, 8000–4350 bc;
(b) ecologically, as postglacial adaptations caused by the replacement of tundra by forest formations;
(c) economically, as practising hunting, fishing and gathering;
(d) culturally, as microlithic assemblages with some degree of geometric standardisation of the industry.

Table 2. *Terminology applied to postglacial assemblages with some mesolithic characteristics: (microlithic toolkit, unpolished stone axes, absence of pottery, hunting-gathering economy, early postglacial period)*

=====

Epipalaeolithic: refers mainly to the continuation of the late palaeolithic hunter-gatherer system in the postglacial period. Characterised by assemblages similar to the preceding late Palaeolithic (Kozłowski and Kozłowski, Chapter 7; for further discussion see Rowley-Conwy, Chapter 2).

Protoneolithic: cultures with certain elements of animal husbandry occurring in predominantly food-gathering economies (Kozłowski and Kozłowski, Chapter 7).

Paraneolithic: Pottery-using hunter-gatherer cultures (Kozłowski and Kozłowski, Chapter 7).

Forest Neolithic: Pottery-using, hunter-gatherer cultures, originally identified with the forest zone of Eastern Europe (Sulimirski 1970; Dolukhanov 1979; a term generally accepted in the Soviet Union).

Pre-pottery neolithic: refers to aceramic food-producing cultures, mostly found in the nuclear zone of the Near East.

Subneolithic: refers to formerly food-producing groups that are thought to have subsequently become hunters and gatherers. This is presumed to have taken place in some regions of the boreal zone of Eurasia, at the natural limit of tolerance of cultigens and domesticates (Broadbent 1981).

straints from those encountered by their counterparts in the Old World. Though superficially similar, the development of post-glacial societies in North America differed in several important aspects (Aikens 1981; Bender 1985a).

Obviously, the above is not a perfect definition; the hunter-gatherer nature of the concept is especially open to criticism as ill defined: where does wild resource management end and domestication begin? Nevertheless, it could be argued that within the limits set above, human groups shared a particular way of coping with their social and natural environment which was markedly different from the societies in the New World or those existing out of the reach and the consequences of the last glaciation.

Models of postglacial hunter-gatherers

From the beginning, the mesolithic period tended to be identified with hunter-gatherers, even though it was not originally linked to the hunting-gathering mode of subsistence explicitly. The fortunes of the Mesolithic as a concept, therefore, closely followed the archaeological perception of hunting and gathering societies. At the general level, it is possible to distinguish two approaches: the traditional, and the more recent, affluent hunter-gatherer concept.

The traditional view of hunter-gatherers arose at first from the experience of the colonisation of hunting-gathering

development was simultaneous with that of the agro-pastoral farming further south and was never replaced by the Neolithic, but by the Bronze Age, Iron Age, or even more recent societies. The Mesolithic should be viewed as both the predecessor of, and an alternative to, the neolithic agro-pastoral farming societies.

Essentially, the Mesolithic is a northern Old World temperate and boreal adaptation. Comparable cultural adaptations from the southern hemisphere are best left out of the mesolithic ambit for historical reasons, while in the New World, postglacial societies faced different conditions, which played an important role in their development. The mountain ranges in North America are aligned from north to south, contributing to a markedly different distribution of flora and fauna in temperate North America from that in comparable areas of the Old World. Moreover, North America was colonised by man only recently, late during the last glaciation; consequently, the early postglacial societies in North America must have been facing very different opportunities and con-

societies by the European settlers and then was enhanced by the aftermath of the colonisation. Neither of these two situations did justice to the hunter-gatherer way of life and could not have been representative of the hunter-gatherer condition in general (Sahlins 1974; Dennell 1985). Consequently, the early view of mesolithic hunter-gatherer culture was also the impoverished view: postglacial hunter-gatherers were held to be mobile, egalitarian and opportunistic in their food quest, predatory on their environment and incapable of transforming their way of life beyond their narrow social and economic constraints (viz. the frontispiece). Rowley-Conwy (Chapter 2) shows how this perception of the hunter-gatherer society affected the earlier and some recent interpretations of the Mesolithic.

The traditional view of recent hunter-gatherers came increasingly under fire as various strands of anthropological, ecological and archaeological evidence combined to show the diversity and adaptiveness of hunter-gatherer culture (see Rowley-Conwy, Chapter 2). Although this process was gradual, the publication of *Man the Hunter* (Lee and DeVore 1968) can be taken as a convenient point of departure for the emergence of the 'affluent forager' view (e.g. Suttles 1968; Watanabe 1968). The tenets of this approach are based on the recognition of cultural variability as coping mechanisms in different habitats, of the existence of both mobile and sedentary hunter-gatherers, with various modulations in between, and of social and economic complexity, including techno-economic specialisation, storage and social ranking. So the affluent forager paradigm allows for the existence of much more culturally dynamic, adaptable and socio-economically complex hunter-gatherers than the traditional perspective.

The affluent forager approach engenders the concept of complex foragers. The two terms, however, are not the same. 'Affluence' refers to hunter-gatherer material security and wealth; 'complexity' to their socio-economic organisation and technology. Although most affluent hunting-gathering societies, such as the Northwest Coast Indians, the Ainu, Aleuts and the Amur River groups are also complex by hunter-gatherer standards, there are cases which are said to be merely 'affluent' (e.g. Sahlins 1974) or merely complex (Great Basin Shoshoneans, Maritime Chukchi, Maritime Koryaks, some Eskimo peoples; for further discussion, see Koyama and Thomas 1981; Price and Brown 1985). Although both affluence and complexity are ill-defined terms, complexity is less so and it has greater potential for being detected in the archaeological record.

To date, the most comprehensive attempt to define complex hunting-gathering societies in the ethnographic and archaeological context was made by Testart (1982a, b). In Testart's view, the existence of complex hunter-gatherer societies is contingent on the development of a techno-economic system based on the large-scale storage of food. The fundamental features of such systems also include reduced residential mobility, increased population density, socio-economic differentiation, social division of labour, developed systems of exchange, presence of warfare and intensive ceremonial and social activities.

Although the occurrence of all these attributes are difficult to demonstrate archaeologically, and although the causal links between the various aspects of the system have been criticised by some authors (Hayden 1982; Ingold 1982; Binford 1983), this model of sedentary, logistic hunter-gatherers has obvious implications for the prehistoric hunter-gatherers of the temperate zone. Indeed, most of the ethnographic examples of complex foragers, even though it is not clear whether this complexity arose from affluence or over-crowding (Cohen 1981), come from the coastal regions of the temperate zone (Lee and DeVore 1968; Koyama and Thomas 1981; Testart 1982a; Perlman 1980).

A number of recent studies have attempted to interpret the archaeological remains of temperate hunter-gatherers in the light of a complex hunter-gatherer model (Akazawa 1981; Aikens 1981; Testart 1982a; Rowley-Conwy 1983; King 1978; Yesner 1980, n.d.; Perlman, 1980; Burley n.d.; Price and Brown 1985; Hayden *et al.* 1985). This has met with only partial success, mainly because of the lack of archaeological correlates which would clearly indicate affluence or complexity among prehistoric hunter-gatherers. The sometimes uncritical eagerness with which 'affluent' hunter-gatherers were being discovered prompted some scholars, notably Binford (1983, pp. 199–203), to dismiss the whole idea as a 'Garden of Eden'.

Despite such criticism, the notion of complex hunter-gatherers remains important so long as we define clearly what is meant by complexity (e.g. Price and Brown 1985). In this volume, we adhere to the indices of complexity proposed by Testart (1982a, b) and outlined above. The advantages of the model are clear: it extends the spectrum of potential hunter-gatherer adaptations at the socio-economically complex end of the range, and it is particularly applicable to non-marginal environments such as the temperate zone. The major problem lies in developing a methodology which would test effectively for the indications of complexity in the prehistoric, hunting-gathering context, such as storage, sedentism, surplus production and social ranking.

Models of the transition to farming

At a fine scale of resolution, there are as many approaches to the transition to farming as there are people writing about it. But within a broader perspective, this fragmented picture can be organised into three competing paradigms. Within these, the transition to farming is generally determined by the attitudes towards the hunting-gathering adaptation which preceded it.

The earliest explanation for the transition to farming is based on the notion of agriculture as the superior mode of production, regardless of circumstances. Since the advantages of farming were self-evident, it would be adopted automatically if ecological circumstances were favourable and if the adequate level of knowledge was reached to render some hunter-gatherers 'culturally ready' (e.g. Caldwell 1977). Once converted to farming, these populations would colonise new areas, displacing or absorbing those groups which failed to reach the required level of cultural readiness and remained hunting and gathering. Within this paradigm, knowledge was the limiting factor, and the gradual accumulation of knowledge provided an explanation for the transition to farming. Dating back to Darwin (1868), this view was adopted by Childe (1928) and was implicit in Braidwood's (1958) approach to the problem. Within such a paradigm, it was quite natural that hunter-gatherer territories would be colonised by expanding farming populations or that the surviving foragers would rapidly adopt farming.

Perhaps the most concise statement in favour of the diffusionist approach is Ammerman and Cavalli-Sforza's (1973, 1984) 'wave of advance' model for the spread of farming across Europe. The model, simulating the demic diffusion of farmers, colonising new habitats from the centre of origin in the Near East, is tested against, and found to be compatible with, the actual rate of spread of farming across Europe and with the patterns of genetic variation in European populations. Despite its simplicity and elegance, the model provides no real explanation for the adoption of farming in Europe, while its authors make some untenable assumptions. These include the minimal view of hunter-gatherers (*ibid.* 1984, p. 9), the assumption that the discontinuity in settlement pattern and lithic assemblages between the Mesolithic and the Neolithic are the norm, rather than the exception (*ibid.*, pp. 46–7, 55), the assumption that pottery and food production were introduced simultaneously (*ibid.*, p. 46) and the assumption of little or no overlap between the mesolithic occupation and the onset of early farming (*ibid.*, p. 60). Some of the sites used in recording the rate of spread of farming have no positive evidence for cereals and only a few bones of domesticates in otherwise wild faunal assemblages (*ibid.*, p. 52), while others are clearly hunting-gathering sites without a trace of farming, which have been included in the analysis because of the presence of pottery (i.e. Sarnate and Piestina; *ibid.*, appendix). Because of the underlying assumptions about the poverty of foragers and the dynamism of farming economy, hunter-gatherer populations and their ability to resist farming colonisation are underestimated, while the colonising potential of farmers is probably overestimated (Dennell 1985). Despite these shortcomings, the model amounts to a quantified and well argued, if somewhat biased, case for the introduction of farming to Europe by farmer colonisation.

The palaeo-economic approach, developed by Eric Higgs and his associates (Higgs and Jarman 1969; Higgs 1972; Higgs 1975), though concerned mainly with the methodological issues of early domestication and cultivation, can be said to belong within the scope of the 'knowledge' paradigm (Binford 1983, p. 198). The 'Higgsians' have convincingly argued that domestication was a much more gradual and widespread process than has been previously acknowledged. They can be credited with identifying husbandry practices, such as selective culling or various forms of herd management, which could be interpreted as early domestication. In this sense, they extended the domestication process chronologically into the late glacial and early postglacial period (Legge 1972; Jarman 1972; Sturdy 1975; Bahn 1983; Higgs and Jarman 1972) and geographically to include regions outside the Fertile Crescent in western Asia, the Mediterranean and parts of temperate Europe (Dennell 1983). For the most part, however, they continued to regard domestication as a 'continuously developing natural process of great selective value' (Higgs and Jarman 1972), the advantages of which are self-evident and whose adoption is self-explanatory, and in so doing they merely extended the spatial and chronological range of domestication without providing an adequate explanation of its causes.

The second major school of thought is based on the notion of population–resource imbalance as a direct or an underlying cause of the transition to farming. With the realisation that farming is often a more labour-requiring activity than foraging, leading often to no immediate change in living standards (Clark and Haswell 1967; Lee and DeVore 1968; Binford 1968; Lee 1972, 1979), the status of farming as an inherently superior mode of subsistence was revised. The attention focused on the role of demographic variables and on changes in the natural environment as the two major forces affecting the balance between the population and resources. This led to the generation of a whole series of models of agricultural origins (Binford 1968; Flannery 1969; Harner 1970; Smith and Young 1972; Cohen 1977; Hassan 1978; MacNeish 1977) based on the premise that an unfavourable change in the balance between population and food resources may result in economic intensification and domestication. Disequilibrium between populations and their resources is generally held to occur as a result of population increase, either on a global (Cohen 1977) or regional (Hassan 1981; Binford 1983) scale, or because of a decline in the available resources (Zvelebil 1981; Rowley-Conwy 1983). It has been observed, however, that a range of biological and cultural mechanisms such as marriage rules, birth spacing, and depressed fertility regulate population numbers before catastrophic controls, such as death by starvation, come into effect. Most of these non-castastrophic, selective mechanisms were observed to operate among the mobile hunter-gatherers, thus limiting population growth (Binford 1968; Lee 1972, 1979: for opposite view, see Hassan 1981; Hayden 1981). Binford (1968), Sussman (1972), Lee (1972) and others have argued that most of these controlling mechanisms will be relaxed with the shift to sedentism. Hence sedentism came to be perceived as the crucial link in the shift to farming, responsible for relaxing population controls, which in turn permitted population growth, which would generate the search for more intensive forms of resource use, such as domestication.

The complex forager model forms an integral part of this approach: it was, after all, the appreciation of the complexity of recent hunter-gatherer adaptations that led to the rejection of the inherent superiority of agriculture. As a part of this perspective, sedentism was held to occur in areas of exceptional density of food resources (Rowley-Conwy 1983) or where technological developments, such as intensive food storage, permitted it (Testart 1982*a, b*). The demographic paradigm, then, has the following implications: (1) hunter-gatherers will adopt farming only under pressure and (2) residential permanence is crucial as a bridging mechanism in the transition to farming.

The principal weaknesses of the demographic approach consist in the indiscriminate treatment of human populations as a uniform demographic variable and in failure to estimate effectively from archaeological data crucial parameters such as sedentism, population density, economic productivity and population pressure. Dissatisfaction with the way these parameters were sometimes applied (Bender 1975; Hayden 1975; Cowgill 1975; Bronson 1977; Hassan 1978) has led to the elaboration of demographic perspectives (Hassan 1981; Binford 1983). Following the work by Wobst (1974, p. 76), Newell (1984) considered the implications of increased population density on social evolution and on territorial nucleation during the Mesolithic, while Binford (1983) in presenting his 'packing model' showed how population increase at a regional level could result in more closely spaced bands, the reduction in mobility and resource-use territory, and consequently in an increase in the exploitation of sub-optimal resources. Both of these recent approaches represent a more sophisticated, second generation of models within the demographic paradigm.

Finally, the third paradigm has its roots in social anthropology. It is based on the notion of social competition within and between the individual segments of a hunter-gatherer society. This basic premise led to the generation of several 'social disequilibrium' models (Sahlins 1974; Bender 1978, 1981, 1985*a, b*; Godelier 1977), where farming is adopted as the means of maintaining social control or as a consequence of competition for status, spouses or power. All these forms of competition are expensive in terms of subsistence and require surplus resources, a situation which eventually (for delaying mechanisms, see Sahlins 1974) leads to the adoption of some form of farming as the more intensive means of production than hunting and gathering.

This approach assumes that human society is essentially competitive, where (*a*) competition and disequilibrium are the natural state, (*b*) relations of dominance are latent, and (*c*) egalitarian systems are an exception (Faris 1975; Bender 1978). These basic assumptions have the following implications: one has to accept that human societies are, by and large, non-egalitarian, i.e. that dominance patterns and competition came into existence in the pre-hominid stage and form a part of the baggage that makes humans animal, or one has to explain somehow the evolution of social ranking from the original egalitarian state. The attempts to find the original causes of social intensification failed so far to provide an explicit answer (e.g. Bender 1978, 1981), lending some support to the idea of the inherently non-egalitarian nature of human societies. On a biological time scale of human evolution, it is conceivable that socially egalitarian but biologically competitive species will, at a certain point in their evolution, reinforce patterns of dominance by projecting them to a symbolic level. On the present evidence, symbolic expressions of status date to the Upper Palaeolithic and may be a mark of *Homo sapiens sapiens* in hominid evolution. One then has to explain the development of this behaviour from the Upper Palaeolithic onwards (see Lewthwaite, Chapter 5).

The social disequilibrium paradigm is potentially of great interest to students of the Mesolithic–Neolithic transition. Just as it is difficult to isolate population pressure archaeologically, however, so it is to define operational variables of social competition, ranking and surplus production: we are facing here the same problems as those attendant on the recognition of complex hunter-gatherers in the archaeological record.

The concept of an agricultural frontier

The idea of an agricultural frontier has usually been associated with models of agricultural colonisation, involving advancing farming populations and rapidly disappearing hunter-gatherers. The distinctly mobile character of the frontier is largely due to the adoption of the agricultural expansion of the eighteenth and nineteenth centuries as the historical analogue for the prehistoric event. As Dennell (1985) points out, however, the situation in prehistoric Europe as well as in other areas, would have been very different. Early farming groups would not have had the same technological superiority over the indigenous hunter-gatherers, nor would they be able to attain the same levels of agricultural productivity or population growth as the agricultural colonists of the modern times. Nevertheless, the nature of the agricultural frontier in prehistory, and the impact of early farmers on the resident foraging groups, are widely disputed issues (compare Vencl, Chapter 4, and Dennell, 1985).

A large amount of literature has been written recently on the subject of the agricultural frontier (Thompson 1973; Alexander 1977, 1978; Bohanan and Plog 1967; Miller and Steffen 1977; Lewis 1984; Ammerman and Cavalli-Sforza 1984; Green and Perlman 1985). On the basis of recent ethno-historical data, frontier zones share special features which encourage population growth, extensive system of land-use, frequent relocation of settlement, relaxed social control, sex and age structure biased towards males and younger age groups, low subsistence costs and high labour costs (Thompson 1973; Green 1980). These conditions should argue for the rapid expansion of colonising populations; to what extent these conditions can be applied, however, to the temperate zone in prehistory, remains to be seen.

Perhaps the most simplified version of the agricultural frontier occurs in Ammerman and Cavalli-Sforza's (1973, 1984) 'wave of advance' model, where this complex phenomenon is reduced to the notion of a uniform front of colonists sweeping across Europe in the manner of German

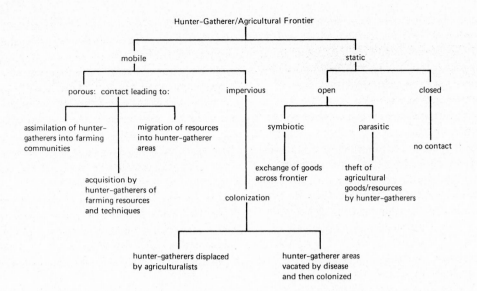

Fig. 1. Dennell's classification of agricultural frontiers (from Dennell 1985).

Panzer divisions (Fig. 2). A more sophisticated version of agricultural advance is characterised by selective colonisation taking place in stages, with frequent halts in the process of expansion. The colonisation is selective in that it proceeds at first along the most fertile regions, leaving other regions unoccupied; secondary colonisation of suboptimal areas takes place only at a later date. This model allows for the existence of hunter-gatherer survivals in regions not initially colonised by farmers, and for the adoption of farming by the local mesolithic groups. This is a much more realistic approach and such regional studies as were carried out support this model (i.e. Kruk 1973). The different rates of advance within this scenario led Alexander (1978) to distinguish 'moving' and 'stationary' frontiers, which were further elaborated by Dennell (1985) to incorporate various degrees of participation by the indigenous hunter-gatherers in the process (Fig. 1). The range of variation described by Dennell is useful in that it illustrates the different mechanisms by which farming could have dispersed through Europe with or without the aid of immigrant farming populations.

The availability model of the transition to farming, put forward by Zvelebil and Rowley-Conwy (1984), represents, at least in some aspects, the extension of this. In our view, the process towards the adoption of farming passes through several forms of frontier situations, which can occur simultaneously in geographical space (Fig. 2). At the same time, the transition to farming, when viewed in terms of the replacement of hunting-gathering adaptations by farming as a way of life, rather than as an introduction of elements of farming economy, is likely to have taken much longer to complete than is usually supposed. So we regard the entire zone of foraging–farming interaction, rather than merely the line of forager–farmer contact, as the frontier.

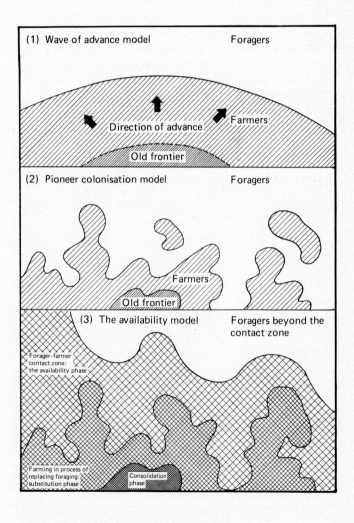

Fig. 2. Spatial models of agricultural frontiers.

In our model, we distinguish three phases of transition, each phase being defined by the relationship between the farming and non-farming elements within a region and by the intensity of farming practices: (1) the availability phase, (2) the substitution phase, and (3) the consolidation phase (Fig. 3).

During the availability phase, farming is known to the foraging groups in question and some exchange of materials and information goes on between farming and foraging settlements, yet farming is not adopted by the hunter-gatherer societies. From this definition it is obvious that the availability phase exists in the early stages of the agricultural frontier, when farmers and foragers are developing contacts but while the two still operate as culturally and economically independent units.

The availability phase ends with the adoption of at least some elements of farming by the foragers, or with the settlement of farmers in the territory hitherto used by hunter-gatherers. Through these two mechanisms, the early frontier zone moves to the adjacent region. The diffusionist model of farming colonisation (Ammerman and Cavalli-Sforza 1971, 1984), based on the notion of inherent farming superiority and rapid dispersal by agricultural colonists, does not pay adequate attention to this phase, since its very existence is not accounted for by the model. In areas where the transition to farming was slow, however, the availability phase might have existed for several hundred years (see Zvelebil and Rowley-Conwy, Chapter 6; Dolukhanov, Chapters 8 and 9).

The substitution phase can have two forms: external, after farmers had moved into the hunting-gathering territory and settled, thus competing with the remaining foragers for land and food resources; and internal, after foragers had added elements of farming to their range of subsistence strategies.

In both cases, competition between two mutually incompatible ways of life is the key concept. In their effort to stress the gradual nature of the transition from foraging to farming, research workers have focused on biological and economic rather than social aspects of the transition, thereby neglecting the incompatible elements within the process (Higgs 1972, 1975). However, it can be shown that farming and foraging compete at several levels: directly for land, food resources and raw materials (Anderson 1976, 1981; Alexander 1978); indirectly for space, access to information, time, manpower and social status (Moore 1981; Bender 1978, 1985*a*; Sahlins 1974).

At an operational level, these incompatible aspects of the foraging—farming interface are responsible for the eventual decline of hunting-gathering groups or for the abandonment of the foraging element in a mixed economy. The substitution phase ends when hunter-gatherer survivals no longer compete with farmers for resources (i.e. whatever foragers remain, they operate in a niche so marginal as to be virtually useless to farmers), or when foraging ceases to be a major contribution to the economy in terms of food supply, organisation of labour and other socio-economic conditions.

The consolidation phase denotes the final stage in the

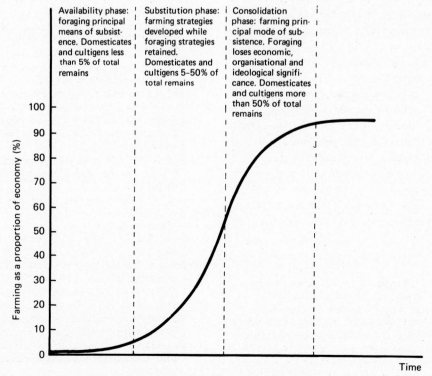

Fig. 3. The availability model of the transition from foraging to farming. The sigmoid shape of the curve represents an idealised situation. In actual situations, the shape of the curve will be determined by the length of the phases.

transition to farming, during which the social and economic structures of the old frontier mature to hinterland conditions. Economically, this is the first stage of a predominantly neolithic economy, marked by both the extensive and intensive growth of food production: having occupied the best soils, the farming settlement extends to new, secondary areas and, having exhausted the possibilities of the extensive form of land-use, more intensive farming practices are employed. The use of wild resources continues only as an emergency strategy or as an industrial activity, designed primarily for the procurement of fur, hides and other non-dietary items. The phase comes to an end when the socio-economic conditions of an area become identical with those of earlier settled areas and the effects of the transition disappear.

Our model does not attempt to find an underlying cause for the transition to farming. Rather, it provides a descriptive framework for the process. This framework stresses the importance of early stages in the transition and emphasises its length. In our view, the adoption of farming must have had a number of causes which were variable from region to region and were contingent on the regional environmental and socio-economic conditions. The regional circumstances of the transition to farming are examined in Chapters 5 to 12.

Conclusions

I have tried to provide a broad theoretical background to the study of postglacial hunter-gatherers in temperate Eurasia and their transition to farming. Most of the models and approaches outlined above have their roots in the anthropology and ethnography of recent hunter-gatherers. When considering the prehistoric hunter-gatherer of temperate Eurasia, however, the anthropological perspective can reveal only part of the story.

Not all the models and approaches offered by anthropology may be relevant to the Mesolithic. The methodology of analysis and of interpretation of material remains which make up the Mesolithic raises problems specific to archaeology and to the early postglacial period in Europe and Asia. Moreover, the historical circumstances of the early postglacial period may have produced conditions which were outside the range of variability accountable for by models derived from anthropology. All these issues must form an integral part of any attempt to understand the material culture and the society of the mesolithic hunter-gatherers and to account for their transition to farming.

Note

1 The distinction between hunting and gathering and farming is in fact poorly researched within the archaeological perspective. On one hand, genetically undomesticated, and therefore morphologically undetectable, animals may have been tended as domesticates; on the other, various forms of herding and plant husbandry may have existed within an essentially hunting-gathering society. In the present definition, the hunter-gatherer mode of subsistence allows for the existence of intensive plant and animal management, carried out within the hunter-gatherer social and economic organisation.

References

Aikens, C. M. (1981) 'The last 10 000 years in Japan and Eastern North America: parallels in environment, economic adaptation, growth of societal complexity and the adoption of agriculture', in S. Koyama and D. H. Thomas, eds., *Affluent Foragers*, pp. 261–74, Senri Ethnological Studies 9, National Museum of Ethnology, Osaka.

Akazawa, T. (1981) 'Maritime adaptation of prehistoric hunter-gatherers and their transition to agriculture in Japan', in S. Koyama and D. H. Thomas, eds., *Affluent Foragers*, pp. 213–60, Senri Ethnological Studies 9, National Museum of Ethnology, Osaka.

Alexander, J. (1977) 'The frontier in prehistory', in J. V. S. Megaw, ed., *Hunters, Gatherers and First Farmers Beyond Europe*, pp. 25–41, Leicester University Press, Leicester.

(1978) 'Frontier studies and the earliest farmers in Europe', in D. Green, C. Haselgrove and M. Spriggs, eds., *Social Organisation and Settlement*, pp. 13–29, BAR International Series 47, British Archaeological Reports, Oxford.

Ammerman, A. J. and Cavalli-Sforza, L. L. (1971) 'Measuring the rate of spread of early farming in Europe'. *Man* 6, 674–88.

(1973) 'A population model for the diffusion of early farming in Europe', in C. Renfrew, ed., *The Explanation of Culture Change*, pp. 343–57, Duckworth, London.

(1984) *The Neolithic Transition and the Genetics of Population in Europe*, Princeton University Press, Princeton, N.J.

Anderson, A. (1976) Prehistoric economies and competition in the Stone Age of northern Sweden. Ph.D. thesis, University of Cambridge.

(1981) 'Economic change and the prehistoric fur trade in Northern Sweden: the relevance of a Canadian model'. *Norwegian Archaeological Review* 14, 1–38.

Bahn, P. (1983) *Pyrenean Prehistory*, Aris and Phillips, Warminster, Wiltshire.

Bender, B. (1975) *Farming in Prehistory*, John Baker, London.

(1978) 'Gatherer-hunter to farmer: a social perspective'. *World Archaeology* 10, 204–22.

(1981) 'Gatherer-hunter intensification', in A. Sheridan and G. Bailey, eds., *Economic Archaeology*, pp. 149–57, BAR International Series 96, British Archaeological Reports, Oxford.

(1985a) 'Emergent tribal formations in the American midcontinent'. *American Antiquity* 50, 52–62.

(1985b) 'Prehistoric developments in the American midcontinent and in Brittany, northwest France', in T. D. Price and J. A. Brown, eds., *Prehistoric Hunter-Gatherers. The Emergence of Complexity*, pp. 21–58, Academic Press, Orlando, Fl. and London.

Binford L. R. (1968) 'Post-pleistocene adaptations', in S and L. Binford, eds., *New Perspectives in Archaeology*, pp. 313–41, Aldine, Chicago.

(1983) *In Pursuit of the Past*, Thames and Hudson, London.

Bohanan, P. and Plog, F. (eds.) (1967) *Beyond the Frontier,* Natural History Press, New York.

Braidwood, R. (1958) 'Near Eastern prehistory'. *Science* 127, 1419–30.

Broadbent, N. (1981) 'The Epimesolithic and the Subneolithic cultures of Northern Sweden and Finland', in B. Gramsch, ed., *Mesolithikum in Europa*, pp. 165–76, Deutscher Verlag, Berlin.

Bronson, B. (1977) 'The earliest farming: demography as a cause and consequence', in S. Polgar, ed., *Population, Ecology and Social Evolution*, pp. 53–78, Mouton, The Hague.

Brown, A. (1893) 'On the continuity of the neolithic and palaeolithic periods'. *Journal of the Royal Anthropological Institute* 22, 66–98.

Burkitt, M. (1925) 'The transition between palaeolithic and neolithic times'. *Proceedings of the Prehistoric Society of East Anglia* 5, 16–33.

Burley, D. (n.d.) 'Specialisation and the evolution of complex society in the Gulf of Georgia'. Paper presented at the 44th Annual Meeting of the Society for American Archaeology, Vancouver, 1979.

Caldwell, J. R. (1977) 'Cultural evolution in the Old World and the New, leading to the beginnings and spread of agriculture', in C. A. Reed, ed., *Origins of Agriculture*, pp. 77–88, Mouton, The Hague.

Childe, V. G. (1925) *The Dawn of European Civilisation*, Kegan Paul, London.

(1928) *The Most Ancient East: The Oriental Prelude to European Prehistory*, Kegan Paul, London.

(1935) *The Prehistory of Scotland*, Kegan Paul, London.

(1947) *The Dawn of European Civilisation*, 4th edn, Kegan Paul, London.

Clark, C. and Haswell, M. R. (1967) *The Economics of Subsistence Agriculture*, Methuen, London.

Clark, J. G. D. (1932) *The Mesolithic Age in Britain*, Cambridge University Press, Cambridge.

(1934) 'The classification of a microlithic culture'. *Archaeological Journal* 90, 52–77.

(1936) *The Mesolithic Settlement of Northern Europe*, Cambridge University Press, Cambridge.

(1946) 'Seal-hunting in the Stone Age of North-Western Europe: a study in economic prehistory'. *Proceedings of the Prehistoric Society* 12, 12–48.

(1948a) 'The development of fishing in Prehistoric Europe'. *Antiquaries Journal* 28, 45–85.

(1948b) 'Fowling in prehistoric Europe'. *Antiquity* 22, 116–30.

(1952) *Prehistoric Europe: The Economic Basis*, Methuen, London.

(1954) *Excavations at Star Carr, an Early Mesolithic Site at Seamer, near Scarborough, Yorkshire*, Cambridge University Press, Cambridge.

(1962) 'A survey of the Mesolithic phase', in *The Prehistory of Europe and South-west Asia*, pp. 97–111, Atti VI Congresso Internazionale Scienze Preistoriche e Protostoriche, Rome. Relazione Generale.

(1976) *The Earlier Stone Age Settlement of Scandinavia*, Cambridge University Press, Cambridge.

(1978) 'Neothermal orientations', in P. Mellars, ed., *The Early Postglacial Settlement of Northern Europe*, pp. 1–10, Duckworth, London.

(1980) *Mesolithic Prelude*, Edinburgh University Press, Edinburgh.

Cohen, M. N. (1977) *The Food Crisis in Prehistory*, Yale University Press, New Haven, Conn.

(1981) 'Pacific coast foragers: affluent or overcrowded?', in S. Koyama and D. H. Thomas, eds., *Affluent Foragers*, pp. 275–95, Senri Ethnological Studies 9, National Museum of Ethnology, Osaka.

Cowgill, G. L. (1975) 'Population pressure as a non-explanation', in C. E. Swedlund, ed., *Population Studies in Archaeology and Biological Anthropology*, American Antiquity Memoir 40, 127–31.

Darwin, C. (1868) *The Variation of Animals and Plants under Domestication*, vol. 1, 1st edn, Murray, London.

Dawkins, W. B. (1894) 'On the relation of the Palaeolithic to the Neolithic period'. *Journal of the Anthropological Institute* 22, 242–54.

de Mortillet, G. (1983) *Le Préhistorique Antiquité de l'Homme*, Paris.

Dennell, R. (1983) *European Economic Prehistory*, Academic Press, London.

(1985) 'The hunter-gatherer/agricultural frontier in prehistoric temperate Europe', in S. Green and S. M. Perlman, eds., *The Archaeology of Frontiers and Boundaries*, pp. 113–40, Academic Press, New York.

Dolukhanov, P. (1979) *Ecology and Economy in Neolithic Eastern Europe*, Duckworth, London.

Faris, J. C. (1975) 'Social evolution, population and production', in S. Polgar, ed., *Population, Ecology and Social Evolution*, pp. 235–73, Mouton, The Hague.

Flannery, K. V. (1969) 'Origins and ecological effects of early domestication in Iran and the Near East', in P. J. Ucko and G. W. Dimbleby, eds., *The Domestication and Exploitation of Plants and Animals*, pp. 73–100, Aldine, Chicago.

Godelier, M. (1977) *Perspectives in Marxist Anthropology*, Cambridge University Press, Cambridge.

Green, S. (1980) 'Broadening least-cost models for expanding agricultural systems', in T. K. Earle and A. L. Christenson, eds., *Modeling Change in Prehistoric Subsistence Economies*, pp. 209–41, Academic Press, New York.

Green, S. and Perlman, S. (1985) *The Archaeology of Frontiers and Boundaries*, Academic Press, New York.

Gurina, N. N. (1966) 'Sources of ancient culture (mesolithic epoch)'. *Materialy i Issledovaniya po Arkheologii SSSR* 126.

Harner, M. J. (1970) 'Population pressure and the social evolution of agriculturalists'. *Southwestern Journal of Anthropology* 26, 67–86.

Hassan, F. (1978) 'Demographic archaeology', in M. Schiffer, ed., *Advances in Archaeological Method and Theory*, vol. 1, pp. 49–103, Academic Press, New York.

(1981) *Demographic Archaeology*, Academic Press, London.

Hayden, B. (1975) 'The carrying capacity dilemma', in C. E. Swedlund, ed., *Population Studies in Archaeology and Biological Anthropology*, American Antiquity Memoir 40, 205–21.

(1981) 'Research and development in the Stone Age: technological transitions among hunter-gatherers'. *Current Anthropology* 22, 519–48.

(1982) 'Comment on the significance of food storage among hunter-gatherers, by A. Testart'. *Current Anthropology* 23, 531.

Hayden, B., Eldridge, M., Eldridge, A. and Cannon, A. (1985) 'Complex hunter-gatherers in interior British Columbia', in T. D. Price and J. A. Brown, eds., *Prehistoric Hunter-Gatherers. The Emergence of Complexity*, pp. 181–200, Academic Press, Orlando, Fl. and London.

Higgs, E. S. (ed.) (1972) *Papers in Economic Prehistory*, Cambridge University Press, Cambridge.

(1975) *Palaeoeconomy*, Cambridge University Press, Cambridge.

Higgs, E. S. and Jarman, M. (1969) 'The origins of agriculture: a reconsideration'. *Antiquity* 43, 31–41.

(1972) 'The origins of animal and plant husbandry', in E. S. Higgs, ed., *Papers in Economic Prehistory*, pp. 3–15, Cambridge University Press, Cambridge.

Ingold, T. (1982) 'Comment on the significance of food storage among hunter-gatherers, by A. Testart'. *Current Anthropology* 23, 531–2.

Jarman, M. (1972) 'European deer economies and the advent of the Neolithic', in E. Higgs, ed., *Papers in Economic Prehistory*, pp. 125–47, Cambridge University Press, Cambridge.

King, T. F. (1978) 'Don't that beat the band? Nonegalitarian political organisation in prehistoric central California', in C. Redman, W. P. Langhorne, M. J. Burman, N. M. Verfaggi, E. Curtin and J. Wanser, eds., *Beyond Subsistence and Dating*, pp. 225–248, Academic Press, New York.

Koyama, S. and Thomas, D. H. (1981) *Affluent Foragers*, Senri Ethnological Studies 9, National Museum of Ethnology, Osaka.

Kozłowski, S. and Kozłowski, J. (1978) 'Le rôle du substrat mésolithique dans la néolithisation de la partie nord de l'Europe central'. *Godišnjak – Centar za Balkanoloska Ispitivanja* 14.

Kruk, J. (1973) *Studia Osadnicze nad Neolitem Wyzyn Lessowych*, Polska Academia Nauk, Institut Historii Kultury Materyalnei, Warsaw.

Lee, R. B. (1972) 'Work effort, group structure and land use in contemporary hunter-gatherers', in P. J. Ucko, R. Tringham and G. W. Dimbleby, eds., *Man, Settlement and Urbanism*, pp. 177–85, Duckworth, London.

(1979) *The !Kung San*, Cambridge University Press, Cambridge.

Lee, R. B. and DeVore, I. (eds.) (1968) *Man the Hunter*, Aldine, Chicago.

Legge, A. J. (1972) 'Prehistoric exploitation of the gazelle in Palestine', in E. S. Higgs, ed., *Papers in Economic Prehistory*, pp. 119–25, Cambridge University Press, Cambridge.

Lewis, K. E. (1984) *The American Frontier*, Academic Press, New York.

Macalister, R. A. S. (1921) *Textbook of European Archaeology*, Cambridge University Press, Cambridge.

MacCurdy, G. C. (1924) *Human Origins: A Manual of Prehistory*, D. Appleton, New York, London.

MacNeish, S. (1977) 'The beginning of agriculture in Peru', in C. A. Reed, ed., *Origins of Agriculture*, pp. 753–802, Mouton, The Hague.

Matyushin, G. N. (1976) *Mezolit Yuzhnogo Urala*, Nauka, Moscow.

Mellars, P. (1981) 'Towards a definition of the Mesolithic'. *Mesolithic Miscellany* 2 (2), 13–16.

Miller, D. H. and Steffen, J. O. (1977) *The Frontier: Comparative Studies*, University of Oklahoma Press, Norman.

Moore, J. (1981) 'The effects of information networks in hunter-gatherer societies', in B. Winterhalder and E. A. Smith, eds., *Hunter-Gatherer Foraging Strategies*, pp. 194–217, University of Chicago Press, Chicago.

Newell, R. (1984) 'On the mesolithic contribution to the social evolution of Western European society', in J. Bintliff, ed., *Social Evolution*, pp. 69–82, University of Bradford, Bradford.

Osborn, H. F. (1918) *Men of the Old Stone Age*, G. Bell and Sons, London.

Perlman, S. (1980) 'An optimum diet model, coastal variability and hunter-gatherer behaviour', in M. B. Schiffer, ed., *Advances in Archaeological Method and Theory*, vol. 3, pp. 257–99, Academic Press, Orlando, Fl. and London.

Price, T. D. and Brown, J. A. (eds.) (1985) *Prehistoric Hunter-Gatherers. The Emergence of Complexity*, Academic Press, Orlando, Fl. and London.

Rowley-Conwy, P. (1983) 'Sedentary hunters: the Ertebølle example', in G. Bailey, ed., *Hunter-Gatherer Economy in Prehistory*, pp. 111–26, Cambridge University Press, Cambridge.

Sahlins, M. (1974) *Stone Age Economics*, Aldine, Chicago.

Smith, P. E. L. and Young, T. C. (1972) 'The evolution of early agriculture and culture in greater Mesopotamia: a trial model', in B. Spooner, ed., *Population Growth: Anthropological Implications*, pp. 1–59, MIT Press, Cambridge, Mass.

Sturdy, D. A. (1975) 'Some reindeer economies in prehistoric Europe', in E. S. Higgs, ed., *Palaeconomy*, pp. 55–95, Cambridge University Press, Cambridge.

Sulimirski, T. (1970) *Prehistoric Russia. An Outline*, John Baker, Humanities Press, London.

Sussman, R. M. (1972) 'Child transport, family size and the increase of human populations during the Neolithic'. *Current Anthropology* 13, 258–69.

Suttles, W. (1968) 'Coping with abundance: subsistence on the Northwest Coast', in R. Lee and R. DeVore, eds., *Man the Hunter*, pp. 56–68, Aldine, Chicago.

Testart, A. (1982*a*) *Les Chasseurs-Cueilleurs ou L'Origine des Inégalités*, Société d'Ethnographie, Paris.

(1982*b*) 'The significance of food storage among hunter-gatherers: residence patterns, population densities and social inequalities'. *Current Anthropology* 23, 523–37.

Thompson, S. (1973) 'Pioneer colonisation: a cross-cultural view'. *Modules in Anthropology* 33, Addison-Wesley, Reading, Mass.

Vavilov, N. I. (1926) *Studies on the Origin of Cultivated Plants*, Institut de Botanique Appliquée et d'Amélioration des Plantes, Leningrad.

Watanabe, H. (1968) 'Subsistence and ecology of Northern food gatherers with special reference to the Ainu', in R. B. Lee and R. DeVore, eds., *Man the Hunter*, pp. 69–77, Aldine, Chicago.

Westropp, H. M. (1872) *Prehistoric Phases*, London.

Wobst, M. (1974) 'Boundary conditions for Palaeolithic social systems: a simulation approach'. *American Antiquity* 39, 147–78.

(1976) 'Locational relationships in Palaeolithic society'. *Journal of Human Evolution* 5, 48–58.

Yesner, D. R. (1980) 'Maritime hunter-gatherers: ecology and prehistory'. *Current Anthropology* 21, 727–50.

(n.d.) 'Life in the "Garden of Eden": causes and consequences of the adoption of marine diets by human societies'. Unpublished manuscript, available from the author.

Zvelebil, M. (1981) *From Forager to Farmer in the Boreal Zone*, BAR International Series 115 (i and ii), British Archaeological Reports, Oxford.

Zvelebil, M. and Rowley-Conwy, P. (1984) 'Transition to farming in northern Europe: a hunter-gatherer perspective'. *Norwegian Archaeological Review* 17, 104–28.

Chapter 2

Between cave painters and crop planters: aspects of the temperate European Mesolithic

Peter Rowley-Conwy

Introduction: occupational hiatus and cultural hiatus

The Mesolithic was the last of the major prehistoric periods of Europe to be recognised and defined. It emerged piecemeal through the last decades of the nineteenth and the first decades of the twentieth centuries, and filled the gap between late glacial hunters and neolithic farmers. The 'hiatus theory', claiming that Europe was not occupied during this interval, was proved false. Nevertheless, the period was initially of significance only because it bridged the gap between the brilliant, cave-painting Palaeolithic and the dynamic, crop-planting Neolithic. Archaeological views of the Mesolithic have never entirely escaped from the straitjacket imposed upon them by this fact.

The story of the arrival and subsequent development of the Mesolithic as an age has been told elsewhere (Clark 1978, 1980). Important are the unflattering comparisons between the Mesolithic and the preceding and succeeding epochs. These have their background in the hiatus theory, which, as Grahame Clark writes, 'can be shown to have warped much of our thinking' (1978, p. 2). European prehistory in the middle years of this century was dominated by the figure of Gordon Childe. His views are symptomatic of the interpretative wilderness in which mesolithic studies, with few exceptions, found themselves. In the first edition of *The Dawn of European Civilization*, he wrote that 'the contribution of [the Mesolithic] to European culture is negligible. The hiatus is

only recreated. The traditional picture may thus be retained' (Childe 1925, p. 3). In the sixth and final edition of *The Dawn* he wrote of 'cultures that are termed mesolithic because in time—but only in time—they occupy a place between the latest palaeolithic and the oldest neolithic cultures' (*ibid*. 1957, p. 35). The occupational hiatus has become a *cultural hiatus* instead.

Many developments have recently taken place to affect this picture. Some of these are described below. There has been a tendency, however, for these developments to be interpreted against the backdrop of the cultural hiatus theory, and thus to provide unintentional support for that theory rather than to generate possible alternatives. The intention of this essay is to show how this has come about, and then to argue that some recent work is in fact pointing in a different direction. What Grahame Clark (1978, p. 6) has described as 'the broken-backed European tradition' is giving way to more flexible models of the European Mesolithic.

Terminology

Any examination of the European Mesolithic must inevitably include a definition of the term 'Mesolithic'. I prefer a deliberately loose definition, and will here use the term as a label for human groups and their material remains in the period from the end of the Ice Age until the start of a predominantly farming economy. There seems little point in trying to pin it down more closely — if it becomes necessary to agonise over whether groups from the Allerød warm phase should be called mesolithic, and if so whether groups from the subsequent Younger Dryas cold phase should in some sense revert to the Palaeolithic, then it is clear that we know far more about environment, society and economy than can be contained within any tight definitions of Palaeolithic and Mesolithic. These terms thus lose their value except as broad and loose descriptive labels.

Some discussion of terminology is unfortunately necessary, as different authorities may use different terms to mean the same thing, or the same terms to mean different things. The recently published papers from the Potsdam conference, *Mesolithikum in Europa*, provide a classic example. The first two papers deal respectively with 'the start of the Epipalaeolithic' (Rozoy 1981) and 'the end of the Epipalaeolithic and the start of the Mesolithic' (Thévenin 1981). One might reasonably suppose that these two papers complemented one another chronologically, Rozoy discussing an earlier period than Thévenin. This is not the case: both deal with the same period. Thévenin uses epipalaeolithic to describe the *late glacial* predecessors of the postglacial Mesolithic. For Rozoy, the degree of continuity between glacial and postglacial groups is such that he uses epipalaeolithic to describe all *postglacial* hunter-gatherer groups. Thus Thévenin's Mesolithic is Rozoy's Epipalaeolithic; Thévenin's Epipalaeolithic is the final part of Rozoy's Upper Palaeolithic.

Problems also arise at the other end of the period. The West European definition of 'Neolithic' is usually based upon the appearance of cultivated cereals and domestic animals, while the East European is usually defined as the appearance of pottery. Thus the pottery-using cultures north of the Black Sea, with few or no domestic animals, are called neolithic (e.g. Dolukhanov 1979; Gurina 1981). The pottery-using cultures of the southwest Baltic coast, with few or no domestic animals, are usually called mesolithic (e.g. Clark 1975, 1980), except when domestic animals are definitely claimed, when some would call them neolithic (Schwabedissen 1981), or until they occur in the East European Baltic states when they are once again called neolithic on the basis of their pottery (e.g. Loze 1981). Use of ceramics as the definition of neolithic can lead to problems. Sulimirski (1970) describes pottery-using hunter-gatherers of the Upper Volga Pit-Comb culture as neolithic. Neighbouring, contemporary groups have similar settlements in similar locations, and similar material culture except for an absence of pottery. Sulimirski (1970, p. 137) is trapped into calling these classic microlithic hunter-gatherer groups 'pre-pottery neolithic'.

There is little point in becoming embroiled in such terminological problems; mention is made of them to avoid the confusion that could otherwise arise from the use of palaeolithic, mesolithic and neolithic all to refer to the same thing.

Cultures and chronologies
Culture and function

One of the main pursuits of mesolithic studies in Europe has been to classify industries into cultures. Since the Second World War, there has been a great proliferation of cultural groupings and schemes. The result has been the erection of a cumbersome and controversial edifice of ever increasing complexity. Precisely how helpful such elaboration might be is a topic of current discussion. Some would regard many of the claimed cultural units as questionable entities, based on finds of uneven provenance and of dubious palaeo-ethnic significance. Terminology, as one might expect, is a source of confusion — it surely makes little difference whether we should regard Star Carr as part of the Maglemose group (Clark 1955) or as part of the Duvensee group (Kozłowski 1973, 1975). This is further complicated by the fact that the names are used in different senses. Clark uses Maglemose as a general label to cover a number of related industries over a wide area (including Duvensee), while Kozłowski elevates both Maglemose and Duvensee to the status of culture groups, each containing various cultures of implied palaeo-ethnic status.

The biggest terminological debate concerns the terms Tardenoisian and Sauveterrian, and some discussion of this is unfortunately essential. Before the mid 1950s, Tardenoisian was used indiscriminately to refer to nearly all West-European microlithic industries. Re-examination of the material led Barrière (1956) to use the terms chronologically, defining a late mesolithic Tardenoisian horizon, following an early mesolithic Sauveterrian horizon over much of Europe. This usage has been strongly contested by Rozoy (1971, 1973), who insists that these terms should each be applied to the *entire* mesolithic sequence in their own area only, Tardenoisian referring to the north and Sauveterrian to the south of France (Fig. 1). Rozoy refers to this as a methodological problem. We may note, however, that there is no methodology for determining nomenclature; the debate is subjective, and the issue not of great significance. It is, however, a source of confusion which must be understood before the position of an authority on other matters can be appreciated.

Recent years have seen something of a move away from such culture-oriented studies on the part of some authorities. A good example of this is recent work on the British Mesolithic. When Grahame Clark (1932) wrote *The Mesolithic Age in Britain* over 50 years ago, he distinguished two main cultures: a predominantly microlithic culture in upland regions, similar to Franco-Belgian Tardenoisian groups (that term being used in its general, pre-1950s sense); and a more lowland culture with an axe-adze component and bone tools, paralleling the Maglemose cultures of northern Europe (*ibid*.). Table 1 gives the frequencies of some tool types on some British mesolithic sites (after Mellars 1976*a*), and it is clear that the two assemblage types do to some extent divide up by altitude.

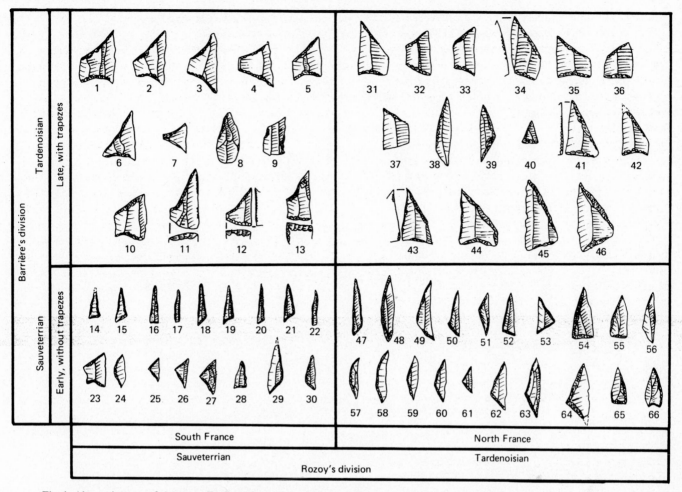

Fig. 1. Alternative uses of the terms Tardenoisian and Sauveterrian. (Flints redrawn after Rozoy 1971.) 1–9, Châteauneuf les Martigues 7 & 8; 10–13, Rouffignac 3; 14–22, Montclus lower levels; 23–30, St Laurent Médoc; 31–42, Montbani 13; 43–46, Allée Tortue; 47–56, La Sablonnière de Coincy; 57–66, Piscop.

It was against this backdrop that the major lowland site of Star Carr was excavated, fitting into the Maglemose group (Clark 1954). Recent developments, however, have changed interpretations of the pattern. Clark himself has not made use of the 'two culture model' for Britain since 1955 (*ibid.* 1955); since then, Radley and Mellars (1964) have emphasised the similarity between the microlithic component of the upland and lowland assemblages, and point out that axes do indeed occur in the uplands, albeit as stray finds. Most authorities would now regard the two assemblage types as seasonal manifestations of the same human groups. The differences are seen as the result of functional variability and differing conditions of preservation, not as separate cultures. The absence of bone on upland sites is probably due to poor preservation; the higher percentages of microliths on the smaller, mainly upland sites are the product of a restricted range of activities; the higher percentages of scrapers on the larger sites are evidence of a wider range of activities; and the rarity of axe-adzes in the uplands is put down to the thinner nature of the woodland in those areas (Clark 1972, 1973; Jacobi 1978, 1979; Mellars 1976a) (see Table 1).

Some problems remain, however: exact site size is often difficult to determine, especially in the case of smaller excavations. Changes in artefact frequency may vary with time as well as space, and there is some evidence that scrapers decrease in the later Mesolithic (R. M. Jacobi, personal communication). Reanalysis of the fauna from Star Carr also emphasises the complexity of the situation. Star Carr has usually been regarded as a winter site (Clark 1972), in keeping with the nomadic model of upland exploitation in summer. Reanalysis suggests, however, that Star Carr was certainly occupied in the summer (Legge and Rowley-Conwy, 1986).

Many similar developments are visible on the European mainland. Grahame Clark (1936) put foward the same dichotomy between Maglemose cultures (with axes and art) and Tardenoisian cultures (with neither). This was followed by later writers (e.g. Childe 1957; Schwabedissen 1944). More recently, however, this dichotomy has been seen to be due in considerable measure to variable preservation and research emphasis (Newell 1973). One regional study has made the point that there is no sharp boundary between axe-adze and non axe-adze cultures; rather, there is a gradual trend for axes

Table 1. *Site size and percentages of some tool types on some British mesolithic sites (after Mellars 1976a, Tables 3 and 4)*

Site	Area (m^2)	% Microliths	% Scrapers	% Axe-adze
Type A: microlith dominated assemblages				
Upland				
Broomhead 5	14.9	90	10	–
Dunford A	4.5	93	–	–
Dunford B	3.9	90	–	–
Rocher Moss	?8.0	91	6	–
White Hill	?12.0	92	8	–
Lowland				
Thorpe Common	8.4	94	–	–
Oakhanger VIII	8.8	93	–	–
Iping Common	?44.0	91	8	–
Type B: assemblages with fewer microliths				
Upland				
Deepcar	44	60	32	–
Warcock North	>100	61	32	–
Warcock South	>40	62	35	–
Windy Hill 3	>42	51	37	–
Mickleden	44	67	29	–
Lowland				
Star Carr	185	27	35	1
Flixton I	50	29	62	1
Broxbourne	?50	44	49	4
Thatcham	116	57	26	2
Oakhanger V	100	46	38	1
Oakhanger VII	210	37	49	1
Downton	60	47	33	4
Peacehaven	>100	39	50	6
Morton	>150	27	61	–
Low Clone	54	46	32	–
Barsalloch	>50	42	47	–

Only sites of known area are included. Percentages are to the nearest whole number. Mellars' type B1 assemblages are omitted.

to diminish towards higher ground (Geupel 1973), just as in Britain.

Much of the current work on the European Mesolithic is concerned with establishing the presence of cultural units. Two main developments are occurring: radiocarbon dating now permits the establishment of a number of broad horizons (horizontal dividing lines); and an increased study of flint typology has resulted in attempts at more precise definition of local cultural groupings (vertical dividing lines).

Chronological divisions and radiocarbon dating

The advent of radiocarbon dating has been of immeasurable importance for the establishment of chronological divisions. Within Britain a two-fold division has been established, based on a now considerable number of radio-

carbon dates. The Early Mesolithic, in which obliquely blunted points dominate among the microliths, dates to before a point in the early seventh millennium bc, perhaps around 6800 bc. Such assemblages are usually termed *broad blade*. The Late Mesolithic, after about 6800 bc, is characterised by smaller, more varied microlithic forms, among which scalene triangles are important. Such assemblages are termed *narrow blade* (see Jacobi 1973, 1976; Mellars 1974, 1976b; Switsur and Jacobi 1979).

Many would now agree that radiocarbon dating indicates three main phases within the Mesolithic of continental Europe. The *first phase* is characterised by a low range of microlithic forms, among which obliquely blunted points (= K points, Kozłowski 1976a) are important (Fig. 2). This phase corresponds to the British broad blade industries (see above) and

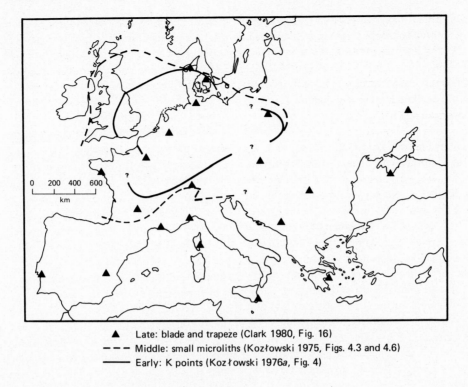

▲   Late: blade and trapeze (Clark 1980, Fig. 16)
‐ ‐ ‐   Middle: small microliths (Kozłowski 1975, Figs. 4.3 and 4.6)
——   Early: K points (Kozłowski 1976*a*, Fig. 4)

Fig. 2. Approximate distribution of main northwest European phases.

comes to an end at about the same time – early in the seventh millennium bc. The *second phase* displays a proliferation of microlithic forms on narrow blades, triangular and lanceolate forms being particularly important. Some K points continue to be found. This phase lasts approximately a millennium, and corresponds to the first part of the British narrow blade industries. It forms Jacobi's 'Late Mesolithic' and Kozłowski's S component. The *third phase* is characterised by the wide-spread appearance of blade and trapeze industries throughout Europe (except Britain), earlier microlithic forms taking a subordinate place. This phase starts early in the sixth millennium bc and continues until the advent of the Neolithic. It forms Jacobi's 'Latest Mesolithic' and Kozłowski's K component (not to be confused with the K points of the first phase). (See particularly Jacobi 1976; Kozłowski 1976*c*; also Clark 1958; Kozłowski 1976*a, b*.)

Just how synchronous these events are in different areas is still a matter for debate. Radiocarbon and pollen dating would suggest that they are indeed quite closely synchronous at any rate within northern and western Europe. The second phase starts on present evidence slightly earlier in southern France and apparently spreads from there (Jacobi 1976; Kozłowski 1976*b, c*). No such area of origin can be discerned for the third phase on the basis of the radiocarbon dates, all of which lie very close together.

These three phases have been distinguished in a restricted area of Europe (France, Britain and the North European Plain as far east as Poland). Beyond these areas the picture is less clear. K points do not seem to penetrate south of the Pyrénées, Alps or Carpathians, nor do they spread east

of the Vistula (Fig. 2) (Kozłowski 1976*a*). Elements of the second phase seem to be restricted to approximately the same area. Elements of the third phase appear to spread more widely. This may partly be due to problems of definition, and to the uncertain status of finds in southern and southwestern Europe. In Russia, industries sometimes called Swiderian and Azilian, after their earlier West-European counterparts (Sulimirski 1970), apparently occur contemporaneously with the first and second phases of the western sequence; Kozłowski (1975) groups some of these in his 'north-eastern technocomplex', characterised by long, narrow parallel-sided bladelets rather than microliths of more western type. Trapezes characteristic of the western third phase do on the other hand spread quite far east. Sulimirski (1970) therefore terms these industries Tardenoisian (using that name in its chronological sense).

Social territories

Recent cultural studies have emphasised regional con-tinuity, despite the cross-cutting of large areas by the three main phases outlined above. The results of these studies are inevitably less clear cut and more controversial than the chronological stages. Evaluations often have a subjective element and thus do not have the independent validity of radiocarbon dates. The most complete considerations of the European material are by Kozłowski (1973, 1975). Some problems do arise – for example, the Kormonica/Chojnice-Pienki culture sequence of Poland displays considerable spatial and temporal overlap with the unrelated Janisławice culture, and it is uncertain what this might mean in terms of the human occupation of the area — but these works do represent the clearest and most thorough attempt to organise the various European groupings. Rozoy has carried out a very detailed survey of the French material and distinguishes some 20 local groups (Rozoy 1978). Despite the encyclopaedic nature of this work, understanding of the French groupings reaches an impasse when a reviewer can still write that 'none of the twenty cultural groups defined by Rozoy fits the actual cultural differentiation of Europe' (Gob 1981, p. 19).

One avenue which, although problematic, may eventually provide a way out of these difficulties is the search for the 'social territories' of individual human groups, signalled by 'characteristically idiosyncratic' traits in their material culture (Clark 1975, pp. 70, 72). What marks out some of the modern work in this field (e.g. Clark 1975; Jacobi 1978, 1979; Price 1981; Switsur and Jacobi 1979) is a much clearer understanding of the size and nature of the human group it attempts to locate. This is largely due to comparisons with ethnographic situations assumed to be relevant. The type of behavioural unit regarded as most relevant to the Mesolithic is the mating network as defined by Wobst (1976). In order to ensure an adequate supply of mates, a minimum mating network size of about 500 individuals is necessary. Such systems may be *open*, with each local band (average size 25) in contact with a sufficiency of neighbouring bands to ensure adequate numbers of mates. In this case, no sharp cultural boundaries would be expected. Alternatively such systems may be *closed*, with a unit of about 500 individuals forming a discrete entity. In this case cultural boundaries would exist and should be visible archaeologically (Wobst 1976). It is such units that social territory studies seek to recognise.

The most ambitious work in this direction is that carried out by Price (1981). He notes that four main groups are visible during the tanged point phase at the end of the Late Glacial (those shown by Clark (1975, p. 70) and the Creswellian of Britain). By the boreal period, eight to ten groups are visible, and this has risen to over 15 by the Atlantic. The average diameter of the area they occupy is around 100 to 200 km; this agrees with the areas that average-sized mating networks should occupy at ethnographically documented population densities. On this basis, Price (1981) calculates that the entire North European Plain might contain around 54 such mating networks, probably with greater densities being attained in coastal regions. Areas occupied by networks not so far recognised archaeologically may be predicted in some cases by reference to natural obstacles such as mountain ranges, major rivers and bodies of water etc. (Price 1981).

Work within Britain has been carried out on a systematic basis by Jacobi (1978, 1979; Switsur and Jacobi 1979), who uses cluster analysis to attempt to demonstrate groupings within the broad blade and narrow blade periods. The broad blade (early) industries are remarkably similar over most of Britain; the major area of divergence is in the southeast (the Weald), which appears as a distinct group. The narrow blade (later) industries show rather more diversity. Britain is broadly divided into northern and southern areas; in addition, a more localised group appears in the Pennine and Cleveland hills, dating from the fourth millennium bc (Switsur and Jacobi 1979). The Weald area continues as a local group in the seventh millennium bc, and the major southern grouping may be further subdivided into southwestern and Midlands/East Anglia groups (Jacobi 1979).

It seems, therefore, that the progressively greater fragmentation noted by Price (1981) for the North European Plain also takes place in Britain. The later groups seem to be about the same size as their continental counterparts. However, added complexities arise. The Pennine—Cleveland group (the most clearly differentiated one in Jacobi's cluster analysis) is known only from the Pennine and Cleveland hills above 300 m altitude, and not in the intervening lowland. The main northern group is spread over a wider area, including the Pennine and Cleveland hills and the surrounding lowlands, and at least partially overlaps the smaller group chronologically. It is not certain that the existence of the markedly different Pennine—Cleveland group represents — cultural difference is only one of several possible explanations. Another might be that particular specialised activities were being carried out at these sites by the individuals elsewhere responsible for the main northern industries. In the southwest of England, however, it was the fact demonstrated by cluster analysis that the lowland/coastal and inland sites *shared* so many traits that caused seasonal movement between the two to be suggested. Why the Pennine—Cleveland group in contrast should be so different from its lowland counterpart must be a question for future research. Analysis of faunal remains to determine the season of occupation would be one way of shedding light on the problem.

The need for integration

In the above an attempt has been made to describe some of the recent developments concerning the 'horizontal' and 'vertical' dividing lines seen in the European Mesolithic. Different authorities choose to emphasise the one or the other — the debate over the usage of Tardenoisian and Sauveterrian (above) is a reflection of this. Despite these differences, it is clear that major strides have been, and continue to be, made in both areas. One of the major areas for future research will probably be an integration of the two types of patterning into a single model.

Extreme proponents of the vertical divisions (emphasising local continuity and implying separate, closed mating networks) ignore the fact that the elements initiating the second and third phases (S. K. Kozłowski's intercultural S and K components) spread very rapidly across large areas of Europe — the mating network boundaries are evidently not culturally impermeable. Britain after about 6500 bc forms an interesting exception that emphasises this general rule. As Jacobi has clearly demonstrated, after Europe was cut off from Britain in the mid seventh millennium bc, European developments played no further part in the British Mesolithic.

The third European phase (blade and trapeze industries starting in the early sixth millennium bc) is completely unrepresented in Britain, and the narrow blade industries continue with little change. Evidence of isolation is indeed visible earlier than the start of the third phase — elements characteristic of the later part of the second phase (after about 6500 bc) make no appearance in Britain, although the marine barrier was only some 24 km wide (Jacobi 1976).

On the other hand, the fact that the S and K components do spread so fast does not disprove the existence of the local groupings. The Mesolithic is clearly not organised only as a widespread open network. Some theoretical reconciliation of these two apparently opposed pieces of evidence is to be looked for.

The minimal view and the affluent alternative

I hope that the above presents the impression that recent years have contributed more than any comparable period to our knowledge of the Mesolithic. Despite this, the view frequently found concerning mesolithic economies and societies is still often a minimal one. The cultural hiatus theory (described above) still colours views of many recent developments:

> it is a fact that not only in Britain but in Europe as a whole Mesolithic man has left little of artistic wealth. We have few clues to his beliefs, and burials, apart from a few examples such as the horrible nest of skulls at Ofnet in Bavaria, are rare. There is nothing of the brilliance of the upper palaeolithic hunters living as they were in the stimulating landscape of the Ice Age, nor anything of the vital urgency with which later farming communities were to settle and cultivate the lands of Western Europe and the British Isles (Evans 1975, p. 90).

This view in which mesolithic man is caricatured as neither brilliant, stimulated nor urgent (unlike men of earlier and later periods) is rather extreme; nevertheless, the likelihood that mesolithic groups were at the most basic level of organisation and culture known to man is commonly expressed. In the period 8000–5000 bc:

> there was a sudden decline followed by a further impoverishment of European culture . . . Judging from their modest achievements it is thought that Palaeolithic religious art finally ceased to exist, that larger units were scattered into smaller groups of hunters who pursued their prey in the dense forests, that every sense of building craft was lost, as well as the capacity for creating any more complex forms of economic and social relations (Srejović 1972, p. 14).

This is in part due to two major areas of research, both outside archaeology, yet having a major influence upon the formulation of archaeological viewpoints.

The first research area: ecological considerations

The first research area is ecology, primarily pollen analysis. Early descriptions of the deciduous forests of the atlantic period emphasised how hostile these environments were to man. In particular, early pollen work in Denmark made this point.

> In the Atlantic period, Denmark was covered by continuous woodland . . . Conditions of living in it were unfavourable for animals, which means man too. The mesolithic hunter and fisher cultures had to subsist under severe conditions, and large parts of the country must have been almost empty of human beings in the Atlantic period (Iversen 1949, p. 6).

In a later article, Iversen mentions that, with the appearance of the atlantic forests, 'the golden age was over' (1973, p. 73). These works have been widely quoted, and the view that population declined drastically from a late glacial high point is often found — Troels-Smith (1960) believes that the population of Denmark was about 120 in the late glacial; by the atlantic this had fallen to scarcely 30.

There is little reason to believe that this view is correct. Each successional stage in postglacial forest history is likely to have seen an increase in basic ecological productivity.

Ecosystem type	Net primary productivity g dry wt/m^2 per yr	
	Mean	Normal range
Tundra and alpine	140	10–400
Boreal forest	800	400–2000
Temperate forest	1250	600–2500
NB also:		
Swamp and marsh	2000	800–3500
Lake and stream	250	100–1500
Estuaries	1800	500–4000

Figures from Whittaker (1975).

It is particularly notable how much less productive is tundra than the forest ecosystems. High net productivity is of course no indication of utility — savanna has a much lower productivity and biomass than temperate forest, but is capable of supporting much greater numbers of grazing animals because much of the productivity is near ground level and so accessible to herbivores. Much of the temperate forest biomass is in the form of wood, or leaves above the reach of grazing animals; but many kinds of deciduous woodlands do have well-developed lower layers which may be exploited (Rackham 1980). Reasons for the absence of undergrowth pollen in pollen diagrams have been discussed elsewhere (Rowley–Conwy 1982).

The change from glacial to postglacial probably saw an increase of ungulate biomass. Mellars (1975) gives a range of 1000–2500 kg/km^2 for ungulate biomass in mixed deciduous woodland. This is considerably higher than the value of 800 kg/km^2 given for caribou in the Canadian tundra (Bourlière 1963), or of 440 kg/km^2 for total animal biomass in tundra (calculated from Table 5.3 of Whittaker 1975). It should be remembered that these figures do not take into account the possibility of burning areas of forest, which, by increasing available grazing, may markedly increase ungulate biomass (Mellars 1976c). Evidence of widespread systematic burning of forests has been claimed during the British Mesolithic (Jacobi, Tallis and Mellars 1976).

The increased availability of plant foods exploitable by man in the postglacial forest is also an important point and has been stressed by Clarke (1976).

A further important point is the replacement of a single ungulate species (reindeer) in the Late Glacial by a range of ungulates and other animals in the postglacial. The importance of this has been emphasised (Clark 1968, 1975, 1980; Newell 1973). A wider range of exploited species confers greater security on the exploiters. This is in notable contrast to the reindeer, which displays marked cyclical fluctuations in population numbers (Burch 1972).

The relative reliability of mesolithic hunting, the presence of a larger ungulate biomass, and the increased availability of plant foods are therefore factors likely to ensure an *increase* of population in the Mesolithic (Rowley-Conwy 1982).

Considerations such as the above have been taken into account in some recent studies of the Mesolithic. However, many of those who accept that population may have increased in the Mesolithic argue that, because of the more static nature and even spread of resources across the landscape (in contrast to the concentrated and mobile reindeer herds of the Late Glacial), human populations are likely to have been more evenly spread. This would have meant a drop in both group size and mobility (Meiklejohn 1978; Price 1978).

This may be true for certain areas of Europe, but other areas are likely to have seen very different demographic arrangements. Temperate Europe is indeed a less seasonal environment than late glacial Europe would have been; but seasonal migrations are marked and the availability of resources fluctuates. Many of the local ungulates migrate seasonally in certain environments. The seasonal availability of important high-yield plant foods like hazel nuts and acorns may also be mentioned. Aquatic resources are particularly seasonal. Coasts and estuaries are highly productive in ecological terms (see p. 87). Temperate seas are highly seasonal in plankton production, and the effects of this in terms of seasonal movements of many animals throughout the food chain are great (Coull 1972; Cushing 1975). Seasonally available concentrations of marine, anadromous and catadromous fish, and of seals, whales and waterbirds would have had a major effect on human settlement patterns. In some cases this would mean seasonal concentrations of human groups larger than those envisaged by the proponents of fragmentation. Resource storage could extend the period of

occupation of such sites. Permanent settlements are to be expected in areas where several migratory or otherwise seasonally available resources of high productivity are available within a small area. Storage and the seasonal use of continually available local resources such as non-migratory mammals and shellfish are to be expected to plug any gaps in the cycle. Sedentary groups are, by analogy with modern groups, likely to be larger than mobile ones, and it is precisely in the areas where sedentism can be expected to develop that migratory, storable agglomerations of resources make larger populations viable (Rowley-Conwy 1981, 1983). Groups of such complexity and size in other regions have been described as 'affluent foragers'.

It is thus argued that no single, ecologically derived model of mesolithic settlement patterns is adequate. Postglacial Europe was sufficiently temperate for the environment to be relatively productive and reliable; and yet also sufficiently far north for parts of this productivity to be concentrated into particular restricted locations and/or seasons. The interplay of the availability of resources would vary greatly; and this variability is likely to have had a profound effect on human settlement. Price (1981), as mentioned above, states that rivers and bodies of water are likely to have been *boundaries* between separate mating networks. This will in some cases be correct, but it will surely depend on the river, lake or coast in question — some are certain to have been *foci* of such groups. Site size in certain areas may indeed have been such that the minimum mating network of *c.* 500 people, so useful in any consideration of interfluvial and interlacustrine areas, may lose much of its significance as a demographic unit.

Before moving on, a word is necessary on the use of coastal resources. It has been suggested that the hostile nature of the atlantic forests forced people to move towards the coasts, the increased density of the forest being matched by an increase in finds of coastal sites (Troels-Smith 1960; Waterbolk 1968; Iversen 1973; Bradley 1978). Newell has, however, forcibly reminded us that:

> In those areas where geologic and hydrographic conditions have fortuitously conserved coastal sites, and these have been discovered and excavated, we find a continuous series of coastal sites, complementing the inland sites, from the late glacial and early postglacial into the mid Atlantic (Newell 1973, p. 411).

In other words, the submergence by the rising sea of almost all coastlines of older than atlantic age means that the apparent increase of coastal sites in the atlantic period is not the result of a new adaptation; merely of a newly visible one.

The second research area: anthropological considerations

The second research area which has led some archaeologists to take a minimal view of the Mesolithic is anthropology. The problems here are: which recent hunter-gatherers are suitable analogies for the European Mesolithic and how should these analogies be employed?

The ethnographic model put forward by Lee and

DeVore (1968), based primarily on the Kalahari Bushmen, is often used. They write: 'we make two basic assumptions about hunters and gatherers: (1) they live in small groups and (2) they move around a lot' (*ibid*. 1968, p. 11). Mobility limits personal property to what can be carried, so society is generally egalitarian; group size is small, usually below 50; local groups do not own or identify with particular resources; and food surpluses are rare (*ibid*. 1968).

The assumption has often been made that such hunter-gatherers are the kind that was to be found throughout the Mesolithic (cf. Jensen 1982; Milisauskas 1978). Our understanding of the European mesolithic environment as a hostile one (see above), populated by small, nomadic groups hanging on only by the skin of their ecological teeth, has prepared us well to accept the simplest social type known to anthropology as our model for the Mesolithic.

Recent work has developed and refined the application of the mobile band model to Europe, and some predictions have been put forward. The best examples of this are those of Gamble (1978) and Binford (1980). The Lee and DeVore model (above) is derived from, and relevant to, hunter-gatherers in lower latitudes. Environments in these regions tend to be *generalised* (Gamble 1978), with a large number of species each represented by relatively few, evenly spaced individuals forming a relatively stable ecosystem. Hunter—gatherer settlement, following this, consists of small, dispersed groups, moving camp frequently as local exhaustion of the evenly spread resources takes place. Binford (1980) terms this *residential mobility*.

Higher latitude environments, on the other hand, are more uneven in productivity and reliability, having fewer species in relatively larger numbers: they are *specialised* (Gamble 1978). Group movement takes place less frequently and is usually directed towards a single or a particular set of resources. Larger population units may occur seasonally. Special purpose camps are used alongside the base camps and resources are sometimes transported back to the base camps and stored. Binford (1980) calls this *logistic mobility*.

Definition of the logistic strategy in specialised environments results from work among the recent Eskimo (Binford 1980) and on glacial Europe (Gamble 1978). Both environments are more extreme than postglacial Europe, but as argued in the preceding section, there would have been many areas in postglacial Europe where seasonal resource availability would have been marked enough for the specialised, logistic option to be necessary.

The excellence of this work on band hunters should not blind us to the possibility that other options might have been available in mesolithic Europe. The ethnographic record is very truncated as far as hunter-gatherers are concerned; but even among the fragmentary remnants of this once worldwide mode of production are groups diverging, often in major fashion, from the band models generally applied to the European Mesolithic. The Ainu and the Northwest Coast groups are but two examples of such 'affluent foragers'. Such

groups, living in permanent settlements, often with larger-than-band-group size and more complex social organisation, should serve to remind us that our prehistoric hunter-gatherers were by no means obliged to conform to any single model of settlement and society.

A model of variability

In the introduction to this paper, I wrote that new developments in mesolithic studies sometimes tend to be used in tacit support of the cultural hiatus theory. I hope that this review of ecological and anthropological factors has made it clear that neither of these fields in fact offers any support to the cultural hiatus. On the contrary, the ecological and anthropological considerations discussed above contain some of the basic elements of an alternative view of the temperate Mesolithic.

This view would emphasise the degree of variability in mesolithic settlement and subsistence. At one end of the range would be groups varying between generalised hunter-gatherers practising residential mobility, and more specialised groups practising logistic mobility (cf. Gamble 1978; Binford 1980). At the other end of the range, beyond the specialised logistic groups, would be permanently settled, 'affluent' hunter-gatherers in favourable environments. By analogy with recent hunter-gatherers, such groups might have larger, more complex social units.

This is not the place for a discussion of the European evidence as it relates to this model. Mention may be made briefly of two groups, however, who appear to have corresponded to the more complex end of the range. Lepenski Vir and other sites in the Iron Gates region of the Danube consisted of large villages. They exploited a variety of resources, riverine ones being of particular importance. Osteological evidence shows that the sites were permanently occupied (Bökönyi 1972; Bolomey 1973). The Ertebølle culture of the western Baltic consists of large and small sites. The latter reveal economic specialisation and seasonal occupation, and appear to have been special-purpose camps. The large sites are, on osteological grounds, believed to have been permanently occupied, and were apparently base-camps (Rowley-Conwy 1983). Both the Iron Gates and the west Baltic mesolithic groups appear, therefore, to be good candidates for temperate European affluent foragers.

These developments are explicitly seen against the environmental background of temperate Europe; ecological factors have been viewed as crucial to the variability of social and economic patterns in the Mesolithic. There are various alternatives to this, some of which may be grouped under two main headings. These are discussed in the next sections.

Intensification: a European agriculture?

Domestication of both plant and animal species native to western temperate Europe has been suggested. The purpose of this section is to evaluate the likelihood of anything approaching an agricultural system emerging within the temperate European Mesolithic, using native plant and animal species.

The domestication of deer

The herding of red deer has been proposed as a possibility for mesolithic Europe (Jarman 1972; Chaplin 1975). It will be argued here, however, that there are reasons for doubting whether red or roe deer would be a likely candidate for early domestication. This conclusion results from a comparison of deer behaviour with that of cattle and sheep.

Recent reviews of the behaviour of African ungulates are helpful here. The family Bovidae contains all antelope species, as well as cattle, sheep, goats and their relatives. The family has been divided up into two fundamentally different behavioural types (e.g. Estes 1974; Leuthold 1974; Walther, Mungall and Grau 1983). On the one hand there are species in which at least some of the males are territorial at least some of the time. Territorial males space themselves out over the landscape, attempt to herd females within their territories, and will not tolerate the presence of other males. On the other hand there are species in which the males establish a dominance hierarchy, and do not become territorial or intolerant of other males. Although separate groups of bachelor males, adult females etc. form in both types, herd membership is more constant among the non-territorial species, and correspondingly weaker among the territorial ones.

This division has had the greatest importance on the human choice of domesticated animals. Domestic cattle (subfamily Bovinae), sheep and goats (subfamily Caprinae) are not territorial, nor are their wild relatives (Leuthold 1974; Walther *et al.* 1983). Domestication within the Bovidae has followed quite narrow taxonomic pathways, ignoring territorial species such as the subfamilies Cephalophinae (15 species), Antilopinae (23 species) and Alcelaphinae (7 species). Exercising control over groups of animals which insist on exploding over the landscape would obviously be difficult. Describing one territorial member of the Bovidae, P. J. and M. V. Jarman write:

> The behaviour of the impala does not seem to be compatible with their domestication, for which animals with fixed-membership herds, like buffalo or eland, are more appropriate. The problems experienced by territorial male impala trying to restrict the movements of a female herd should be observed by anyone who wishes to put himself in the male's position (Jarman and Jarman 1974, p. 880).

Mention of the eland raises an interesting point. This species is the only 'antelope' which is both gregarious and hierarchical; it does not form territories. 'The eland, as every Masai herdsman knows, is more like an ox than an antelope' (Estes 1974, p. 194), and some would indeed classify it within the subfamily Bovinae, with cattle. Two domestication experiments have proved successful, and in both cases the animals were treated just like cattle (Posselt 1963; Treus and Kravchenko 1968). Bigalke (1974) describes experiments with

a range of other animals, all territorial. The problems are great when these animals are confined. The young of the more solitary species frequently die or are killed, and among more gregarious species male aggression results in vigorous fighting and frequent deaths.

The moral of the African examples is that it takes two to form a man—animal relationship. It is clear that the behaviour and social system of the ungulate is as important in influencing the range of possible relationships as are the needs and intentions of the humans. Various aspects have been little explored — it would be interesting to know the effects of castration, for example. Artificial herd structures have been imposed in some zoos, such as putting only a single male in with the females. This does not remove the problem. The unsatisfied aggressive tendencies of the male find outlets in attacks on inanimate objects, human handlers, or the females and young (Walther *et al.* 1983).

Turning to temperate Europe, we may note that red and roe deer are members of the superfamily Cervoidea. Studies of deer behaviour show that these animals are behaviourally close to the territorial antelopes.

Roe deer are territorial for a longer period than just the rut, and the males are virtually solitary. Females are also largely solitary, at least in woodland, and move from one male's territory to another's (Prior 1968; Strandgaard 1972). For these reasons it is concluded that roe deer would have been unsuitable as an early domesticate.

Red deer may in open country form larger herds, but the dominant stags are still decidedly territorial during the rut (de Nahlik 1974; Clutton-Brock, Guinness and Albon 1982). Under forested conditions, red deer break down into much smaller groups, mean group size being as low as two or three (Ratcliffe and Staines 1982).

Current red deer domestication experiments in Scotland have high-lighted some of the problems that would have faced early domesticators. If a group of mixed stags and hinds are put into a paddock, the usual pattern is for one stag to establish dominance, herd the hinds into a corner, and attempt to hold the remaining stags at bay — the territorial pattern carries on. The chasing of a subordinate by a dominant stag can induce the subordinate to leap over fences of more than 2 m in height (Blaxter *et al.* 1974). That experimental deer farming has achieved such success as it has in recent years is due to a large investment of capital and labour, particularly in the erection of many high fences (not always deer proof). Deer are unpredictable during the rut and, in the Scottish example, on occasion attacked farm workers (*ibid.*).

This behaviour is in marked contrast to that of domestic cattle, sheep and goats and their relatives. The behaviour of deer just does not seem to be compatible with their becoming a herd domesticate in the Mesolithic.

Local domestication of cattle and pig

Various claims have been put forward regarding the domestication of cattle and pig in mesolithic Europe. These animals are of course domestic in the Neolithic, being (unlike deer) suitable for close herding. The evidence presented is frequently enigmatic, however, usually consisting of bones claimed to be too small to come from wild animals. As demonstrably wild animals are often present on the same sites, the question arises as to whether the wild-size ranges are really fully known, and whether the claimed domestic animals might not merely be small (i.e. female) wild individuals.

To some extent the search for local domestication is a result of the minimal view sometimes taken of the Mesolithic. The claims are often made where 'un-mesolithic' features such as pottery or permanent settlement occur. The assumption can follow that such 'semi-neolithic' technology ought to be paralleled by a 'semi-neolithic' economy, and that such developments are unlikely in a pure mesolithic context. The foregoing discussion has presented the alternative view, that a degree of complexity can be achieved without the European Mesolithic having to emulate the Near Eastern.

The most important claims in Western temperate Europe are put forward for the south Scandinavian region. These are discussed elsewhere (Zvelebil and Rowley-Conwy, Chapter 6, this volume; Rowley-Conwy 1985). For Eastern Europe, evaluation of the claims is more difficult, as little of the primary data are published in a form accessible to Western readers.

Claims of domestication are sometimes made for the area north of the Black Sea. Claims of early domestic cattle at Kammenaya Mogila and pigs at Zamil Koba and Taš Ayir are regarded as uncertain due to dating problems (Tringham 1971). The best-dated sites are those at Soroki on the River Dniester, belonging to the Bug–Dniester culture. Aceramic layers at Soroki II, dating from 5565 ± 120 bc and 5470 ± 80 bc are claimed to contain a small proportion of domestic cattle and pigs (Dolukhanov 1979). The site location 'ruled out the possibility of effective agriculture and stock breeding in the area' (*ibid*., p. 92), so the domestic animals are regarded as evidence of contact with the Criş neolithic culture on the River Prut (*ibid*.). There is no good evidence that the Criş culture is to be dated this early, however, particularly at the northeastern end of its spread, so the likelihood of such contacts between farmers and fishers is questionable. Local domestication is perhaps also doubtful given the apparent unsuitability of the terrain. In the absence of direct evidence in the form of the publication of measurements, the splitting of the cattle and pig bones into wild and domestic on these sites should perhaps be regarded as tentative.

A largely unexplored aspect of neolithic economies is the degree of interdependence of the various components. In temperate contexts it is uncertain how domestic pigs would be integrated with an otherwise foraging economy. On agricultural settlements, pigs often forage for themselves, and convert organic waste into useful meat. This organic waste is largely the inedible parts of cultivated plants, for example chaff from cereal growing. At other times, pigs may be used to uproot stubble in harvested fields. It is doubtful whether a mesolithic site would provide so many opportunities for pigs –

fruits, nuts, berries, roots etc., even if brought to the site, would probably not result in much waste edible by pigs. Special efforts would thus have to be made to feed the pigs, which would lose the most valuable attribute they have on agricultural settlements: their ability to be partially self-supporting.

Plant cultivation
The wild ancestors of cultivated cereals were not available in temperate Europe, but other plant resources were numerous, and claims for the domestication of one have been put forward.

Primary cultigens in early agricultural systems are usually annuals. These plants give a quicker return, and so are more flexible than plants with a slower turnover. Hazel, for example, is enormously productive, and may be made more so by coppicing. It does not reach maximum nut production, however, until the tree is about 15 years old (Howes 1948). This slow turnover makes the hazel less likely to be the foundation of a temperate agricultural or quasi-agricultural system.

Considerations like this led Clarke (1976) to suggest that plants with a faster turnover might have been cultivated. In particular, he examined bracken (*Pteridium aquilinum*) from this point of view, suggesting that 'late mesolithic exploitation of the Atlantic temperate deciduous forest already closely approached varieties of asexual horticulture and forest husbandry' (*ibid*., p. 32). Annual productivity, he states, may be about 20 to 50 tonnes of edible rhizome/km^2, and he points out that bracken rhizomes were important in the Maori economy.

Merely to point out how much there is, however, is to ignore many factors. There may be 1 000 000 earthworms per hectare of soil, and their weight may be greater than that of the cattle grazing the surface of the same area (Evans 1975), yet an earthworm Mesolithic has not, so far as I know, been suggested. The New Zealand comparison is not directly relevant – New Zealand bracken may form a dense growth up to 3 m in height (Laing and Blackwell 1940), and is sometimes regarded as a different species, *Pteridium esculentum* (Heath and Chinnock 1974). Only the rhizomes of the largest plants were worth digging up, and then only in areas not well suited to the cultivation of the introduced Pacific cultigens (Shawcross 1967). European plants are much smaller; even the rhizomes of the largest are only some 1–1.5 cm in diameter, and are buried about 25 cm below the ground (Watt 1940). On average, roots have a calorific value around one-fifteenth of that of an equivalent weight of hazel nut kernel (although no specific figures are available for bracken). This, the small size of the European rhizomes, and above all the sheer hard labour of digging them up with a digging stick or antler pick, make bracken rhizomes an unlikely cultigen.

It seems, therefore, that there are good arguments against the emergence of an agricultural or quasi-agricultural system based on native temperate European species. The model of mesolithic settlement proposed in the preceding section allows for alternative forms of intensification in certain environments, and we do not need a mimic of Near-Eastern agricultural systems for some European groups to be 'affluent'. This can be achieved in other, more strictly temperate European ways. The local domestication models have, however, caused mesolithic exploitative strategies to be re-examined in a new light. Although the details of the models remain controversial, this alone is sufficient to emphasise the importance of these models to studies of the temperate Mesolithic.

Intensification: the social impetus
The 'Domestic mode of production'

Many strands of the 'social view' can be traced back to Sahlins' (1974) essays on the 'Domestic mode of production'. No household is ever economically autonomous: some under-produce, some overproduce. Overproduction by some house-holds is institutionalised to various degrees in various societies.

Bender (1978, 1981) points out that hunter-gatherer bands are similarly interdependent. She concentrates specifically on mechanisms of change, in particular the intensi-fication of overproduction. Her main unit of study is the alliance network, linking many bands together. The reciprocal social relations involved in the alliance network are the stimulus for intensification and its consequences.

'The political life is a stimulus to production. But it is so to varying degrees' (Sahlins 1974, p. 135). The crucial point is clearly why intensification sometimes occurs and sometimes does not. The placing of Sahlins' scheme into a developmental framework does not in itself demonstrate causation.

Bender (1978, p. 210) invokes environmental factors to account for the existence of reciprocal relations — 'gatherer-hunter bands cannot be autonomous . . . [resources fluctuate, so] it is therefore essential to have reciprocal social relations' (cf. also the similar argument of Tilley 1981*a*). It is a short step from this to the notion that different degrees of reciprocal relations may be suited to different environments. The social view appears entirely compatible with the eco-logical, and the two views seem to be two essential aspects of the same model. The social view needs the ecological factor to account for the variability between systems (why some intensify and some do not). The ecological view needs the social factor to account for the ability to take up environ-mental opportunities. This, however, is probably where many proponents of the social view part company with ecologically inclined colleagues.

It is often argued that many social forms are viable in the same environment, so the environment only sets the broad limits (Ingold 1981). If this is so, the environmental factors cannot explain why one option rather than another (e.g. intensification or no intensification) is taken up.

At one level this is certainly correct. Many organisational aspects are probably evolutionarily neutral, i.e. they incur neither positive nor negative selection in environmental terms.

The evolutionary–ecological perspective takes the view, how-ever, that major alternatives are unlikely to be equally viable and that selection will occur. This will be discussed regarding the interlinked fields of sedentism and storage.

Sedentism is conventionally linked with larger group size. The development of large, sedentary communities would entail a decrease in flexibility, and risk local resource over-exploitation, in some environments. In these environments, interannual resource fluctuations mean that sedentism is a higher risk option. Some environments must therefore be more suited to the appearance of large, sedentary groups than others. In suitable environments the option is likely to be taken up, because the variability in human behaviour offers ample scope for the operation of selection (Rowley-Conwy 1983). The degree of social complexity varies broadly as a function of group size (Carneiro 1967). It therefore seems inescapable that the general levels of complexity (though not the details) of social forms such as alliance networks are fundamentally linked to environmental factors.

Resource storage or its absence in a society is paralleled by ideologies for or against hoarding (Testart 1982; Woodburn 1980). Whether the ideological chicken comes before the environmental egg is another matter. Woodburn (1980) dis-tinguishes between systems of immediate return (without storage) and systems of delayed return (with storage), and writes:

> Although I can imagine ecological and other factors which might favour one approach rather than another, I cannot imagine any environment in which either of the two strategies is impracticable (*ibid.* 1980, p. 101).

> Systems of immediate return and systems of delayed return can both occur in any environment. I do not believe that abundance and scarcity of food and other resources are, in themselves, likely to be crucial variables (*ibid.* p. 111).

This view may be questioned. In seasonal environments there are often seasons when few or no resources are available, so that storage is quite simply a prerequisite for survival. In environments with lesser seasonal variation there is little point in storing food, because 'since everyone knows where the food is, in effect the environment itself is the storehouse' (Lee and DeVore 1968, p. 12). There seems little difficulty in viewing storage in explicitly environmental terms.

The evolutionary–ecological view, then, stresses that, at least at the level of the major alternatives discussed here, selection will favour one or other choice. The broad options are seen as environmentally ranked, not equal. All that is required to articulate this view, and to set in motion the sorts of development described by Bender (1978) where these are environmentally suitable, is the notion of behavioural varia-bility allowing scope for the selection for, and adoption of, particular activities.

A note on 'determinism'
The insistence of the evolutionary–ecological viewpoint

on behavioural variability casts an interesting sidelight on accusations of 'determinism'. Tilley (1981*b*, p. 131) deplores the ecological view for depicting people as 'reified, helpless spectators, always subject to external forces . . . Human intentions, motivations and meanings become dependent variables, functions of social, psychological or biological forces'. This view is hard to maintain, given the *necessity* of behavioural variation to the ecological view. As Grahame Clark (1970, p. 98) points out, 'an individual man or for that matter an individual mosquito enjoys at any particular moment a freedom of choice limited only by organic attributes and the constraints of the environment'. An evolutionary viewpoint attempts to understand why certain traits are selected, not which ones will occur (Dunnell 1980), and makes no claims concerning 'human intentions, motivations and meanings'. Critics have misunderstood this fundamental point.

All constructive approaches to prehistory attempt to see what determined the broad course of visible events. Which approach makes greater claims regarding the actions of individuals is open to argument. Meillassoux (1973) describes the Mbaka pygmies, hunters in the process of becoming farmers. Many new features appear in their social organisation, 'not due to imitative processes, but to the requirements of their new activities' (*ibid*. 1973, p. 197). Once the differences between hunters and farmers have been pointed out, however, they acquire a certain rigidity:

> We do not detect a continuous development from one economic system to another; nor do we find in hunting societies any sign of those internal contradictions which might have led to change . . . This leads us to question the usually assumed notion that, in the successive stages of human evolution, agriculture proceeded from hunting and foraging. Actually hunting may well be unable to develop into any other mode of production and the origins of agriculture should be looked for among other activities, such as fishing (*ibid*., p. 201).

In this view, culture is pictured as being as variable and flexible as a brick. Individuals appear as free to vary their behaviour as the particles of clay that make up the brick. This in turn necessitates stadial transformations as the only way to change from one 'brick' to another. This view achieves a level of determinism concerning the actions of individuals unheard of in the present practice of ecological archaeology. It ignores the fact that no cultures ever live purely by hunting (or fishing, or farming), but must have a flexible organisation capable of switching from one to the other. If hunters are unable to develop into farmers, and if fishers are so similar to farmers, how did hunters ever develop into fishers?

This view runs counter to the idea that biological evolution has developed organisms that are increasingly flexible in their responses, the level of genetic determination of behaviour diminishing as complexity of response increases (Bonner 1980). Man is, of course, *unique* in his flexibility of behaviour. From the evolutionary perspective, the appearance of culture is causally linked with behavioural flexibility (Bonner 1980). It would be strange for the evolution of flexibility to culminate in producing such rigid behavioural forms as sociocultural determinism would have us believe in.

Conclusion

I hope it is now clear why I wrote in the introduction that a minimal view is still sometimes taken of the temperate European Mesolithic. I hope it is also clear that various strands of current work are emphasising that the minimal view is no longer applicable. 'Free and careless families of bowmen' (Rozoy 1978, p. 1192) is not an adequate expression of all that was taking place. The various lines of research emphasising this are still in their infancy, and often resist integration with one another with customary bellicosity. It will be interesting to see whether a more general view will emerge with the maturing of these research directions.

One reason for the minimal view has been the assumption that the European Mesolithic, unlike that of the Near East, led nowhere. An avenue of future research must be to compare various mesolithic traditions on a broad scale. Why was it, for example, that the European Mesolithic was not left alone to continue its development for much longer, as was the Jomon of Japan? At another level, European mesolithic adaptations must be studied for their own sake, and the epoch must not be relegated to the status of a period of 'waiting' (Kozłowski 1973, p. 333) or 'gestation' (Srejović 1972, p. 15). Mesolithic groups on the ground did not know that they were to be followed, centuries or millennia later, by farmers; and had they known, it is unlikely they would have cared. If this essay has made the point that the Mesolithic is not just a pregnant pause in European prehistory, then it has succeeded in its purpose.

Acknowledgements
I would like to express my thanks to the following for many interesting discussions and helpful suggestions, and for comments on an earlier draft of this paper: Grahame Clark, Paul Halstead, Roger Jacobi, Glynis Jones, Jim Lewthwaite, Paul Mellars, Robin Torrence and Marek Zvelebil. All views and errors remain my own.

References
Barrière, C. (1956) *Les Civilisations Tardenoisiennes en Europe Occidentale*, Bière, Paris.
Bender, B. (1978) 'Gatherer-hunter to farmer: a social perspective'. *World Archaeology* 10, 204–22.
  (1981) 'Gatherer-hunter intensification', in A. Sheridan and G. N. Bailey, eds., *Economic Archaeology*, pp. 149–58, BAR International Series 96, British Archaeological Reports, Oxford.
Bigalke, R. C. (1974) 'Ungulate behaviour and management, with special reference to husbandry of wild ungulates on South African game ranches', in V. Geist and F. Walther, eds., *The Behaviour of Ungulates and its Relation to Management*, pp. 830–52, IUCN, Morges, Switzerland.
Binford, L. R. (1980) 'Willow smoke and dogs' tails: hunter-gatherer settlement systems and archaeological site formation'. *American Antiquity* 45, 4–20.
Blaxter, K. L., Kay, R. N. B., Sharman, G. A. M., Cunningham, J. M. M. and Hamilton, W. J. (1974) *Farming the Red Deer*, HMSO, Edinburgh.

Bökönyi, S. (1972) 'Zoological evidence for seasonal or permanent occupation of prehistoric settlements', in P. J. Ucko, R. Tringham and G. W. Dimbleby, eds., *Man, Settlement and Urbanism*, pp. 121–6, Duckworth, London.

Bolomey, A. (1973) 'An outline of the late epipalaeolithic economy at the "Iron Gates": the evidence of bones'. *Dacia* 17, 41–52.

Bonner, J. T. (1980) *The Evolution of Culture in Animals*, Princeton University Press, Princeton, N.J.

Bourlière, F. (1963) 'Observations on the ecology of some large African mammals'. *Viking Fund Publications on Anthropology* 36, 43–54.

Bradley, R. (1978) *The Prehistoric Settlement of Britain*, Routledge and Kegan Paul, London.

Burch, E. S. (1972) 'The caribou/wild reindeer as a human resource'. *American Antiquity* 37, 339–68.

Carneiro, R. L. (1967) 'On the relationship between size of population and complexity of social organisation'. *Southwestern Journal of Anthropology* 23, 234–43.

Chaplin, R. E. (1975) 'The ecology and behaviour of deer in relation to their impact on the environment of prehistoric Britain', in J. G. Evans, S. Limbrey and H. Cleere, eds., *The Effect of Man on the Landscape: the Highland Zone*, pp. 40–2, Council for British Archaeology Research Report 11.

Childe, V. G. (1925) *The Dawn of European Civilisation*, 1st edn, Routledge and Kegan Paul, London.

(1957) *The Dawn of European Civilisation*, 6th edn, Paladin, St Albans.

Clark, J. G. D. (1932) *The Mesolithic Age in Britain*, Cambridge University Press, Cambridge.

(1936) *The Mesolithic Settlement of Northern Europe*, Cambridge University Press, Cambridge.

(1954) *Excavations at Star Carr*, Cambridge University Press, Cambridge.

(1955) 'A microlithic industry from the Cambridgeshire fenland and other industries of Sauveterrian affinities from Britain'. *Proceedings of the Prehistoric Society* 21, 3–20.

(1958) 'Blade and trapeze industries of the European stone age'. *Proceedings of the Prehistoric Society* 24, 24–42.

(1968) 'The economic impact of the change from late-glacial to post-glacial conditions in northern Europe'. *Proceedings VIIIth Congress of Anthropological and Ethnological Sciences – Ecology*, pp. 241–4.

(1970) *Aspects of Prehistory*, University of California Press, Berkeley.

(1972) *Star Carr: A Case Study in Bioarchaeology*, Addison-Wesley Module in Anthropology 10, Addison-Wesley, Reading, Mass.

(1973) 'Seasonality and the interpretation of lithic industries', in J. Maluquer de Motes, ed., *Estudios Dedicados al Professor Dr Luis Pericot*, pp. 1–13, University of Barcelona, Publicaciones Eventuales 23.

(1975) *The Earlier Stone Age Settlement of Scandinavia*, Cambridge University Press, Cambridge.

(1978) 'Neothermal orientations', in P. Mellars, ed., *The Early Postglacial Settlement of Northern Europe. An Ecological Perspective*, pp. 1–10, Duckworth, London.

(1980) *Mesolithic Prelude*, Edinburgh University Press, Edinburgh.

Clarke, D. L. (1976) 'Mesolithic Europe: the economic basis' in G. de G. Sieveking, I. H. Longworth and K. E. Wilson, eds., *Problems in Economic and Social Archaeology*, pp. 449–81, Duckworth, London.

Clutton-Brock, T. H., Guinness, F. E. and S. D. Albon (1982) *Red Deer. Behaviour and Ecology of Two Sexes*, Edinburgh University Press, Edinburgh.

Coull, J. R. (1972) *The Fisheries of Europe. An Economic Geography*, Bell, London.

Cushing, D. H. (1975) *Marine Ecology and Fisheries*, Cambridge University Press, Cambridge.

Dolukhanov, P. (1979) *Ecology and Economy in Neolithic Eastern Europe*, Duckworth, London.

Dunnell, R. C. (1980) 'Evolutionary theory and archaeology', in M. B. Schiffer, ed., *Advances in Archaeological Theory and Method*, vol. 3, pp. 35–99, Academic Press, London.

Estes, R. D. (1974) 'Social organisation of the African Bovidae', in V. Geist and F. Walther, eds., *The Behaviour of Ungulates and its Relation to Management*, pp. 166–205, IUCN, Morges, Switzerland.

Evans, J. G. (1975) *The Environment of Early Man in the British Isles*, Paul Elek, London.

Gamble, C. (1978) 'Resource exploitation and the spatial patterning of hunter-gatherers: a case study', in D. Green, C. Haselgrove and M. Spriggs, eds., *Social Organisation and Settlement*, pp. 153–85, BAR International Series 47, British Archaeological Reports, Oxford.

Geupel, V. (1973) 'Zur kenntnis des mesolithikums im Süden der DDR', in S. K. Kozłowski, ed., *The Mesolithic in Europe*, pp. 157–76, Warsaw University Press, Warsaw.

Gob, A. (1981) 'Review of *Les Derniers Chasseurs. L'Epipaléolithique en France et en Belgique*, by J. G. Rozoy'. *Mesolithic Miscellany* 2(1), 18–19.

Gurina, N. N. (1981) 'Zur Frage der Genesis des Frühneolithikums in der Russischen Tiefebene oberes Wolgagebeit und Wolga-Oka Zwischenströmland', in B. Gramsch, ed., *Mesolithikum in Europa*, pp. 191–200, Veröffentlichungen des Museums für Ur- und Frühgeschichte, Potsdam 14/15, Deutscher Verlag, Berlin.

Heath, E. and Chinnock, P. R. (1974) *Ferns and Fern Allies of New Zealand*, Reed, Wellington.

Howes, F. N. (1948) *Nuts. Their Production and Everday Uses*, Faber, London.

Ingold, T. (1981) 'The hunter and his spear: notes on the cultural mediation of social and ecological systems', in A. Sheridan and G. N. Bailey, eds., *Economic Archaeology*, pp. 119–30, BAR International Series 96, British Archaeological Reports, Oxford.

Iversen, J. (1949) 'The influence of prehistoric man on vegetation'. *Danmarks Geologiske Undersøgelse* IV, 3, 6, 6–23.

(1973) 'The development of Denmark's nature since the last glacial'. *Danmarks Geologiske Undersøgelse* V (7-C), 7–126.

Jacobi, R. M. (1973) 'Aspects of the "Mesolithic Age" in Great Britain', in S. K. Kozłowski, ed., *The Mesolithic in Europe*, pp. 237–65, Warsaw University Press, Warsaw.

(1976) 'Britain inside and outside mesolithic Europe'. *Proceedings of the Prehistoric Society* 42, 67–84.

(1978) 'Northern England in the eighth millennium b.c.: an essay', in P. Mellars, ed., *The Early Postglacial Settlement of Northern Europe. An Ecological Perspective*, pp. 295–332, Duckworth, London.

(1979) 'Early Flandrian hunters in the south-west'. *Proceedings of the Devon Archaeological Society, Jubilee Conference Volume*, pp. 48–93.

Jacobi, R. M., Tallis, J. H. and Mellars, P. A. (1976) 'The southern Pennine mesolithic and the ecological record'. *Journal of Archaeological Science* 3, 307–20.

Jarman, M. R. (1972) 'European deer economies and the advent of the neolithic', in E. S. Higgs, ed., *Papers in Economic Prehistory*, pp. 125–48, Cambridge University Press, Cambridge.

Jarman, P. J. and Jarman, M. V. (1974) 'Impala behaviour and its relevance to management', in V. Geist and F. Walther, eds., *The Behaviour of Ungulates and its Relation to Management*, pp. 871–81, IUCN, Morges, Switzerland.

Jensen, J. (1982) *The Prehistory of Denmark*, Methuen, London.

Kozłowski, S. K. (1973) 'Introduction to the history of Europe in the early Holocene', in S. K. Kozłowski, ed., *The Mesolithic in Europe*, pp. 331–66, Warsaw University Press, Warsaw.

(1975) *Cultural Differentiation of Europe from 10th to 5th millennium B.C.*, Warsaw University Press, Warsaw.

(1976*a*) 'Studies on the European mesolithic – K points'. *Archaeologia Polona* 17, 7–25.

(1976*b*) 'Studies on the European mesolithic. II. Rectangles, rhomboids and trapezoids in northwestern Europe'. *Helinium* 16, 43–54.

(1976*c*) 'Les courants interculturels dans le mésolithique de l'Europe occidentale'. *9th Congrès International des Sciences Préhistoriques et Protohistoriques, Nice*, Collogue XIX, pp. 135–60.

Laing, R. M. and Blackwell, E. W. (1940) *Plants of New Zealand*, Whitcombe and Tombs, Christchurch.

Lee, R. B. and DeVore, I. (1968) 'Problems in the study of hunters and gatherers', in R. B. Lee and I. DeVore, eds., *Man the Hunter*, pp. 3–12, Aldine, Chicago.

Legge, A. and Rowley-Conwy, P. A. (1986) 'A reconsideration of the fauna from Star Carr', in C. Bonsall, ed. *Proceedings of the 3rd International Symposium on the Mesolithic in Europe, Edinburgh, 1985*, Edinburgh University, Edinburgh, in press.

Leuthold, W. (1974) 'Observations on home range and social organisation of lesser kudu, *Tragelaphus imberbis* (Blyth 1869)', in V. Giest and F. Walther, eds., *The Behaviour of Ungulates and its Relation to Management*, pp. 206–34, IUCN, Morges, Switzerland.

Loze, I. (1981) 'Spätmesolithikum and frühneolithikum in Lettland', in B. Gramsch, ed., *Mesolithikum in Europa*, pp. 183–90, Veröffentlichungen des Museums für Ur- und Frühgeschichte, Potsdam, 14/15, Deutscher Verlag, Berlin.

Meiklejohn, C. (1978) 'Ecological aspects of population size and growth in late glacial and early postglacial north-western Europe', in P. Mellars, ed., *The Early Postglacial Settlement of Northern Europe. An Ecological Perspective*, pp. 65–79, Duckworth, London.

Meillassoux, C. (1973) 'On the mode of production of the hunting band', in P. Alexandre, ed., *French Perspectives in African Studies*, pp. 187–203, Oxford University Press, Oxford.

Mellars, P. A. (1974) 'The palaeolithic and mesolithic', in C. Renfrew, ed., *British Prehistory*, pp. 41–99, Duckworth, London.

(1975) 'Ungulate biomass, economic patterns and the mesolithic landscape', in J. G. Evans, S. Limbrey and H. Cleere, eds., *The Effectof Man on the Landscape: the Highland Zone*, pp. 49–56, Council for British Archaeology Research Report 11.

(1976*a*) 'Settlement patterns and industrial variability in the British mesolithic', in G. de G. Sieveking, I. H. Longworth and K. E. Wilson, eds., *Problems in Economic and Social Archaeology*, pp. 375–99, Duckworth, London.

(1976*b*) 'The appearance of "narrow blade" microlithic industries in Britain: the radiocarbon evidence'. *9th Congrès International des Sciences Préhistoriques et Protohistoriques, Nice*, Colloque XIX, pp. 166–74.

(1976*c*) 'Fire ecology, animal populations and man; a study of some ecological relationships in prehistory'. *Proceedings of the Prehistoric Society* 42, 15–45.

Milisauskas, S. (1978) *European Prehistory*, Academic Press, London.

de Nahlik, A. J. (1974) *Deer Management. Improved Herds for Greater Profit*, David and Charles, London.

Newell, R. R. (1973) 'The postglacial adaptations of the indigenous population of the northwest European plain', in S. K. Kozłowski, ed., *The Mesolithic in Europe*, pp. 399–440, Warsaw University Press, Warsaw.

Posselt, J. (1963) 'The domestication of the eland'. *Rhodesian Journal of Agricultural Research* 1, 81–7.

Price, T. D. (1978) 'Mesolithic settlement systems in the Netherlands', in P. Mellars, ed., *The Early Postglacial Settlement of Northern Europe. An Ecological Perspective*, pp. 81–113, Duckworth, London.

(1981) 'Regional approaches to human adaptation in the mesolithic of the north European plain', in B. Gramsch, ed., *Mesolithikum in Europa*, pp. 217–34, Veröffentlichungen des Museums für Ur- und Frühgeschichte, Potsdam, 14/15, Deutscher Verlag, Berlin.

Prior, R. (1968) *The Roe Deer of Cranbourne Chase*, Oxford University Press, Oxford.

Rackham, O. (1980) *Ancient Woodland. Its History, Vegetation and Uses in England*, Edward Arnold, London.

Radley J. and Mellars, P. (1964) 'A mesolithic structure at Deepcar, Yorkshire, and the affinities of its associated flint industries'. *Proceedings of the Prehistoric Society* 30, 1–24.

Ratcliffe, P. R. and Staines B. W. (1982) 'Red deer in woodlands: research findings', in *Roe and Red Deer in British Forestry*, pp. 42–53, British Deer Society, London.

Rowley-Conwy, P. A. (1981) 'Mesolithic Danish bacon: permanent and temporary sites in the Danish mesolithic', in A. Sheridan and G. Bailey, eds., *Economic Archaeology. Towards an Integration of Ecological and Social Approaches*, pp. 51–5. BAR International Series 96, British Archaeological Reports, Oxford.

(1982) 'Forest grazing and clearance in temperate Europe with special reference to Denmark', in S. Limbrey and M. Bell, eds., *Archaeological Aspects of Woodland Ecology*, pp. 199–215, BAR International Series 146, British Archaeological Reports, Oxford.

(1983) 'Sedentary hunters: the Ertebølle example', in G. N. Bailey, ed., *Hunter-Gatherer Economy in Prehistory. A European Perspective*, pp. 111–126, Cambridge University Press, Cambridge.

(1985) 'The origins of agriculture in Denmark: a review of some theories'. *Journal of Danish Archaeology* 4, 188–95.

Rozoy, J. G. (1971) 'Tardenoisien et Sauveterrien'. *Bulletin de la Société Préhistorique Française* 68, 345–74.

(1973) 'The Franco-Belgian epipalaeolithic: current problems', in S. K. Kozłowski, ed., *The Mesolithic in Europe*, pp. 503–30, Warsaw University Press, Warsaw.

(1978) *Les Derniers Chasseurs* (3 vols., English summaries), Bulletin de la Société Archéologique Champenoise, special number.

(1981) 'Les changements dans la continuité. Les débuts de l'épipaléolithique dans l'Europe de l'Ouest', in B. Gramsch, ed., *Mesolithikum in Europa*, pp. 11–24, Veröffentlichungen des Museums für Ur- und Frühgeschichte, Potsdam, 14/15, Deutscher Verlag, Berlin.

Sahlins, M. (1974) *Stone Age Economics*, Tavistock, London.

Schwabedissen, H. (1944) *Die Mittlere Steinzeit in westlichen Norddeutschland*, Wachnolz, Neümunster.

(1981) 'Ertebølle/Ellerbek – mesolithikum oder neolithikum?', in B. Gramsch, ed., *Mesolithikum in Europa*, pp. 129–42, Veröffentlichungen des Museums für Ur- und Frühgeschichte, Potsdam, 14/15, Deutscher Verlag, Berlin.

Shawcross, K. (1967) 'Fern root, and the total scheme of 18th century Maori food production in agricultural areas'. *Journal of the Polynesian Society* 76, 330–52.

Srejović, D. (1972) *Europe's First Monumental Sculpture: New Discoveries at Lepenski Vir*, Thames and Hudson, London.

Strandgaard, H. (1972) *The Roe Deer* (Capreolus capreolus) *Population at Kaló and the Factors Regulating its Size*, Danish Review of Game Biology 7(1).

Sulimirski, T. (1970) *Prehistoric Russia. An Outline*, John Baker, Humanities Press, London.

Switsur, V. R. and Jacobi, R. M. (1979) 'A radiocarbon chronology for the early postglacial stone industries of England and Wales', in

R. Berger and H. E. Suess, eds., *Radiocarbon Dating*, pp. 41–68, University of California Press, Berkeley.

Testart, A. (1982) 'The significance of food storage among hunter-gatherers: residence patterns, population densities, and social inequalities'. *Current Anthropology* 23, 523–37.

Thévenin, A. (1981) 'La fin de l'épipaléolithique et les débuts du mésolithique dans le nord du Jura français', in B. Gramsch, ed., *Mesolithikum in Europa*, pp. 25–32, Veröffentlichungen der Museums für Ur- und Frühgeschichte, Potsdam, 14/15, Deutscher Verlag, Berlin.

Tilley, C. (1981*a*) 'Conceptual frameworks for the explanation of sociocultural change', in I. Hodder, G. Isaac and N. Hammond, eds., *Pattern of the Past*, pp. 363–86, Cambridge University Press, Cambridge.

(1981*b*) 'Economy and society: what relationship?', in A. Sheridan and G. N. Bailey, eds., *Economic Archaeology*, pp. 131–48, BAR International Series 96, British Archaeological Reports, Oxford.

Treus, V. and Kravchenko, D. (1968) 'Methods of rearing and economic utilisation of eland in the Askaniya-Nova Zoological Park'. *Symposium of the Zoological Society of London* 21, 395–411.

Tringham, R. (1971) *Hunters, Fishers and Farmers of Eastern Europe 6000–3000 B.C.*, Hutchinson, London.

Troels-Smith, J. (1960) 'Ertebølletidens fangstfolk og bønder' *Fra Nationalmuseets Arbejdsmark 1960*, 95–119.

Walther, R. R., Mungall, E. C. and Grau, G. (1983) *Gazelles and their Relatives. A Study in Territorial Behaviour*, Noyes, Park Ridge, New Jersey.

Waterbolk, H. T. (1968) 'Food production in prehistoric Europe'. *Science* 162, 1093–102.

Watt, A. S. (1940) 'Contributions to the ecology of bracken (*Pteridium aquilinum*). I. The rhizome'. *New Phytologist* 39, 401–22.

Whittaker, R. H. (1975) *Communities and Ecosystems*, Macmillan, New York.

Wobst, H. M. (1976) 'Locational relationships in palaeolithic society'. *Journal of Human Evolution* 5, 49–58.

Woodburn, J. (1980) 'Hunters and gatherers today and reconstruction of the past', in E. Gellner, ed., *Soviet and Western Anthropology*, pp. 95–117, Duckworth, London.

Chapter 3

The mesolithic sandwich: ecological approaches and the archaeological record of the early postglacial

Clive Gamble

'To be excitingly right in general is better than to be dully accurate in particular'
Gore Vidal *Burr*

The postglacial period presents archaeologists with a test bed between ecological and social theories of culture change. The archaeological and environmental evidence that has now been accumulated suggests two main lines of approach. On the one hand, the upturn in world climate that was felt in a myriad of ways and at many spatial scales throughout the five continents *may* have been the decisive factor in bringing to fruition fundamental changes in human survival strategies.

Alternatively, the geographical selectivity of where these changes in the structures of production took place *can* be used as an argument against looking for such determinism in the archaeological record. This, in turn, lends weight to an argument for the role of social forces in the progress.

In this paper I want to take a third view and look at the Postglacial in terms of *variation* in human survival strategies rather than *change* to novel systems of organisation and exploitation. I shall do this by considering aspects of the archaeological record associated with the Eurasian Mesolithic, sandwiched, as archaeologists often describe it, in terms of long-run stability and short-run change, between hunters and farmers, cold and warmth, tundra and forests, reindeer and wheat, simple and complex environments. My main aim is to raise methodological issues concerning the interpretation of this record rather than providing explanations for all the patterns we can identify in the data.

Pleistocene background

As might be expected, many views about the post-glacial period are closely associated with the data base from Europe and the wider boreal/temperate zones of Asia. Depending upon the type of axe you wish to grind, the archaeology of the early postglacial period, traditionally associated with mesolithic assemblages, becomes a prelude, a waiting room, a failed experiment or the finest hour of the hunter-gatherers before they succumbed to the inevitable as agricultural groups realised their full potential. This usually implies the utilisation of the latent productivity in the temperate latitudes with their 'inherent' suitability for agri-culture, and the possibility of sustained demographic growth leading to the development of complex systems of social and economic organisation. In other words, studying this period in temperate Eurasia has either everything or nothing to tell us about cultural evolution, adaptive strategies and the process of culture change.

With a longer perspective, we can see that anatomically modern human populations were present in parts of this huge territory at least 35 000 years ago. Although climates at this date were cold and arid they were still some way from those associated with the maximum extension of the last glacial ice sheets at 18 000 bp. For many regions, the conditions at this time spike must have established a bottom line in resources. From this perspective 'things could only get better'.

The common ground in these familiar scenarios recognises that there were indeed differences in terms of climate, resources and the distribution of energy which distinguished the scale of human adaptations in postglacial temperate latitudes from those practised during the last glacial. Moreover, at the other end of the period a major restructuring clearly took place in the organisation of society which had implications for the appropriation, distribution and utilisation of resources.

Archaeologists have devoted considerable effort to defining the slices in this period sandwich. Much more attention has been given to examining how the loaf should be cut rather than to examining the manner in which the commonly agreed interpretations are made.

My aim is not to enter demarcation disputes about the relative thicknesses of these early/middle/late slices. Instead I want to examine ways of dispensing with these divisions and predetermined categories. This will be achieved by examining the way we attach significance to the archaeological record and the processes we believe it enshrines during this period. The purpose is to look at three rather different archaeological records which have been variously interpreted as three different cultural periods, three contrasted economies, and at least two types of society and to see if such divisions can be supported. I will do this by considering:

(a) the relative costs to human populations of exploiting, when available, highly productive resources;
(b) the implications for human mobility patterns based on the use of these resources;
(c) the interpretation of temporal and spatial variation in regional archaeological records where these resources were used.

Resources

The proportional use of resources is one major way of classifying contemporary hunters and gatherers. This is done by categorising their diets according to the broadly defined activites of hunting—gathering—fishing (for discussion see Davidson 1981; Hayden 1981*a*). When it was introduced (Lee 1968; Murdock 1967), such an approach was undeniably a step forward in looking at band society subsistence in terms of the degree of dependence upon groups of resources rather than classifying them by either one distinctive or abundant element such as moth, wallaby or reindeer hunters. However, this approach, while used by pre-historians, has done little to promote any greater understanding of how variable dependence on any one group of resources will show up in the archaeological record as variation in such aspects as settlement location, occupational density and systemic organisation.

These general approaches have been criticised before. In a major paper, Clarke (1976) examined several of these weaknesses by critically examining the stereotypes into which

archaeologists had fitted the postglacial Mesolithic. His aim was to suggest alternative interpretations of the same data base. One of his main points was that archaeologists should abandon their preconceptions of mesolithic economies as meat-orientated and look instead at the associated technologies as solutions to plant exploitation.

His warrant for this shift in emphasis rested with an ecological appraisal of the distribution and abundance of resources within Europe. In particular, the Postglacial was characterised by the appearance of highly productive environments, in the ecological and food sense, along coasts, around lakes, rivers, lagoons and in forests. One of this aims was to identify the *hot-spots* for postglacial settlement. The emphasis was on ecological production, on the prediction of the good areas to live in, which could be tested by examining the archaeological record for settlement location and occupation density.

It is interesting that while Clarke was discussing the prime areas for human occupation in mesolithic Europe, Jochim (1976) was providing an elegant analysis of mesolithic settlement in southern Germany, an area in the centre of the continent where ecological productivity was comparatively low (Clarke 1976, p. 24). This case-study has contributed to the development of wider methodological principles concerning the formation and interpretation of the archaeological record. Jochim presented his analysis in the form of a game played against the environment and where human groups set about achieving particular goals. Understanding why a particular solution, from among many alternatives, was adopted, lies in reviewing the relative costs incurred in the various possible options. The archaeological outcome of such subsistence decisions would be seen, for example, in the location of population to resources. Thus at a sub-regional scale of analysis there would be considerable variation in the formation of the archaeological record as the costs of resources fluctuated according to cycles of abundance. Emphasis was laid on the importance of assessing the potential food resources in the environment, since this allowed hunters and gatherers to draw up the all-important *resource use schedule*, based on their attributes.

The predictive nature of the model presented archaeologists with the possibility that by identifying the food resources on a prehistoric shopping list they could conduct similar case-studies. Such lists are usually determined by digging up and identifying the resources. If the preservation of these vital ecofacts is poor then historical and ecological evidence has been used to supply the missing resources and so account for the location of settlement, as in the case with salmon bones from mesolithic rock shelter sites along the Rhine (Jochim 1979).

The utility of a case-study approach based upon the study of resource attributes has been demonstrated in a number of later studies (Bailey 1983; Gamble 1978; Mellars 1978; Weniger 1982) where the broad palaeoecological picture is discussed and then a smaller scale selected in order to demonstrate the archaeologists's apparent ability to identify and understand variation in the materials of the archaeological record and to interpret them as changes in survival strategies.

These case-studies proved valuable in integrating artefactual and ecofactual data in a spatial framework. However, they were limited by aspects of the general model they employed where the particularities of any situation were stressed. Indeed, while the model systematised a great deal about prehistoric subsistence, much of this fell into the category of demonstrating how a system worked rather than how and why systems changed. Moreover the assumptions of optimality in subsistence behaviour led to the search for a single solution and hence played down the possible importance of variation within a survival strategy in the long term. They imply a constant appreciation by human groups of variables such as exploitation costs, levels of demand and the intensity of extraction rates. But there is no guarantee that this appreciation of resources was characteristic of all prehistoric hunters and gatherers. Indeed this is highly improbable.

As a result, by far the most convincing examples of these models, now loosely grouped under applications of optimal foraging theory, have been restricted to the analysis of short-run contemporary foragers rather than long-run prehistoric hunters (Winterhalder and Smith 1980; Smiley *et al.* 1980).

One way to develop these approaches in order to consider variation (i.e. alternative solutions) and change (i.e. new assumptions determining strategies) is to characterise resources on the basis of their exploitation costs relative to their productivity.

The productivity of plants and animals is a measure of energy accumulation over a specific period and given area (Jones, G. 1979, p. 14). As a general rule the rate of energy accumulation is faster and thus productivity is greater among small-bodied species and at particular stages of environmental succession (Table 1). High productivity is characteristic of resources such as grasses, acorns, shellfish, small mammals and birds. This has been commented upon on many occasions (e.g. Deevey 1968). Hayden (1981*b*), for example, has examined this productivity by using the biological models of *K* and *r* selection. Among animal species, *r* strategists are often small bodied, short lived, produce many offspring and are con-

Table 1. *The characteristics of different successional stages*

Characteristic of organism	Developmental stages	Mature stages
Niche style	Broad	Narrow
Size of organism	Small	Large
Life cycles	Short, simple	Long, complex
Growth form, selection pressure for	Rapid growth	Feedback control
Production, selection for	Quantity	Quality

Putman and Wratten 1984, Table 4.2.

sequently more productive than their large-bodied *K* counterparts.

However, while these biological models are informative in understanding the varied strategies employed by plant and animal species to cope with variable environmental factors, it it not easy to fit human food resources into such a neat dichotomy. For example, there are many bird species which, although small bodied, are classified as *K* strategists. Many plant and animal species change both their selection and dispersal strategies according to competition, crowding and many other environmental factors (Horn 1982; Putman and Wratten 1984). Changes in these strategies are not always neatly linked to a change in the successional stage of the environment.

For human foragers, the small package size in which these highly productive food resources occur represents the most significant exploitation cost. The costs of utilising such production can principally be measured by the time taken in harvesting and preparation. One example would be the seed-harvesting strategies employed by many Aboriginal groups in the semi-arid zones of Australia (Allen 1972; Cane 1984; Latz and Griffin 1978; O'Connell and Hawkes 1981). The yield from these grass seeds can be prodigious although the costs involved in collection and processing time are almost always very high. Cane (1984, pp. 84–5) provides figures that, among the Gugadja/Pintupi of the Western Desert, a woman will have to work for six hours collecting and preparing in order just to feed herself on a grass seed diet. The advantage of seeds lay not in their abundance but in their potential for storage as well as being found throughout the local landscape at all seasons. They are a guaranteed resource. High exploitation costs relative to yields are also a feature of grain-based subsistence agriculture (Pimentel and Pimentel 1979).

Food management strategies which aim to meet group requirements from these small-package resources will bring into play the tactical options contained within the time and labour budgets. From the former budget, technology can play its part although variation will be enormous as, for example, between extremely complex facilities, e.g. fish traps designed to cope with the brief availability of a resource such as salmon, and the simplicity of seed-grinding equipment. Indeed the mobility of the resource is reflected in the different technological response as Torrence (1983) and Satterthwait (1979) have pointed out. This of course also applies to the large-bodied resources such as reindeer or seals which, in turn, are only available either for brief periods of the year or fleetingly in the hunter's search for food. Also within the time budget there will be variation in the tactical use of storage to cope with problems of the limited availability of food resources. The suitability of a resource for bulk storage will be important and may occur in either a large- or a small-package resource.

High productivity can also be maintained by interrupting the process of ecological succession. Early seral stages are often characterised by plant dispersal strategies which cope with factors of stress, disturbance and competition by the spectacular quantity of seed production (Grime 1977). Both agriculturalists and hunter-gatherers manage and maintain these highly productive environments. Among hunters and gatherers this is primarily achieved by the global practice of burning (Jones 1969; Mellars 1976).

Variation in the labour budget is equally flexible in order to meet the variable costs in exploiting resources of many different sizes and types of productivity. The composition of work groups based on age and sex categories is one example (Carlstein 1982, p. 307). Further costs, however, will be incurred in the co-ordination of these activities. The information required to guide the schedule of resource use is moreover only acquired at considerable cost. Equally, the wider mechanisms of risk sharing among regional populations are only achieved at considerable expense to the contributing parties.

While these high costs can apply both to hunters of large mammals and to seed foragers, it is interesting to note that the archaeological evidence for the first systematic use of small-package resources indicates a late date (Dennell 1983; Freeman 1981; Gamble 1986; Meehan 1982) and probably correlates with the global appearance of anatomically modern human populations.

Further changes in the archaeological record would be associated with this addition of small-package resources to food management strategies. This would include the purposive maintenance, where applicable, of the productivity of environments at an early successional stage. However, once this change in strategy was instituted, I would anticipate variation in the archaeological record reflecting the management of food resources in these productive but demanding environments. This of course makes divisions, based on the species exploited, between different types of hunters (e.g. nomadic and complex; Rowley-Conwy 1983) or between hunter-gatherers and agriculturalists largely unnecessary.

In summary, small-bodied, highly productive resources were always potentially available for exploitation but were only employed comparatively recently because of the high-cost tarifs involved. The 'breakthrough' has to be seen in terms of an overall strategy rather than a single innovation such as domesticating wheat or inventing the sickle. The spatial and temporal tactics that serviced this strategy were apparently available in Eurasia from at least 35 000 bp.

Mobility

Far from offering congratulations to mesolithic populations for being the first groups to cope with these high-cost tarifs and so break into 'new' resource environments, we must place the credit with pleistocene groups who, for example, were exploiting anadromous fish runs in the Dordogne (Jochim 1983), rabbits in south-eastern Spain (Davidson 1976), catfish on the Nile (Wendorf and Schild 1980) or grass seeds in the Western Desert of Australia (O'Connell and Hawkes 1981).

However, we might still want to differentiate among

and between hunters and agriculturalists by contrasting their degree of residential mobility. It is commonplace to regard agriculture as a settling down process that required novel, domesticated resources as population growth occurred. Once again we need to ask whether the archaeological record really confirms this view of major change, or whether an alternative interpretation is possible that links a variable survival strategy with the impact of ecological structure.

In the last section, I identified mobility as possibly the key attribute of resources in understanding aspects of their use by human groups; for example, variation in technology (Satterthwait 1979, Fig. 9.2). The mobility of resources is also reflected in the size and extent of hunter–gatherer territories (Gamble 1978) and there is no doubt that between the Late Glacial and Postglacial in Europe the annual territory size of local groups shrank quite considerably. The smaller-bodied resources, both plant and animal, found within these smaller territories were now exploited. Moreover the widespread evidence for burning (Mellars 1976) points to the management of a particular successional stage. This reduction in spatial area occurred as a function of the density and predictability of such resources within the environment. This of course waited, in Europe at least, upon the upturn in climate and a change in plant productivity.

The size of territories is not, however, a very sensitive indicator of mobility strategies. The Nunamiut, for example, move within a territory of 63 000 km^2 while the G/wi bushmen exploit an area of 782 km^2. However, both groups move on average some 10 or 11 times per annum (Kelly 1983, Table 1). As Kelly points out, those groups which move most are generally associated with high primary biomass conditions (expressed as kg/m^2). Examples of such environments, coupled with low effective temperatures (Binford 1980), would be the boreal forests, where primary biomass in the form of trees is high but where food choices in the shape of animals and vegetable resources are extremely low. This results in a great deal of commuting time before a hunter can begin to search for, pursue and hopefully secure some game (Kelly 1983, pp. 290–1). High primary biomass linked with high effective temperatures also results in groups with comparatively small territories and very high mobility. The Punan in a food-rich environment move, on average, some 45 times per annum within a total area of 861 km^2. The value of such comparative studies of hunter-gatherer mobility (Binford 1980; Kelly 1983) lies in the demonstration that mobility varies according to general principles of ecological organisation. Rather than being amazed at the variety of hunter-gatherer mobility strategies, we can see instead that they are a structured transformation of small group interactions with the environment. If we can understand differences in mobility among hunter-gatherer groups in terms of such ecological transformations, then there seems little reason to cite major changes in the use of space and mobility between the late glacial Palaeolithic and the Mesolithic. What we are seeing in the archaeological record is equally a structured transformation by prehistoric groups in response to changed ecological conditions. Human behaviour in this instance was variable with respect to a set of ground-rules and did not change because of new ground-rules. In this instance, a degree of sedentism should not be seen as a radical departure from 'normal' hunter-gatherer mobility tactics but as part of the spectrum of variation.

A greater degree of sedentism is of course well known for recent hunter-gatherer groups along the Northwest Coast of America. The key resource among these and other Pacific groups with comparable low residential mobility is the availability of anadromous fish stocks. Kelly (1983, Table 6) emphasised the importance of these bulk resources and their suitability for storage. Such groups should, according to his ecological model, exhibit a high degree of mobility, since they are in an environment which combines high primary biomass and low effective temperature. He argues, however, that the strategy they adopted was a solution to the very high commuting costs that would have been incurred if the primary biomass of the land alone were exploited (*ibid*., p. 292). Bulk resources are also important for explaining the low number of residential moves undertaken every year by the Nunamiut. In this case such a strategy is based on a large-bodied resource, caribou. As a general point, the key to sedentism, reduced mobility, rests on guaranteeing access to scarce resources, as Hitchcock (1982, p. 246) has shown for groups in the Kalahari.

These consequences of sedentary behaviour for population should not be modelled as growth in a single population as Hitchcock's (1982) study of recently settled Kalahari groups also shows. Here local group size remained constant as hunters and gatherers settled down, due to an increasing dependence on stores and missions. The growth came in the proliferation of local groups and the consequent problems of integration and packing. This could also occur if sedentism were based on the presence of highly nucleated and abundant resources. There is of course no implication in either situation that further organisational complexity will occur as a result of sedentism.

Finally, variation in mobility can also be linked to the degree of territoriality and the defence of resources. According to Dyson-Hudson and Smith (1978), the presence of territoriality depends on the existence of predictable and dense resource distributions. Their argument is that the economic defensibility of resources can be measured in terms of a cost/benefit ratio where energy input for energy return is the appropriate measure. The costs of territoriality will have particular importance for the time budgets of groups. We have seen repeatedly that behaviour in this budget is under strong selection to cope with scheduling factors; hence the application to variation in technology and storage options. It will also be under selection from the information strategies that are required to integrate groups so as to minimise conflict and reduce risk in the exploitation of resources. It is important to appreciate that a high degree of territoriality with regard to

defended resources can be predicted on ecological grounds for hunters and gatherers. This needs to be considered when interpreting the archaeological record of earthworks and assigning cultural, economic and social status to the groups responsible for their construction.

Regional records

In the preceding section I have argued that the archaeological record associated with sedentary communities is no easier to decipher than that associated with mobile adaptations (Cribb 1982; Foley 1981, 1984; Gould 1980; Gamble 1986). The examples underscore the role that ecology has played in measuring variation in the archaeological record of such mobile systems. If it is difficult to interpret the archaeological record for sedentary hunters and gatherers, why should it be any different for early agricultural groups, especially when the degree of sedentism is also dependent upon the exploitation of varieties of small-bodied resources and the maintenance of early seral stages (Barker and Gamble 1985)?

For the moment let us consider the methodological limitations of the first approach, based as it is on ethnographic observation. An example is provided by the current trend among archaeologists to identify complex systems of organisation in the archaeological record of hunters and gatherers (Price 1981). In a recent paper, Rowley-Conwy (1983, p. 112) has argued that sedentism is a primary feature of what he terms *complex* as distinct from the more familiar *nomadic* hunting and gathering groups. He generalises from a small ethnographic sample that the former will be found in environmental situations with 'the overlapping seasonal appearance of various migratory resources' (*ibid*., p. 118). The combined result is to encourage sedentism in order to take advantage of such bountiful resource conditions where different food sources, e.g. birds, shellfish, plants, fish and land mammals, come on stream at different times of the year and within easy, if not immediate, reach of a fixed location.

With such importance attached, in his definition, to the existence of a suitable resource base, we would have to recast our characterisation of most of the world's hunters and gatherers from nomadic to complex. For example, overlapping sets of resources in Arnhem land (Jones 1980; Meehan 1982) or along the rivers of southeastern Australia (Allen 1972; Lourandos 1980, 1983), or even within some of the subarctic areas of inland North America (Helm 1981) might be expected to produce 'dramatic' archaeological evidence equalling that cited by Rowley-Conwy (1983) from a small area in northern Europe.

There are also examples of where bulk storage was possible but did not take place. In this context, the Tasmanians are of especial interest, since the archaeological record they created without bulk storage, even though it was possible, is particularly impressive. A recent survey of the West Point midden sites (Stockton 1983) has plotted some 125 middens of various sizes along *c.* 3 km of coastline. Of these, the largest covers an area of almost 0.5 km^2 (Bowdler 1982).

An excavation of 75 m^3 into this midden produced 30 000 stone artefacts, including grinding slabs, and 20 000 faunal remains. There is abundant evidence among these for the harvesting of shellfish, elephant seal, birds, land mammals and other food resources, but no fish. Pit depressions on the surface of the midden mounds represent habitation traces and it has been estimated that the midden was occupied by *c*. 40 people for one-third of the year (Jones 1966). Despite such evidence, the Tasmanians are not regarded as having been complex hunters even though there is this evidence for some degree of residential permanence and only a limited amount of annual movement within the immediate hinterland (Jones 1977). Moreover, at Mount Cameron West, north of West Point, there exist some monumental engravings that rival in scale some of the artistic achievements of the Northwest Coast (Flood 1983, Plate 15). It is possible that lower commuting costs in the hinterland of the northwest Tasmanian tribe may be one reason why these bulk resources, seal and the ignored fish, were not utilised as the basis for a 'complex' hunting adaptation.

My point here is quite simple. Goodness of fit between models of organisational complexity derived from a segment of ethnography and matched to a segment of archaeology is not by itself a demonstration of complexity in the archaeological record. The use of descriptions such as *complex* to describe hunter-gatherer systems has, in the first instance, to be separated from expected variation in universal tactics such as mobility, the organisation of time and labour budgets and the deployment of technology. We have already seen above that many small-bodied resources carry implications for the organisation of time budgets and labour schedules, which will structure the regional archaeological record. This occurs irrespective of the wider economic systems (e.g. the varieties of hunter-gatherer economy and between these and agriculturalists) that we are often trying to identify.

The essential problem is that we have collected data to fit definitions, such as hunter or farmer, rather than developed methodologies for investigating behaviour. As a result we are happy to attribute our identifications of sedentary behaviour with consequences for population growth, the intensification of production and many other key stages in the complex process of becoming complex.

We can now see that sedentism has less to do with identifying changes in the archaeological record of hunters and gatherers than is commonly argued. Reduced mobility was always a tactical option for hunter-gatherer groups which were utilising both small- and large-bodied food resources.

At the other end of the period sandwich, sedentism is often seen as a key factor in the transition towards systems of food production based, characteristically, on the local abundance of small-bodied resources. This is followed by the population explosion that sedentism is supposed to trigger (Rowley-Conwy 1983; Price 1981; Harris 1977*a, b*) and after which societies are trapped in agriculture. Indeed sedentism linked to rapid population growth based on the use of

domesticated grass seeds is regarded by most authors as the main factor distinguishing the Neolithic from earlier economies. As with many of the attributes normally associated with the definition of agricultural communities there is none, however, which is exclusive. For example, low yield agriculture in the Kalahari did not require hunting and gathering groups to become sedentary. Instead crops were planted and then left as groups continued their annual rounds, only returning to the fields when the crops had ripened (Hitchcock 1982, p. 246). In this instance traditional archaeological inferences about residential mobility and organisational complexity based on the recovery of carbonised seeds could be misleading.

These examples bring us back once again to recognising *change* (new assumptions determining strategies) and *variation* (alternative solutions) in the archaeological record.

I have argued elsewhere (Gamble 1983, 1984, 1986) that the palaeolithic record from Europe reveals only a single restructuring in the organisation and use of resources. This can be identified archaeologically at the middle/upper palaeolithic interface. The change cannot be identified by inferring new approaches to resource management by speculating on the relative advantages of the shapes of new tools, or of the cultural, mental or behavioural implications of the first appearance of art and ornament but rather through the evidence of regional settlement histories. These establish a quantitative advance, associated with the Upper Palaeolithic, in the use of regional resources, compared to the responses to similar environmental conditions that existed in earlier climatic cycles of the Middle and Upper Pleistocene.

This ability to cope with some extreme resource conditions is an integral part of the upper palaeolithic 'package'. Moreover, these refer to the extremes of both full glacial and interglacial environments. We can follow the latter outcome in the archaeological record of the Postglacial. Here, a comparison of the settlement histories of England at the time of the last interglacial (128 000−118 000 bp) and the Early Postglacial shows that, in the former period, no occupation took place while, in the latter, there are abundant archaeological traces under broadly comparable environmental conditions (Gamble 1984). While the list of potential resources may have been similar, the adaptive responses were not. It is therefore shown by this evidence that a change occurred in the organisation of subsistence and the appropriation of resources between these two periods (Gamble 1986, Chapter 8). Furthermore, settlement histories also show a greater success in coping with the resources available in the period 35 000−10 000 bp than for comparable conditions in the earlier part of the last glaciation (Gamble 1983), when parts of Europe were abandoned. In other words, the restructuring in the use of resources that took place at *c*. 35 000 bp solved the problems of exploiting many different combinations of resources. These occurred in both glacial and interglacial (holocene) environments and presumably at a variety of seral stages. While these examples are drawn from Europe (Gamble 1986), it is also clear that what occurred as part of this continent's upper palaeolithic package had a global significance in terms of human adaptive strategies. As a result what we are seeing in the archaeological record is a single change in human adaptive patterns which appears at different times in different areas; probably since it is related to the process of colonisation associated with anatomically modern *Homo sapiens*. Once this restructuring occurs in any given region, it is only followed by variation as the tactics cope with particular distributions of resources and communities. Viewed in the archaeological record, the variation may, on occasion, as with the Ertebølle middens (Price 1981) or the sites of Dolní Věstonice/Pavlov (Klíma 1962), seem to provide spectacular and unequivocal evidence that another restructuring step, in other words a change, has been documented. I would argue, however, that rather than dealing with either subsequent changes in the organisation of subsistence economies or trends towards complexity and intensification, we are seeing instead the implementation of a food management strategy designed to cope with extremely variable combinations of resources.

The subsistence aspects of what Dennell (1983, p. 102) has called fully modern behaviour involved food management strategies in which a great variety of demands upon time and labour budgets were now incorporated, via a number of tactics, into a comprehensive schedule that could cope with almost anything. These tactics no doubt included systems of information sharing as well as developments in technology. We can measure their success in the settlement histories of regions as diverse as the Willandra lakes of New South Wales, the tundras of the Don river and the boreal forests of northern England. Moreover, we can also see one aspect of food management strategies associated with domestic plant and animal communities: namely, the ability to schedule time and labour budgets to cope with differential growing seasons, soil productivity, frosts and all other environmental hazards which result in variation in agricultural strategies aiming to maintain productivity to meet targets determined by population needs and social requirements.

But, however useful an ecological framework might be for examining variation, it is less successful when used to partition the archaeological record into different economic types and levels of organisational complexity. Any major difference between hunter-gatherers and agriculturalists must therefore be related to the systems of appropriation, the husbanding of resources marked by concepts of ownership and property (Ingold 1980). If we can demonstrate such a fundamental restructuring in social relations in the archaeological record then it would be appropriate to recognise a change.

A useful perspective on these questions of recognising change and variation is supplied by current research in Australia. In a range of different environments, beginning 4000–5000 years bp, there is a significant shift in regional archaeological signatures (Bowdler 1981). Not only is there a dramatic increase in the number of sites and artefact distri-

butions (e.g. Ross 1981) but new foods are included in the diet. These include such species as cycads (*Macrozamia moorei*) (Beaton 1977), boogong moths (Flood 1980), bunya nuts (Sullivan 1977), yams (Hallam n.d.) and a variety of grass seed strategies (Allen 1972), as well as evidence for eel traps and fish weirs on a massive scale (Coutts, Frank and Hughes 1978; Lourandos 1980, 1983). This is associated with a continent-wide change in technology known as the small tool tradition (Mulvaney 1975; White with O'Connell 1983). What is also now apparent is the considerable evidence for earth mound 'villages' in southwestern Victoria (Lourandos 1980, 1983) and in Western Australia (Hallam n.d.). These have to be combined with an upward revision of population estimates for the continent (Butlin 1983).

How is this evidence for significant additions to the archaeological records of regional populations relevant to a study of the Eurasian Mesolithic?

Just suppose for a moment that *Macrozamia* or daisy yams had become staples as important as maize or wheat due, perhaps, to changes acquired during the process of domestication. Then delay Captain Cook's arrival long enough for society to have diverged from its hunter-gatherer roots. Any early-dated finds of *Macrozamia* or daisy yams would then assume great significance in current archaeological interpretations for the origins of the process that Cook interrupted. The evidence for villages, eel traps etc. would no doubt be seen as proof beyond reasonable doubt for a major shift in society and subsistence that began at *c.* 4000–5000 bp. Australia would, on this evidence, be yet another independent centre of food production. Moreover, we would not be surprised in this distortion of prehistory to discover, on contact, many different types of societies and economies rubbing shoulders in the continent. As Beaton (1983, p. 95) points out, this bothers no-one studying the prehistory of the Americas.

What these data from Australia splendidly challenge are the assumptions behind the European models for recognising postglacial developments in food production. The challenge is a methodological one that stems from a too literal reading of the archaeological record; where undue emphasis is placed on new additions to the record rather than on arguing that they represent variation within existing strategies to exploit highly productive small-bodied resources. The Australian data emphasise the global nature of such strategies. Moreover, by considering both the Australian and Eurasian cases it is difficult to argue that climate and environmental change played a significant role in precipitating a global shift during these postglacial millennia.

Alternatively, there is Cohen's (1977) argument that by this time colonisation had filled the world and that subsequent population growth would produce stress at a regional level and begin to select for change in exploitation strategies. This does rather imply a dampening on fertility rates and on population increase during the Pleistocene which is difficult to explain, since so many environments are represented and in areas both near to, and far from, the polar ice sheets.

A further explanation, currently in favour, is that an intensification in the exploitation of resources took place and was promoted by the changed demands of social relations on appropriation and production (Bender 1978; Lourandos 1983). Why this should occur in several different continents during the second half of the postglacial is as difficult to explain as population increase.

Conclusion

I have now briefly examined the test bed of social and ecological theory mentioned at the beginning of the paper. What I hope to have indicated is that the transitions in this particular period sandwich do not stand up to close scrutiny if an ecological approach is adopted. Many patterns used by archaeologists to draw up the major divisions in the sandwich can be accounted for by variation in mobility and resource use, predicted from the changing combinations of small-package food resources in early seral stages.

Neither is there as yet an alternative methodology, based on a social theory of culture change, to help unravel and partition the archaeological record of the Postglacial in a more relevant manner. Consequently, I am unconvinced by arguments put forward for either the European or the Australian data that what happens in the Early Postglacial is a change in the social relations of production; either to food production based on different social premises (Europe), or to more complex hunters and gatherers with premises equally different from those of their predecessors in the region (Australia). I do not deny that change and restructuring occurred but in Europe this is archaeologically difficult to detect because at present we lack an adequate methodology for interpreting the material evidence from this end of the sandwich. Of one thing I am sure, it is not synonymous with neolithic assemblages. The patterning in many of these might profitably be examined within an ecological framework and as variation within hunter-gatherer strategies. In Australia such restructuring arrived with Captain Cook.

It has, however, been possible to provide an unambiguous measure of the change in society and economy that took place during the Upper Pleistocene (Gamble 1986). This uses the ecological framework to compare the performance of systems in time and seeks an explanation in terms of the guiding principles behind subsistence behaviours which create archaeological signatures. These changes in upper pleistocene strategies not only produced a much greater range of choice in resource combinations but also a greater degree of dependence upon networks and alliances which were costly to maintain. Here lay the nexus for variation as such alliance networks exploited interregional differences in ecological structures of productivity, limiting resources and degrees of risk. I see no convenient marker, no comparable 'Big Surprise', in the Eurasian archaeological record to focus our search for a comparable change in human organisation during the early postglacial period. Consequently we need to examine alternative explanations for the patterns we recover rather than continue to confirm existing interpretations in ever more detail. After all, who would know that by eating their sandwiches they could someday eat cake?

Acknowledgements
Earlier drafts of this paper were read by Marek Zvelebil, Rory Putman and Iain Davidson. I am very grateful for all their comments and hope they still disagree with the final result.

References
Allen, H. (1972) 'Where the crow flies backward', Ph.D. thesis, Australian National University.
Bailey, G. N. (ed.) (1983) *Hunter-gatherer Economy in Prehistory*, Cambridge University Press, Cambridge.
Barker, G. W. W. and Gamble, C. (eds.) (1985) *Beyond Domestication in Prehistoric Europe. Investigations in Subsistence Archaeology and Social Complexity*, Academic Press, New York.
Beaton, J. M. (1977) 'Dangerous harvest', Ph.D. thesis, Australian National University.
     (1983) 'Does intensification account for changes in the Australian holocene archaeological record?' *Archaeology in Oceania* 18, 94–7.
Bender, B. (1978) 'Gatherer-hunter to farmer: a social perspective'. *World Archaeology* 10, 204–22.
Binford, L. R. (1980) 'Willow smoke and dog's tails: hunter–gatherer settlement systems and archaeological site formation'. *American Antiquity* 45, 4–20.
Bowdler, S. (1981) 'Hunters in the highlands: aboriginal adaptations in the eastern Australian uplands'. *Archaeology in Oceania* 16, 99–111.
     (1982) 'Prehistoric archaeology in Tasmania', in F. Wendorf and A. Close, eds., *Advances in World Archaeology*, vol. 1, pp. 1–49, Academic Press, New York.
Butlin, N. (1983) *Our Original Aggression*, George Allen and Unwin, Sydney.
Cane, S. (1984) 'Desert camps', Ph.D. thesis, Australian National University.
Carlstein, T. (1982) *Time Resources, Society and Ecology,* vol. 1, *Preindustrial Societies*, George Allen and Unwin, London.
Clarke, D. L. (1976) 'Mesolithic Europe: the economic basis', in G. de G. Sieveking, I. H. Longworth and K. E. Wilson, eds., *Problems in Economic and Social Archaeology*, pp. 449–82, Duckworth, London.
Cohen, M. N. (1977) *The Food Crisis in Prehistory*, Yale University Press, New Haven, Conn.
Coutts, P. J. F., Frank, R. K. and Hughes, P. J. (1978) 'Aboriginal engineers of the Western District, Victoria'. *Records of the Victorian Archaeological Survey* 7.
Cribb, R. L. D. (1982) 'The archaeological dimensions of Near Eastern nomadic pastoralism', Ph.D. thesis, Southampton University.
Davidson, I. (1976) 'Les Mallaetes and Monduver: the economy of a human group in prehistoric Spain', in G. de G. Sieveking, I. H. Longworth and K. E. Wilson, eds., *Problems in Economic and Social Archaeology*, pp. 483–99, Duckworth, London.
     (1981) 'Can we study prehistoric economy for fisher–gatherer–hunters?' in A. Sheridan and G. N. Bailey, eds., *Economic Archaeology*, pp. 17–33, BAR International Series 96, British Archaeological Reports, Oxford.
Deevey, E. (1968) 'Discussions, Part II', in R. B. Lee and I. DeVore, eds., *Man the Hunter*, pp. 94–5, Aldine, Chicago.
Dennell, R. W. (1983) *European Economic Prehistory*, Academic Press, London.
Dyson-Hudson, R. and Smith, E. A. (1978) 'Human territoriality: an ecological reassessment'. *American Anthropologist* 80, 21–41.

Flood, J. M. (1980) *The Moth Hunters*, Australian Institute of Aboriginal Studies, Canberra.

(1983) *The Archaeology of the Dreamtime*, Collins, London.

Foley, R. (1981) 'A model of regional archaeological structure'. *Proceedings of the Prehistoric Society* 47, 1–17.

(ed.) (1984) *Hominid Evolution and Community Ecology*, Academic Press, London.

Freeman, L. G. (1981) 'The fat of the land: notes on palaeolithic diet in Iberia', in R. S. O. Harding and G. Terleki, eds., *Omnivorous Primates*, pp. 104–65, Columbia University, New York.

Gamble, C. S. (1978) 'Resource exploitation and the spatial patterning of hunter-gatherers: a case study', in D. Green, C. Haselgrove and M. Spriggs, eds., *Social Organisation and Settlement*, pp. 153–85, BAR International Series 47(i), British Archaeological Reports, Oxford.

(1983) 'Culture and society in the upper palaeolithic of Europe', in G. N. Bailey, ed., *Hunter-gatherer Economy in Prehistory*, pp. 201–11, Cambridge University Press, Cambridge.

(1984) 'Regional variation in hunter-gatherer strategy in the upper pleistocene of Europe', in R. Foley, ed., *Hominid Evolution and Community Ecology*, pp. 237–60, Academic Press, London.

(1986) *The Palaeolithic Settlement of Europe*, Cambridge University Press, Cambridge.

Gould, R. A. (1980) *Living Archaeology*, Cambridge University Press, Cambridge.

Grime, J. P. (1977) 'Evidence for the existence of three primary strategies in plants and its relevance to ecological and evolutionary theory'. *American Naturalist* 111, 1169–94.

Hallam, S. J. (n.d.) 'Yams, alluvium and 'villages' on the west coastal plain', AIAS, Canberra, in press.

Harris, D. R. (1977a) 'Alternative pathways toward agriculture', in C. A. Reed, ed., *Origins of Agriculture*, pp. 179–243, Mouton, The Hague.

(1977b) 'Settling down: an evolutionary model for the transformation of mobile bands into sedentary communities', in J. Friedman and M. J. Rowlands, eds., *The Evolution of Social Systems*, pp. 401–17, Duckworth, London.

Hayden, B. (1981a) 'Subsistence and ecological adaptations of modern hunter/gatherers', in R. S. O. Harding and G. Terleki, eds., *Omnivorous Primates*, pp. 344–421, Columbia University Press, New York.

(1981b) 'Research and development in the stone age: technological transitions among hunter-gatherers'. *Current Anthropology* 22, 519–48.

Helm, J. (1981) *Handbook of North American Indians*, Vol. 6, *Subarctic*, Smithsonian Institute, Washington DC.

Hitchcock, R. K. (1982) 'Patterns of sedentism among the Basarwa of eastern Botswana', in E. Leacock and R. B. Lee, eds., *Politics and History in Band Societies*, pp. 223–67, Cambridge University Press, Cambridge.

Horn, H. S. (1982) 'Optimal tactics of reproduction and life-history', in J. R. Krebs and N. B. Davies, eds., *Behavioural Ecology: An Evolutionary Approach*, pp. 411–29, Blackwell Scientific Publications, Oxford.

Ingold, T. (1980) *Hunters, Pastoralists and Ranchers*, Cambridge University Press, Cambridge.

Jochim, M. A. (1976) *Hunter-Gatherer Settlement and Subsistence*, Academic Press, New York.

(1979) 'Catches and caches: ethnographic alternatives for prehistory', in C. Kramer, ed., *Ethnoarchaeology*, pp. 219–46, Columbia University Press, New York.

(1983) 'Palaeolithic cave art in ecological perspective', in G. N. Bailey, ed., *Hunter-gatherer Economy in Prehistory*, pp. 212–19, Cambridge University Press, Cambridge.

Jones, G. (1979) *Vegetation Productivity*, Longman, London.

Jones, R. (1966) 'A speculative archaeological sequence for north-west

Tasmania'. *Records of the Queen Victoria Museum, Launceston* 25.

(1969) 'Firestick farming'. *Australian Natural History* 16, 224–8.

(1977) 'The Tasmanian paradox', in R. V. S. Wright, ed., *Stone Tools as Cultural Markers*, pp. 189–204, Australian Institute of Aboriginal Studies, Canberra.

(1979) 'The fifth continent: problems concerning the human colonization of Australia'. *Annual Review of Anthropology* 8, 445–66.

(1980) 'Hunters in the Australian coastal savanna', in D. R. Harris, ed., *Human Ecology in Savanna Environments*, pp. 107–46, Academic Press, London.

Kelly, R. L. (1983) 'Hunter-gatherer mobility strategies'. *Journal of Anthropological Research* 39, 277–306.

Klíma, B. (1962) 'The first ground-plan of an upper palaeolithc loess settlement in middle Europe and its meaning', in R. J. Braidwood and G. R. Willey, eds., *Courses Towards Urban Life*, pp. 193–210, Edinburgh University Press, Edinburgh.

Latz, P. K. and Griffin, G. F. (1978) 'Changes in aboriginal land management in relation to fire and food plants in Central Australia', in B. S. Hetzel and H. J. Frith, eds., *The Nutrition of Aborigines in Relation to the Ecosystem of Central Australia*, pp. 77–85, CSIRO, Melbourne.

Lee, R. B. (1968) 'What hunters do for a living, or how to make out on scarce resources', in R. B. Lee and I. DeVore, eds., *Man the Hunter*, pp. 30–48, Aldine, Chicago.

Lourandos, H. (1980) 'Change or stability?: hydraulics, hunter-gatherers and population in temperate Australia. *World Archaeology* 11, 245–66.

(1983) 'Intensification: a late pleistocene–holocene archaeological sequence from southwestern Victoria'. *Archaeology in Oceania* 18, 81–94.

Meehan, B. (1982) *Shell Bed to Shell Midden*, Australian Institute of Aboriginal Studies, Canberra.

Mellars, P. A. (1976) 'Fire ecology, animal populations and man: a study of some ecological relationships in prehistory'. *Proceedings of the Prehistoric Society* 42, 15–45.

(ed.) (1978) *The Early Postglacial Settlement of Northern Europe*, Duckworth, London.

Mulvaney, D. J. (1975) *The Prehistory of Australia*, 2nd edn, Pelican, Melbourne.

Murdock, G. P. (1967) 'Ethnographic atlas; a summary'. *Ethnology* 6, 109–236.

O'Connell, J. F. and Hawkes, K., (1981) 'Alyawara plant use and optimal foraging theory', in B. P. Winterhalder and E. A. Smith, eds., *Hunter-gatherer Foraging Strategies*, pp. 99–125, University of Chicago Press, Chicago.

Pimentel, D. and Pimentel, M. (1979) *Food Ecology and Society*, Edward Arnold, London.

Price, T. D. (1981) 'Complexity in "non-complex" societies', in S. E. van der Leeuw, ed., *Archaeological Approaches to the Study of Complexity*, pp. 54–86, CINGVLA VI, Amsterdam.

Putman, R. J. and Wratten, S. D. (1984) *Principles of Ecology*, Croom Helm, London.

Ross, A. (1981) 'Holocene environments and prehistoric site patterning in the Victorian Mallee'. *Archaeology in Oceania* 16, 145–54.

Rowley-Conwy, P. (1983) 'Sedentary hunters: the Ertebølle example'. In G. Bailey, ed., *Hunter-gatherer Economy in Prehistory* pp. 111–26, Cambridge University Press, Cambridge.

Satterthwait, L. D. (1979) 'A comparative analysis of Australian Aboriginal food-procurement technologies', Ph.D. thesis, University of California Los Angeles.

(1980) 'Aboriginal Australia: the simplest technologies?' *Archaeology and Physical Anthropology in Oceania* 15, 153–6.

Smiley, F. E., Sinopoli, C. M., Jackson, H., Wills, W. H. and Gregg, S. A. (1980) 'The archaeological correlates of hunter-gatherer societies: studies from the ethnographic record'. *Michigan Discussions in Anthropology* 5.

Stockton, J. H. (1983) 'The prehistoric geography of northwest Tasmania', Ph.D. thesis, Australian National University.

Sullivan, H. (1977) 'Aboriginal gatherings in south-east Queensland', B.A. (Honours) thesis, Australian National University.

Torrence, R. (1983) 'Time budgeting and hunter-gatherer technology', in G. N. Bailey, ed., *Hunter-gatherer Economy in Prehistory* . pp. 11–22, Cambridge University Press, Cambridge.

Wendorf, F. and Schild, R. (1980) *Prehistory of the Eastern Sahara*, Academic Press, New York.

Weniger, G. C. (1982) *Wildbeuter and ihre Umwelt*, Archaeologica Venatoria 5, Tubingen.

White, J. P. with O'Connell, J. F. (1983) *A Prehistory of Australia, New Guinea and Sahul*, Academic Press, Sydney.

Winterhalder, B. P. and Smith, E. A. (eds.) (1980) *Hunter-gatherer Foraging Strategies*, University of Chicago Press, Chicago.

Chapter 4

The role of hunting-gathering populations in the transition to farming: a Central-European perspective

*Slavomil Vencl**

The pioneering work of Grahame Clark in the study of Mesolithic Europe, beginning in 1932 and, continuing some 50 years later with the latest addition (Clark 1932, 1980), created a significant research tradition which enjoys well-deserved authority and exerts considerable influence on current thought. His understanding of the European Mesolithic emerged above all from the profound knowledge of the British and North-European evidence, a geographical orientation which tended to determine the view of the European Mesolithic in general. The active part played by the North-European mesolithic groups in the transition to food production came to be regarded as a model for other, as yet little explored, parts of mesolithic Europe. The belief in the importance of the local mesolithic groups in the emergence of food production in Europe remains a characteristic feature of the Anglo-Saxon school of thought, elaborated in a number of imaginative variations (Clarke 1976; Ashbee 1982; Dennell 1983). It forms the backbone of the paradigm prevailing today, as illustrated in the following passage by Price (1983, p. 771):

> In virtually every area of Europe, the transition from Mesolithic foraging to Neolithic farming witnesses distinct aspects of continuity in human adaptation . . . The end of the Mesolithic is not brought about by an advance of invading farmers but rather reflects a period of readaptation and adjustment to changing environment

and new subsistence practices, often within the context of existing societies.

In the present contribution I shall argue that such an understanding of the mesolithic−neolithic continuity does not correspond to the actual situation in Europe as a whole, because it is based on a simplified model historically rooted in the North-European evidence. Such models simply cannot form the basis for a pan-European interpretation of the transition to farming.

This point is best illustrated by David Clarke's (1976) influential study of the economic basis of the Mesolithic of Europe. Clarke correctly regarded the archaeological evidence for the use of plant food in the Mesolithic as inadequate; to compensate, he based his own interpretation of the mesolithic economy on the dietary potential of different resources in temperate Europe, where plants form a significant portion of the standing biomass. He concluded that:

> the subsistence basis was probably focused on various root/foliage/fruit and nut combinations exploited in techniques which perhaps in some areas already approximated to simple forest horticulture (*ibid*. 1976, p. 477).

Quoting the work of Higgs and Jarman (1969, 1972), Clarke (1976, p. 459) considers the Mesolithic−Neolithic interface as

*Translated, from the Czech original, by the editor.

an artifically created dichotomy, because in reality we are
dealing with mere acculturation:

> many areas of the European Temperate forest *c.* 7000–
> 4000 BC were areas of very high edible productivity, as
> rich in wild foods as any areas of the world at that
> latitude: areas in which it was not so much a matter of
> the late arrival of advanced food production, diffused
> from distant sources, as of the local continuance of rich
> wild-food resources and stable population pressure.
> Here, temperate-forest husbandry had probably
> developed over the millennia in a rather different
> direction, of which we are only now beginning to catch
> glimpses. The northward spread of the productive
> species of hazel-nut, apple, pear, and other food species
> in the oak–hazel forest, although part of an ecological
> and climatic succession, may well have been extensively
> and deliberately assisted by fire-clearance and even
> planting (Waterbolk 1968). (Clarke 1976, p. 460)

In my view, the suggested trend toward the indigenous
evolution of farming remains an unrealistic hypothesis which is
at variance with the existing archaeological data: nowhere in
Europe can we find neolithic economies based on cultigens
and domesticates of local origin. On the contrary, the
economic basis of the European Neolithic originated in regions
outside Europe (Wijnen 1981; Waterbolk 1982). To date, not
a single culture in neolithic Europe can be shown to have been
based, economically, on the tending of apple, pear or hazel
trees. Clarke (1976) based his examination of the European
Mesolithic on the conventional analysis of lithic industries;
unconventionally, he added the ecological perspective. But the
whole problem is considered from the mesolithic perspective
only, with important sources of information, such as the
human fossil record, left unexplored.

Regional data to aid the reconstruction of mesolithic
societies and their development remain too incomplete to
allow more than the presentation of an alternative hypothesis;
the speculative essay presented here should be seen in this
light. The main difference between the view expressed here
and the model developed by Clarke (1976) and others consists in the more balanced approach to the Mesolithic–
Neolithic transition, with due emphasis given to (1) the
existence and the autonomous evolution of the neolithic
cultures and (2) the historical significance of developments in
Central and southeastern Europe. In addition, I support the
view that the problem of the Mesolithic–Neolithic transition
should not be regarded in isolation, but, while acknowledging
its specific chronological and geographical context, one should
see it in common with other historical situations, where similar
events took place (such as the demise of hunter-gatherers as a
result of Greek and Roman colonisation in antiquity or the
more recent expansion of European civilisation). At the
archaeological level, the transformation of mesolithic cultures
should be considered systematically and *in toto*, rather than
by reference to those elements of material culture which are

least affected by the processes of deposition and attrition of
the archaeological record.

Palaeoanthropological aspects of the problem

Data obtained from the study of past human populations can be used to distinguish between hunter-gatherers
and food-producing groups in those areas where farming was
introduced by the neolithic colonists. It can be also used as an
indication of continuity where farming was adopted by the
indigenous population. The chronological and geographical
deficiency of sources, as well as methodological contradictions
between the typological and statistical analysis of the material
(for a discussion, see Schwidetzky 1978*a*, p. 317), as for
instance those arising from the genetics of small populations
(Bach 1978, p. 57), will make any conclusions about the
Mesolithic–Neolithic transition based on the human fossil
record arguable. On the other hand, extensive data are now
available regarding individual areas of Europe (Schwabedissen
and Schwidetzky 1973, 1978) which indicate a number of
distinct correlations between anthropological types and
archaeological remains in the Neolithic and Eneolithic of
Europe: groups responsible for the Dnieper–Donetsk, the
Tripolye, the Corded Ware, the Bell Beakers, the Seine-
Oise-Marne (SOM) culture in France, the Funnel-Neck Beaker
(TRB) in Scandinavia, and the *vasi a bocca quadrata* in Italy
all differ markedly in their morphological characteristics from
the surrounding population. The correspondence between the
new anthropological elements and the introduction of new
cultural traits would seem to be more than coincidental and
indicates a relationship between the two phenomena (see also
Schwidetzky 1978*a*, p. 319).

Reliably-dated, culturally identifiable and sufficiently
numerous osteological material is fundamental to any reliable
analysis of the fossil evidence. In addition, the data must be
continuous in time and space. The latter condition prevents
us, for example, from considering seriously the assumptions
about the continuity between the upper palaeolithic and
neolithic populations in Czechoslovakia, since the investigator
(Jelínek 1978, p. 249) based his judgement on the comparison
of a number of Gravettian skeletons with finds 20 000 years
younger, separated not only by a very long time-interval, but
also by multiple cultural transformations. Similarly, the
statistical analysis of metric measurements of neolithic crania
by Xirotiris (1981*a, b*) can only be viewed with caution, as he
did not take into account the geographical and chronological
variability of his sample.

Despite the fragmentary nature of the existing skeletal
evidence, it is possible to use the data at a simplified, broad
level of resolution. From this perspective, we are in a position
to distinguish two fundamentally different entities: the first
is characterised by populations with a predominance of
cromanoid or palaeo-europoid traits, who, despite the coarse-
grained nature of the evidence, can be said to represent the
indigenous mesolithic populations. In contrast, the second

complex is characterised by leptodolichomorphic (particularly mediterranoid) populations who, from the sixth and fifth millennia bc onwards, expanded from the Balkans and Greece to the Danubian basin and, partially, along the Mediterranean coasts into Western Europe as well. The appearance of these populations in Europe coincides with the introduction of the neolithic economy. These populations appear to have been responsible for the Starčevo, Criş and Linear Pottery cultures, as well as for their derivatives: the Stroke-Ornamented Ware, Rössen, Jordanów and Lengyel (Bernhard 1978, p. 158). The close correspondence between the core area of the expansion of the mediterranoid populations and the regions ecologically most favourable for farming is striking. In fertile areas of Europe, the productive capacity of farming could find its full realisation; this acted as a catalyst to population growth, which in turn led to the progressive colonisation and the establishment of fully neolithic societies in secondary areas.

The spread of leptodolichomorphic neolithic populations was no doubt accelerated by the existing Climatic Optimum, which increased the productivity and reliability of farming. The expansion of the mediterranoid traits and the corresponding regression of the palaeo-europoid ones can be traced, according to Schwidetzky (1978a), down to the second millennium bc, by which time the palaeo-europoid-dominated populations remained only in areas of Northern and Western Europe marginal to farming (Fig. 1).

In the north of Europe, the rapid spread of farming practices, adapted to the more favourable conditions of Southern and Central Europe, were arrested by the conditions of the natural environment. As a result, the development of farming had a tenuous and temporary character and was supplemented by the exploitation of wild resources. Such a mixed economy must have had a greater resemblance to that of the food collectors and must have been subject to similar constraints of productive potential and population capacity. Consequently, the farming population could not have greatly exceeded the indigenous hunting and gathering one. Acculturation, rather than the displacement of indigenous groups, would be the likely development under these conditions. In fact, the acculturation process is attested by the perserverance in the skeletal morphology of the original palaeo-europoid traits detectable, for instance, in the skeletal populations of the TRB or Corded Ware culture.

In reality, the initial process of expansion of the neolithic colonists can be expected to have been less uniform than would appear and may have included the assimilation of numerically insignificant groups of the indigenous hunters and gatherers. The subsequent reappearance of paleo-europoid traits in the Eneolithic of Central Europe, instead of indicating the persistence of hunting-gathering populations, was probably the result of intrusions of paleo-europoid populations from the north (Vencl 1982, p. 652). During the Eneolithic, the neolithic populations became exposed to the return pressure of the remaining palaeo-europoid populations, as worsening environmental conditions contributed to the reversal of the previous trend. By late neolithic/eneolithic

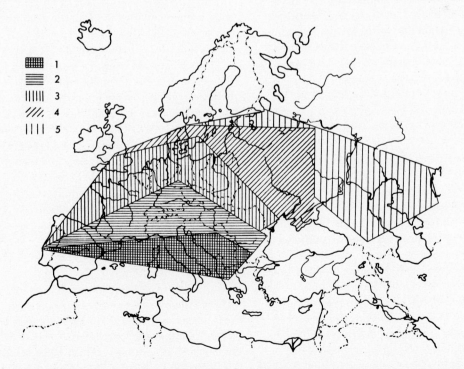

Fig. 1. The spread of leptodolichomorphic anthropogenic characteristics in Europe during the fifth to second millennium bc. 1, spread before 4000 bc; 2, expansion during the fourth millennium bc; 3, expansion 3000–2500 bc; 4, expansion 2500–2000 bc; 5, expansion during the second millennium bc. (After Schwidetzky, 1978a, p. 320, Abb. 80.)

times, the northern populations of local origin succeeded in developing an effective variant of the original neolithic economy, adapted to the north temperate conditions. This economic breakthrough was followed by regional population growth and by the expansion of the archaeologically detectable cultural traits from the north. This picture is matched by the human fossil evidence: Chochol, for instance, has observed remarkable similarities between the populations of the Baalberg phase of the Funnel Beaker culture in Bohemia and the mesolithic population (Chochol 1969, p. 496). Similarly, a close resemblance was noted between Central-European Corded Ware populations and those of the mesolithic period (Schwidetzky 1978*b*; Chochol 1981). While this cannot imply a direct acculturation of the Central-European Mesolithic groups, delayed until the end of the neolithic period (*c.* 3000 bc) it may indicate the influx of people from the northern margins of Europe, who remained unaffected by the neolithic colonisation of the Danubian farmers.

Even though cemeteries first occur during the mesolithic period (Vencl 1984), the palaeoanthropological reconstruction of the prehistoric populations in mesolithic Europe remains far from comprehensive. Large or recurrent burial grounds, such as those in the Iron Gates region along the Danube, occur only exceptionally (Mikić 1982). The fragmentary nature of the evidence should not, however, allow us to ignore the skeletal evidence, as has commonly been the case (Dolukhanov 1975, 1981; Clarke 1976; Clark 1980; Waterbolk 1982; Gob 1983).

In summary, a number of archaeological cultures can be shown to correlate with two discrete populations: a palaeo-europoid population which is related to the local mesolithic (for instance Tiefstich, Steinkisten and Walternienburg groups; Bernhard 1978, p. 158) cultures, and a leptodolichomorphic one, whose appearance and diffusion coincides with the spread of farming (e.g. LBK and derivatives, Tripolye). Such a coincidence seems too great to be purely accidental and supports, in my view, the proposition that a gradual migration was responsible for the origin of the Danubian Neolithic.

The demographic aspects of the Mesolithic—Neolithic transition

The current disregard for the implications of the different population dynamics of mesolithic and neolithic societies stems from the original concept of the Mesolithic as a period comparable to that of the Palaeolithic or Neolithic. This served to disguise the essential historical inequality of the Mesolithic in relation to both the Old and the New Stone Age.

From the economic and the demographic points of view, post-glacial food-gatherers operated a far more restricted and far less dynamic system than did food producers. In areas favourable to farming, the neolithic colonists were bound to gain numerical superiority over the indigenous mesolithic population in the course of a few generations (see below). This demographic difference was bound to create direct or indirect pressures to dislodge hunter-gatherers (Vincent 1979, p. 423),

and must have been one of the main factors influencing the development of neolithic society in Europe.

The population dynamics of both systems are, of course, restricted by the productive potential of their economies. While hunter-gatherer population densities are ultimately determined by the naturally occuring biomass, or, more precisely, by the food potential of the leanest season in the hunter-gatherer seasonal cycle, the food producers are capable of increasing their carrying-capacity thresholds through the genetic manipulation of cultigens and domesticates and through increasing the input of their labour. In geographical terms, the vast difference in the productive potential of foragers (Clarke 1976, Fig. 3) and farmers can be explained by the fact that farmers were able to increase the naturally low productivity of large continental areas by farming: hence the shift in settlement pattern to agriculturally favoured inland areas, many of which had previously been avoided by the mesolithic groups. Ecotonal areas along watercourses, lakes and marine shorelines are relatively restricted in size, yet they alone could have been exploited by hunter-gatherers intensively. In increasing the productivity of the interfluvial areas such as the steppes, the food producers opened vast new areas for intensive settlement. The increase in population during the Neolithic compared with the Mesolithic is estimated as tenfold (Rozoy 1978, pp. 1105–9; Schwidetzky 1978*a*, p. 327).

In such regions, the attempts at understanding the Mesolithic—Neolithic transition through 'contact finds' seem unrealistic: whatever the early nature of contacts between the two populations, the mesolithic groups were bound to become vastly outnumbered by the neolithic colonists within a few generations, while their contribution to further cultural and demographic development would have become insignificant.

In contrast, in areas of sub-optimal agricultural potential, the conditions for a rapid population increase and the subsequent expansion did not obtain, thereby giving the hunter-gatherers an adequate time to adjust to a new situation. This led to the genesis of technologically and economically mixed cultures, such as the Ertebølle or the Pitted or Combed Ware cultures. Only with the development of farming better adjusted to the poorer climatic and edaphic conditions of Northern Europe in the Late Neolithic and Eneolithic did the acculturated descendants of the hunter-gatherer groups experience demographic growth and expansion, which took place at the expense of the remaining food-gatherers/collectors and of the less adaptable farmers of the Danubian tradition.

A number of economic, social, ideological and ecological variables combine to generate the population growth among food producers which stands in such marked contrast to the foragers (Hassan and Sengel 1973; Cohen 1977). Among the hunter-gatherers, population-controlling practices, carried out in the full knowledge of the limited availability of food resources, are generally held to be responsible for the near-static population growth (Vincent 1979, p. 422, with references). In contrast, farmers are able to exploit the reproductive potential inherent in human populations to its full capacity.

The hunter-gatherer population might also have been maintained at a low level through warfare, carried on for the control of space and resources by the territorially organised communities. This is evidenced by the presence of dozens of individuals, killed by arrows, spears or by other weapons, in the mesolithic cemeteries in Europe and North Africa (Vencl 1984, with references). Warfare among hunter-gatherers and the subsequent annihilation of the vanquished is also recorded by the classical sources. Despite the increase in population, comparable phenomena do not occur in the cemeteries of the neolithic period.

The shift to sedentism, a consequence of the adoption of the neolithic farming practices, played an important role in this process. While the reproductive capacity of a hunting-gathering female in a nomadic society is limited by her ability to carry her offspring — usually to one child in three to four years (Sussman 1972) — a female in a sedentary society could raise several infants simultaneously (Sussman 1972). Although there are also other dietary and economic conditions which seem to favour a higher population growth rate among farming populations (Hassan and Sengel 1973, p. 535), the degree of sedentism may be considered as the decisive influence. Stuart (1980), for instance, was able to demonstrate that hunter-gatherers travelling by canoe were able to maintain a higher birth rate than those who travelled by foot.

While it would be superfluous, in the present context, to discuss the issue of the population growth as a cause or consequence of food production (c.f. Bronson 1977; Cohen 1977), it remains a fact that a regional population increase remains firmly associated with the development and diffusion of farming. Given favourable conditions, farming groups were capable of multiplying their original populations many times over in a short time (Neustupný 1981). The conventional outlet for population increase stimulated by the requirements of farming was, in many cultural contexts, a scaled emigration to new areas underpopulated from the agricultural point of view.

This process alone might have contributed to further population growth. Emigrating colonists left behind them a demographically active territory, stimulated by the need to fill the gap in social relations created by the departure of segments of the original community (Neustupný 1983, p. 12).

The high reproductive potential of farming populations allows us to explain a number of archaeological observations, such as the widespread diffusion of the Linear Pottery (LBK) culture. The local differences in the skeletal morphology of the LBK populations, observed by Bernhard (1978, p. 158) need not reflect the assimilation of the local mesolithic groups, but can be seen as a result of secondary colonisation. As Dobzhansky has observed, the genetic pool of a breeding population in itself represents a source of variability, since the genetic make-up of individuals within a breeding population is not identical (Bach 1978, p. 57; Drvota 1979, p. 336). The idea of a direct migration from the nuclear Near East to southeastern and Central Europe is not supported by the radiocarbon dates, the archaeological evidence, or by the requirements of the farming practices of the colonists themselves, which required at least a temporary establishment of permanent settlement. The morphological variability observed within the neolithic population can be explained by the generation of secondary, tertiary and subsequent chains of colonisation, as the original centres of settlement became saturated and the continuing population growth fuelled the colonisation of new, hitherto underpopulated areas. Interbreeding between various waves of colonists, interrupted by temporary isolation during the periods of the establishment of new settlements, can be seen as responsible for anthropological differences between the secondary colonists and the original population.

Ecological aspects of the problem

The notion of a gradual penetration of the European interior by neolithic colonists is also supported by certain ecological aspects of the problem which help to explain why the initial colonisation of temperate Europe was likely to pass unchallenged by the local mesolithic groups. Despite the incomplete and regionally variable quality of the data relating to the mesolithic and early neolithic settlement pattern, it is clear that (a) the mesolithic settlement was dispersed over a greater area than the more agglomerated early neolithic settlement, raising automatically the question of the co-existence of foragers and farmers during the Early Neolithic; and (b) the ecological requirements of the mesolithic and neolithic settlers were markedly different. While the earliest agriculturalists selected good soils with sufficient moisture and higher temperatures (Rulf 1983, p. 75), the mesolithic groups, though not selecting any types of soils, preferred open, less forested locations, which tended to occur on poor soils such as dunes, terrace and morainic gravels or sands, which were within easy reach of watercourses (Gramsch 1973, p. 64; Kozłowski and Kozłowski, Chapter 7). During the humid atlantic period, fertile soils were colonised by mixed oak forest, which produced a greater amount of shade than did previous forms of vegetation, thus restricting the growth of game-supporting undergrowth (Waterbolk 1968, p. 1096). The evidence from areas with a well-developed local chronology, such as southern Germany, indicates that the density of settlement on fertile soils declined in the later as compared with the earlier mesolithic period (Taute 1973–4), p. 94). Mesolithic settlement is on the whole absent from the loess soils of central Europe (Kozłowski and Kozłowski 1977, p. 316, and Chapter 7, this volume; Kaufmann 1979, p. 114, Fig. 4). In such situations, the initial colonisation of the European interior by farmers would create a residential dichotomy: the areas settled by the neolithic colonists were only of secondary importance to the local mesolithic groups, if utilised by them at all. The initial neolithic colonisation would not provoke resistance, then, because it did not pose a threat to the indigenous resource base. Unharassed, the colonists were allowed to increase their economic potential and to build up their population numbers, until, in a short time, they outnumbered the original groups of hunter-gatherers.

Discussion

It is the practice prevalent in the analysis of genetic relationships between archaeological cultures, to base such an analysis on the mutual relationship of those archaeological remains which are the most accessible. Such evidence is often considered at its face value, regardless of its original role within the societies under investigation. However, the availability of data may not be the best criterion in establishing the parenthood of archaeological cultures.

The relationship between the Mesolithic and the Neolithic is most frequently examined in terms of: (1) the mutual interdependence of chipped-stone industries, these being the sole class of artefacts common to both complexes; (2) interpretations of 'contact finds'; (3) interpretations of radiocarbon dates; (4) palaeobotanical and palynological evidence; (5) differences in the organisation of neolithic and eneolithic societies, often explained by the cultural contribution of the mesolithic substratum. Too often are the common features of such investigations characterised by (*a*) the comparative analysis of possibly trivial features, which are held to express genetic relationships, whatever their significance in the context of the whole culture; this regardless of the fact that there are bound to be hundreds of such attributes (the selective consideration given to the trapeze at the expense of other elements of the chipped-stone industry is a case in point), most of which are ignored in the analysis; (*b*) a propensity to use the regional framework of analysis as an excuse to ignore the wider ramifications, often resulting in the translocation of the problems of origin into some convenient *terra incognita*; (*c*) a similar propensity to shift the question of ancestry into chronological oblivion, in other words, before or after the period with which the investigator is familiar. These practices reflect the inherent weakness of archaeological sources, when it comes to recording the periods of rapid change, when gradual quantitative changes become transformed into qualitative ones.

Attempts to solve the problem of the Mesolithic–Neolithic transition through the analysis of lithic industry have often been plagued by stratigraphic problems (such as secondary mixed complexes of 'contact' surface finds, erroneously held to be 'in association'; see Vencl 1960, p. 65); and by the reliance on type-fossils of little chronological or cultural significance (Mazálek 1954; Krzak 1980). In the recent analysis of chipped-stone industries of the Balkan and Central-European Neolithic, J. K. Kozłowski (1982) considers the differences among the individual neolithic assemblages as being due to the local mesolithic traditions, even though he is prepared to acknowledge the possible influence of later

neolithic colonisation. The mesolithic contribution is open to question, however; this can be illustrated in the case of the Linear Pottery culture: although within the area of its distribution the mesolithic settlement consisted of several lithic traditions (cf. Kozłowski and Kozłowski, Chapter 7) with a number of microlithic elements, the Linear Pottery culture bearers adopted only one, the trapeze (Kozłowski 1982, p. 166, and Chapter 7, this volume). This is the least diagnostic element, however, as it also occurs in a whole range of the early neolithic cultures (Vencl 1971, p. 75; Clark 1980, pp. 19, 54). It seems far more important that the Linear Pottery culture's chipped-stone industry as a whole cannot be compared with any stone assemblage belonging to the Mesolithic of Europe. Another illustration of the failure of the lithic analysis to demonstrate conclusively a parental relationship can be seen in the recent work on the Funnel Beaker culture in Poland: while Lech and Młynarczyk (1981) argue for a genetic relationship between the Linear Pottery and Funnel Beaker cultures, Niesołowska-Śreniowska (1981) use the same data base to argue for the local origin of the Funnel Beaker assemblage in the Janisławice culture (see also Kozłowski and Kozłowski, Chapter 7). The point is that the origin of the neolithic cultures cannot be inferred on the basis of the lithic industries alone. Other forms of material culture should be included in such considerations.

The material evidence of contact between the mesolithic and neolithic groups is mostly limited to funerary contexts, cases of the re-utilisation of neolithic artefacts and to finds of mesolithic and neolithic artefacts in stratigraphically unambiguous association. In Central Europe, such finds are rare and, moreover, belong mostly to the later neolithic and eneolithic contexts (Vencl 1982, p. 664). These finds can best be regarded as instances of incidental contacts between neolithic settlers and peripheral mesolithic survivals, which were without significance for the evolution of neolithic material culture and society. Neolithic cultures consisted of mature, well-adapted, integrated systems, which were likely to reject, rather than adopt, isolated elements of a foreign, hunter–gatherer culture. Archaeologists are in error when they regard cultural loans as a free circulation of elements; in reality every aspect of culture is firmly tied to the economic, social and ideological structures. The adoption of a new element will therefore lead to a change in the structure of the system.

The attempts to monitor the transition from foraging to farming, with the help of radiocarbon dating, too, is not without problems. These arise from the often far too wide standard deviations of the dates, accentuated by the changes in the magnetic field of the earth, for which no correction can be made (Waterbolk 1971; Schwabedissen 1978; Campbell *et al.* 1979; Barbetti and Flude 1979); and from the failure to separate with precision the contaminated samples (cf. Bagniewski 1981) from the real instances of mesolithic groups surviving into later periods.

Recently, some workers have pointed to the occurrence

of cereal pollen in preneolithic layers as the evidence for the development of the mesolithic economy in the direction of food production (Milojčić 1960, 1973; Kossack and Schmeidl 1977; Menke 1978; Schwaar 1980). Others have consistently rejected this interpretation as unreliable on account of the high risk of erroneous identifications, arising from the strong similarities between the pollen of Cerealia and the wild grasses (Smolla 1960, p. 108; Vencl 1968, p. 54, 1982, p. 657; Narr 1982, p. 50). A similar danger affects the pollen evidence for cereal cultivation in the later palaeolithic layers at Abu Hureyra and at Mureybit (Moore 1979; Leroi-Gourhan 1974; Cauvin 1977), where the alleged pollen of Cerealia was probably confused with the pollen of certain aquatic plants (Zeist and Woldring 1980). Similarly, efforts to identify a phase of pre-ceramic and therefore indigenous domestication in Central Europe (Lichardus and Pavúk 1963; Menke 1978) have met with no success (Vencl 1968, 1982, p. 657; Clason 1980, p. 171).

Finally, those who hold local mesolithic traditions responsible for the cultural differentiation of the neolithic period underestimate the likelihood of an independent cultural divergence arising from the process of demographic expansion of the neolithic groups. Basic features of all reconstructions involving the mesolithic substratum are (*a*) the total lack of positive cultural bonds between the Mesolithic and the Neolithic, (*b*) a lack of awareness of the marked demographic differences between the Mesolithic and the Neolithic, and (*c*) the efforts to bridge seemingly irreconcilable differences in the material culture of two neolithic groups (such as ceramics, for instance) by vague references to the influence of local mesolithic traditions.

These critical comments should not detract from the task of unravelling the conditions under which the neolithic people and culture replaced the indigenous hunter-gatherers. The traditional approaches, criticised above as inadequate, could be much enhanced by the addition of palaeoanthropological, demographic and ecological evidence. Last, but not least, ethnohistorical sources provide us with the opportunity to extend the archaeological perspective on the Mesolithic–Neolithic transition by informing us about those aspects of society which did not find any reflection in the archaeological record.

To illustrate the point, a survey of classical sources (Vencl 1982, pp. 666–78) indicates that in the classical world, including Europe, hunting-gathering cultures were still surviving at the time of Christ (Caesar IV, 10; Tacitus: *Germania* II, 46) in areas marginal to farming. Such a pervading co-existence of hunter-gatherers and food producers demonstrates a remarkable resistance to the adoption of farming on the part of the former, a resistance which is confirmed by the more recent examples from the colonial period in Africa and Asia.

At the other end of the range of farmer–forager interactions, classical as well as mediaeval and more recent sources document many cases of the genocide of hunter-gatherers by the more powerful agricultural populations, 'barbaric' and 'civilised' alike (Herodotus 4, 183; Pertold 1926, pp. 529–32). As victims were seldom buried, genocide would not leave archaeological traces. Consequently, it is seldom considered by archaeologists in their reconstruction of hunter-gather–food-producer relationships.

The above two examples are intended to show that the forager–farmer interaction was not one of equal partnership, and that contacts between the two could generate outcomes other than rapid acculturation. The economic superiority of the food-producing system, so obvious and acceptable from the point of view of European civilisation, does not appear to have been uniformly desirable to hunter-gatherers, for their criteria of desirability were not confined solely to the economic considerations. Although this is a theme familiar to prehistorians (Cohen 1977; Bender 1978) the diachronic implications of the hunter-gatherer reluctance to adopt farming have not been fully appreciated: the longer such a situation persisted, the more profound the demographic and socio-economic differences became between the two societies. Correspondingly, the chances of acculturation would diminish while the likelihood of a violent end to the hunter-gatherer way of life would increase. The end of the mesolithic period has been described as undramatic (Bosinski 1983, p. 108), but does this impression reflect the true situation, or does it merely reflect the silence of the archaeological record?

Conclusions

In the context of chronologically and geographically variable conditions in Europe, it would be impossible to postulate a simple and uniform solution to the transition from foraging to food production. I have attempted to argue here that archaeological sources provide only a limited amount of information, which leaves room for several interpretations. For a greater understanding of the transition, other sources, such as palaeodemography, palaeoanthropology and ethnohistory must be taken into consideration. From these expanded perspectives, it seems clear that the relations between food gatherers and food producers span a whole range of behaviours; at the same time, some of these forms of behaviour will not be reflected clearly in the archaeological record, while others are in danger of not being reflected at all. As a general observation, it may be stated that the rate of disintegration of hunting–gathering societies is in a large measure determined by the suitability of their habitats to farming: the precipitate demise of food-gatherers in areas favourable to farming contrasts with the gradual transformation of food-gathering societies in areas less suitable for agriculture.

References

Ashbee, P. (1982) 'A reconsideration of the British Neolithic'. *Antiquity* 56 (217), 134–8.

Bach, A. (1978) *Neolithische Populationen im Mittelelbe-Saale Gebiet*, Museum für Ur- und Frühgeschichte Thüringens, Weimar.

Bagniewski, Z. (1981) 'Das Problem der Koexistenz mesolithischer und neolithischer Gesellschaften im Südteil des mitteleuropäischen Flachlandes', in B. Gramsch, ed., *Mesolithikum in Europa*, pp. 113–19, Veröffentlichungen des Museums für Ur- und Frühgeschichte Potsdam 14/15, Deutscher Verlag, Berlin.

Barbetti, M. and Flude, K. (1979) 'Geomagnetic variation during the Late Pleistocene period and changes in the radiocarbon time scale'. *Nature* 279, 202–5.

Bender, B. (1978) 'Gatherer-hunter to farmer: a social perspective'. *World Archaeology* 10, 204–22.

Bernhard, W. (1978) 'Anthropologie der Bandkeramik', in H. Schwabedissen and I. Schwidetzky, eds., *Die Anfänge des Neolithikums vom Orient bis Nordeuropa*, Teil VIIIb, *Anthropologie 2*, *Fundamenta* B3, pp. 126–63, Böhlau Verlag, Köln, Wien.

Bosinski, G. (1983) 'Die Jägerische Geschichte des Rheinlandes'. *Jahrbuch des Römisch-Germanischen Zentralmuseums Mainz* 30, 81–112.

Bronson, B. (1977) 'The earliest farming: demography as a cause and consequence', in Ch.A. Reed, ed., *Origins of Agriculture*, pp. 23–48, Mouton, The Hague.

Caesar, G. I. *Commentariorum de bello Gallico libri septem*, Teubner, Leipzig.

Campbell, J. A., Baxter, M. S. and Alcock, L. (1979) 'Radiocarbon dates for the Cadbury massacre'. *Antiquity* 53, 31–8.

Cauvin, J. (1977) 'Les fouilles de Mureybet (1971–1974) et leur signification pour les origines de la sédentarisation au Proche-Orient'. *Annual American School Oriental Research* 44, 19–48.

Chochol, J. (1969) 'K antropologii české baalberské skupiny KNP'. *Památky archeologické* 60, 488–97.

(1981) 'Anthropologické vztahy skupin obyvatelstva v pravěkém vývoji', in J. Poulík and J. Zeman, eds., *Současné úkoly československé archeologie*, pp. 220–25, Archeologický ústav ČSAV, Praha.

Clark, J. G. D. (1932) *The Mesolithic Age in Britain*, Cambridge University Press, Cambridge.

(1980) *Mesolithic Prelude. The Palaeolithic–Neolithic Transition in Old World Prehistory*, Edinburgh University Press, Edinburgh.

Clarke, D. (1976) 'Mesolithic Europe: the economic basis', in G. de G. Sieveking, I. H. Longworth and K. E. Wilson, eds., *Problems in Economic and Social Archaeology*, pp. 449–81, Duckworth, London.

Clason, A. T. (1980) 'Padina and Starčevo-game, fish and cattle'. *Palaeohistoria* 22, 142–73.

Cohen, M. N. 1977) *Food Crisis in Prehistory*, Yale University Press, New Haven, Conn.

Dennell, R. (1983) *European Economic Prehistory*, Academic Press, London.

Dolukhanov, P. M. (1975) 'Die ökologische und ökonomische Grundlagen der Neolithisierung Mittel- und Osteuropas', in K.-H. Otto and H.-J. Brachmann, eds., *Moderne Probleme der Archäologie*, pp. 73–82, Akademie Verlag, Berlin.

(1981) 'Ökologie und Chronologie des Mesolithikums in Europa', in B. Gramsch, ed., *Mesolithikum in Europa*, pp. 211–15, Veröffentlichungen des Museums für Ur- and Frühgeschichte Potsdam 14/15, Deutscher Verlag, Berlin.

Drvota, S. (1979) *Od zvířete k člověku*, Panorama, Praha.

Gob, A. (1983) 'Du Mésolithique au Néolithique entre Rhin et Seine: un modèle de néolithisation', in S. J. de Laet, ed., *Progrès récents dams l'étude du Néolithique ancien*, pp. 55–61, Université de Gand, Brugge.

Gramsch, B. (1973) *Das Mesolithikum im Flachland zwischen Elbe und Oder*, VEB Deutscher Verlag der Wissenschaften, Berlin.

Hassan, F. A. and Sengel, R. A. (1973) 'On the mechanism of population growth during the Neolithic'. *Current Anthropology* 14, 535–42.

Herodotus *Herodoti Historiarum libri IX*, Teubner, Leipzig.

Higgs, E. S. and Jarman, M. R. (1969) 'The origins of agriculture: a reconsideration'. *Antiquity* 43, 31–41.

(1972) 'The origins of animal and plant husbandary', in E. S. Higgs, ed., *Papers in Economic Prehistory*, pp. 3–15, Cambridge University Press, Cambridge.

Jelínek, J. (1978) 'The racial history of Czechoslovakia'. *Anthropologie* 16(3), 249–70.

Kaufmann, D. (1979) 'Gedanken zur Neolithisierung im Südwesten der DDR', in W. Wojciechowski, ed., *Początki neolityzacji Polski poł.-zachodniej*, pp. 105–19, Wrocław.

Kossack, G. and Schmeidl, H. (1977) 'Vorneolithischer Getreidebau im bayerischen Alpenvorland'. *Jahresbericht der Bayerischen Bodendenkmalpflege* 15/16 (1974–75), 7–23.

Kozłowski, J. K. (1982) 'La néolithisation de la zone balkano-danubienne du point de vue des industries lithiques', in J. K. Kozłowski, ed., *Origin of the Chipped Stone Industries of the Early Farming Cultures in Balkans*, pp. 131–70, Państwowe Wydawnictwo Naukowe Warszawa, Kraków.

Kozłowski, J. K. and Kozłowski, S. K. (1977) *Epoka kamienia na ziemiach polskich*, Panstwowe Wydawnictwo Naukowe Warszawa, Kraków.

Krzak, Z. (1980) *Geneza i chronologia kultury ceramiki sznurowej w Europie*, PWN Wrocław, Warszawa, Kraków, Gdańsk.

Lech, J. and Mlynarczyk, H. (1981) 'Uwagi o krzemieniarstwie społeczności wstęgowych i wspólnot kultury pucharów lejkowatych. Próba konfrontacji', in T. Wiślański, ed., *Kultura pucharów lejkowatych w Polsce*, pp. 11–36, Polska Akademia Nauk, Poznań.

Leroi-Gourhan, A. (1974) 'Etudes palynologiques des derniers 11 000 and en Syrie semidésertique'. *Paléorient* 2, 443–51.

Lichardus, J. and Pavúk, J. (1963) 'Bemerkungen zum präkeramischen Neolithikum in der Argissa-Magula und zu seiner Existenz in Europa'. *Slovenská archeológia* 11(2), 459–76.

Mazálek, M. (1954) 'Na okraj československého mesolitu'. *Anthropozoikum* 4, 373–86.

Menke, M. (1978) 'Zum Frühneolithikum zwischen Jura and Alpenrand'. *Germania* 56, 24–52.

Mikić, Z. (1980) 'Anthropologische Typen der Djerdap (Eisernen-Tor)-Serie', in J. K. Kozłowski and J. Machnik, eds., *Problèmes de la néolithisation dans certaines régions de l'Europe*, pp. 151–61, Kraków.

(1982) 'Penroseova distanca mezolitskih (epipaleolitskih) populacija podunavskih oblasti'. *Godišnjak* 20, 211–20.

Milojčić, V. (1960) 'Präkeramisches Neolithikum auf der Balkanhalbinsel'. *Germania* 38, 320–35.

(1973) 'Zur Frage eines präkeramischen Neolithikums in Mitteleuropa', in G. Novak, ed., *Actes du VIIIe Congrès Internationale des Sciences Préhistoriques et Protohistoriques*, Vol. II, pp. 248–51, Beograd.

Moore, A. M. T. (1979) 'A pre-Neolithic farmer's village on the Euphrates'. *Scientific American* 241, 50–8.

Narr, K. J. (1982) 'Struktur und Ereignis: Einige urgeschichtliche Aspekte'. *Grenzfragen* 11, 35–61.

Neustupný, E. (1981) 'Mobilität der äneolithischen populationen'. *Slovenská Archeológia* 29, 111–19.

(1983) 'The demography of prehistoric cemetries'. *Památky archeologické* 74, 7–34.

Niesołowska-Sreniowska, E. (1981) 'Niektóre problemy związane z materialami krzemiennymi kultury pucharów lejkowatych z fazy A/B, pochodzącymi z grobowca 8 w Sarnowie, woj. wloclawskie', in T. Wiślański, ed., *Kultura pucharów lejkowatych w Polsce*, pp. 37–57, Polska Akademia Nauk, Poznań.

Pertold, O. (1926) *Perla Indického Oceánu*, Vilímek, Praha.

Price, T. D. (1983) 'The European Mesolithic'. *American Antiquity* 48, 761–78.

Rozoy, J. G. (1978) *Les Derniers Chasseurs. L'Epipaléolithique en France et en Belgique*, Vols. I–III, Charleville, Reims.

Rulf, J. (1983) 'Přírodní prostředí a kultury českého neolitu a eneolitu'. *Památky archeologické* 74, 35–95.

Schwaar, J. (1980) 'Getreideanbau vor 4,000 v. Chr. im niedersächsischen Tiefland?' *Nachrichten aus Niedersachsens Urgeschichte* 49, 261–3.

Schwabedissen, H. (1978) 'Konventionelle oder kalibrierte C14-Daten?' *Archäologische Informationen* 4, 110–17.

Schwabedissen, H. and Schwidetzky, I. (1973) (eds.) *Die Anfänge des Neolithikums vom Orient bis Nordeuropa*, Teil VIIIa, *Anthropologie 1, Fundamenta* B3. Böhlau Verlag, Köln, Wien.

   (eds.) (1978) *Die Anfänge des Neolithikums vom Orient bis Nordeuropa*, Teil VIIIb, *Anthropologie 2, Fundamenta* B3, Böhlau Verlag, Köln, Wien.

Schwidetzky, I. (1978a) 'Stand und Aufgaben der prähistorischen Anthropologie unter besonderer Berücksichtung des Neolithikums', in H. Schwabedissen and I. Schwidetzky, eds., *Die Anfänge des Neolithikums vom Orient bis Nordeuropa*, pp. 317–40, Böhlau Verlag, Köln, Wien.

   (1978b) 'Anthropologie der Schnurkeramik- und Streitaxtkulturen', in H. Schwabedissen and I. Schwidetzky, eds., *Die Anfänge des Neolithikums vom Orient bis Nordeuropa*, pp. 241–64, Böhlau Verlag, Köln, Wien.

Smolla, G. (1960) *Neolithische Kulturerscheinungen*, Antiquitas, Bonn.

Stuart, D. E. (1980) 'Kinship and social organisation in Tierra del Fuego: evolutionary consequences' in L. Cordell and S. Beckerman, eds., *The Versatility of Kinship*, pp. 269–84, Academic Press, New York.

Sussman, R. W. (1972) 'Child transport, family size, and increase in human population during the Neolithic'. *Current Anthropology* 13, 258–9.

Tacitus, C. *De origine et situ Germanorum liber*, E. Koestermann, ed., Leipzig 1962.

Taute, W. (1973–4) 'Neolithische Mikrolithen und andere neolithische Silexartefakte aus Süddeutschland'. *Archäologische Informationen* 2–3, 71–125.

Vencl, S. (1960) 'Kamenné nástroje prvních zemědělců ve střední Evropě – Les instruments lithiques des premiers agriculteurs en Europe central'. *Sborník Národního musea v Praze* 14(1–2), 1–91, XXI pl.

   (1968) 'Zur Frage des Bestehens eines präkeramischen Neolithikums in der Slowakei'. *Acta Archaeologica Carpathica* 10, 39–61.

   (1971) 'Současný stav poznání postmesolitických štípaných industrií v Československu'. *Z badań nad krzemieniarstwem neolitycznym i eneolitycznym*, pp. 74–99, Polskie Towarzystwo Archeologiczne, Kraków.

   (1982) 'K otázce zániku sběračsko-loveckých kultur – Zur Frage des Untergangs von Jagd- und Sammlerkulturen'. *Archeologické rozhledy* 34, 648–94.

   (1984) 'Stopy zranění zbraněmi jako archeologický pramen poznání vojenství'. *Archeologické rozhledy* 36, 533–52.

Vincent, J. (1979) 'On the sexual division of labour, population, and the origins of agriculture'. *Current Anthropology* 20, 422–5.

Waterbolk, H. T. (1968) 'Food production in prehistoric Europe'. *Science* 162, 1093–102.

   (1971) 'Working with radiocarbon dates'. *Proceedings of the Prehistoric Society* 37, 15–33.

   (1982) 'The spread of food production over the European continent', in T. Sjøvold, ed., *Introduksjonen av jordbruk i Norden*, pp. 19–37, Tromsø, Universitetsvorlaget Oslo, Bergen.

Wijnen, M. H. (1981) 'The early neolithic I settlement at Sesklo: an early farming community in Thessaly, Greece'. *Analecta Praehistorica Leidensia* 14, 1–146.

Xirotiris, N. I. (1981a) 'Anthropologie des Äneolithikums und der Frühbronzezeit im Mittel- und Südosteuropa'. *Slovenská archeológia* 29, 235–41.

   (1981b) 'Die Neolithisierung Südost-Europas. Ein anthropologischer Versuch'. *Godišnjak* 19, 5–12.

Zeist, W. van and Woldring, H. (1980) 'Holocene vegetation and climate of Northwestern Syria'. *Palaeohistoria* 22, 111–25.

PART TWO

Regional studies

Chapter 5

The transition to food production: a Mediterranean perspective

James Lewthwaite

Modern research has confirmed V. G. Childe's proposition that the rate of growth of mesolithic population and the processual rate of the transition to food production differed between the eastern and western basins of the Mediterranean: in effect, the very success of the western Mesolithic appears to have significantly delayed the adoption of crop cultivation and animal husbandry. This regional variation is the product of three major variables: the productivity, diversity and stability of the environment; the tolerance levels of the food-production system affecting its capacity to penetrate vacant niches; finally the effects of natural, theoretical and methodological biases favouring the survival, identification, excavation and analysis of different classes of sites. The critical role of islands as 'filters' of the transmission of food production from one mainland region to another receives particular attention.

Introduction

The very inclusion of the Mediterranean region within a volume devoted to the postglacial adaptations of the temperate zone may occasion some surprise; however, recent palaeoecological research has conclusively demonstrated the chronological priority of deciduous over evergreen woodland over a wide swathe of territory from Catalunya (Catalonia) to Crete. The expansion of evergreen species from the mid-third millennium bc onward (the so-called sub-boreal period of the palynologists) must be attributed to the effects of human activities (Reille *et al.* 1980).

It is argued below that, although the archaeological and palaeoecological data are both patchy, there is an evident correlation between the areas in which postglacial adaptations were most successful (in terms of population growth, economic and technical innovation and perhaps social complexity) and the distribution of primary temperate forest. The humid northern and western areas were therefore favoured during the mesolithic period over the more arid south and east, and in particular over the islands, which had suffered a severe impoverishment of terrestrial fauna during the Pleistocene.

No uniformity of pattern can be teased out of the data concerning the regional transition to food production: in the eastern basin the abrupt inception of the village farming way of life appears to occur with minimal continuity from the Mesolithic, while in the west a more gradual transformation spanning two or more millennia is indicated. Selective site loss to the holocene eustatic sea level rise cannot entirely explain this contrast, so that it is reasonable to suppose that this resistance was due to the greater stability and success of the western adaptations. It is proposed that crop plants may have been adopted initially only as a seasonal complement to foraging-based subsistence, and that domesticated animals, especially sheep, spread particularly rapidly through the major western islands because they provided a palliative for the dearth of indigenous game.

Problems and issues in the Mediterranean Mesolithic and the beginnings of food production
The Mediterranean Mesolithic

This period has never been accorded the same level of attention as in the more northerly regions: the data base is poorer, the time-span limited and there is not the same intellectual puzzle of an apparent decline from a palaeolithic golden age. Consequently, mesolithic developments have been studied neither in their own right, nor as permutations of the Upper Palaeolithic, but rather as an interlude setting the scene for the introduction of neolithic food production. Therefore, the purely typological and chronological ordering of lithic artefacts has retained a pre-eminence long since supplemented or supplanted elsewhere by palaeo-ecological and palaeo-economic approaches.

Over the past quarter of a century, some scholars have proposed the hypothesis of a mesolithic socio-economic adaptation to the changed postglacial environment: as large game grew scarcer, the mobile hunting bands of the Epipalaeolithic responded by exploiting a broader resource spectrum (small game, fish, birds, shellfish and plant foods) from more circumscribed territories.

The most highly elaborated presentation of this argument was put forward by the late D. L. Clarke (1976, pp. 449–81): as temperate forest became progressively replaced from south to north by less-productive Mediterranean woodland and scrub, and as the coastal lowlands which provided winter ranges for large herbivores underwent flooding through the postglacial eustatic rise in sea level, the epipalaeolithic transhumant big-game strategy became less and less adaptive. Mesolithic communities therefore increasingly settled along coasts and around wetlands in order to exploit aquatic resources, thereby becoming pre-adapted to the eventual

adoption of cereals and ovicaprids (Fig. 1).

According to Clarke, the key technical innovation of the mesolithic period consisted of the replacement of the palaeolithic toolkit (a few highly specialised artefacts) by a more flexible system based on composite tools: geometric microliths easily replicated and replaced on wear surfaces set in organic hafts and holders (Clarke 1976, pp. 452–7). Since this toolkit would have been adopted in the course of the reorientation of subsistence strategies away from hunting towards fishing and gathering, it would be logical to predict that geometric microliths would replace the epipalaeolithic industries from south to north. In fact, the Sauveterrian and Tardenoisian microlith industries occur in the northern temperate zone (Fig. 2), while epipalaeolithic industries persist throughout the mesolithic period in the southern Mediterranean (Broglio 1980, pp. 13–21, 24, Fig. 7; Biagi *et al.* 1981, p. 32), down to the very threshold of the Neolithic, only in the north evolving into a true Mesolithic. Much turns on the definition of the Mesolithic in terms of characteristic tool-types and manufacturing techniques: Broglio points out that although microlithic segments and triangles can be found in final epigravettian contexts in Italy from the Alpine piedmont to Sicily, the toolkits of extremely small (narrow blade) lithics with the predominance of isosceles and scalene triangles which characterises the Sauveterrian are confined to certain regions – specifically the Po Plain, the Trieste carst, Tuscany and Le Marche, during the period 8000–5800 bc. The Tardenoisian (Castelnovian) assemblages, defined by a massive preponderance of trapezes formed from broad, thin blades, occur in the same regions. In each case the formal similarities are much stronger with the contemporary industries of north-eastern Spain and southern France than with the remainder of peninsular Italy (Broglio 1980, p. 24).

If, as Clarke (1976) has argued, the use of microlithic toolkits in general, and of the trapeze-based industries in particular, indicate the intensified exploitation of vegetal resources, then such a shift in subsistence strategies must have taken place first in the northern rather than the southern Mediterranean. Furthermore, the widespread adoption of blade and trapeze industries coincides with the expansion and enrichment of the deciduous mixed oak forests during the atlantic Climatic Optimum (Reille *et al.* 1980). The development of both the blade and trapeze industries and the temperate forest was confined to the northern regions of the Mediterranean; in which case the south–north trend in the intensification of the exploitation of plant resources predicted by Clarke did not occur. The innovations postulated by Clarke only affected the northern Mediterranean; the correlation between the intensification of the use of plant food and the Mediterranean evergreen forest does not hold good.

The beginnings of food production from a traditional perspective – processual inference from the east–west pattern of culture change

The most succinct presentation of the diffusionist model of the beginnings of food production in the Mediterranean has

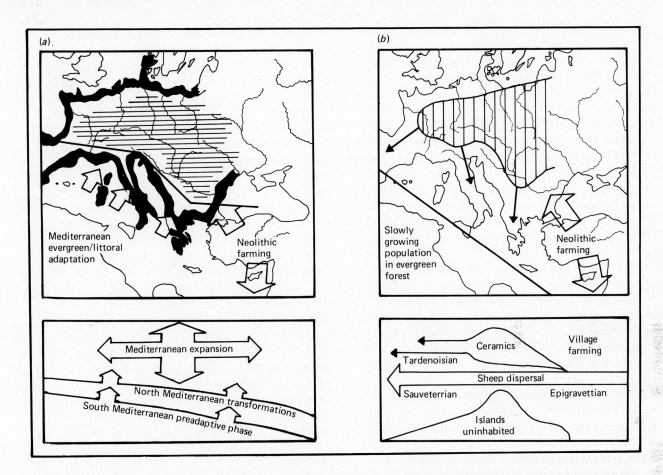

Fig. 1. Models of the transition to food production. (*a*) Schematised by D. L. Clarke (1976); (*b*) this chapter. Horizontal hatching, sparse population in European interior; black, dense population in coastal zones; vertical hatching, expanding population in temperate forests.

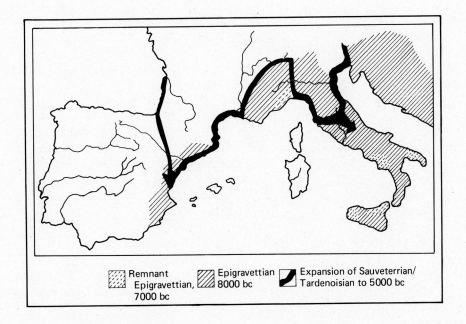

Fig. 2. Mesolithic cultural distribution in the Mediterranean. Schematised on the basis of Fig. 7 of Broglio (1980).

been made by Childe (1957, p. 16):

> Farming must of course have started in South-West
> Asia . . . Fishing communities along the Levant coasts
> could perfectly well have learned to supplement the
> products of food gathering by cultivating cereals and
> breeding stock. Such incipient food-producers, forced
> to colonize fresh territories, might perfectly well have
> taken to their boats and paddled or sailed on the alluring
> waters of the Mediterranean to the next landfall — and
> then the next.

One of Childe's most enduring observations was to emphasise
the contrast between the eastern and western basins in respect
of the continuity of the way of life from the Mesolithic, inso-
far as known, into the Neolithic. For whereas, in the eastern
basin, from Greece and Crete as far west as Sicily, evidence of
cereal cultivation and animal husbandry appeared abruptly and
in close conjunction with the manufacture of ceramics and the
practice of permanent settlement in villages and homesteads,
from the key site of Arene Candide (Finale Ligure) westward
to the Iberian peninsula, the earliest domestic fauna and
ceramics occur only in coastal caves previously occupied
during the Mesolithic, without the major shift to village settlement (Childe 1957, pp. 17, 58, 230–1, 244, 265–7) (Fig. 3);
(for the opposite view, see Geddes 1984).

Childe none the less recognised the possibility of the
contrasts in pattern being due to sample bias alone. Referring
to Cardial ware, he commented:

> It was carried by groups of hunters and stock-breeders,
> known almost exclusively from their occupation of
> caves. This circumstance has unduly exaggerated the

rôle attributed to animal husbandry in the economy; for
herdsmen periodically shelter in caves even though they
have homes in permanent farming villages (Childe 1957,
p. 266)

Similarly, he admitted that the apparent absence of mesolithic
precursors of the Greek *tell*-dwellers might be deceiving
'merely because no systematic search for such remains has
been made' (Childe 1957, p. 58). Therefore, both the apparent
patterns in each region, and the contrast between them, might
be the result of different forms of bias and sample error.

Nearly three decades of subsequent research have only
confirmed the essential validity of Childe's two points: in the
first place, the apparent duality of regional patterning; in the
second, the resultant explanatory dilemma — to accept the
distinction as real or to postulate the effect of various biases
on a pristine uniformity?

The duality is clear (Figs. 4 and 5): whereas the dates for
the first appearance of sheep and ceramics are broadly synchronous throughout the Mediterranean, mixed-farming
villages occur significantly later in the western basin than in
the eastern, indeed belatedly enough to be regarded by some
authors as a properly middle neolithic development (Guilaine
1976, pp. 42–59, 1980, pp. 5–10; Mills 1985). In the west
Mediterranean, therefore, there is a gap of at least 2000 years
between the earliest appearance of pottery and caprines, and
the adoption of other farming practices (6000–4000 bc).
Recent research has eliminated two out of the four possible
explanations:

(1)   The possibility that a similar transitional period occurred
       in Greece during the millennium prior to the establish-

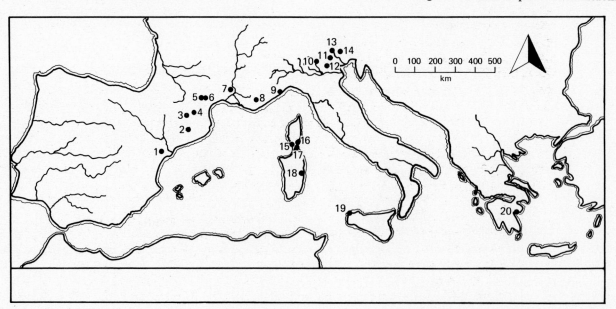

Fig. 3. Key sites of the Mesolithic and Early Neolithic in the Mediterranean. 1, Cova Fosca (Castellón); 2, Balma del Gai (Moià); 3, Balma
Margineda (Andorra); 4, Abri du Roc de Dourgne (Fontanès-de-Sault); 5, Grotte Gazel (Sallèles-Cabardès); 6, Balma de l'Abeurador (Fé-
lines-Minervois); 7, Baume de Montclus (Montclus); 8, Baume de Fontbrégoua (Salernes); 9, Arene Candide (Finale Ligure); 10, Riparo
Valtenesi (Manerba); 11, Colbricon; 12, Riparo Tagliente (Grezzana); 13, Riparo Battaglia (Asiago); 14, Piancavallo; 15, Basi (Serra-di-
Ferro); 16, Curacchiaghiu (Levie); 17, Araguina-Sennola (Bonifacio); 18, Corbeddu Cave (Oliena); 19, Grotta dell'Uzzo (Trapani); 20,
Franchthi Cave (Koilada).

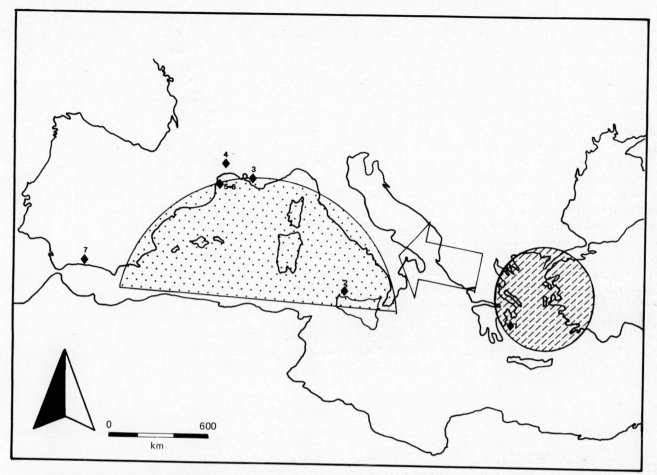

Fig. 4. Spread of coastal fishing in the Mediterranean: hatched area, intensified coastal fishing prior to the Neolithic, 7000 bc, dotted area, intensified coastal fishing parallel with or subsequent to the emergence of farming, 6000–5000 bc. 1, Franchthi Cave (Koilada); 2, Grotta dell'Uzzo (Trapani); 3, Cap Ragnon (Le Rove); 4, Balma de l'Abeurador (Félines-Minervois); 5, L'Ile de Corrège (Leucate); 6, Cova de l'Espérit (Salses); 7, Cueva de Nerja (Málaga).

ment of farming villages appears to be excluded by the excavations at the key site of Franchthi cave (Koilada), which shows a sudden replacement of the Mesolithic by a fully developed neolithic economy (Jacobsen 1981).

(2) The hypothesis that the sheep was independently domesticated within the western Mediterranean prior to the introduction of farming, formerly accepted by Guilaine (1976, pp. 48–51), now seems implausible (Guilaine 1980, p. 5; Poplin 1979; Vigne 1985; Geddes 1984). The Tyrrhenian moufflon, formerly thought to have been the wild progenitor of the local domesticated sheep has now itself been shown to have developed from primitive domestic sheep (Vigne 1983, p. 346).

Research now focuses on the two remaining hypotheses (Lewthwaite 1981):

(1) Mixed-farming villages in the western basin might have existed from the sixth millennium bc but have been drowned by the holocene eustatic rise in sea level. In order to explain why this should have selectively affected the west, it is necessary to consider in detail the relative size and topography of the drowned continental shelves and surviving coastal plains (van Andel and Shackleton 1982; Shackleton, van Andel and Runnels 1984; Geddes, Guilaine and Monaco 1983).

(2) The mixed-farming settlement–subsistence system may have encountered natural or cultural selective pressures which favoured the westward diffusion of ovicaprine husbandry and ceramic technology while delaying the adoption of the village settlement mode.

Late mesolithic economic and social organisation
Southern France and the Iberian peninsula

The early holocene vegetational succession of this region is well known as a result of recent extensive palynological and anthracological research (Ros Mora and Vernet 1985; Vernet, Badal Garcia and Grau Almero 1985; Jalut 1977; Triat-Laval 1978). At the end of the Pleistocene, the vegetation consisted of pines, junipers, and pioneer species yielding edible fruits and nuts (Rosaceae, Rhamnaceae, Oleaceae).

During the preboreal and boreal periods, the pine retreated to higher ground before the expansion of deciduous

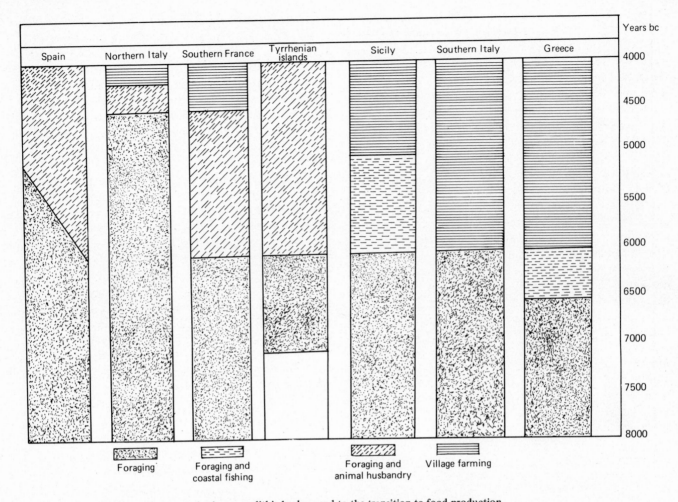

Fig. 5. Regional temporal patterns in the preneolithic background to the transition to food production.

oaks, with local peaks of hazel, while the onset of the Atlantic was marked by the further expansion of thermophilous plants at low altitudes and of fir in the mountains. Compared with the mixed oak forest of Central Europe, the temperate Mediterranean variant was poor in species such as elm, lime and alder, the marcescent white oak (*Quercus pubescens*) being the dominant species. The evergreen oaks, restricted to edaphically arid microenvironments in southern France, formed a major component of the vegetation of south-eastern Spain.

The rapid eustatic rise in sea level from 50 m below the present sea level at *c*. 8000 bc successively to 20 m at *c*. 6000 bc and to approximately the present day level at *c*. 4000 bc created the lagoons, estuaries, embayments and eventually deltas, the high edible productivity of which Clarke has emphasised (Clarke 1976, pp. 464–7). However, detailed investigations into the palaeogeography and palaeo-ecology of the Camargue (Rhône delta) by Pons, Toni and Triat (1979, pp. 13–30) have uncovered a more complex sequence of developments: temporary pauses and retreats of sea level periodically changed the extent, location and openness to the sea of coastal lagoons. Such fluctuations in salinity and accessibility to

migrant marine species could have recurrently limited the productivity and stability of the aquatic ecosystem.

The settlement–subsistence system of the late mesolithic period is best known from western Languedoc (particularly the Aude valley), the flanks of the Pyrénées, Catalunya and the Spanish Levant, but is even so obscured by sampling biases in favour of inland cave sites and faunal rather than palaeobotanical remains. Within this region, two major classes of site may be recognised. In the one, the faunal assemblage consists predominantly of large game – pig, ibex and red deer in the main, the proportions varying with antiquity and altitude, besides lower frequencies of roe deer, bovines and equids. In the other, small game (particularly the rabbit, *Oryctolagus cuniculus*) accounts for the bulk of the bone remains and gathering activities are known or believed to have been important.

The sites of the Aude valley studied by Geddes (1983*a*) are representative of the first category. The ibex and chamois, which were the principal prey of epipalaeolithic hunters in the region at about 10 000 bc, disappeared from low-lying sites such as the Grotte Gazel (Sallèles-Cabardès), altitude 250 m, and the Abri du Roc de Dourgne (Fontanès-de-Sault), altitude

710 m, before 5000 bc, although these continued to be hunted at the higher lying (970 m) Balma Margineda (Andorra) (Gascó and Gutherz 1983, pp. 68–72) (Fig. 3). Although Jarman has picked out the red deer as the faunal staple of the European Mesolithic (Jarman 1972, pp. 125–47), in the Aude valley it was rather the wild swine which replaced the ibex during the early neothermal (Geddes 1983*b*, p. 120).

Typical of the sites with small game are the Cova Fosca (Castellón) in eastern Spain (Olaría de Gusí, Estévez Escalera and Y11 1982, pp. 107–20), the Balma del Gai (Moià) in Catalunya (Guilaine *et al.* 1982), the Balma de l'Abeurador (Félines-Minervois) in Languedoc and the Baume de Fontbrégoua (Salernes) in Provence (Gascó and Gutherz 1983, pp. 67–8, 82–3) (Fig. 3). Although the remains of larger mammals were encountered, rabbits were numerically the most important game, while birds were consumed with surprising frequency. In the case of the Balma del Gai, only the skull and lower extremities of the larger mammals were left at the site, the meat-bearing joints being taken elsewhere. At all sites, remains of nuts and fruits were found: acorns, chestnuts and *piñones* at the Cova Fosca; at Abeurador, hazelnuts, wild grapes and wild cherry; acorns, hazelnuts and wild grapes at the Baume de Fontbrégoua; while the presence of wood charcoal of the genera *Amygdalus* and *Prunus* at the Balma del Gai indicates the availability of such resources. Three species of indigenous legumes were culled at the French sites: *Lathyrus cicera*, *Ervum ervilia* and a vetch, *Vicia* sp., but the greater surprise has been the discovery at Abeurador, in a Sauveterrian (Montclusian) level dated to 6790 ± 90 bc (MC-2144) of three species of supposedly eastern Mediterranean or western Asiatic provenance, possibly cultivated; the chickpea *Cicer arietinum*, the lentil *Lens esculenta* and the pea *Pisum sativum* (Erroux 1980; Vaquer 1980; Vaquer and Barbaza 1985).

The two classes of site appear to be complementary, indicating an element of mobility, but it is not necessary to postulate altitudinal migration. Thus, while the activities represented are clearly appropriate to different periods of the year — big-game hunting to the cold months, the gathering of pulses, nuts and fruit to the warm season or as late as the autumn — the sites of the second category are located at no greater an altitude than those of the former (Balma de l'Abeurador 560 m, Baume de Fontbrégoua 450 m). Again, the evidence of the Balma del Gai suggests a pattern of logistic movements within a limited radius between the base camps and outstations rather than true transhumance. Finally, it is not clear whether the widespread settlement and seasonal movements, attested for the eighth millennium bc at the sites quoted, continued unchanged into subsequent millennia, as the density of edible terrestrial resources would have been increasing towards the Boreal–Atlantic transition.

The still controversial claims for the garden-scale cultivation of legumes at Balma de l'Abeurador (for which the criteria have not been elaborated) may indicate that the summer was the critical seasonal threshold limiting the annual carrying capacity of Mediterranean regions. Adaptations which would have offset this seasonal shortfall include not only intensified plant collection but fishing, since migratory species are easily captured during their entry into and exit from coastal lagoons, while pelagic migrants are best exploited during the summer, when they are near the shore. Although such coastal sites, especially on the shelving coast of Languedoc, must now lie under water, inland freshwater fishing sites such as the Baume de Montclus (Montclus) survive. This site on the banks of the Cèze was occupied in the spring, according to the excavator, but the remains of fish-smoking hearths suggest that resources may have been processed for later consumption (Gascó and Gutherz 1983, p. 75). There is no direct evidence of increasing social complexity, but the recently discovered case of scalping and head-hunting in the context of the Provençal Mesolithic (Bouville and Courtin 1985) may indicate the crystallisation of self-conscious territorial groups and perhaps a degree of competition for limited resources. The same phenomenon may be reflected in the proliferation of the parietal art of the Spanish Levant, which records hunting activities.

In summary, late mesolithic groups in the Mediterranean regions of France and Spain appear to have taken full advantage of the increasing density of edible resources to be found in the warm-temperate forest, and may have been intensifying summer fishing and plant-harvesting activities.

Italy and the west Mediterranean islands
Palaeoecological research has not been carried out with the same intensity in all the regions of peninsular Italy and in the adjacent islands: palynological samples for the early Holocene are very rare outside a restricted region (Corsica and mainland Italy north of Rome), while anthracological investigations have been concentrated on waterlogged sites in the Po Plain. Despite the proximity of refuges, the colonisation by temperate species of the north Italian plain and piedmont may have been delayed by an insufficiency of rainfall during the preboreal period; however, during the Boreal, mixed oak forest appears to have colonised the whole of this region. The increased humidity of the atlantic period would have favoured the expansion of beech and fir at the expense of oak even in the lowlands (Broglio 1980, p. 13). Corsican vegetation developed in a broadly similar pattern, with the exception that the boreal peak of the hazel did not occur. The Boreal was the period of the maximum extension of the Corsican laricio pine, although deciduous and evergreen species were already present. During the Atlantic, deciduous oaks (particularly *Quercus pubescens*) formed a climax down to sea level, at least in the humid southeast, while the tree heath (*Erica arborea*) colonised the thinner soils of the slopes (Reille 1984). As in other Mediterranean regions, the evergreen oaks (*Quercus ilex*, *Q. suber*) did not become widespread until the Sub-boreal (Reille 1976, pp. 52–8). Costantini's (1981) palaeobotanical research at the Grotta dell'Uzzo (Trapani) in northwestern Sicily suggests that evergreen oaks and species typical of

macchia (wild olives, vines) were already features of the landscape by the eighth millennium bc.

Postglacial adaptations in northern Italy appear to have been highly correlated with changes in the distribution of terrestrial resources brought about by the vegetational succession and by the loss of the extensive upper Adriatic lowlands under the encroaching postglacial sea (Shackleton *et al.* 1984). As the ibex retreated before the rising treeline, the predation practised during the eleventh millennium bc at the final epigravettian site of Riparo Tagliente (Grezzana), altitude 225 m, in the Alpine foothills, continued during the ninth and eighth millennia at stations such as the Riparo Battaglia (Asiago), altitude 1050 m, or Piancavallo (1360 m) and during the seventh at the Sauveterrian site of Colbricon (1900 m). The specialised Sauveterrian ibex-hunting sites which surround the Trento basin and in the Dolomites at heights of 1900–2200 m would have been uninhabitable in winter and could only have been used by communities or task groups practising seasonal movements (Broglio 1980, pp. 7–13). During the atlantic period, however, the Castelnovian–Tardenoisian groups appear to have drawn their subsistence from a narrower zone of high productivity – red deer, boar, freshwater fish and vegetal products of the lowland forest and rivers. By the fifth millennium bc, specialised lakeside fishing settlements existed, such as the Riparo Valtenesi (Manerba) on Lake Garda (Bagolini and Biagi 1980; Biagi *et al.* 1981, p. 27).

A very different situation developed on the Tyrrhenian islands. Although claims have recently been made for the presence of human settlers on Sardinia as early as the twelfth millennium bc and for their predation on the now extinct endemic deer *Megaceros (Nesoleipoceros) cazioti* at the Corbeddu cave (Oliena) (Sondaar *et al.* (1984), the earliest reliably documented evidence of the colonisation of either island consists of the seventh millennium bc levels in the southern Corsican sites (Fig. 3) of Curacchiaghiu (Levie) and Araguina–Sennola (Bonifacio) (Lewthwaite 1983, pp. 146–83). The extreme dependence of the occupants of the latter shelter on the predation of the extinct small-game species *Prolagus sardus*, eked out with fish, shellfish, birds and seals (Vigne 1984, 1985) reflects the absolute lack of indigenous medium-sized game.

No such faunal impoverishment affected early postglacial Sicily; however, the mesolithic occupants of the Grotta dell'Uzzo (Trapani), despite their location on a coastal promontory, made little use of the sea except to harvest shellfish, for the most part hunting red deer and pig and collecting acorns, wild grapes and grass peas (*Lathyrus* sp.) from the evergreen oak forest and macchia which surrounded the site (Costantini 1981). Calculations of the requirements of a model band of 30 suggests that the site could have been occupied all the year around if the deer of the surrounding two-hour territory were rationally culled (Piperno, Scali and Tagliacozzo 1980). The duration and intensity of the eighth and seventh millennia bc occupation is confirmed by the thick deposits,

density of artefacts and food debris and construction of fixed hearths; the site may have served as a ritual centre as well, since several burials occur therein and there are traces of graffiti on the walls.

An upsurge in the exploitation of marine resources is indicated during a period of economic and artefactual transition which developed at the very end of the seventh millennium bc (*terminus post quem*, 6180 ± 90 bc, P-2734). Three species of cetaceans were exploited, neolithic-style blade-based lithic technology began to replace that of the Mesolithic, while a few fragments of ceramics and of obsidian have been found. This transitional period came to an end at *c.* 5500 bc (extrapolation from P-2733, 4990 ± 70 bc, higher up in the sequence) with the inception of food-producing activities (cereals, legumes, domesticated animals) and, paradoxically, with the first bone and artefactual evidence for intensive line-fishing of rocky-coast species (Piperno, Tusa and Valente 1980; Durante 1980; Costantini, Piperno and Tusa 1985; Piperno 1984).

Consideration of this rather superficial north–south transect suggests a general tendency towards an intensification of the food quest. The preneolithic inhabitants of Corsica must clearly have pursued a mobile subsistence strategy simply in order to survive, while the seasonal exploitation of ibex during the Sauveterrian period in northern Italy almost certainly represented no more than a seasonal facies of a more broadly based foraging strategy. The dynamism of the sixth millennium bc is common to the Po Plain and Sicily. In the Po Plain case, it took the form of an intensified exploitation of the indigenous resources of the temperate forests and rivers, and of the concurrent adoption of blade and trapeze industries. In Sicily, the innovations may plausibly be regarded as having been derived from the eastern Mediterranean (improved watercraft, blade and ceramic technology).

The growth of widespread interaction spheres is indicated by the petrological evidence for the dispersion of lithic raw material into and across the Po Plain from the adjacent highlands (Biagi *et al.* 1981, pp. 28–32, Fig. 12).

Greece
Palynological data from Greece is scarcer than elsewhere, but from a number of sources van Zeist and Bottema (1982, pp. 277–321) have assembled a general tableau. In east-central Greece, an open oak forest (below 600 m) and a mixed deciduous oak forest (600–1200 m) began to develop from *c.* 8500 bc, driving the conifers of the late pleistocene pine parkland to heights above 1600 m. Between 7300 and 6200 bc increases in *Pistacia* and *Poterium* indicate warmer, drier conditions and a more open forest structure, precipitation thereafter increasing and the forest becoming denser.

The Franchthi cave (Koilada) in the Argolid is not only the most important mesolithic site in Greece, but one of the most important in the entire Mediterranean (Jacobsen 1981). At the beginning of the postglacial period a band of perhaps 30 occupied the cave, if not permanently, then on several occasions throughout the year. The hunting of red deer and pig replaced that of equids, bovids and a caprine (ibex?) practised during the Upper or Final Palaeolithic on the adjacent coastal lowlands, as they were progressively flooded (van Andel and Shackelton 1982; Payne 1975, pp. 120–31); since the final Pleistocene, a wide variety of plant foods had also been consumed, including cereals (native wild oats and barley), legumes (lentils and vetch) and nuts (pistachio and almonds), peas and wild pears being added during the Mesolithic proper (Hansen, 1978), but few and only small fish.

At the beginning of the seventh millennium bc, dramatic developments occurred: firstly, large fish bones appeared and soon accounted for a half of all large animal bones deposited, 95% of these belonging to the bluefin tunny (which can reach a weight of 200 kg); secondly, claims have been made for the incipient cultivation of local lentils; finally, obsidian came to be employed more frequently and geometric microliths (not made on microblades) to replace the cruder industry of the Final Palaeolithic (Payne 1975; Jacobsen 1981). Although the unique nature of the site precludes any generalisation at the regional level, it is evident that, at Franchthi at least, there was a gradual shift to sedentism and an intensification of fishing and plant gathering.

Discussion

According to Clarke (1972, pp. 1–60), the process of archaeological argumentation consists of a conscious and repeated dialectic between a set of operational models and the corpus of empirical evidence, neither induction nor deduction from axiomatic first principles receiving undue emphasis. When the set of operational models is drawn from too narrow a spectrum of perceived possibilities and the quantity of data is slender, slow-growing and unevenly scattered, then such a closed system of reasoning will tend towards a complacent equilibrium, periodically punctuated by catastrophic reversals of opinion as the intrusion of fresh evidence admits some sensational surprise from a hitherto overlooked source.

Clarke himself perpetuated certain stereotypes drawn from his awareness of the burgeoning archaeologically oriented ethnography of surviving foragers, as in his evocation of a nuclear family as a functioning minimal adaptive unit or in repeated references to a 'seasonal circuit' involving 'transhumance' within a 'territory' (Clarke 1976, pp. 456, 468–70).

One of the most fundamental axioms to enter the archaeology of foragers thus holds that egalitarian society constitutes a sort of state of nature, an entropic baseline from which social complexity has subsequently been conjured up by some sort of social energy-capture on the part of individuals or groups (Bender 1978). This is to confuse the equality of outcome with that of the equality of opportunity.

An alternative reading of the ethnographic literature suggests that, to paraphrase Pearson's (1957, p. 339) dictum concerning surpluses, there are always and everywhere potential inequalities available. What counts is the institutional

means for bringing them to nought. In other words, the egalitarian social system of many (but not all) foragers can just as easily be seen as a precarious equilibrium between dynamically opposed forces, a high-energy situation, in which potential rights *in rem* and *in personam* are dissipated through a constant 'Red Queen' competitiveness among the adult male contenders, which leaves none relatively better off despite the exertion of much effort, and through homeostatic devices which burden the successful hunter with extra hangers-on through the institution of flexible bilateral kinship. Clearly, it only requires the relaxation of such feedbacks for social inequalities to emerge, for instance in respect of the universality of access to technological resources and to the harvesting of seasonally abundant and storable foods. In the same way, as mesolithic population densities rose, the necessity of band exogamy would be progressively reduced, the breeding groups coming to coincide with the social group (Newell 1984). Negative reciprocity would tend, therefore, to characterise intergroup relationships, particularly as the intensification of resource exploitation resulted in investment in fixed facilities within circumscribed territories. Collective burial rites, parietal art, scalping and headhunting (*vide supra*) may signal precisely such social developments.

From foraging to food production
The transition at the regional level

Given the evidence of apparently well adapted yet also innovative mesolithic communities from Greece to Languedoc, the regional differences in the pattern of the transition to food production appear all the more surprising. For it is in the eastern basin, where the preneolithic intensification of foraging was the most advanced, as demonstrated at Franchthi, that the adoption of mixed-farming and village settlement took place most abruptly, while the farther west one looks (l'Uzzo, Sicily; l'Abeurador, Languedoc), the better the congruence between a low level of mesolithic experimentation and the belated adoption of village farming (Figs. 4 and 5). None the less, the horizon of the beginnings of ceramic manufacture and ovicaprine husbandry is more or less synchronous in its date of 6500–6000 bc throughout the Mediterranean, as if unconnected with either subsequent or preceding developments. Since neither total diffusion nor totally independent evolution predicts such a lack of congruence, more complex scenarios deserve consideration which may be termed the 'social' and the 'island filter' models.

Put succinctly, the 'social model' postulates that ovicaprines might have spread in advance of farming for reasons other than simple subsistence. Ethnographic accounts suggest that over and above their 'secondary products' livestock possess the tertiary quality of expressing prestige and serving as instruments whereby transient social ranking can rapidly be established, even among societies at a very low level of technology (Lewthwaite 1986). If the socio-economic organisation of the northern temperate-forest zone of the

Mediterranean was the more developed at the time of the dispersion of ovicaprines, then it is worth investigating the possibility that the mixed hunting—herding economy which persisted for some time consisted not of two modes of subsistence, but of one of subsistence and one of prestige or capital accumulation. A similar hypothesis may explain the dispersion of the finer Impressed wares (Lewthwaite 1981).

The 'island filter' model takes as a point of departure the application of island biogeographic theory to the pattern and process of Mediterranean island settlement pioneered by Cherry (1981), who concludes that island biogeographic theory accurately predicts the sequence of colonisation, in that proximity to the mainland and areal extent correlate positively with early settlement; that colonisation has probably been effected by very small groups, highly vulnerable to physical extinction and to the attrition of cultural traits (founder effect); and that the constraints of insular environments deterred both foraging and farming populations from settling many islands long after this was feasible simply in terms of achieving the watercrossing.

One conclusion which emerges with particular clarity from Cherry's analysis is the surprising fact that it was the western basin which developed the higher level of colonising activity between the sixth and the fourth millennia bc, when, moreover, the material homogeneity of the Impressed ware culture group contrasted markedly with the cultural isolation of Crete and Cyprus; indeed the Cyclades may have been frequented only by fishermen until the fourth millennium bc (Cherry 1981, pp. 58–64). Since it is generally assumed that the preneolithic settlers of Corsica and Sardinia made the shortest watercrossing from the nearest mainland, i.e via the Elban archipelago from Tuscany, it follows that the pattern of western priority can be traced still further back, into the seventh millennium bc, with the implication that mesolithic communities of the warm-temperate zone of the northwestern Mediterranean achieved the first and the most extensive island settlement, whatever the precocity of deep-sea fishing and obsidian procurement at Franchthi might suggest.

It is equally apparent that the extreme variability in the beginnings of food production among the various Mediterranean islands alerts us to the boundary conditions under which the otherwise banal circumstances of the introduction of cereals, legumes and the common farmyard animals to mainland contexts holds good. The aceramic neolithic colonists of Cyprus imported, along with the usual run of domesticates, the Syrian fallow deer *Dama mesopotamica* (Watson and Stanley Price 1977); the early settlers of Mallorca depended for more than a millennium on the exploitation of the now extinct endemic *Myotragus balearicus* prior to the appearance in the third millennium bc of the commoner domesticates (Waldren 1982, pp. 105–22). A model of the transition to food production which could accommodate or, better still, predict such singular anomalies would surely be judged superior to one which could only satisfactorily explain the mainstream pattern, even if this includes 99% of

recorded instances. The 'island filter model' meets these conditions. In this model, islands, or other discrete regions, act as a filter in selecting certain elements from a more complex phenomenon such as food production in response to their own particular requirements. Any other region dependent on the filter region for access to such an innovation therefore receives only the limited version transmitted by the filter. This process reduces their range of choice.

If it is assumed that the Tyrrhenian islands formed such an obligatory filter to southern France and the Iberian peninsula, then it is clear that any such selective decision would determine the variables transmitted further down the line, reducing the options available to Franco-Iberian mesolithic populations, despite their possibly greater 'receptivity' as a result of population growth in the temperate forest environment. In effect, until such time as the Tyrrhenian 'filter' was bypassed or ceased to operate selectively, the inception of cereal cultivation and the aggregation of population into permanent villages would be delayed.

If it is accepted that in general the exploitation of medium-sized mammals represents an optimal type of resource for management by human populations (McCullough 1970), then it is evident that the importation of the ovicaprines and swine found at the sixth millennium bc Impressed Ware site of Basi (Serra-de-Ferro) in south-western Corsica (Vigne 1984, 1985) would have raised the carrying capacity significantly closer to that of a contemporary and equivalent mainland region; the adoption of cereal cultivation and cattle-raising would not necessarily have been advantageous until the population grew further.

The central position of the Corsico-Sardinian island block as a medium of diffusion between southern Italy and Sicily on the one hand, and southern France on the other, is given some support by the patterning of Guilaine's tripartition of the Impressed Ware culture grouping into regional facies (Guilaine 1980, pp. 8–12): in effect, the transmission of ceramic technology and design passed not along the western coast of Italy but through the interaction sphere of the Tyrrhenian sea consisting of Corsica, Sardinia and an arc of coastland extending from Toulon to the Tiber (Fig. 6).

This model can be contrasted with the rather different sort of filter-effect likely to have been generated by the Aegean archipelago (see above), thus conforming to Cherry's findings that the western basin overtook the eastern in the rate of colonisation during the Impressed Ware period (sixth to fourth millennia bc). Whereas on Corsica and Sardinia, an established but sparse population multiplied rapidly on acquiring the first mammals of worthwhile size through which to exploit the terrestrial environment, in the case of the Aegean archipelago the environment itself may have been so poor as to inhibit even this level of population, given their exiguity and aridity. Consequently, innovations would have spread through the Aegean without causing structural change, whereas in the Tyrrhenian case some sort of structural transformation must be postulated to explain their further diffusion.

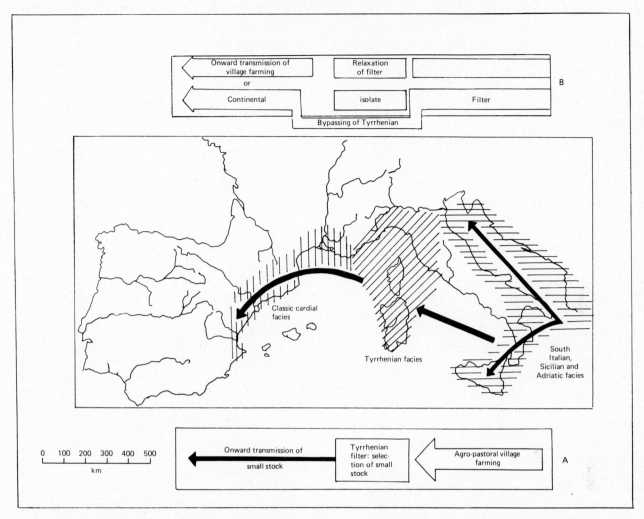

Fig. 6. The Tyrrhenian filter model of the Early Neolithic of the western Mediterranean; A, sixth millennium bc; B, fifth millennium bc.

The transition at the local level

Although the long-term effect of the adoption of crop cultivation and animal husbandry may have been that of permitting the achievement of higher population densities, it is reasonable to suppose that the initial advantages to groups still largely dependent on foraging for subsistence lay in their utility in stabilising the existing systems, perhaps by resolving the recurrent seasonal crises, which on ethnographic grounds would be expected to have occurred during the summer (Clark Forbes 1976, p. 131, Figs. 1 and 2). The cultivation of cereals and legumes as supplementary or complementary resources would have been periodically important for populations unable to resolve the summer crisis through the exploitation of the resources of the sea or of adjacent non-Mediterranean life zones.

Models of early Mediterranean farming practices such as those of Sherratt (1980, pp. 316–22) or Halstead (1981, pp. 307–39) envisage adaptations by pioneer settlers to virgin environments, making hardly any allowances for the constraints likely to have been imposed by the persistent priority of foraging strategies. Despite Rowley-Conwy's (1981, pp.

85–96) recent rejection of swiddening as a universal stage of early food production, it is likely that temporary, dispersed clearances preceded the tilling of fixed plots adjacent to permanent, agglomerated settlements; groups moving seasonally among altitudinally stratified resource zones might well have cultivated crops at several points in the seasonal round in order to enjoy a succession of harvests thanks to staggered growing seasons.

One indication of such pre-village farming cultivation may be provided by the anomalously early (sixth millennium bc) occurrence of clearance horizons associated with cereal pollen which have been detected by palynologists as far apart as in Crete (Bottema 1980, p. 210) and the lower Rhône (Triat-Laval 1978, pp. 263–5) and at altitudes of up to 1510 m in the east central Pyrénées (Jalut 1980, pp. 63–4). Settlement patterns are another source of clues: Ammerman's intensive research into the Early Neolithic of Calabria has uncovered a pattern very different from that commonly predicted on theoretical grounds, sites being small, dispersed and located on relatively poor-quality soils (Ammerman 1985; Ammerman and Shaffer 1981).

If the assumption that the rate of the adoption of food production was determined by the intensity of the seasonal food crisis holds good, then the capacity and direction of the spread of crop cultivation and animal husbandry ought to be correlated with the severity of the summer drought. As agriculture in the Mediterranean is traditionally dependent on winter and spring rainfall, it would not have been affected by the summer lack of moisture.

Some four situations can be recognised which can be arranged along the humid–arid axis from southeast to northwest, modified by the special properties of the islands:

(1) The Aegean archipelago appears to have been so hostile an environment that neither foraging nor farming permanent settlements became established during the period in question, although this may be a false impression created by the loss of sites due to drowning and the paucity of systematic field survey attuned to the recognition of lithic scatters.

(2) A zone from mainland Greece to the south-central Mediterranean (southern Italy and Sicily) supported a sparser population of foragers among whom the food-producing economy spread relatively rapidly. This may have included the actual dispersion of farmers from the eastern Mediterranean.

(3) The paucity of large mammals on the major Tyrrhenian islands stimulated the rapid adoption of animal husbandry as the major subsistence strategy, pre-empting the acceptance of crop cultivation in conformity with the island filter model.

(4) The dense mesolithic population of the northwestern mainland, exploiting a temperate forest ecosystem, diversified by the complementary resources of montane zones, perennial rivers and lagoons, adopted food production particularly gradually and tardily. In this area, the selective adoption of certain forms of farming may have acted as a seasonal complement to foraging and probably as a medium for the expression of status and for the accumulation of power.

This patterning appears to confirm the strength of the correlation between the constraints on the resources available to foragers and the rapidity of the local transition to food production.

Conclusions

(1) During the first two millennia of the postglacial period, the population of the Mediterranean region not only grew simply in proportion to the increasing resources of the developing terrestrial ecosystem as the temperate forest expanded, but began to settle the larger and closer islands (Corsica) and to appropriate additional resources such as pelagic fish (Franchthi) or possibly exotic legumes (l'Abeurador).

(2) From *c.* 6000 bc alternative modes of intensifying and stabilising food procurement began to impinge on the northwestern and southeastern margins of the region,

respectively; on the one hand, the further intensification of the exploitation of the indigenous resources of the temperate forest as the atlantic peak of humidity increased its productivity, a phenomenon archaeologically represented by the Tardenoisian–Castelnovian culture; on the other, the intrusion of the food-production system based on the cultivation of cereals and pulses and the husbandry of domestic animals.

(3) Between *c.* 6000 bc and *c.* 4000 bc the latter system replaced the former, but with significant differences in respect of the rate of adoption between the eastern and Western basins and between the mainlands and the islands, which are indicative of the stability and complexity of the indigenous foraging subsistence strategy. Where the mesolithic population appears to have been particularly sparse, as in Greece and the Aegean Sea, it is difficult to envisage a non-diffusionist model of the introduction of food production. Elsewhere, the evidence favours the continuity of population from Mesolithic into Early Neolithic.

(4) The rapidity of the adoption of ovicaprid husbandry and of ceramic technology compared with fully developed village farming in the western basin requires particular attention. Unless the western site sample has suffered disproportionately from coastal site loss, the discrepancy must be explained in terms of the positive properties of the indigenous cultural systems – e.g. a high degree of interconnection through voyaging, social complexity necessitating prestige goods etc. ('filter' and 'social' models); the practice of cereal cultivation may have spread in the same manner in advance of the integrated agro-pastoral system as a resource complementary to foraging strategies.

(5) Consideration of ethnographic analogues (California, Japan) suggest that the cultural complexity of Mediterranean Europe could have progressed still further on the basis of purely indigenous resources had the diffusion of the western Asiatic farming system been delayed. However, there is no evidence that the mesolithic populations of the Mediterranean were on the point of developing a farming system of comparable productivity based upon local resources.

Acknowledgements

I would like to thank all those friends and colleagues who have generously donated offprints and even whole books: A. Ammerman, P. Biagi, J. Cherry, L. Costantini, D. Geddes, T. Jacobsen, G. Jalut, A. Pons, M. Piperno. F. Poplin, M. Reille, P. Rowley-Conwy, J. Shackleton, A. Sherratt, J. L. Vernet, J. D. Vigne, and W. Waldren. I am especially grateful to Marek Zvelebil for inviting me to contribute to this volume; to both David Geddes and Marek Zvelebil for reading and making valuable comments upon earlier drafts, although all errors and omissions remain my responsibility; to Robin Zvelebil for undertaking the typing and to John Howell for preparing the original illustrations. This publication was written during tenure of a Research Assistantship in the Undergraduate School of Studies in Archaeological Sciences of the University of Bradford.

References

Ammerman, A. J. (1985) 'Neolithic occupation in Calabria', in J. Guilaine, ed., *Premières Communautés Paysannes en Méditerranée Occidentale*, Centre National de Recherche Scientifique, in press.

Ammerman, A. J. and Shaffer, G. D. (1981) 'Neolithic settlement patterns in Calabria'. *Current Anthropology* 22, 430–2.

Bagolini, B. and Biagi, P. (1980) 'The mesolithic and early neolithic settlement of northern Italy', in J. K. Kozłowski and J. Machnik eds., *Problèmes de la Néolithisation dans Certaines Régions de l'Europe*, Krakow.

Bender, B. (1978) 'Gatherer–hunter to farmer: a social perspective'. *World Archaeology* 10, 204–22.

Biagi, P., Castelletti, L., Cremaschi, M., Sala, B. and Tozzi, C. (1981) 'Popolazione e territorio nell'appennino tosco – emiliano e nel tratto centrale del bacino del Po, tra il IX e il V millennio'. *Emilia Preromana* 8, 13–36.

Bottema, S. (1980) 'Palynological investigation on Crete'. *Review of Palaeobotany and Palynology* 31, 193–217.

Bouville, C. and Courtin, J. (1985) 'Les restes humains de la grotte de Fontbrégoua (Salernes-Var)', in J. Guilane, ed., *Premières Communautés Paysannes en Méditerranée Occidentale*, Centre National de Recherche Scientifique, in press.

Broglio, A. (1980) 'Culture ed ambienti della fine del paleolitico e del mesolitico nell'Italia nord-orientale'. *Prehistoria Alpina* 16, 7–29.

Cherry, J. (1981) 'Pattern and process in the earliest colonisation of the Mediterranean Islands'. *Proceedings of the Prehistoric Society* 47, 41–68.

Childe, V. G (1957) *The Dawn of European Civilization*, 6th edn, Routledge and Kegan Paul, London.

Clarke, D. L. (1972) 'Models and paradigms in contemporary archaeology', in D. L. Clarke, ed., *Models in Archaeology*, pp. 1–60, Duckworth, London.

(1976) 'Mesolithic Europe: the economic basis', in G. de G. Sieveking, I. H. Longworth and K. E. Wilson, eds., *Problems in Economic and Social Archaeology*, pp. 449–81, Duckworth, London.

Clark Forbes, M. H. (1976) 'Farming and foraging in prehistoric Greece: a cultural ecological perspective'. *Annals of the New York Academy of Sciences* 268, 127–42.

Costantini, L. (1981) 'Semi e carboni del mesolitico e neolitico della Grotta dell'Uzzo, Trapani'. *Quaternaria* 23, 233–47.

Costantini, L., Piperno, M., Tusa, S. (1985) 'La néolithisation de la Sicile Occidentale d'après les résultats des fouilles à la grotte de l'Uzzo (Trapani)', in J. Guilaine, ed., *Premières Communautés Paysannes en Méditerranée Occidentale*, Centre National de Recherche Scientifique, in press.

Durante, S. (1980) 'Nota preliminare sulla ittiofauna e sullo sfruttamento delle risorse marine'. *Sicilia Archeologica* 21, 65–6.

Erroux, J. (1980) 'Les graines préhistoriques de la grotte de l'Abeurador'. *Les Dossiers de l'Archéologie* 44, 20–1.

Gascó, J. and Gutherz, X. (1983) *Premiers Paysans de la France Méditerranéenne*, Direction du Patrimoine, Montpellier.

Geddes, D. S. (1983a) 'Neolithic transhumance in the Mediterranean Pyrenees'. *World Archaeology* 15, 51–66.

(1983b) *De la Chasse au Troupeau en Méditerranée Occidentale*, Centre d'Anthropologie des Sociétés Rurales, Toulouse.

(1984) 'Settlement and subsistence during the Mesolithic and Neolithic in the Aude river valley (France)', in W. H. Waldren, R. Chapman, J. Lewthwaite and R. C. Kennard, eds., *The Deya Conference of Prehistory: Early Settlement in the Western Mediterranean Islands and their Peripheral Areas*, pp. 179–92, BAR International Series 229, British Archaeological Reports, Oxford.

Geddes, D. S., Guilaine, J. and Monaco, A. (1983) 'Early neolithic occupation on the submerged continental plateau of Roussillon', in P. M. Masters and N. C. Flemming, eds., *Quaternary Coastlines and Marine Archaeology: Towards the Prehistory of Land Bridges and Continental Shelves*, pp. 175–87, Academic Press, London and New York.

Guilaine, J. (1976) *Premiers Bergers et Paysans de l'Occident Méditerranéen*, Mouton, The Hague.

(1980) 'Problèmes actuels de la néolithisation et du néolithique ancien en Méditerranée Occidentale', in J. G. P. Best and N. M. W. de Vries, eds., *Interaction and Acculturation in the Mediterranean I*, pp. 3–22, B. K. Grüner, Amsterdam.

Guilaine, J., Barbaza, M., Geddes, D., Vernet, J. L., Llongueras, M. and Hopf, M. (1982) 'Prehistoric human adaptations in Catalonia (Spain)'. *Journal of Field Archaeology* 9, 407–16.

Gusí, C. Olaría de, Estévez Escalera, J. and Yll, E. (1982) 'Domesticación y Paleoambiente de la Cova Fosca', in *Le Néolithique Ancien Méditerranéen*, pp. 107–20, Fédération Archéologique de L'Hérault.

Halstead, P. L. J. (1981) 'Counting sheep in Neolithic and Bronze Age Greece', in I. Hodder, G. Isaac and N. Hammond, eds., *Pattern of the Past*, pp. 307–40, Cambridge University Press, Cambridge.

Hansen, J. (1978) 'The earliest seed remains from Greece: palaeolithic through Neolithic at Franchthi Cave'. *Berichte der Deutsche Botanische Gesellschaft* 91, 39–46.

Jacobsen, T. W. (1981) 'Franchthi Cave and the beginnings of settled village life in Greece'. *Hesperia* 50 (4), 303–19.

Jalut, G. (1977). *Végétation et Climat des Pyrénées Méditerranéennes Depuis Quinze Mille Ans*, Centre d'Anthropologie des Sociétés Rurales, Toulouse.

(1980) 'Les débuts de l'agriculture en domaine méditerranéen: l'apport de la palynologie'. *Les Dossiers de l'Archéologie* 44, 60–4.

Jarman, M. R. (1972) 'European deer economies and the advent of the Neolithic' in E. S. Higgs, ed., *Papers in Economic Prehistory*, pp. 125–48, Cambridge University Press, Cambridge.

Lewthwaite, J. G. (1981) 'Ambiguous first impressions: a survey of recent work on the early Neolithic of the West Mediterranean'. *Journal of Mediterranean Anthropology and Archaeology* 1 (2), 292–307.

(1983) 'The Neolithic of Corsica', in C. J. Scarre, ed., *Ancient France 6000–2000 BC. Neolithic Societies and their Landscapes*, pp. 146–83, Edinburgh University Press, Edinburgh.

(1986) 'Essai pour faire sortir de sa coquille le facteur social dans le cadre du Néolithique Ancien Méditerranéen', in J. Guilaine, ed., *Premières Communautés Paysannes en Méditerranée Occidentale*, Centre National de Recherche Scientifique, in press.

McCullough, (1970) 'Secondary production of birds and mammals', in E. D. Reiche, ed., *Temperate Forest Ecosystems. Ecological Studies*, vol. 1, pp. 107–30, Springer Verlag, Berlin.

Mills, N. T. W. (1985) 'Questions méthodologiques et l'étude des premières communautés paysannes dans le Midi de la France, in J. Guilaine, ed., *Premières Communautés Paysannes en Méditerranée Occidentale*, Centre National de Recherche Scientifique, in press.

Newell, R. (1984) 'On the mesolithic contribution to the social evolution of western European society', in J. L. Bintliff, ed., *European Social Evolution: Archaeological Perspectives*, pp. 69–82, University of Bradford Archaeological Press, Bradford.

Payne, S. (1975) 'Faunal change at Franchthi Cave from 20,000 BC to 3000 BC', in A. T. Clason, ed., *Archaeozoological Studies*, pp. 120–131, North-Holland and American Elsevier, New York.

Pearson, H. W. (1957) 'The economy has no surplus: critique of a theory of development', in K. Polanyi, C. M. Ahrensberg and H. W. Pearson, eds., *Trade and Market in the Early Empires*, pp. 320–41, Free Press, Glencoe, Ill.

Piperno, M. (1984) 'Alcune date C-14 per l'evidenza paleoeconomica dai livelli olocenici della Grotta dell'Uzzo (Trapani)', in S. Stoddart and C. Malone, eds., *The Third Conference of Italian Archaeology*, pp. 83–6, BAR International Series 244, British Archaeological Reports, Oxford.

Piperno, M., Scali, S., and Taglicozzo, A. (1980) 'Mesolitico e Neolitico alla Grotta dell'Uzzo (Trapani). Primi dati per un'interpretazione paleoeconomica'. *Quaternaria* 22, 275–300.

Piperno, M., Tusa, S. and Valente, I. (1980) 'Campagne di Scavo 1977 e 1978 alla Grotta dell'Uzzo (Trapani)'. *Sicilia Archeologica* 21, 49–64.

Pons, A., Toni, C. and Triat, H. (1979) 'Edification de la Camargue et histoire holocène de sa végétation'. *La Terre et la Vie*, suppl. 2, 13–30.

Poplin, F. (1979) 'Origine du mouflon de Corse dans une nouvelle perspective paléontologique: par marronnage'. *Annales Génétique et Sélection Animale* 11 (2), 138–43.

Reille, M. (1976) 'Histoire de la végétation de la montagne Corse depuis le Tardiglaciaire', in J. Guilaine, ed., *La Préhistoire Française*, vol. 2, *Les Civilisations Néolithiques et Proto-historiques*, pp. 52–8, Centre National de Recherche Scientifique, Paris.

 (1984) 'Origine de la végétation actuelle de la Corse sudorientale; analyse pollinique de cinq marais côtiers'. *Pollen et Spores* 26 (1), 43–60.

Reille, M., Triat-Laval, H. and Vernet, J. L. (1980) 'Les témoignages de structures actuelles de végétation méditerranéenne durant le passé contemporain de l'action de l'homme'. *Naturalia Monspeliensia* No. hors série, 79–87.

Ros Mora, T. and Vernet, J. L. (1985) 'L'environnement végétal de l'homme, du Néolithique à l'âge du Bronze, dans le Nord-Est de la Catalogne, d'après l'analyse anthracologique de la Cova del Frare, St Llorenç del Munt (Matadepera, Barcelona)' in J. Guilaine, ed., *Premières Communautés Paysannes en Méditerranée Occidentale*, Centre National de Recherche Scientifique, in press.

Rowley-Conwy, P. A. (1981) 'Slash and burn in the temperate European Neolithic', in R. Mercer, ed., *Farming Practice in British Prehistory*, pp. 85–95, Edinburgh University Press, Edinburgh.

Shackleton, J., van Andel, T. and Runnels, C. (1984) 'Late Quaternary coasts: central and western Mediterranean'. *Journal of Field Archaeology* 11(3), 307–14.

Sherratt, A. G. (1980) 'Water, soil and seasonality in early cereal cultivation'. *World Archaeology* 11 (3), 313–30.

Sondaar, P., Sanges, M., Kotsakis, T., Esu, D. and Boer, P. de (1984) 'First report on a palaeolithic culture in Sardinia', in W. H. Waldren, R. Chapman, J. Lewthwaite and R. C. Kennard, eds., *The Deya Conference of Prehistory: Early Settlement in the Western Mediterranean Islands and Their Peripheral Areas*, pp. 29–60, BAR International Series 229, British Archaeological Reports, Oxford.

Triat-Laval, H. (1978) 'Contribution pollenanalytique à l'histoire tardi-et postglaciaire de la végétation de la basse vallée du Rhône'. Thèse de Dr des Sciences, Université Aix-Marseille III.

van Andel, T. and Shackleton, J. (1982) 'Late palaeolithic and meso-lithic coastlines of Greece and the Aegean'. *Journal of Field Archaeology* 9(4), 445–54.

van Zeist, W. and Bottema, S. (1982) 'Vegetational history of the eastern Mediterranean and the Near East during the last 20,000 years', in J. L. Bintliff and W. van Zeist, eds., *Palaeoclimates, Palaeo-environments and Human Communities in the Eastern Mediterranean Region in Later Prehistory*, pp. 277–321, BAR International Series 133, British Archaeological Reports, Oxford.

Vaquer, J. (1980) 'De la cueillette à l'agriculture: la grotte de l'Abeurador'. *Les Dossiers de l'Archéologie* 44, 18–19.

Vaquer, J. and Barbaza, M. (1985) 'Balma de l'Abeurador et les débuts de l'horticulture dans le Midi Méditerranéen Français', in J. Guilaine, ed., *Premières Communautés Paysannes en Méditerranée Occidentale*, Centre National de Recherche Scientifique, in press.

Vernet, J. L., Badal Garcia, E. and Grau Almero, E. (1985) 'Première synthèse de la végétation néolithique du Sud-Est de l'Espagne (Valence-Alicante) d'après l'analyse anthracologique', in J. Guilaine, ed., *Premières Communautés Paysannes en Méditerranée Occidentale*, Centre National de Recherche Scientifique, in press.

Vigne, J. D. (1983) Les mammifères terrestres non volants du post-glaciaire de Corse et leurs rapports avec l'homme: etude paléo-ethno-zoologique fondée sur les ossements, Thèse 3me Cycle Université P. et M. Curie, Paris VI.

 (1984) 'Premières données sur le début de l'élevage du mouton, de la chèvre et du porc dans le Sud de la Corse (France)', in J. Clutton-Brock and C. Grigson, eds., *Animals and Archaeology, vol. 3 Early Herders and Their Flocks*, pp. 47–65, BAR International Series 202, British Archaeological Reports, Oxford.

 (1985) 'L'exploitation des ressources alimentaires carnées en Corse, du 7e au 4e millénaire BC', in J. Guilaine, ed., *Premières Communautés Paysannes en Méditerranée Occidentale*, Centre National de Recherche Scientifique, Paris, in press.

Waldren, W. H. (1982) *Balearic Prehistoric Ecology and Culture: The Excavation and Study of Certain Caves, Rock Shelters and Settlements*, BAR International Series 149, British Archaeological Reports, Oxford.

Watson, J. P. N. and Stanley Price, N. P. (1977) 'The vertebrate fauna from the 1972 sounding at Khirokitia'. *Report of the Department of Antiquities, Cyprus 1977*, 232–60.

Chapter 6

Foragers and farmers in Atlantic Europe

Marek Zvelebil and Peter Rowley-Conwy

You do not enter into a new level of awareness merely by
drawing milk from the udder of a cow

J. G. D. Clark
Comment on the mesolithic–neolithic transition
at the Carrowmore Conference, Ireland, August 1982

Introduction

The aim of this paper is to examine the spread of farming into the Atlantic fringes of Europe. Comparisons between
the situation in Finland (Zvelebil 1981) and Denmark
(Rowley-Conwy 1983, 1984*b*) led us to the conclusion that a
broadly similar sequence of events was visible in the two areas
– although the events took place at different times and speeds
and for different reasons. This, in turn, led us to put forward a
three-stage model for the process (Zvelebil and Rowley-Conwy
1984; and Chapter 1, this volume). This chapter attempts to
see whether the model is applicable to other Atlantic areas,
and presents a series of case-studies extending the analysis
from Finland to Portugal.

The most important result of our earlier examination
was the conclusion that farming did *not* spread into either
Denmark or Finland until long after it had become available
quite close by. We suggested that local foraging adaptations
were relatively productive and reliable, and therefore remained

a viable alternative to farming – which, on the northern fringe
of its spread, would initially be less well adapted than it was
elsewhere.

Marine resources were clearly of crucial importance to
the productivity and reliability of the foraging economies of
the Atlantic fringe. The nature of the resource spectrum
would, of course, vary considerably from area to area, and
human exploitative patterns would have varied in keeping with
this. Some areas would have supported small, more mobile,
human groups, others larger and more stable ones. A consideration of the coasts of North America emphasises this.

This adaptability and versatility has implications for
change through time as well as across space. The Atlantic
fringe in the millennia preceding the appearance of agriculture
was highly variable through time due to factors such as the rise
in, and fluctuations of, sea levels, the vegetational succession,
and the changes in the distributions and migrations of marine
and terrestrial resources in keeping with this. For example, the
estuaries of the rivers flowing across the (then dry) North Sea
bed in the ninth and eighth millennia bc 'would for these two
millennia have provided a concentration of food resources
unparalleled elsewhere in Northern Europe' (Jacobi 1973, p.
245). The exploitation of this environmental opportunity
(of which the Maglemosian fringe is all that is left to us)
must have played a significant role in the colonisation of

Atlantic Europe during the early postglacial. After the initial concentration of foraging settlement in what is today the North Sea, the population rapidly fell to zero as the area was inundated.

This kind of example leads us to conclude that long-term, slow, background increases in forager population density are less relevant than local or regional variations. Local or regional fluctuations in population (both increases and decreases) are likely to have been more rapid and severe, to the extent that they would obscure or negate background trends measured in amounts of much less than 1% per year. Such regional events would have had the greatest importance for local economic change. Fluctuations in foraging economies can be documented in some of the case-studies presented here. All other things being equal, a resource decline would mean a decline in population and perhaps group size among foragers. If, on the other hand, farming was established nearby, then one consequence of a resource decline could be the adoption of agriculture. This involves the opportunistic use of farming when the need arose, in just the same way as the range of foraging strategies had offered a choice of alternatives earlier on. Steamroller models, emphasising inexorable population growth or stadial socio-economic change, are not helpful in this context (see also Hassan 1981; Binford 1983).

Regional survey of the evidence from Atlantic Europe
Portugal

Information from Portugal is at present very incomplete. There are signs, however, that the picture may fit the model well, and it is hoped that work currently in progress will go a long way towards filling the gaps in our knowledge.

The shell middens on the River Muge are justly famous. The best published of these is Moita do Sebastião (Roche 1972a), although several others have also been excavated (ibid. 1972b). Radiocarbon dates suggest that occupation took place in the fifth and fourth millennia bc: Cabeço da Amoreira was formed mainly between 4480 ± 350 bc and 4100 ± 300 bc, and Cabeço da Arruda between 4480 ± 300 bc and 3200 ± 300 bc (ibid. 1972b). Shell middens with a similar artefactual inventory are also known from the River Sado (Morais Arnaud 1982). These middens are all sited on what were shallow, lagoon-like estuaries, and consist largely of cockles.

The fauna from Moita do Sebastião consists of aurochs, red and roe deer, pig, fox, lynx, badger, otter, hare, rabbit and hedgehog, as well as a few birds and fish (quoted by Roche (1972a)). The other Muge middens are believed to be similar (ibid.). Of the Sado middens, the fauna of Cabeço do Pez has been analysed. This is similar to the Muge fauna, consisting entirely of wild animals (Rowley-Conwy, unpublished).

Cemeteries are known from Moita do Sebastião, Cabeço da Amoreira and Cabeço da Arruda (Roche 1972b). Following the model of Chapman (1981), these are regarded as being evidence suggestive of residential stability, and thus probably of increased group size and social complexity.

The late continuation of this mesolithic economy is of the greatest interest in view of the early dates for the Neolithic now available from the west Mediterranean. Many go back to the sixth millennium bc (see Guilaine 1979). The earliest-quoted date for the Iberian peninsula is 6000 ± 150 bc from Verdelpino level 4, on the upper Tagus. The associated fauna, however, consists entirely of horse, pig, aurochs, ibex, red deer, lynx and rabbit (Morales Muñiz 1977), so that this seems to be a good *mesolithic* date. The earliest neolithic date from Iberia is thus Barranco de los Grajos, 5220 ± 160 bc. At the time of writing, no dates are available from Portugal that are older than 4370 ± 350 bc from Salema; but Morais Arnaud (1982) suggests that the earliest Neolithic may go back well into the fifth millennium bc, with the Middle Neolithic dating to the fourth millennium bc. Morais Arnaud's map is reproduced in Fig. 1. Given the lack of information concerning the date and nature of the coastal Mesolithic, the littoral situation cannot be described. What is clear from the distribution and dates of the settlements and tombs, however, is that there was (as far as the Muge and Sado middens were concerned) an

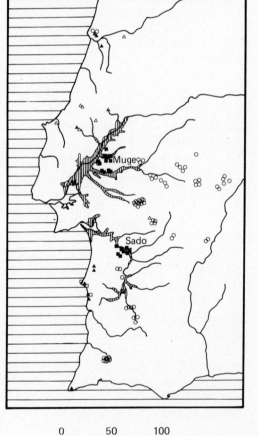

■ Mesolithic shell midden

□ Mesolithic site (possible)

▲ Early neolithic settlement

△ Early neolithic cave occupation

○ Proto megalith (? 4500 bc)

0   50   100
km

Fig. 1. Mesolithic–Neolithic interface in southern Portugal: vertical shading, post-mesolithic alluvium. (From Morais Arnaud 1982, Fig. 1.)

availability phase lasting for a millennium or more. During this time the shell midden inhabitants continued to subsist on wild mammals and marine foods.

The role of plant foods is unclear. Oak and pine are the predominant trees in the area today, and some exploitation of acorns and pine nuts is likely in the Mesolithic (charcoal of *Pinus* was recovered from Cabeço da Amoreira: Roche 1972*b*). In the broadest environmental terms one is tempted to speculate on parallels or differences between Portugal and California, another area in which marine resources, ungulates, acorns and pine nuts were exploited by hunter-gatherers. California never adopted agriculture despite the latter's availability – probably due to the effectiveness of an economy based on wild resources (Baumhoff 1963) – and thus never went beyond the availability phase until European contact.

The process of neolithisation in Portugal is only beginning to be understood (cf. Morais Arnaud 1982), so the reasons for, and nature of, the substitution phases cannot be further examined.

Spain

Cantabrian Spain is without doubt the best-investigated area of the Atlantic rim of the Iberian peninsula. Building on the work of earlier investigators (Vega del Sella 1914, 1923, 1930; Carballo 1926, 1960), Spanish and American archaeologists have recently attempted a palaeo-economic reconstruction of the prehistoric settlement of Cantabrian Spain extending back about 20 000 years (Altuna 1972, 1980; Straus *et al.* 1980, 1981; Clark 1983*a,b*; Straus and Clark 1983, Clark and Yi 1983; Straus 1979). Despite many interesting questions remaining unanswered, this recent research allows us to make a few observations which pertain to our model outlined above (see also Zvelebil, Chapter 1).

Most late palaeolithic sites on the North Atlantic coast of Spain consist of caves and rock shelters. At one such cave, La Riera, a sequence of 30 layers, spanning the period from *c.* 20 000 to 6500 bc, was excavated (Straus *et al.* 1980, 1981; Clark and Straus 1983). The palaeo-economic record shows that while major land mammals such as red deer, ibex and chamois were the principal sources of food throughout the cave's existence as a dwelling site, marine resources, especially molluscs, were in use from the earliest (Solutrean) layers, despite the fact that the contemporary pleistocene shoreline was some 10 km away from the site. At the same time, there is a steady trend towards broadening the marine resource base. From about level 20 (Magdalenian, *c.* 11 000 bc) the variety of marine species increases, reflecting the extension of the site's catchment to include open shorelines and rock coastlines as well as previously exploited estuaries, while the occurrence of intact, rather than shattered shellfish would suggest boiling for the first time (Straus *et al.* 1980). From about 8800 bc, ocean fishes make their first appearance, while in the final layers (27–30) the amount of shellfish increases to the point when they become virtually shell middens. Crab shells make their

first appearance, and the bones of ocean fishes are common. These last layers contained the early postglacial Azilian and Asturian assemblages and date to about 8500–6500 bc.

Most of the early postglacial sites in Cantabrian Spain consist of shell middens and there is some evidence for an increase in the density of coastal sites. From all this evidence it is clear that coastal and marine resources played some important role in prehistoric Cantabria and that this role was increasing with time. What is not clear is the position of shell middens in the overall subsistence–settlement system. If they were refuse dumps deposited as a result of seasonal activity at the entrance of caves and rock shelters which had earlier been used for more permanent settlement (Clark 1983*a*, p. 109), then we are yet to find the residential sites, which would give us a more balanced picture of the overall economy. If, on the other hand, we accept that the middens 'had similar functions as settlement sites, supported by a mixed subsistence economy' (Bailey 1983, p. 163) or even that 'Asturian sites are the remains of base camps situated among the hills and along the estuaries near the coast' (Clark 1983*b*, p. 139) then we are dealing with a strongly maritime-oriented economy.

This picture is further complicated by the possible contemporaneity of Asturian and Azilian sites. If this is the case, then the two assemblages may have been two functional facies of the same culture, the Azilian forming the sophisticated, specialised and curated (Clark and Straus 1983, p. 135) counterpart to the expedient and casual coastal facies. Some support for this interpretation comes from recent radiocarbon dates and from a number of retouched 'small tools' shared by both assemblages (Clark 1983*a, b*; Clark and Straus 1983).

These considerations will, of course, affect our assessment of the importance of marine resources to the early postglacial hunters. Most of the marine food remains consisted of shellfish. As Bailey (1978) and others have pointed out, shellfish are calorically an expensive resource to collect, as the caloric yield in return for the effort expended in procuring and processing them is low. In caloric terms shellfish contributed only 0.4% of the diet (Clark and Yi 1983, p. 195). Yet, Perlman (1980, p. 289) and Yesner (n.d.) have argued, calories alone may not have been the reason why shellfish were collected in such abundance, not only in northern Spain but along the entire Atlantic seaboard, as far as Narva in Estonia (Dolukhanov 1979). Apart from being a rich source of protein (Yesner n.d.), shellfish are a reliable resource (Yesner n.d.; Perlman 1980, p. 289) and moreover one which can be collected by the old, children and the infirm, who would not be able to procure many other foods. Meehan's (1977, p. 524) analysis of shellfish-collecting among Australian Anabara indicates, for instance, that skilled women could collect shellfish equivalent to about 2000 kcal in two hours. Shellfish collection would therefore lower the dependency ratio without detracting from the time devoted by hunters to the capture of more desirable resources, such as deer.

Returning to Cantabrian Spain: the decline in the size of the favoured mollusc *Patella vulgata*, and the broadening of the resource base to include less productive shellfish at the end of the Pleistocene and during the Early Postglacial led Straus *et al.* (1980) and Clark (1983*a*) to suggest that a steady increase in population pressure was responsible for the initial collection of seafood in the first place and for the subsequent increase in the reliance on marine resources. In summary, therefore, it would appear that shellfish and other seafood provided a supplementary resource to fall back on in the situation of a steadily increasing pressure on more productive resources.

The earliest evidence for farming is both late and partial. Although late Asturian and post-Asturian deposits were sampled for the presence of bones of domesticated animals, none was recovered (Clark 1983*b*, p. 2). Contact with farming communities and a knowledge of farming is attested from petroglyphs depicting wheeled vehicles drawn by oxen, from Argaric imports, both dating to the Bronze Age (*c.* 1500–750 bc), and from faunal evidence for early domesticates in the neighbouring Basque country, dated to 3015 ± 195 bc (Arenaza) and 3335 ± 65 bc (Marizulo) (Clark 1983*b*, p. 2). According to Clark and Yi (1983, p. 187) the 'neolithisation' of Cantabria began *c.* 3500 bc but was characterised mainly by the persistence of the foraging economies of earlier periods (see also Altuna 1980). Until the end of the Neolithic, the bones of wild and domesticated fauna occur in roughly the same proportion (Clark and Yi 1983, p. 197; Altuna 1980, p. 28). The incidence of hunted species declines only after the Eneolithic–Bronze Age transition *c.* 1900 bc. There is no primary or indirect evidence for cereal cultivation until the Bronze Age.

It could be argued that the late evidence for farming in Cantabrian Spain is a product of the archaeological invisibility of transhumant pastoral economies. The northern coast of Spain, while too wet for arable farming, is an ideal pastoral country, equipped with sufficient altitudinal variation to counteract seasonal climatic fluctuations and to ensure fresh grazing all year round; consequently, transhumant pastoralism has been the traditional occupation of Cantabrian peasants (Clark and Yi 1983, p. 187). Such husbandry practices may be notoriously difficult to detect archaeologically. Yet it is significant that no bones of domesticated animals have been found at coastal sites in Cantabria itself, arguing for the long existence of coastal economies and for a late and very gradual shift to farming (see Fig. 7).

France
The evidence forthcoming from regions along the Atlantic coast of France indicates much the same picture as the Cantabrian data (Fig. 2). Despite the fact that, except for a small area of the foothills of the Pyrénées, where the amount of land lost due to the rise in the sea level was limited, the late glacial and early postglacial shorelines of Aquitaine were flooded by the neothermal rise in the sea level, the evidence forthcoming from the coastal regions of southwest France indicates that hunter-gatherer culture lasted longer than was previously thought.

In those areas where flooding was limited, material similar to the Asturian assemblage of northern Spain was found. With wide strips of coastal land submerged, however, it is impossible to evaluate the importance of marine resources.

Within the broader regional perspective, Bahn (1983, p. 188) has noted a continuity of material culture, site location and of economic strategy through postglacial times into the protohistoric period on the French side of the Pays Basque. Cervids, caprines and boars formed the basis of a foraging economy. On the one hand, a broadening of the resource spectrum and a selective manipulation of resources took place, leading to the suggestion of the domestication of local resources and even inducing Bahn to postulate mesolithic snail husbandry at sites such as Poeymaü (Bahn 1984, p. 49). On the other hand, a remarkable lack of the conventional, neolithic-introduced domesticates and cultigens can be observed. A good deal of material has been regarded as neolithic simply because it includes pottery sherds and polished stone (Bahn 1983, p. 189); yet on the basis of the economic evidence, the period between 3800 and *c.* 2700 bc could be regarded with justification as one of a ceramic-using hunting and gathering culture.

Subsistence strategies during the Chalcolithic and Early Bronze Age consisted of a mixture of pastoralism, hunting and fishing. The practice of farming is implied only indirectly through the presence of sickles and grinding equipment and the palynological evidence of clearance; cereal grains are reported only from the eastern end of the Pyrénées. Hunting and fishing continued to be important during the Middle Bronze Age, and it was not until the Late Bronze Age that an increase in farming activities can be detected (Bahn 1983, 1984); at the same time, pastoralism remained the dominant subsistence activity in both the prehistoric and the historic periods (Bahn 1983, 1984). On the basis of this admittedly limited information, we can tentatively postulate the availability phase as lasting from *c.* 4000 bc or before to *c.* 2700 bc, the substitution phase 2700–Late Bronze Age, and the consolidation phase as thereafter.

The coastal regions further north, between the Garonne and the Loire, were, of course, further inland during the early postglacial, the coastline assuming its present position only at the end of the sixth millennium bc. Most of the earlier post-glacial settlement has, therefore, been lost to the sea. Recent research has uncovered coastal sites dating to the middle and the second half of the fifth millennium bc. These sites contained Impressed ware pottery together with a microlithic industry, which could be traced to earlier aceramic layers further inland (Scarre 1983, p. 228). Further to the south, a similar tradition, combining the local mesolithic assemblage with crude pottery, has been identified in the Dordogne, Quercy and other areas of southwest France which form a part

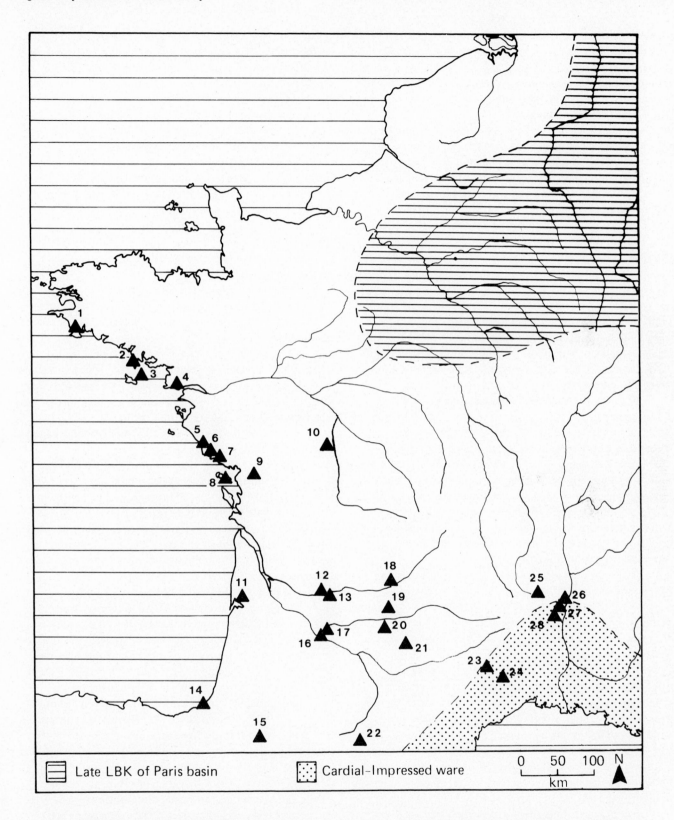

Fig. 2. Mesolithic–Neolithic interface along the west Atlantic coast of France, 4500–4000 bc. Sites containing ceramics and/or isolated remains of cultigens or domesticates associated with predominantly hunting-gathering, mesolithic contexts: 1, Beg-An-Dorchenn; 2, Téviec; 3, Hoëdic; 4, Dissignac; 5, Bretignolles-sur-Mer; 6, Longeville; 7, La Tranche-sur-Mer; 8, Les Gouillauds; 9, Benon; 10, Chambon; 11, Le Betey; 12, Rouffignac; 13, Abri Pageyral; 14, Mouligna Bidart; 15, Arudy; 16, Le Martinet; 17, La Borie del Rey; 18, Chez Jugie; 19, Cuzoul du Gramat; 20, Roucadour; 21, Rocamadour; 22, Terrier Ferrages; 23, Puechmargues; 24, La Poujade; 25, Rond du Barry; 26, Les Estables; 27. Longetraye; 28, Baulmes d'Arlempdes. (After Roussot-Larroque and Thévenin 1981, and several other sources.)

of the Garonne basin (Roussot-Larroque 1977; Scarre 1983). The vessels of the latter group, named Roucadourian after the type-site, were made by the coil technique, and had rounded or pointed bases, features which provoked comparisons with the Ertebølle culture of Denmark and led to speculation about the common origin of the two (Scarre 1983, pp. 327–8).

Although Scarre (1983, p. 228) notes that both of these groups have given evidence of agriculture and stockrearing, on closer examination the evidence quoted is either equivocal or negligible when compared with the remains of wild animals. Thus at Cuzoul, we have a single ovicaprid molar in the Tardenoisian I layer, and a single ovicaprid astragalus, accompanied by the remains of a single small bovine in the Tardenoisian II layer (Roussot-Larroque 1977, p. 578). At Roucadour C domestic fauna is rare, while '*presque toute la viande consommée provenait de la chasse*' (*ibid.*, pp. 578–9). At La Tranche, the bones of domestic animals are also rare (Scarre, personal communication). This leaves cereal grain from Roucadour C, and the bones of cattle and sheep from Rouffignac 2 to account for food production along the west Atlantic seaboard of France. Intriguing as these finds are, it brings us back to the same question: does a single swallow make a summer?

Both the Roucadourian (Roussot-Larroque 1977, p. 569) and the Impressed ware group in west-central France can be dated to 4500–4000 bc (Scarre 1983, pp. 227–30). A hypothesis worth considering is that this period is one of contacts and exchange between the resident foragers and the groups with established farming strategies in *circum*-Mediterranean France, which accounts for certain neolithic traits and occasional finds of grain and domesticates on the settlements within the region. At the same time we must acknowledge that only future research can show whether the 'ceramic mesolithic' hypothesis is correct.

If our hypothesis holds good, then the actual incorporation of the neolithic cultigens and domesticates into subsistence activities took place in the Middle Neolithic, beginning at about 4000 bc. Although little attention has been paid to the economic data from this period, other forms of evidence indicate a gradual development of the neolithic culture. Scarre (1983, p. 235) noted that agriculture was probably well established in the region by the middle of the fourth millennium bc. This would tentatively suggest a substitution phase covering the first half of the Middle Neolithic (4000–3500 bc), while the consolidation phase would cover its latter part, characterised by the Chasseen pottery (3500–2800 bc). For the present, this scheme must remain speculative, but the pattern emerging here is very similar to other regions along the Atlantic seaboard.

Turning our attention now to Brittany, we are confronted with the rise in the sea level, which reached its present state by about 3800 bc, even though fluctuations about the present shoreline continued throughout the later prehistoric period (Hibbs 1983, p. 274). This again means that any concentration on marine or littoral resources during the earlier postglacial period will be minimised in the archaeological record through the drowning of ancient shorelines, and through the loss of both the individual sites and of their resource use territories (*ibid.*, p. 274).

Bearing this in mind, little can be said about the development of coastal adaptations during the earlier part of the Holocene. The presence of foraging groups is attested by the late palaeolithic and early mesolithic assemblages in the caves and rockshelters of the peninsula but the economic data are lacking (Giot, L'Helgouach and Monnier 1979). The earliest coastal sites date to the fifth millennium bc and consist of midden settlements, incorporating, in the cases of Téviec and Hoëdic, burial grounds as well. As Hibbs (1983, p. 279) notes, 'the economy of these sites was based on the exploitation of coastal and marine resources, shellfish in particular, with elements of hinterland hunting and gathering'. As in earlier instances mentioned here, the token presence of domesticates has led to suggestions of a pastoral element in the economy (L'Helgouach 1971). We are dealing, however, with a single tooth of *Capra* or *Ovis* at Téviec (Newell *et al.* 1979, p. 133); and, although bovine remains have been claimed for Hoëdic and Beg-an-Dorchenn (L'Helgouach 1971), their domesticated status is called into question by Newell and others (1979, p. 121), at least at Hoëdic, which is said to contain the debris of 'a totally wild fauna'. Radiocarbon dating has yielded the dates of 4625 ± 350 bc for Hoëdic and 4010 and 3490 for Beg-An-Dorchenn.

At Hoëdic and at Téviec, 14 and 23 persons, respectively, were buried. Inhumations were interred in stone-lined cists, covered with hearths and more stone, and contained a variety of ritual objects, such as engraved antler, ochre and worked shells. Although no statistical analysis has been carried out on the distribution of the grave goods, the apparent variation in the mortuary equipment suggests the existence of social hierarchies (Testart 1982, p. 135).

The Breton Late Mesolithic appears to conform to our model of sedentary, or semi-sedentary, hunter-gatherer communities, characterised by a social system of some complexity and a reliance on a range of resource-use strategies, including marine resources. Evidence of contacts with food-producing societies would suggest that the availability phase occurred here in the course of the fifth millennium.

The subsequent development of the Breton Neolithic (Giot *et al.* 1979; L'Helgouach 1971; Hibbs 1983) indicates a very gradual transition to farming, an impression no doubt enhanced by the paucity of settlement sites. Tentatively, this period, lasting between *c*. 4000 and 2500 bc would fit our substitution phase. Major developments took place in the middle and the second half of the third millennium, such as the increase in forest clearance and the extension of settlement to the central areas of Brittany (Hibbs 1983). Superficially, at least, this would appear to indicate the consolidation of the farming economy which characterises the last phase of our model.

On the whole, the evidence from the Atlantic seaboard

of western France shows that, during the late mesolithic period hunting and gathering communities adopted technological innovations and developed socio-economic strategies which Testart (1982) has characterised as belonging to '*chasseurs-cueilleurs sédentaires stockeurs*'. These included the adoption of a broader range of food-procuring strategies, the increased reliance on aquatic resources, and the adoption of ceramics. In some areas, this was probably associated with a decrease in spatial mobility and the development of social hierarchies. The development of blade and trapeze industries in this context may be significant: Roussot-Larroque (1977, pp. 578–80); Matyushin (1976; and see Chapter 10, this volume) and Grahame Clark (1980) have linked their appearance to economic intensification, or even to the initial stages of domestication.

Britain

A great deal of work of general relevance to the appearance of farming has been carried out in Britain. Despite this, the picture is far from clear, and more problems remain than in many areas of Europe. Most of the evidence is either derived from pollen analysis for from dating (radiocarbon or typological), while little evidence of settlement and economy is available from the crucial period. Despite this, there are indications that the model may be, at least in part, applicable.

Pollen evidence

Traditionally, mesolithic peoples were not thought to have cleared forests; clearances visible in pollen diagrams were thus evidence of the arrival of farming (e.g. Iversen 1941). This view was modified by an increasing number of sites in Britain with evidence of clearance so early that a neolithic origin was ruled out on chronological grounds. An early example of this was Ehenside Tarn in Cumbria, showing a pre-elm decline clearance (Walker 1966; but see the comments of Smith (1981, caption to Fig. 4.7) on the date of this clearance). Other early clearances were soon found, so that Simmons (1979) mentions that over 100 are now known. Important examples come from Cumbria, such as Blea Tarn and Barfield Tarn, where the start of clearing has been radiocarbon dated to 3700 bc (Pennington 1975). Other dated examples are West House Moss in Yorkshire, before 4700 ± 290 bc (Jones 1976); North Gill, Yorkshire, at 4416 ± 69 bc (Spratt and Simmons 1976); and Hockham Mere, Norfolk, at 5497 bc (Sims 1973, 1978).

As this evidence multiplied, it became clear that mesolithic peoples were capable of clearing areas of woodland (e.g. Simmons 1969; Smith 1970). Mellars (1976) presented widespread ethnographic examples of recent hunter-gatherers clearing woodland, and evidence has been put forward suggesting a large-scale and sophisticated clearance regime in the southern Pennines (Jacobi, Tallis and Mellars 1976).

Recently, however, the pendulum has swung a little way back again — for archaeological reasons. As the beginnings of the Neolithic in Britain and Ireland have been pushed ever

further back (cf. the date of 3795 ± 90 bc from Ballynagilly), it has been suggested that some of the later pre-elm decline clearances (such as Blea Tarn and Barfield Tarn in Cumbria) might after all be neolithic (Bradley 1978; Smith 1981). Some pollen studies make the point that the early clearances are identical in kind with those of neolithic date (Pennington 1975; Spratt and Simmons 1976).

Evidence of a few grains of pre-elm decline cereal pollen has recently been presented for a number of sites in Britain and Ireland (Edwards and Hirons 1984). The problems involved in the definite identification of such grains (Andersen 1978), however, must be born in mind. Some 'cereal' grains are known from contexts too early to be neolithic (even of pre-elm decline date); one appears at Oakhanger VII (Rankine, Rankine and Dimbleby 1960), pre-dating a layer with six radiocarbon dates ranging from 7275 ± 170 bc to 6935 ± 160 bc (Switsur and Jacobi 1979). At Loch Pityoulish, O'Sullivan (1976) recorded two 'cereal' grains close to a level radiocarbon dated to 6441 ± 70 bc, and another at 4683 ± 37 bc. Whether these are intrusive or misidentified, they indicate that evidence of 'cereal' pollen should at present be treated cautiously.

Our views of these early clearances are thus closely dependent on current archaeological ideas regarding dating, and not on any palynological factors permitting a distinction between the clearings of farmers and foragers. Archaeological evidence is needed in the areas from which the clearance evidence comes, in order to place them in perspective. A recent survey of part of Cumbria (Bewley 1984) is a case in point. This has failed to reveal any neolithic traces likely to pre-date the elm decline; the tarns (small lakes) from which much of the clearance evidence is derived would likely be foci of mesolithic settlement and activity, so the present evidence suggests that a pre-agricultural origin of the clearances is the most likely (*ibid.*). Coastal Cumbria would have been a favourable area for mesolithic groups and may have been quite densely settled (Bewley 1984; cf. also Bonsall 1981).

In the absence of work like Bewley's in other areas, the nature of the later pre-elm decline clearances remains obscure. Until they can be more closely linked to local archaeological evidence, the clearances remain enigmatic and offer no definite evidence of the presence of farming as far back as 3700 bc.

Dating evidence and the availability phase

Many radiocarbon dates are now available. Figure 3 plots neolithic dates older than 3100 bc. It is apparent that the majority (13 of 19 sites plotted) lie in the far south of Britain; there are five outliers in the north and one in northwest Wales. The extent to which this is an accident of research remains to be seen, but the present pattern does not conflict with the arrival of farming into Britain across the two narrowest waterways: over the English Channel into southern England and over the North Channel into southwest Scotland. At all events Britain is a large and ecologically very diverse island, and it would not be surprising if agriculture was adopted in or taken to various areas for different reasons, in different ways,

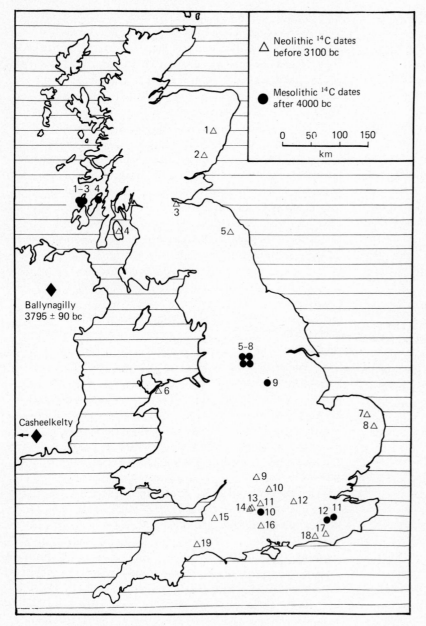

A. Mesolithic ^{14}C dates after 4000 bc:
1. Cnoc Sligeach 3805 ± 180 Gx 1904; 3065 ± 120 Gx 1903; 3476 ± 159 BM 670
2. Caisteal-nan-Gillean II 3900 ± 310 Birm 348a; 3770 ± 140 Birm 348b; 3620 ± 140 Birm 348c; 3500 ± 140 Birm 347; 3200 ± 380 Birm 346a; 2970 ± 400 Birm 346b; 3510 ± 65 Q 1355
3. Cnoc Coig 3545 ± 75 Q1351; 3480 ± 130 Q1352; 3695 ± 80 Q 1353; 3585 ± 140 Q 1354
4. Lussa River 2250 ± 100 BM 555; 2670 ± 140 BM 556
5. Dunford Bridge B 3430 ± 80 Q 799
6. Lominot IV 3660 ± 120 Q 1189
7. Rocher Moss South I 3880 ± 100 Q 1190
8. March Hill II 3900 ± 80 Q 788
9. Thorpe Common 3730 ± 150 Q 1118
10. Wawcott I 3310 ± 130 BM 449
11. High Rocks 3710 ± 150 BM 40; 3780 ± 150 BM 91
12. Stonewall Rockshelter B 3820 ± 100 Q 1143

B. Neolithic ^{14}C dates before 3100 bc:
1. Balbridie 3210 ± 60 ?
2. Dalladies 3240 ± 105 I 6113
3. Nether Kinneil 3110 ± 50 SRR 1486 (a determination from the inner part of the same oyster shell gave 2990 ± 50)
4. Monamore 3160 ± 110 Q 675
5. Thirlings 3280 ± 150 HAR 877
6. Llandegai 3290 ± 150 NPL 223
7. Eaton Heath 3145 ± 49 BM 770
8. Broome Heath 3474 ± 117 BM 679
9. Ascott-under-Wychwood 3248 ± 225 BM 835
10. Abingdon 3110 ± 130 BM 351
11. Lambourn 3415 ± 180 Gx 1178
12. Cannon Hill 3310 ± 110 HAR 1198
13. Horslip 3240 ± 150 BM 180
14. Beckhampton Road 3250 ± 160 NPL 138
15. Sweet Track 3274 ± 75 Q 968; 3268 ± 75 Q 963; 3209 ± 76 Q 966; 3200 ± 65 Q 962; 3190 ± 100 Q 1102; 3158 ± 65 Q 967; 3153 ± 100 Q 1103
16. Fussell's Lodge 3230 ± 150 BM 134
17. Church Hill 3390 ± 150 BM 181
18. Blackpatch 3140 ± 130 BM 290
19. Hembury 3330 ± 150 BM 138; 3240 ± 150 BM 136; 3150 ± 150 BM 130

Fig. 3. Mesolithic–Neolithic interface in Britain.

and at different times. From the Lambourn long barrow to Oronsay, for example, is about 600 km. This is much further than the distance between the neolithic sites of Eitzum and Siggeneben-Süd in Germany, where the appearance of farming is dated to be over 1300 radiocarbon years apart (see the section on South Scandinavia).

Many of the radiocarbon dates from southern England derive from major monuments. In the South Scandinavian section, such monuments are linked to the consolidation phase; agriculture had a history of at least 400 radiocarbon years before such monuments began to be built. For Britain it has been suggested that monument building represents a relatively advanced stage of agricultural development (Case 1969), and that there may have been a lengthy period of

agriculture – perhaps going back to 4000 bc – before monument building began (Jacobi 1982). The status of the later Mesolithic in the area is uncertain: Jacobi (ibid.) has pointed out that the four dates from the three southernmost mesolithic sites in Fig. 3 are to some degree doubtful. A claimed bone of sheep from mesolithic Farnham is no longer available for study, but may well have been a misidentification (Serjeantson 1985). Until settlements from the relevant period are excavated, the picture will remain unclear.

The situation in the north is somewhat different. Of the 25 post-4000 bc mesolithic dates in Fig. 3, no fewer than 16 are from the Inner Hebrides. Fourteen are from the Oronsay middens, associated with a classic mesolithic coastal economy (Mellars 1978; Mellars and Wilkinson 1980). Most of the

Oronsay dates are later than the earliest pollen evidence for farming in the British Isles (see Fig. 3). If the cereal pollen evidence dating to the fourth millennium bc can be taken at its face value, then the radiocarbon dates suggest an availability phase at least in some parts of Britain of some 800 radiocarbon years. Oronsay itself is scarcely prime agricultural land — it would be interesting to know whether areas of southwest Scotland more suited to agriculture were farmed at an earlier date.

Some archaeological evidence can also be interpreted as supporting the notion of a lengthy availability phase. Jacobi (1976) has documented the absence from Britain of trapeze industries characteristic of the latest European Mesolithic (after about the early sixth millennium bc), and indeed tool-types dated by ^{14}C to around 6300–6200 bc in Holland are absent from Britain. This suggests that Britain was culturally isolated very soon after it was separated from mainland Europe in the mid seventh millennium bc (*ibid.*). Bone and antler tools of European type are likewise not found, and there is some evidence that the use of bone and antler decreased in the later British Mesolithic. Some lithic types also disappear, leading Jacobi (1982, p. 21) to describe this as the 'impoverishment of an ancestral technology'. The exception to this is the Obanian, which includes the Oronsay middens and falls late in the Mesolithic (Fig. 3). These sites have a rich bone and antler industry, including T-shaped antler axes and antler harpoons similar to those used by the latest hunter-gatherers in mainland Europe. Their presence in Scotland (*post*dating Ballynagilly) may thus indicate a considerable degree of contact up and down the western seaboard of Britain and Ireland. In this model, certain available traits (such as bone tools or agriculture) were adopted in certain areas, while others were not (Jacobi 1982 and personal communication).

The British situation is thus still rather confused. At present little can be done other than to point to the overlap between hunting and farming indicated by the radiocarbon dates. It is at least beyond doubt that there was an extended availability phase in some areas. In the absence of much information about the later Mesolithic, the reasons for this can only be guessed at, and the substitution phase cannot be discussed. One avenue for future research would be to see whether mesolithic population density, group size and social complexity played the role suggested in some of the other areas discussed. The site of Aveline's Hole in Somerset may represent a major mesolithic cemetery with up to about 100 skeletons (R. M. Jacobi, unpublished data and personal communication; Newell *et al.* 1979). If such cemeteries are indicative of a degree of sedentism and social complexity (Chapman 1981), and if Aveline's Hole is indeed one such, then this aspect cannot be ignored.

Ireland

On theoretical grounds, Ireland presents an interesting test case of our ideas about the transition to farming. As an island since the eighth millennium bc, Ireland's well-defined geographical boundaries have acted as a barrier to the immigration of plants, animals and man. As a result, Ireland has a restricted range of plant and animal species, with a significant number of potential food resources, such as elk, bovids, roe deer and some fish lacking. Ireland also has the distinction of being one of the few areas of Europe without traces of palaeolithic occupation (Woodman 1978). This means that: (1) the initial colonisation probably took place during the Holocene; (2) colonists were entering an environment unaltered by man; (3) the range of alternative resource-use strategies was limited by the simplified ecosystem; (4) after the initial penetration, the postglacial settlement of Ireland was allowed to develop in relative isolation. There is, in fact, little evidence of contact with Britain or the continent during the Irish Mesolithic (Woodman 1981*a*). Such a set of data presents us with simplified 'laboratory' conditions, in which hypotheses about the growth of postglacial hunter-gatherer communities and their transition to the society of the Neolithic could be modelled and tested without the complications and extra-regional interference common to other parts of Europe.

The concrete evidence for the development of the Irish Mesolithic, however, is fragmentary and suffers from the lack of comprehensive palaeo-economic data, the paucity of base-camps and from a regional bias towards the northeast of the country, where most of the research has been done until recently (Woodman 1978). The earliest dated remains, from Mount Sandel in Ulster, confirm mesolithic occupation in Ireland by *c.* 7000 bc, although earlier occupation cannot be precluded. After about 6000 bc the lithic assemblage, which was initially microlithic, with parallels in Britain, turned into a large, heavy-bladed industry without microliths, emphasising the independent development of the Mesolithic in Ireland (*ibid.* 1981*b*, p. 203; 1978, p. 357). From the early stages of its development, the location of settlement had a marked aquatic orientation, with most of the sites situated along the coast or inland along the larger rivers or lakes (*ibid.* 1978). Faunal remains from sites such as Mount Sandel, Newferry, Ormeau Bridge, Sutton, Rockmarshall and Dalkey Island revealed large deposits of salmon and eel remains on the inland sites, and of shellfish, sea fish and sea mammals on the coast (*ibid.*, p. 361). The only terrestrial mammal of any importance appears to have been the wild pig. The aquatic orientation of the Irish Mesolithic is not really surprising in view of the limited choice of strategies open to the foraging communities in Ireland: as Woodman (*ibid.*, p. 362) noted, 'the choice was between small game (which could have been trapped), wild pig and fish'. Limited as it is, then, the available evidence indicates the existence of well-adapted, probably mobile (*ibid.*, pp. 365–6) communities, in possession of a well-organised and probably curated lithic technology (*ibid.* 1981b p. 204; Herity and Eogan 1977, p. 21).

The Neolithic was introduced into this cultural context. There does not seem to be any doubt that farming was brought to Ireland by migration. As Woodman has pointed out, there is no obvious mechanism for introducing a neolithic economy to Ireland other than by a group of people; consequently, 'the case for an evolution from Mesolithic to Neolithic without the movement of at least a small group of people cannot really be justified' (Woodman 1981*b*, p. 203). The questions to be answered, therefore, are how large was the neolithic immigration to Ireland and what was the response of the local mesolithic communities.

Little light at present can be shed on the first question, beyond the general observation that farming appears to have been introduced gradually, by small groups of people and at an earlier date than previously thought. Archaeologically, small, early neolithic settlements, typified by a narrow-bladed industry, by carinated bowls and simple jars, and by refuse deposits containing bones of domesticated sheep and cattle can be dated to between 3500 and 3200 bc (Woodman 1981*b*, p. 201). Palynological evidence, however, suggests a possibly earlier date for the introduction of farming to Ireland. Clearance phases containing cereal-type pollen have been recorded as early as 3900–3500 bc at Casheelkelty, Co. Kerry (Lynch 1981), and as noted above, at Ballynagilly, Co. Tyrone (Pilcher and Smith 1979) — at the two opposite ends of Ireland. Even though Groenman van Waateringe (1983, p. 227) has argued that this and other palynological evidence clearly indicates the existence of agriculture in Ireland during the fourth millennium bc, in view of the reservations outlined above (p. 73), these claims should be treated with some caution.

As to the persistence of hunter-gatherer communities, two views have been expressed on this. Based on his work in the Carrowmore area, Co. Sligo, Burenhult (1980) has resurrected the idea of an extensive mesolithic survival in Ireland, claiming that stock-keeping was negligible throughout the Neolithic and cultivation did not become widespread until the Iron Age, and that some of the megalithic tombs, such as those at Carrowmore, may have been built by mesolithic communities. These claims are based on the early date for the Carrowmore cemetery (3800–2990 bc), the absence of pottery and the presence of shellfish in the graves and in the middens in the vicinity. Shell midden sites, containing layers datable to the late fourth and third millennia bc, i.e. post-dating the earliest evidence for farming, have been recovered at a number of locations in Ireland (Woodman 1978, 1980; Caulfield 1983). This can be contrasted with the paucity of evidence for farming during the Neolithic (Woodman 1985).

The notion of an extensive mesolithic survival in Ireland has recently been challenged by Woodman (1981*b*, 1985), while the alleged mesolithic context of the Carrowmore cemetery has been questioned by Caulfield (1983). Essentially, Woodman argues in favour of an early merger between the initial neolithic colonists and the resident hunter-gatherers, rather than for the persistence of independent mesolithic communities. Such a process can be detected in certain lithic aspects of the neolithic assemblage (Woodman 1981*b*, p. 204)

and would also explain the evidence for the continued exploitation of certain wild resources, particularly the shellfish.

Depending on one's conceptual preference, the fourth millennium can be seen as an 'availability phase' by adherents of the 'mesolithic survival' view, or as a substitution phase, by those who believe in an early merger. The early adoption of animal husbandry makes sense in Ireland because it would fill the gap created by the limited range of larger native mammals (only boar and roe deer were available during the Postglacial). Nevertheless, the case of Ireland cannot be resolved on the present evidence. Our impression is that both processes were taking place during the fourth millennium, and their relative importance varied from region to region; in some areas, the shift to farming, probably aided by colonisation, was rapid; in others, mesolithic communities survived until 3000 bc or later.

Evidence for economic intensification, which in our scheme is a hallmark of the consolidation phase, can be detected in the later Neolithic, with the first traces of ploughing, land division and with the exploitation of poorer habitats (Woodman 1985). Woodman (1985) further notes that late neolithic intensification also included a shift to a broader spectrum economy with increased emphasis on hunting. So, in Ireland, foraging probably made something of a comeback during the consolidation phase, when it was used as an emergency strategy within the context of developed farming economy. The chronology of the later Neolithic in Ireland is not clearly defined, but can generally be dated to the second half of the third millennium bc (Herity and Eogan 1977; Woodman 1985).

The Netherlands

The geology of the western Netherlands complicates any discussion of this region. The higher eastern part of the country consists of Pleistocene deposits, and was settled by neolithic farmers during the Linearbandkeramik (LBK) expansion (cf. the date of 4420 ± 60 (GrN 995) from Geleen). These areas are within the distribution of the mainstream Neolithic cultural sequence of Linearbandkeramik-Rössen-Michelsberg-Funnel Beaker (TRB).

To the west, more recent deposits have been found (Fig. 4). The marine and fluvial deposits derive from the repeated marine transgressions, which have often eroded away earlier deposits of the same type, as well as some of the peat formed at various periods during the transgression sequence. In other areas, this peat is preserved, thus also preserving beneath itself areas of landscape of varying ages (Louwe Kooijmans 1974). Finds dating to the earlier postglacial period are therefore scarce.

The period before 3500 bc

Considerable contact has been documented between the LBK and its immediate successors on the one hand and the local Mesolithic on the other. Mesolithic radiocarbon dates

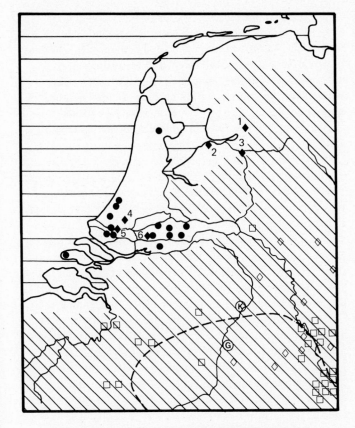

Fig. 4. Mesolithic–Neolithic interface in the Netherlands.
(♦) Western Dutch sites, later fourth millennium bc: 1, De Gaste;
2, Swifterbant; 3, Spoolde; 4, Bergschenhoek; 5, Schiedam; 6,
Hazendonk I. (●) Vlaardingen culture sites. (———) LBK, northwestern boundary. (◊) Rössen sites. (□) Michelsberg sites. K,
Kesseleyk; G, Geleen. Oblique shading, pleistocene deposits;
unshaded, holocene deposits. (After Louwe Kooijmans (1976),
Fig. 5; *ibid.* (1974), Figs. 2 and 5; Schwabedissen (1966), Figs.
3 and 26; *ibid.* (1979b), Fig. 2.)

after 5000 bc are, however, rare and sometimes doubtful
(Lanting and Mook 1977), and no faunal remains have been
preserved at the sites in question. What the cultural contacts
mean in economic terms cannot therefore be determined.

The LBK has a rich and varied flint industry, unlike the
LBK of other areas; Newell (1970, p. 171) seeks to derive this
from the local Mesolithic on technological, morphological and
typological grounds. Louwe Kooijmans (1976) has contested
this, stating that the parallels are not as great as Newell claims,
although there are some similarities. Whatever the degree of
similarity, some contact between farmers on the western
edge of their distribution and foragers is indicated.

A number of factors support this. The mesolithic site of
Maarheeze has been radiocarbon dated to 4280 ± 115 (GrN
2446), thus overlapping in the time with the earliest LBK; two
LBK points were found on this site (Newell, quoted in Lanting
and Mook 1977). So-called Limburg pottery has been found at
Kesseleyk (Modderman 1974) and also apparently as imports
on a number of LBK settlements (Louwe Kooijmans 1976).
No economic information is available from Kesseleyk, but

the pottery is believed to represent the 'neolithisation' of the
local mesolithic population (*ibid.*). A scatter of perforated
stone axes, imported from the east, probably at this time, also
indicates activity beyond the limits of the mainstream farming
cultures (van der Waals 1972; Louwe Kooijmans 1976).

The earliest occupations at Swifterbant (the dune sites)
date from this period. Mesolithic occupation has been dated to
5795 ± 40 bc (GrN 6709) and 4720 ± 35 bc (GrN 6708) at
Site (S) 21, and to 4925 ± 45 bc (GrN 6710) at S 22 (Price
1981). The role of pottery at these sites is unclear: a few
sherds were found (de Roever 1976), but later activity took
place on the sites and there was a tendency for the pottery to
occur rather high up in the profiles (Price 1981). A date of
4290 ± 50 bc (GrN 8248) was obtained from a hearth containing a potsherd at S 23 (Price 1981), and similar dates
(4335 ± 45 bc: GrN 7214, and 4380 ± 45: GrN 7215) have
been obtained from S 11, which also had traces of pottery
(Whallon and Price 1976).

This led Price (1981) to suggest that there was a two-
phase occupation of the Swifterbant dunes: an aceramic phase
at *c.* 4800 bc, and a ceramic mesolithic occupation at *c.* 4300
bc. Others, however, remain uncertain. De Roever (1979)
stated that the pottery in the 4300 bc sites might derive from
the later (*c.* 3300 bc) occupation of the area, and Deckers
(1982) points to a more recent dune excavation (S 61) where
a mesolithic layer (C) has been dated to 4285 ± 50 bc (GrN
10 357). Significantly, this layer contains no pottery, although
it is contemporary with Price's (1981) possible ceramic
mesolithic phase. It seems on present evidence most likely that
all the Swifterbant pottery dates to some time after 4000 bc.

The Swifterbant dune sites have very little bone preservation, so economic aspects cannot be discussed. The sites lay
on a freshwater river (Ente 1976). Whether there might have
been shell middens on the coast at this time is not ascertain-
able because most of the contemporary coastlines have been
eroded away (Louwe Kooijmans 1974).

The period after 3500 bc

A little more information is available from the western
Netherlands for the later fourth millennium bc. The Swifterbant levee sites are dated to the period 3400–3300 bc, and the
base of the peat, which formed during the subsequent flooding
of the levees, is dated to 3005 ± 40 bc (GrN 7507) (van der
Waals 1977).

The sites were on levees along a system of creeks; behind
the levees were extensive back-swamps (Ente 1976;
Hacquebord 1976). Location would thus suggest a major wild
component in the economy. Nevertheless, many cereal grains
(mainly naked six-row barley) were recovered from S 3, and
the presence of chaff suggests that it was grown on the spot,
not imported. Crops could only have been grown on the
highest parts of the levees, so the cultivated area must have
been small (Casparie *et al.* 1977; van Zeist and Palfenier-
Vegter 1981). The animal bones from S 3, S 4 and S 5 include
many wild mammals, birds and fish, as well as domestic cow

and pig, although the relative quantities are not stated (Clason and Brinkhuizen 1978).

A few other sites are known from this period. Hazendonk I has been radiocarbon dated to 3370 ± 40 bc (GrN 6215) (Lanting and Mook 1977). Many fish bones were recovered, as well as grains and chaff of einkorn and barley (Louwe Kooijmans 1976). Many fish bones were also recovered from Bergschenhoek, which has a radiocarbon date of 3465 ± 60 bc (GrN 7764). Artefacts suggestive of a similar date have been recovered from Spoolde, Schiedam and De Gaste (ibid.) (Fig. 4).

Despite the difficulties due to the geological factors discussed above, the Dutch situation shows some similarities with Denmark and north Germany. Quite how far the similarities can be taken is not yet clear. The pottery from the later fourth millennium sites in the western Netherlands is heterogeneous, but has been compared with the site of Hude I in the Dümmer valley (Fig. 5) and to the Erteb∅lle−Ellerbek wares further east (de Roever 1979; Louwe Kooijmans 1976). In south Scandinavia, however, it is associated with virtually no agricultural evidence, while in the Netherlands the evidence from Swifterbant S 3−S 5 and Hazendonk I indicates an agricultural component in the economy. Putting all the south Scandinavian and west Dutch fourth millennium bc sites into one typological group may therefore mean little in economic terms: the acquisition of neolithic economic traits was evidently taking place at different speeds in different parts of the area.

In the western Netherlands, however, foraging remained important. Cereal cultivation was apparently relatively unimportant at Swifterbant due to the small area of cultivable land (see above). Wild animal resources remained predominant until much later: the Vlaardingen culture occupied the western Netherlands in the period 2500−2000 bc (Fig. 4), and wild mammals, birds and fish were predominant at Hekelingen and Vlaardingen itself (Clason 1967). The only relevant stratified site is Hude I (Dümmer) (see Fig. 5). This site presents problems. A radiocarbon date from a level with pointed base pottery gave 4110 ± 115 bc (SHv 1220). Rössen elements begin around 3665 ± 95 bc (Hv 1793), but stratigraphic problems permit no clear separation into layers. The fauna suffers from the same problem. Wild animals are apparently predominant, with (apparently) an increase in domestic mammals towards the top where TRB elements appear. No certain traces of cereal cultivation are known (Deichmüller 1969).

Full publication of the Dümmer and the Schleswig-Holstein sites is thus essential to any understanding of the links between the Netherlands and south Scandinavia. The existence of an extensive availability phase in the western Netherlands is no surprise, because of the difficulties facing farming communities in the area. The marine transgressions suggest one source of pressure on hunter-gatherer adaptations in the area, and after c. 4400 bc farming was established not far away. Explaining the nature of, and reasons for, the substitution phase is a pressing topic for future research.

Southern Scandinavia

The foragers of prehistoric southern Scandinavia are as well studied as any in Europe, due to a combination of a long history of archaeological research, and fortunate geological circumstances resulting in much of the coastline from the immediately pre-farming period being above present sea level. Mesolithic coastal settlements are thus available for study, and the model can be examined in more detail than in many other areas.

Availability phase

(1) The Erteb∅lle as the availability phase. The chronology of the transition from foraging to farming has been examined in detail elsewhere (Zvelebil and Rowley-Conwy 1984). Radiocarbon dating shows that the Erteb∅lle of Denmark and south Sweden and the corresponding Ellerbek and Rosenhof groups from Schleswig-Holstein date to before about 3200 bc (Tauber 1972; Schwabedissen 1979a). Figure 5 shows the earliest dates for the succeeding TRB Neolithic in southern Scandinavia.

The earliest dates for the southern Scandinavian TRB are clearly much later than the earliest dates for the earliest LBK Neolithic of Central Europe (Fig. 5). The LBK sites of Korlat and Eitzum are approximately 1000 km apart, and yet their dates are almost indistinguishable. From Eitzum north to Siggeneben-Süd is less than a quarter of this distance, and yet the dates are 1300 radiocarbon years apart. After the rapid LBK expansion, the neolithic spread virtually stops.

This temporal overlap between farmers in north continental Germany and foragers in southern Scandinavia is a classic availability phase. The Erteb∅lle remained a foraging culture, although contacts between farmers and foragers have been demonstrated. Shoe-last adzes of LBK origin have been found in Denmark (Fischer 1982). Pottery of Baalberg and Michelsberg types has been found at Rosenhof in Holstein (Schwabedissen 1979a), and decoration on some Erteb∅lle pots suggests parallels with the Rössen culture (Fischer 1982). Adzes may have had a symbolic rather than a practical function (ibid.), and the same may indeed have been the case for the imported pottery. An interesting situation is recorded in northern Alaska, where the coastal Eskimo, living in large permanent villages, made large pots for utilitarian purposes. These were traded inland to nomadic groups unable to produce their own pottery. Inland, however, the pots acquired a ritual significance, being used in ceremonials to do with the spring caribou hunt (Spencer 1959). One man's cooking pot may be another man's chalice.

Whatever their significance in the Erteb∅lle context, these finds prove that there were contacts between farmers and foragers during the availability phase. The acquisition of elements of the agricultural economy by the foragers was thus a possibility throughout the existence of the Erteb∅lle, and some have claimed that the Erteb∅lle was indeed semi-agricultural. Detailed consideration of these claims, however, does not offer strong support for agriculture in southern Scandanavia before 3200−3100 bc (Rowley-Conwy 1985b). At

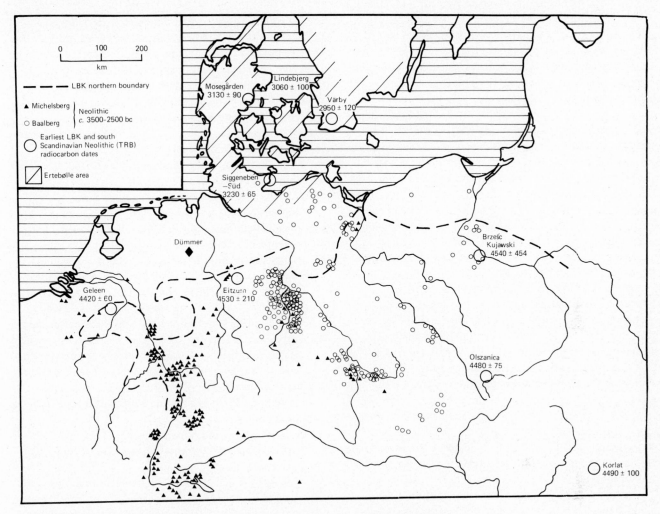

Fig. 5. Mesolithic–Neolithic interface in North European lowland and southern Scandinavia.

all events, farming seems to have played either very little or no part in the economy. The status of the Ertebølle/Ellerbek as the availability phase is thus reaffirmed.

(2) The coastal alternative. Following the model put forward, farming is here regarded as only one of a number of alternative economic strategies. It is probable that it was relatively less attractive in southern Scandinavia than in Central Europe. The more coastal parts of Europe are likely to have had a higher population density in the Mesolithic (Clarke 1976; Vencl, Chapter 4), and this has been particularly argued for Denmark (Paludan-Müller 1978).

It has been suggested that the Jutland Ertebølle occupied large, permanent home bases, also using special purpose camps, because of the appearance of a variety of migratory resources within a restricted area. By analogy with recent sedentary groups, population density and group size may have been relatively high (Rowley-Conwy 1981, 1983). Eastern Denmark and southern Sweden have provided less evidence, and much of the material from northern Germany remains unpublished, but one strong possibility is that sedentary foragers were to be found throughout the area.

Chapman (1981) has linked the appearance of the formal disposal of the dead with the development of residential stability, larger group size, and thus (by implication) greater social complexity. Three of the mesolithic cemeteries in Atlantic Europe are in southern Scandinavia. Vedbaek, dated to *c*. 4100 bc, has 22 graves with some 26 individuals (Albrethsen and Petersen 1976). Two similar cemeteries, of similar age, have been excavated at Skateholm in south Sweden (Larsson 1984*a, b*).

These considerations suggest an explanation for the long continuation of the availability phase in southern Scandinavia. It cannot be assumed that early farming was necessarily more productive and reliable than foraging in a favourable environment, and farming was evidently not automatically adopted whenever it was available. Environmental factors are unlikely to have inhibited the spread of farming, as south Scandinavia is climatically similar to Germany and has light, easily worked soils. The evidence suggests that the sedentary, coastal Ertebølle economy was the reason for the delay in the spread of farming. Coastal foraging apparently offered a viable, alternative way of life, which on present evidence was maintained for some 1300 radiocarbon years despite the availability of farming.

Substitution phase

This phase seems to have occurred rapidly, as part of a single process. It has been suggested that a decline in marine salinity at around 3200–3100 bc had a deleterious effect on the environment, so that coastal foraging was no longer as reliable as previously. The oyster may have been used to plug a critical gap in the resource cycle of the Jutland Ertebølle; its disappearance (archaeologically visible as a change to less productive cockles and mussels as the major shellfish found in shell middens) would have been a serious problem. Other marine resources may also have been affected, so the intensification of these to fill the gap would not have been easy. The marine deterioration would have affected the whole of the region, and so would have been a relevant factor throughout south Scandinavia even though oysters were not equally important everywhere. Farming may have been adopted as a result of this (Rowley-Conwy 1981; 1984*b*).

Jennbert (1984) has suggested that agricultural produce may have arrived in southern Sweden and perhaps elsewhere through gift exchange with farmers. Evidence for cereals from Jennbert's site of Loddesborg is limited to the very end of the Ertebølle, postdating a layer dated to 3310 ± 80 bc. Contacts between foragers and farmers have been demonstrated (see above) and were indeed essential if the foragers were to adopt elements of the neolithic economy when needed. Jennbert's theory can thus be combined with that put forward here: Jennbert discusses the mechanisms whereby farming elements became available, while the changes in marine salinity provide an explanation for the date at which adoption took place.

Archaeological evidence for the details of the process is lacking. It may be guessed that the hunter-gatherers initially adopted farming as a stopgap, to compensate only for the decline in marine resources. Attempts may have been made to integrate farming with the pre-existing pattern of economic activities. There are grounds for believing, however, that such an economy would not remain stable for long. Cereals must be harvested, and animal fodder might in part be collected, in the *autumn*, a time already likely to involve great work effort by hunter-gatherers. This would be a period of peak plant food availability; and if wild resources were stored (as has been suggested for the Ertebølle), autumn would be the main period of procurement and preparation of these resources: nuts were available, and ungulates were in prime condition. If some of these activities were displaced by farming, a further expansion of farming would be required to compensate. Even if all the activities could be carried out at the same time, it might be more efficient to concentrate most effort on one set of activities at a time. Farming at this early stage of development was capable of much further expansion. Hunting and gathering was in difficulties due to the disappearance of the oyster and the decline in marine productivity. If work effort was to be concentrated on one or other set of activities at this stage, it would therefore have had to be on farming.

It is thus suggested that temperate-zone hunter-gatherers practising storage may have faced a scheduling crisis when attempting to integrate an agricultural sector into their economy. The result would be the rapid appearance of an economy based on farming, with hunting playing only a subordinate role. Little direct evidence is to hand from the first few centuries of the Neolithic in Denmark, resulting in disagreement as to the nature of the Early Neolithic. Madsen (1982) suggests a period of mixed foraging and farming (mainly pig keeping), while Skaarup (1982) prefers the view that groups larger than those envisaged by Madsen were mainly dependent on farming from an early date.

In the absence of direct evidence, four factors may be mentioned which offer support to the idea of a rapid change to a predominantly farming economy.

(1)   Many coastal hunting stations continue in use in the Danish Early Neolithic (Skaarup 1973; Madsen 1982; Rowley-Conwy 1983), and Siggeneben-Süd in northern Germany is probably similar (Meurers-Balke 1983).

Hunting was thus of some importance after the appearance of the Neolithic. The continued use of the hunting sites stands in marked contrast to the abandonment of the large sites thought to have been Ertebølle base-camps (Rowley-Conwy 1983). This was apparently rapid and widespread around 3200–3100 bc, at least in Jutland. These were the centres of the complex Ertebølle hunting and gathering economy, and their abandonment implies that another kind of centre had taken their place.

(2)   The various elements of a full neolithic economy were present in the earliest Neolithic (Helbaek 1954; Degerbøl and Fredskild 1970). It seems more likely that these should have been introduced as parts of a functioning system than as minor and disparate elements that were only subsequently reunited into a full neolithic economy.

(3)   The appearance of causewayed camps and megaliths at the end of the Early Neolithic implies an economy of considerable complexity. This might in turn imply a period of established agriculture during at least a part of the Early Neolithic, upon which basis these developments could take place.

(4)   Analysis of the ^{13}C content of human skeletons by Tauber (1982) shows an abrupt change from a marine-dominated mesolithic diet to a terrestrial-dominated neolithic one.

The little evidence available from the Early Neolithic does not therefore suggest the existence of an extended substitution phase beyond the end of that period.

The consolidation phase

This phase is marked by the appearance of causewayed camps, megalithic tombs and major sites with definite evidence of a full neolithic economy. This development starts in the Fuchsberg phase, transitional between the Early and Middle

Neolithic, and radiocarbon dated to around 2650 bc
(Andersen and Madsen 1977).

Causewayed camps like Sarup (Andersen 1980), Toftum
(Madsen 1977) and, in northern Germany, Budelsdorf (Hingst
1971) are regarded as central places (of whatever function)
and thus indicative of a degree of economic complexity
(Andersen 1980; Madsen 1982). The agricultural status of the
economy is not in doubt — bones from Danish middle neolithic sites contain an overwhelming predominance of domestic
animals (Higham 1969), and similar evidence is available from
north Germany from sites like Fuchsberg itself, and thereafter
later Sussau (Nobis 1962, 1971). Cereal finds attest emmer
cultivation (Jørgensen 1976).

Coastal resources apparently still play some part. A
concentration of finds occurs in coastal regions (Andersen
1980; Madsen 1982; Clark 1977). The frequency of sites,
however, actually on (as opposed to near) the coast declines;
many of the sites that are on the coast contain mainly
domestic rather than wild animal bones (Madsen 1982;
Skaarup 1973; Rowley-Conwy 1985a).

Thus Denmark and north Germany provide clear
evidence of the consolidation phase at least as early as 2650
bc. It should not be assumed that this was necessarily an
irreversible development — a renewed increase in the
importance of marine resources is noted in the later Middle
Neolithic, when causewayed camps and megaliths cease to be
constructed (Davidsen 1978; Madsen 1982). This is paralleled
in north Germany by the late neolithic site of Wolkenwehe, a
small settlement containing over 50% wild animal bones
(Lüttschwager 1967). If the decrease of hunting in the earlier
part of the Middle Neolithic is real, rather than an accident
of research, this period conforms to the consolidation phase
of our present framework.

Middle Sweden

Middle Sweden presents an interesting and complex case
study, marked by a temporary return from frontier farming
to hunting and gathering. During the fifth millennium
bc, the hunter-gatherers of the Climatic Optimum employed
what appears to have been a reliable and productive range
of subsistence strategies, based on the exploitation of bays,
lagoons and inner coastlines on the one hand, and of the
interior on the other (Welinder 1981, 1983). The inner coastal
habitats formed the basic food-gathering area. Extraction
forays were made to the lakes and rivers of the interior, but
the outer coasts and archipelagos were not used at this time.
Faunal remains consist mainly of elk, deer, boar, fur game,
seal, water birds and fish.

About 3000 bc, farming was introduced to eastern
middle Sweden with the arrival of the TRB culture. In the
view of most authors, this represents an actual immigration of
farmers from southern Sweden (Welinder 1981). However,
in eastern middle Sweden, as in other parts of Scandinavia, the
TRB economy depended on hunting as well as farming

strategies, although to a lesser extent (*ibid*. 1981, p. 159;
1982, pp. 153–7).

About 2700 bc, amid deteriorating climatic conditions,
the TRB was replaced by the Pitted Ware culture (Moberg
1966). There is some disagreement as to whether the early
Pitted Ware culture developed from the TRB or from the
local mesolithic survivals. Welinder (1981, p. 160) thinks
that the latter is more likely on economic and technological
grounds, yet some elements of material culture, such as
pottery, display traits common to the TRB. The Pitted Ware
economy was more marine-oriented than that of the previous
foragers or the TRB farmers. This is evident from both the
location of the Pitted Ware Settlements and the faunal remains,
which show that seal constituted between 50% and 100% of
the mammalian sample (*ibid*. 1976, 1981). Some sites
contained enormous amounts of freshwater, non-migratory
fish: at Äs, fish formed about 90% of the total bone sample.
This, of course, does not reflect the true importance of fish in
the diet, but, together with seal, it underlines the strongly
aquatic orientation of Pitted Ware economy. Compared with
the earlier mesolithic settlement, a shift in resource use
territory has taken place: the inner coastal areas remained the
basic food-gathering areas, but the extraction forays were now
taking place in the outer archipelago, and concentrating on
seal hunting (*ibid*. 1976, 1981).

At about 2300 bc farming was introduced for the second
time into middle Sweden, within the context of the Battle Axe
culture. During the next 500 years the two cultures coexisted
within the region, but, as Welinder (1981, p. 161) emphasised,
'no acculturation can be demonstrated, that is no adoption of
a neolithic economy by the hunting–gathering groups'. This
was despite the fact that, faced with the Battle Axe settlement, the Pitted Ware territory was becoming gradually displaced towards the outer margins of the littoral. The main
zone of resource use moved into the outer archipelago. In
Welinder's view, this shift can be held responsible for the end
of the hunting–gathering tradition: the Pitted Ware ecological
base became so narrow and dependent on a few species,
mostly seals and other maritime resources, that 'its hunting–
gathering economy did not survive at this end point in the
landscape and (of) nutritional chains' (*ibid*., p. 162). By 1800
bc, the Pitted Ware adaptation had completely disappeared
from the archaeological record.

The course of events in middle Sweden is unusual in
three aspects: (1) farming was most probably introduced by
immigration, (2) the process of neolithic colonisation was
reversed, probably due to climatic deterioration; (3) there is
no evidence of acculturation and the final demise of the
hunting–gathering society was probably due to overspecial-
isation, to the point where the adoption of farming was no
longer possible for ecological as well as social reasons. This
gives us a clear situation of the colonisation, competition and
eventual replacement of one society by another as opposed
to the adoption of farming practices by resident hunter-
gatherers. In terms of our model, the period 3000–2700 bc

represents a substitution phase, and, since the process in this case is reversed, the availability phase follows with the domination of the area by the Pitted Ware culture 2700–2300 bc. A new substitution phase occurs with the Battle Axe penetration of the area, but, since there is no acculturation, the Pitted Ware remains in the availability phase. The period following the demise of the Pitted Ware culture, 1800–1300 bc, can be seen as a consolidation phase for the late neolithic groups.

Southern Finland

Economic reconstruction in southern Finland has always been hampered by the paucity and poor preservation of bone and plant remains. As a result, the economic orientation of different cultures and cultural groups could be described only in terms of a basic division between farming and foraging, and, in doing so, scholars have often relied on extrapolation from related cultural contexts outside Finland (Äyräpää 1952; Kivikoski 1967).

Traditionally, the introduction of farming is associated with the appearance, around 2500 bc, of the Boat Axe assemblage, characterised mainly by its Corded ware and boat-shaped battle axes and related to the Corded Ware/Battle Axe complex of Central and Eastern Europe (Äyräpää 1952; Kivikoski 1967). By reference to related groups in Sweden and Estonia, the Boat Axe groups are thought to have been 'nomadic or half nomadic herdsmen' (ibid., p. 47), with stock-breeding as the chief means of livelihood. In the absence of bone and plant remains, support for this view has been sought in the location of Boat Axe sites and the distribution of the culture as a whole in Finland, both of which seem to select for favourable farming rather than hunting and fishing locations.

The Boat Axe culture did not replace the indigenous hunting and fishing groups, in fact the two cultures continued to coexist until c. 2000 bc, when the Boat Axe intrusion came to an end by being absorbed by the foraging groups. This gave rise to a hybrid culture in southwest Finland, the Kiukainen culture, which is traditionally thought to have had a mixed economy of hunting, fishing, sealing and some agriculture (Meinander 1954; Äyräpää 1952; Kivikoski 1967). With the beginning of the Bronze Age, c. 1300 bc, the farming element increases while foraging declines. This process continues in the Iron Age (roughly first millennium AD), but as Äyräpää (1952, p. 296) pointed out, the dual economy – agriculture and hunting – 'remained characteristic of the Finns far into historical times'.

We would argue, however, that, in the light of recent evidence, the status of Corded Ware and Kiukais cultures as farming and pastoral groups has been brought into doubt, although there are indications that both of these were familiar with agriculture and in contact with farmers. At the same time there is no evidence that the indigenous Combed Ware groups practised farming.

The case for Corded Ware groups being farmers and pastoralists relies on several types of evidence: (1) pollen data

for burning and for Cerealia-type pollen found in profiles of three sites (Huttunen 1980, 1982; Siiriäinen 1982a, b), (2) faunal remains, (3) the location of Corded Ware sites and (4) the paucity of hunting equipment in Corded Ware assemblages (Siiriäinen 1981, 1982a, b). As we have argued in an earlier publication (Zvelebil and Rowley-Conwy 1984), none of these types of data shows unequivocally that farming was practised. Our view has received recent support from Donner's (1984) assessment of palynological evidence in southern Finland and from Edgren's (1984) analysis of Boat Axe/Corded Ware economy, neither whom now consider farming by the Corded Ware groups in Finland as likely.

The palynological case for Corded Ware farming in Finland rests on a few uncertain identifications of cereal pollen – evidence, which in view of the great similarities in size and shape of cereal and other gramineae pollen (Andersen 1978; Vencl 1982; Donner 1984) could hardly justify the belief that the Corded Ware economy was based on farming.

The evidence for the presence of domesticates in the Corded Ware context is similarly thin. Bone remains of any sort have so far been found at only six sites which contained Corded Ware remains. The single ovicaprid bone found at Pisimäki was retrieved in dubious stratigraphic circumstances (Forsten 1972). At Vantaa, no domesticated animals were found apart from dog and the same is true also for Topee and two other sites with mixed layers, which, however, included Boat Axe remains (Ailio 1909; A. Forsten, personal communication). At Jettbole, too, where the cultural material is related to both Corded Ware and Combed Ware groups (Meinander 1957; Kivikoski 1967), no bones of domesticated animals were found.

On the other hand, these sites contained bones of elk, beaver, hare, and especially seal. Perhaps the most important evidence comes from Vantaa, where stratigraphically distinct Corded Ware layers yielded 212 identifiable bones, 173 of which belonged to seal (Forsten and Blomquist 1974). From this it would appear that Corded Ware groups engaged more in hunting than husbanding, though at present there is simply not enough evidence to establish the basis of the Corded Ware economy with any confidence.

The spatial relationships of Corded Ware sites have also been used to argue the case of Corded Ware farming in Finland. These relate, firstly, to the distribution of Corded Ware sites in Finland as a whole and, secondly, to the location of sites in relationship to their immediate vicinity. Neither of these two patterns show convincingly that farming played a role, as other explanations are possible (Siiriäinen 1981; Zvelebil 1981; Zvelebil and Rowley-Conwy 1984).

Finally, Corded Ware groups are said to have been pastoral and agricultural because their assemblages do not contain hunting gear (Siiriäinen 1981, 1982b; Luho 1976; Kivikoski 1967). The fact is that the Corded Ware stone industry is in general very poor, both in number and variety (apart from axes) and the absence of hunting tools is fully matched by the absence of reaping knives, querns or other equipment which might suggest agriculture (Edgren 1970). If anything, this situation suggests an intensive use of perishable materials for tools or, alternatively, it raises questions about the status of Corded Ware as an independent cultural tradition.

The evidence such as we have for the economic orientation of the contemporary Combed Ware groups (Combed Ware III, Pyheensilta) suggests that hunting and fishing were the basis of subsistence, with an increasing reliance on the exploitation of marine resources. This is indicated by the developed fishing and seal-processing slate element within the stone industry (Fitzhugh 1974), by the distribution of late Combed Ware sites (Siiriäinen 1981) and their catchment analysis (Zvelebil 1981), and finally by the overwhelming presence of seal remains on six late Combed Ware sites dated to this period (Forsten and Blomquist in Zvelebil 1978; Siiriäinen 1982*b*).

On the present evidence, three possible solutions to the Corded Ware problem can be considered.

(1) Farming Corded Ware groups entered Finland from Sweden and Estonia in the mid third millennium bc. Because of the adverse environmental conditions, their farming mode of subsistence began to fail and, in the long run, their attempt to settle and farm southwest Finland proved maladaptive. They gradually adopted foraging as the principal means of subsistence and merged with the local population. This is the traditional explanation (Siiriäinen 1981; Edgren 1970). The problem is that despite efforts to find traces of farming in Corded Ware contexts (Alhonen in Edgren 1970; Huttunen 1980; 1982; Siiriäinen 1982; Zvelebil 1981) the evidence for it remains circumstantial and in our view unconvincing. If Corded Ware people did practise farming in Finland, it must have been very limited and carried out on sites difficult to trace through pollen analysis (see Tolonen, Siiriäinen and Hirviluoto 1979).

(2) The Corded Ware horizon in Finland represents not a migration but the adoption of cultural traits by the local people. The inland Corded Ware sites and the coastal Combed Ware III sites would then belong to the same groups with two functionally distinct assemblages. As a corollary, some farming would take place on inland Corded Ware sites, while seal would be seasonally exploited at the coast.

This is really a problem of the recognition of migrations in an archaeological context. With the appearance of the Corded Ware horizon in Finland, new traits were introduced in just about all aspects of culture (lithics, pottery, dwellings, burial, etc.) representing a complete break with previous cultural traditions. So we are really dealing with cultural replacement, rather than with the adoption of isolated cultural traits. Moreover, the attributes of the Corded Ware culture can be traced to similar contemporary groups in south Scandinavia and Estonia (Äyräpää 1933, 1973; Edgren 1970; Luho 1976; Jaanits 1971). These considerations would, in our view, indicate migration rather than imitation. Finally, there are no clear indications of farming going on in the Corded Ware context.

(3) Corded Ware groups used southern Finland as a hunting and trapping zone adjacent to the farming frontier which extended across southern Sweden and the east Baltic (Fig. 6). This scenario would bring the Corded Ware people into competition with the indigenous foragers, although the initial emphasis on specialised hunting and trapping for fur would have led the Corded Ware people to exploit a slightly different niche. Such a hunting emphasis could provide one explanation for the lack of projectile hunting equipment, and for the location of Corded Ware sites, which are sub-optimal for ungulate exploitation and for aquatic resources, but not for trapping (Zvelebil 1981).

In this paper, we favour the last proposition, if only to shift attention from simple hunters/farmers and locals/immigrants dichotomies. The third solution does not exclude the possibility of limited farming by Corded Ware people, or of local Corded Ware development, while, at the same time, maintaining contact with the areas outside of Finland. The evidence for the latter two processes can be found in the changing attributes of Corded Ware assemblages (Äyräpää 1973; Luho 1976; Edgren 1970). At present, this remains a tentative hypothesis in need of vigorous testing; it does, however, place the Corded Ware period provisionally into the 'availability phase'.

At the beginning of the second millennium bc, the Corded Ware was replaced by the Kiukainen culture, which is regarded, on the basis of archaeological material, as a hybrid of Corded Ware and Combed Ware groups. Settlement location (Siiriäinen 1981, 1982*b*), catchment analysis (Zvelebil 1981) and extensive fishing and sealing equipment (Meinander 1954; Zvelebil 1981; Siiriäinen 1981, 1982*b*) point to a developed hunting and fishing economy, with seal as the principal resource. This is confirmed by the recent analysis of faunal remains from three Kiukainen sites (Fortelius in Siiriäinen 1982*b*) where bones of seal ranged from 64 to 95%; while no bones of domesticated animals are reported.

The question that remains is how much farming, if any, was practised by Kiukainen groups. The pollen evidence for cultivation remains equivocal until the very end of the Kiukainen period. It is only from the fifteenth century bc and later that we have more definite remains of Cerealia pollen found on inland, rather than littoral sites (Vuorela 1972, 1975; Nuñez and Vuorela 1979; Siiriäinen 1982*b*; Donner 1984). The Cerealia pollen curve is discontinuous and associated with clearance profiles and weeds of cultivation which suggest regrowth cycles associated with slash and burn rather than permanent field cultivation (Tolonen *et al.* 1979; ; Vuorela 1975; Huttunen 1980). Within our framework, this evidence marks the transition to the substitution phase, a period during which farming gradually replaced foraging as the principal means of subsistence.

There is little doubt that, for the most part, the people of the Kiukainen culture were engaged in hunting marine mammals, particularly ringed (*Phoca hispida*) and grey (*Halichoerus grypus*) seal (Siiriäinen 1981, 1982*a, b*; Forsten 1977; Salo and Lahtiperä 1970; Meinander 1954). The

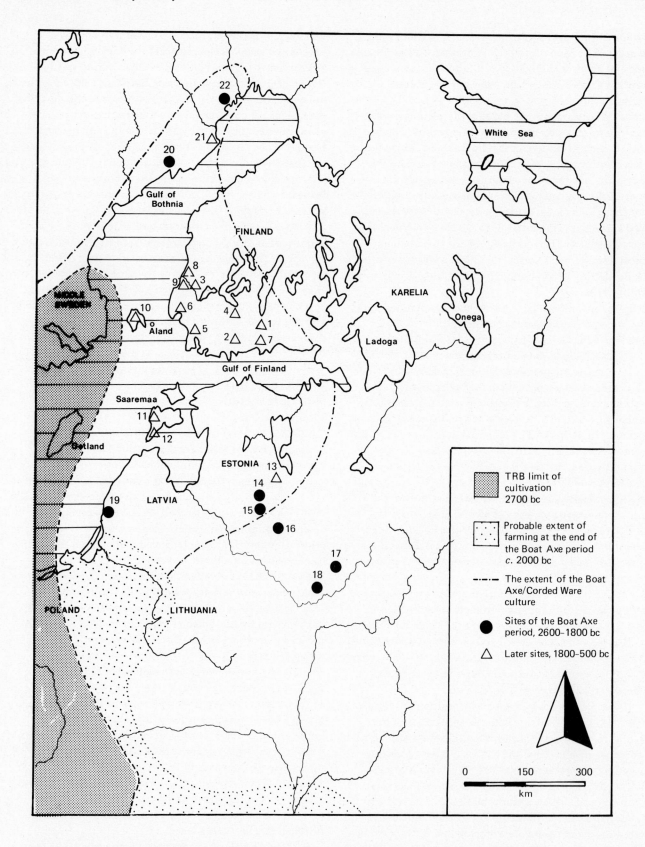

Fig. 6. Mesolithic–Neolithic interface in the north-east Baltic. The earliest evidence for the presence of cultigens and domesticates consists of pollen profiles with isolated Cerealia pollen (nos. 1–7, 20–22); macroscopic remains (11, 19); and/or small numbers of domestic animal bones (8, 9, 10–19, 22). These are usually less than 5% of the faunal sample; only Asva (11) and Loona (12) on Saaremaa have greater proportions of domesticates in samples that contain more than just a few bones.

1, Ahvenainen; 2, Katihännänsuo; 3, Loimansuo; 4, Retula; 5, Ketohaka; 6, Kirkkojärvi; 7, Tyotjärvi; 8, Rieskaronmäki; 9, Uotinmäki; 10, Otterbote; 11, Asva; 12, Loona; 13, Tamula; 14, Abora; 15, Eyni; 16, Kreichi; 17, Usvyaty; 18, Krivina; 19, Šventoji; 20, Norrbole; 21, Umeå; 22, Bjurselet.

availability of the resource, however, is affected by a number of environmental factors related to breeding, such as the sinuosity of the coastline, and the duration and thickness of the ice (McLaren 1962; Zvelebil 1981). These factors changed during the second millennium bc. Accumulation of alluvium and the emergence of lowland plains through continuous isostatic uplift caused a decrease in the sinuosity of the coastline and thus in the number of calving places for ringed seal. As a result of the sub-boreal oscillation of the climate and the changes in the salinity of the Baltic Sea, the ice cover became more extensive: the thickness of ice increased as did its duration, and the edge of the ice moved south towards the mouth of the Gulf of Bothnia (Forsten and Alhonen 1975; Clark 1976) (Fig. 6). This meant that the conditions optimal for the calving of both the grey and probably also the ringed seal shifted from the central and northern shores of the Gulf to the islands in the central Baltic, and so did, presumably, seal populations. Significantly, the exploitation of ringed and/ or grey seal on these islands increased during the second millennium bc (Forsten 1977; Clark 1976; Paaver 1965). However, since the calving season in late winter and early spring is the main hunting season for seals, Kiukainen settlements along the Gulf of Bothnia would find their hunting grounds impoverished during the main hunting season, as seal would be calving in more southerly areas. Zvelebil (1981) has shown that while the overall availability of seal in the coastal waters of Finland was likely to decline as a result of these changes, the sealing potential within the site catchments of the Kiukainen sites had actually increased. This might represent an effort to maximise on sealing through site location to counter the declining availability of the resource.

We believe that the transition to farming in southern Finland must be seen in the context of the diminishing seal resources. In this respect, the coincidence between the decline in seal availability and the increase in the indicators of agriculture from the middle of the second millennium bc resembles closely the situation in Denmark 1500 years earlier where the adoption of farming is associated with the decline in oyster. In both cases it would appear that farming was adopted as a substitute for a shortage of an aquatic resource, which formed an important part in the seasonal-use pattern of the people in question.

On the present evidence, the rate of transition to farming was a slow process retarded by climatic factors, and, possibly, by the role of slash-and-burn agriculture (Zvelebil and Rowley-Conwy 1984). There is general agreement that the early evidence for farming in pollen profiles relates to swidden cultivation (for full discussion of indicators of swiddening as opposed to permanent arable, see Vuorela 1970, 1975, 1976; Tolonen *et al.* 1979; Huttunen and Tolonen 1977; Huttunen 1980). The reconstruction of past landscapes in southern Finland indicates that permanent arable did not become a major component of farming until the mid-first millennium AD (Tolonen *et al.* 1979; Zvelebil 1981). This marks the beginning of a consolidation phase, which continued at least until the end of the Middle Ages. At the household level, however, wild resources, especially fishing, continued to make a contribution to the diet until the growth of towns during the industrial revolution. Wild resource management still continues to play an important part in the Finnish economy. In a sense, therefore, the consolidation phase has never ended.

Discussion and conclusions

The evidence presented here from the Atlantic fringes of Europe brings to attention the slow nature of the transition to farming in coastal areas of Atlantic Europe. We wish to emphasise here two quite separate points: (1) the initial introduction of cultigens and domesticates and the main shift to farming are not the same processes, and (2) the delay in the shift to farming occurred among the more sedentary and socio-economically more complex hunter-gatherer societies.

Our analysis suggests that the transition to farming was a complex phenomenon which proceeded in phases which co-occurred or followed one another within a region. Figure 7 summarises the transitional sequences suggested for the different areas. If viewed from this perspective, the development of the farming economy could have taken 3000–4000 years to complete (i.e. in the case of northern Spain or Finland).

Our scheme covers a period much longer than that traditionally accorded to the transition to farming mainly because we make a distinction between the *introduction* of farming and its *adoption as the mainstay of the economy*. Our data indicate that elements of farming were adopted selectively, to fit the local needs, sometimes after a long period when it was available close by. Knowledge therefore could not have been a limiting factor in the adoption of farming, while the introduction of elements of farming (i.e. ovicaprid husbandry, limited stock keeping or cultivation) into a predominantly hunting–gathering context would not have initially transformed the hunting–gathering way of life. It would be only after a period of adjustment to the requirements of the farming economy, requirements that are often in conflict with the hunting–gathering mode of production (Zvelebil and Rowley-Conwy 1984; Moore 1981; Anderson 1981) that farming fully replaced hunting as the main means of subsistence. The chronological points of introduction and of full adoption are therefore different, and the period in between constitutes our substitution phase. What we emphasise as the critical distinction, therefore, is the replacement of hunting–gathering by the farming way of life, with all the attendant implications, rather than the mere introduction of farming.

As Fig. 7 indicates, the length of the substitution phase differs according to the local conditions of the transition to food production. We can have a predominantly internal or predominantly external situation. In the internal case, farming practices are adopted selectively in time and space (as in France, Finland and probably northern Spain) or all at the

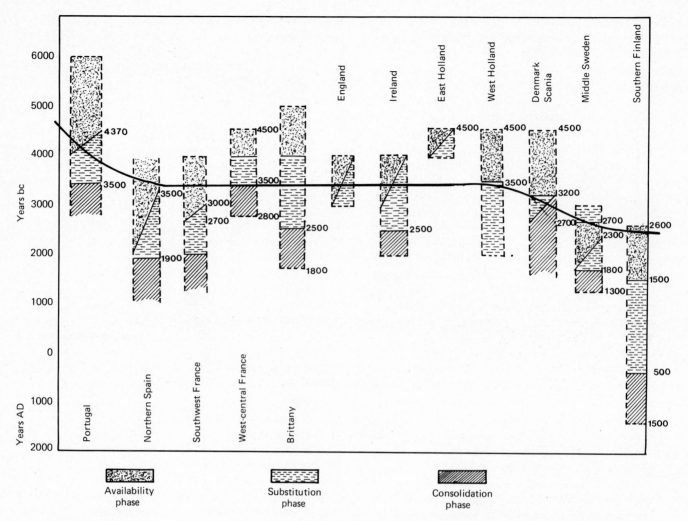

Fig. 7. Transition to farming in the Atlantic fringes of Europe: duration and sequence of phases. Bold line indicates the conventional date for the spread of farming.

same time, as in Denmark or Holland by the local hunter-gatherer communities. In the latter case, the transition to farming may be more rapid, but even so it is likely to take several hundred years, as was the case in Denmark. In an external situation, immigrant farming groups co-exist with the local foragers and eventually become absorbed by (as happened in Sweden) or, more frequently, replace hunter-gatherer societies (as in Ireland).

It is undeniable that the transition to farming has many permutations. Our model operates at a gross level of resolution and cannot account for all the variation within individual sequences. It is principally intended to shift attention from simple frontier dichotomies and to underline the extended duration and the complexity of the process. Yet, in our view, this complex process can be ordered into distinct phases which can be detected in most, if not all, cases of the transition to farming.

We have examined the transition to farming in coastal areas of Western Europe. From the point of view of natural resources, these areas are among the most productive in the temperate zone. This is largely because the Atlantic coasts form an ecotone, either side of which is highly productive:

the continental shelf in marine resources (Fig. 8) and the adjacent land in terrestrial and plant food characteristic of temperate forest zone (see also Rowley-Conwy, Chapter 2). With its lagoons and estuaries, the shoreline itself supports seasonal resources of its own, such as shellfish, water birds and pelagic seals. Hunter-gatherer communities, on the basis of the probable exploitation of these areas, would therefore have a much larger potential resource base than groups further inland. Moreover, as Rowley-Conwy (1983) has suggested, the availability of highly productive seasonal resources throughout the year would make sedentary existence and logistic resource-use patterns a viable alternative to mobile, opportunistic economies. Perlman (1980) has also considered the productivity of coastal zones. In his view, 'estuarine environments, particularly those above 40 degrees latitude provide a subsistence base that minimises mobility, maintains higher population densities by providing a number of high return rates and buffering resources, and involves less risk' (*ibid.*, p. 283).

With this background in mind, it is not really surprising that we find evidence of more stable, sedentary, and possibly socially and economically complex hunter-gatherer com-

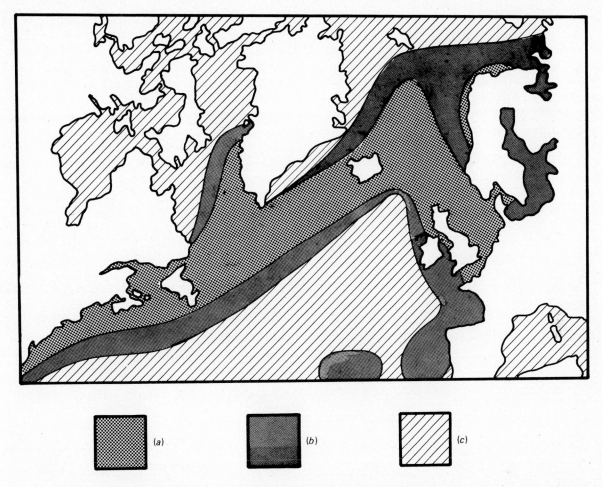

Fig. 8. Productivity of continental-shelf waters in Atlantic Europe. Plankton biomass zones in the North Atlantic (after Coull 1972). (*a*) 301 mg/m³ and over (seasonal peak up to 2000 mg/m³); (*b*) 151–300 mg/m³; (*c*) under 150 mg/m³.

munities at or near the coasts. This is, of course, not the case everywhere. That foragers of the Atlantic fringe were often able to develop a degree of sedentism, however, is emerging from a number of studies. Some Danish sites have long been regarded as permanently occupied. Winter occupation is attested by the presence of migratory birds such as the Bewick's swan, summer occupation by the honey buzzard and Dalmatian pelican as well as bones of immature great auk (Winge 1900). Pig tooth eruption from Ertebølle itself and Norslund/Flynderhage also indicates all-year occupation (Rowley-Conwy, unpublished). At Lundfors in northern Sweden, the presence of seal-netting equipment and bones of young seal indicates occupation from September to April; fish bones were not well preserved, but a few bones were found, suggesting summer occupation (Broadbent 1979). At the site of Nyelv Nedre Vest in northern Norway, reindeer bones testify to winter occupation, whole salmon and other marine fish indicate summer occupation (Renouf 1981, 1984). Remains of sledge runners, and of sealing on the one hand and of boats, fish traps, and waterchestnut on the other, indicate both summer and winter occupation at Sarnate in Latvia.

Faunal assemblages from Finland to Portugal also

imply some degree of dependence on the use of marine resources, in some cases resulting in the development of specialised technologies (such as those used in sealing in Scandinavia; Fitzhugh 1974, 1975). In more extensively researched areas, there is also evidence for the specialised exploitation of other resources, such as waterbirds (Narva-Riigikülä in Estonia, Aggersund and Sølager in Denmark), terrestrial mammals (Brovst and Ringkloster in Denmark), and plants (waterchestnut at Sarnate, Šventoji), (Dolukhanov 1979; Skaarup 1973; Møhl 1978; Rowley-Conwy 1980). In Northern Europe, there is also evidence for various forms of storage (Rowley-Conwy and Zvelebil 1987) and for facilities for the capture of aquatic resources (*sensu* Oswalt 1976; Torrence 1983), while the introduction of pottery in many late mesolithic communities along the western and northern coasts of Europe (see Chapter 12, Fig. 4) must have aided in storing food (i.e. the seal-blubber jars from Åland, or the Combed ware pot filled with waterchestnuts at Orimattila; Zvelebil 1981) and could be seen as another mark of increased sedentism (Testart 1982).

The notion of more sedentary, and perhaps socially stratified, hunter-gatherer societies in the littoral margins of Europe helps to make sense of a particular phenomenon

which, among European hunter-gatherers, is largely restricted
to the Atlantic fringe: cemetries (Fig. 9). Chapman (1981)
and others (Price and Brown 1985) have linked the existence
of such formal disposal areas to population stability and
sedentism, while O'Shea and Zvelebil (1984) were able to
demonstrate that, at least in one case, the Oleneostrovski
Mogilnik in northern Russia, the variation in grave goods
reflected the existence of wealth ranks and of inherited
status positions within the society. Variation in mortuary
equipment has been noted also in other mesolithic cemeteries
in Europe (Zagorski 1973; Clark 1980; Testart 1982;
Khlobistina 1978; Gurina 1956; Oshibkina 1982; Price 1985).
In a broader geographical context, Yesner (n.d.), King (1978),
Osborn (1977) and Perlman (1980) have all argued in favour
of the development of sociocultural complexity among
coastal groups.

Similarly, the link between coastal, 'affluent' foragers
and the transition to farming has been discussed by many
authors (Cohen 1977, 1981; Binford 1968, 1983; Fitzhugh
1975; Osborn 1977; Yesner 1980, n.d.; Akazawa 1981; Stark
and Voorhies 1978; Testart 1982; Rowley-Conwy 1983, 1984b;

Zvelebil 1981). The prevailing argument appears to be that
greater sedentism and more complex socio-economic
structures either pre-adapted the coastal communities to the
adoption of farming (Binford 1983) or compelled them to
adopt farming because of accelerated population growth
(Cohen 1977, 1981; Binford 1968), or both (Yesner n.d.). At
variance with this view, we would like to emphasise that the
adoption of farming was *delayed, not accelerated*, along the
coastal margins of Atlantic Europe. In our view, this was
because coastal hunters and gatherers in the temperate zone
had an alternative to the adoption of farming, namely the
development of intensive aquatic resource use strategies. Such
strategies based on the intensified use of local resources,
remained viable for longer than the hunter–gatherer subsistence strategies based solely or mainly on inland resources.

The eventual decline of maritime-oriented, coastal
economies can best be attributed to a number of causes,
depending on the conditions within each region. In some areas,
such as Denmark or Finland, a decline in the traditional,
aquatic resources precipitated the transition to farming. In
others, however, farming appears to have been adopted for

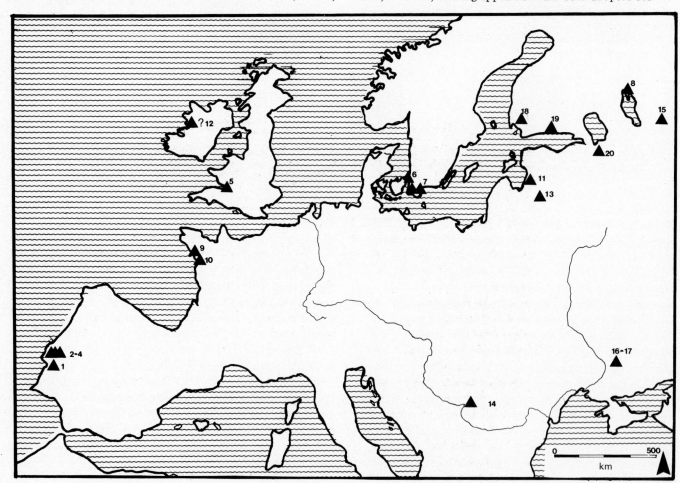

Fig. 9. Mesolithic cemeteries clustering in the northern and western fringes of Europe.
1, Cabeço do Pez; 2, Moita do Sebastião; 3, Cabeço da Amoreira; 4, Cabeço da Arruda; 5, Aveline's Hole; 6, Vedbaek; 7, Skateholm
1–3; 8, Oleneostrovski mogilnik; 9, Hoëdic; 10, Téviec; 11, Zvejnieki; 12, Carrowmore; 13, Abora I; 14, Lepenski Vir (Vlasac, Padina);
15, Popovo; 16, Vasil'evka 1; 17, Vasil'evka 3; 18, Kolmhaara; 19, Jönjas; 20, Sandermokha.

reasons other than demographic stress. Jennbert (1984), Broadbent (1981) and Anderson (1981) have all emphasised the role of forager—farmer contact, exchange and the consequent need for increased production as the contributing causes of the transition to farming in Scandanavia. While this remains an intriguing possibility, badly in need of further investigation, it does stress the importance of the availability phase during which the farmer—forager contacts would have been established and the early impact of the proximity of the farming frontier felt.

Our model, then, presents a framework for the appearance of agriculture in Atlantic Europe. The model itself is descriptive, not explanatory. However, the application of the model provokes a particular series of questions about the cause and the course of events at the transition. By focusing on these questions, explanation of the process is brought closer — and explanation, of course, remains the goal of every archaeologist.

References

Ailio, J. (1909) *Die Steinzeitlichen Wohnplatzefunde in Finland*, Helsingfors.

Akazawa, T. (1981) 'Maritime adaptation of prehistoric hunter-gatherers and their transition to agriculture in Japan', in S. Koyama and D. H. Thomas, eds., *Affluent Foragers: Prehistoric Coastal Adaptations*, pp. 213–60, Academic Press, New York.

Albrethsen, S. E. and Petersen, E. B. (1976) 'Excavation of a mesolithic cemetery at Vedbaek, Denmark'. *Acta Archaeologica* 47, 1–28.

Altuna, J. (1972) 'Fauna de mamíferos de los yacimientos prehistóricos de Guipuzcoa, con catálogo de los mamíferos cuaternarios del Cantabrico y Pirineo Occidental'. *Munibe* 24, 1–464.

(1980) 'Historia de la domesticación animal en el País Vasco desde sus origenes hasta la Romanización'. *Munibe* 32, 1–163.

Andersen, N. H. (1980) 'Sarup. Befaestede neolitiskenalaeg og deres baggrund'. [English Summary.] *Kuml*, 63–103.

Andersen, N. H. and Madsen, T. (1977) 'Skåle og baegre med storvinkelbånd fra yngre stenalder. Overgangen mellem tidling-og mellemneolitikum'. [English summary.] *Kuml*, 131–60.

Andersen, S. T. (1978) 'Identification of wild grass and cereal pollen'. *Danmarks Geologiske Undersøgelse, Arbog 1978*, 69–92.

Anderson, A. (1981) 'Economic change and the prehistoric fur trade in northern Sweden: the relevance of a Canadian model'. *Norwegian Archaeological Review* 14, 1–38.

Äyräpää, A. (1933) 'Über die Streitaxtkulturen in Russland'. *Eurasia Septentrionalis Antiqua* 8.

(1952) 'The settlement of prehistoric age'. *Fennia* 72, 285–300.

(1973) 'Batyxkulturen i Finland'. *Helsingin Yliopisten Arkeologian Laitos* 9, 195–213. *Opera selecta.*

Bahn, P. (1983) 'The neolithic of the French Pyrenees', in C. Scarre, ed., *Ancient France*, pp. 223–70, Edinburgh University Press, Edinburgh.

(1984) *Pyrenean Prehistory*, Wiltshire, Aris and Phillips, Warminster.

Bailey, G. (1978) 'Shell middens as indicators of postglacial economies: a territorial perspective', in P. Mellars, ed., *Early Postglacial Settlement of Northern Europe*, pp. 37–63, Duckworth, London.

(1983) 'Economic change in Late Pleistocene Cantabria', in G. Bailey, ed., *Hunter-Gatherer Economy in Prehistory: A European Perspective*, pp. 149–65, Cambridge University Press, Cambridge.

Baumhoff, M. A. (1963) 'Ecological determinants of Aboriginal Californian populations'. *University of California Publications in American Archaeology and Ethnology* 49 (2), 155–236.

Bewley, R. H. (1984) Prehistoric and Romano-British settlement patterns in the Solway Plain, Cumbria. Ph.D. thesis, University of Cambridge.

Binford, L. (1968) 'Post-pleistocene adaptations', in S. R. Binford and L. R. Binford, eds., *New Perspectives in Archaeology*, pp. 313–41, Aldine, Chicago.

(1983) *In Pursuit of the Past*, Thames and Hudson, London.

Bonsall, C. (1981) 'The coastal factor in the mesolithic settlement of northwest England', in B. Gramsch, ed., *Mesolithikum in Europa*, pp. 451–72, Veröffentlichungen des Museums für Ur- und Frühgeschichte, Potsdam, 14/15, Deutcher Verlag, Berlin.

Bradley, R. (1978) *The Prehistoric Settlement of Britain*, Routledge and Kegan Paul, London.

Broadbent, N. (1979) *Coastal Resources and Settlement Stability. A Critical Study of a Mesolithic Site Complex in Northern Sweden*, Institute of North European Archaeology, Uppsala.

(1981) 'The epimesolithic and the subneolithic cultures of northern Sweden and Finland', in B. Gramsch, ed., *Mesolithikum in Europa*, p. 165–76, Veröffentlichungen des Museums für Ur- und Frühgeschichte, Potsdam, 14/15, Deutcher Verlag, Berlin.

Burenhult, G. (1980) 'The archaeological excavations at Carrowmore, Co. Sligo, Ireland'. *Theses and Papers in North European Archaeology* 9, Institute of Archaeology, Stockholm.

Carballo, J. (1926) *El Esquéleto Humano Mas Antiguo de España*, published privately by the author, Santander.

(1960) *Investigaciones Prehistóricas II*, publicaciones del Museo Provincial de Prehistoria, Santander.

Case, H. (1969) 'Neolithic explanations'. *Antiquity* 43, 176–86.

Casparie, W. A., Mook-Kamps, B., Palfenier-Vegter, R. M., Struijk, P. C. and van Zeist, W. (1977) 'The palaeobotany of Swifterbant. A preliminary report. (Swifterbant Contributions 7)'. *Helinium* 17, 28–55.

Caulfield, S. (1983) 'The neolithic settlement of North Connaught'. in T. Reeves-Smyth and F. Hamond, eds., *Landscape Archaeology in Ireland*, pp. 195–216, BAR British Series 116, British Archaeological Reports, Oxford.

Chapman, R. (1981) 'The emergence of formal disposal areas and the "problem" of megalithic tombs in prehistoric Europe', in R. Chapman, I. Kinnes and K. Randsborg, eds., *The Archaeology of Death*, pp. 71–81, Cambridge University Press, Cambridge.

Clark, G. A. (1983a) 'Boreal phase settlement—subsistence models for Cantabrian Spain', in G. Bailey, ed., *Hunter–Gatherer Economy in Prehistory*, pp. 96–110, Cambridge University Press, Cambridge.

(1983b) 'The Asturian of Cantabria'. *Anthropological Papers of the University of Arizona*, Tucson.

Clark, G. A. and Straus, L. (1983) 'Late pleistocene hunter-gatherer adaptation in Cantabrian Spain', in G. Bailey, ed., *Hunter–Gatherer Economy in Prehistory*, pp. 131–47. Cambridge University Press, Cambridge.

Clark, G. A. and Yi, S. (1983) 'Niche-width variation in Cantabrian archaeofaunas: a diachronic study', in J. Clutton-Brock and C. Grigson, eds., *Animals and Archaeology*, vol. 1, *Hunters and Their Prey*, pp. 183–208, BAR International Series 163, British Archaeological Reports, Oxford.

Clark, J. G. D. (1976) 'A Baltic cave sequence'. Festschrift für Richard Pittioni'. *Archaeologica Austriaca* 13, 113–23.

(1977) 'The economic context of dolmens and passage graves in Sweden', in V. Markotić, ed., *Ancient Europe and the Mediterranean*, pp. 35–47, Aris and Phillips, Warminster.

(1980) *Mesolithic Prelude*, Edinburgh University Press, Edinburgh.

Clarke, D. L. (1976) 'Mesolithic Europe: the economic basis', in

G. de G. Sieveking, I. H. Longworth and K. E. Wilson, eds.,
  Problems in Economic and Social Archaeology, pp. 449–81,
  Duckworth, London.
Clason, A. T. (1967) 'Animal and man in Holland's past'. *Palaeo-
  historia* 13A, 1–247.
Clason, A. T. and Brinkhuizen, D. C. (1978) 'Swifterbant, mammals,
  birds, fishes. A preliminary report. (Swifterbant Contributions
  8)'. *Helinium* 18, 69–82.
Cohen, M. N. (1977) *Food Crisis in Prehistory*, Yale University Press,
  New Haven.
  (1981) 'Pacific coastal foragers: affluent or over-crowded?' in
  S. Koyama and D. H. Thomas, eds., *Affluent Foragers*, pp.
  275–95, Senri Ethnological Studies 9, National Museum of
  Ethnology, Osaka.
Coull, J. R. (1972) *The Fisheries of Europe: An Economic Geography*,
  Bell, London.
Davidsen, K. (1978) *The Final TRB Culture in Denmark. A Settle-
  ment Study*, Arkaeologiske Studier V, Akademiske Forlag,
  Copenhagen.
Deckers, P. H. (1982) 'Preliminary notes on the neolithic flint material
  from Swifterbant. (Swifterbant Contributions 13)'. *Helinium*
  22, 33–9.
Degerbøl, M. and Fredskild, B. (1970) The Urus (Bos primigenius
  Bojanus) and Neolithic Domesticated Cattle (Bos taurus Linne)
  in Denmark, *Det Kongelige Dansk Videnskabernes Selskab,
  Biologiske Skrifter* 17(1).
Deichmüller, J. (1969) 'Die neolithische Moorsiedlung Hude I am
  Dummer, Kreis Grafschaft Diepholz. Vorlaufiger Abschlus-
  sbericht'. *Neue Ausgrabungen und Forschungen in Niedersachsen*
  4, 28–36.
Dennell, R' (1985) 'The hunter-gatherer/agricultural frontier in pre-
  historic temperate Europe', in S. Green and S. Perlman, eds.,
  The Archaeology of Frontiers and Boundaries, pp. 113–39,
  Academic Press, New York.
Dolukhanov, P. (1979) *Ecology and Economy in Neolithic Eastern
  Europe*, Duckworth, London.
Donner, J. (1984) 'Some comments on the pollen-analytical records
  of cereals and their dating in southern Finland'. *Fennoscandia
  Archaeologica* 1, 13–19.
Edgren, T. (1970). 'Studier over den snörkeramiska kulturens keramik i
  Finland'. *Suomen Muinais Muisto Yhdistys/Finska Forminnes
  Förenignen* 72, 1–118.
  (1984) 'On the economy and subsistence of the Battle-Axe culture
  in Finland'. *Suomen Muinais Muisto Yhdistys/Finska Forminnes
  Föreningen Iskos 4* (Fenno-Ugri et Slavi 1983), pp. 9–16.
Edwards, K. J. and Hirons, K. R. (1984) 'Cereal pollen grains in pre-
  elm decline deposits: implications for the earliest agriculture in
  Britain and Ireland'. *Journal of Archaeological Science* 11, 71–
  80.
Ente, P. J. (1976) 'The geology of the northern part of Flevoland
  in relation to the human occupation in the Atlantic time.
  (Swifterbant Contribution 2)'. *Helinium* 16, 15–35.
Fischer, A. (1982) 'Trade in Danubian shaft-hole axes and the intro-
  duction of neolithic economy in Denmark'. *Journal of Danish
  Archaeology* 1, 7–12.
Fitzhugh, W. (1974) 'Ground slate in the Scandinavian Younger Stone
  Age'. *Proceedings of the Prehistoric Society* 40, 45–59.
  (1975) (ed.) *Prehistoric Maritime Adaptations of the Circumpolar
  Zone*, Mouton, The Hague.
Forsten, A. (1972) 'The refuse fauna of the Mesolithic Suomusjärvi
  period in Finland'. *Finskt Museum* 79, 74–85.
  (1977) 'A Bronze Age refuse fauna from Kökar, Aland'. *Finskt
  Museum* 81, 56–61 (1974).
Forsten, A. and Alhonen, P. (1975) 'The subfossil seals of Finland'.
  BOREAS 4, 143–55.

Forsten, A. and Blomquist, L. (1974) 'Refuse faunas of the Vantaa
  Mesolithic and Neolithic periods'. *Finskt Museum* 81, 50–6.
Giot, P. R., L'Helgouach, J. and Monnier, J. L. (1979) *Préhistoire de la
  Bretagne*, Ouest France, Rennes.
Groneman van Waateringe, W. (1983) 'The early agricultural utilization
  of the Irish landscape: the last work on the elm decline', in
  T. Reeves-Smyth and F. Hamond, eds., *Landscape Archaeology
  in Ireland*, pp. 217–32, BAR British Series 116, British
  Archaeological Reports, Oxford.
Guilaine, J. (1979) 'The earliest neolithic in the West Mediterranean: a
  new appraisal', *Antiquity* 53, 22–30.
Gurina, N. N. (1956) 'Oleneostrovski Mogilnik'. *Materialy i Issledo-
  vaniya po Arkheologii SSSR* 47.
Hacquebord, L. (1976) 'Holocene geology and palaeogeography of the
  environment of the levee sites near Swifterbant (Polder Oost
  Flevoland, section G 36–41). (Swifterbant Contributions 3)'.
  Helinium 16, 36–42.
Hassan, F. (1981) *Demographic Archaeology*, Academic Press, New
  York.
Helbaek, H. (1954) 'Store Valby. Kornavl i Danmarks første neolitiske
  fase'. [English summary.] *Aarbøger for Nordisk Oldkyndighed
  og Historie 1954*, 198–204.
Herity, M. and Eogan, G. (1977) *Ireland in Prehistory*, Routledge and
  Kegan Paul, London.
Hibbs, J. (1983) 'The Neolithic of Brittany', in C. Scarre, ed., *Ancient
  France*, pp. 271–323, Edinburgh University Press, Edinburgh.
Higham, C. F. W. (1969) 'The economic basis of the Danish Funnel-
  necked beaker (TRB) culture'. *Acta Archaeologica* 40, 200–9.
Hingst, H. (1971) 'Ein befestigtes dorf aus der jungsteinzeit in Büdels-
  dorf (Holstein)'. *Archäologisches Korrespondenzblatt* 1, 191–4.
Huttunen, P. (1980) 'Early land use, especially the slash and burn culti-
  vation in the commune of Lammi, southern Finland, interpreted
  mainly using pollen and charcoal analysis'. *Acta Botanica
  Fennica* 113, 1–43.
  (1982) 'Spar ar den neolitiska människan: Finlands natur', in
  T. Sjøvold, ed., *Introduksjonen Av Jordbruk i Norden*, pp.
  209–15, Universitetsforlaget Oslo, Bergen, Tromsø.
Huttunen, P. and Tolonen, M. (1977) 'Human influence in the history
  of lake Lovojärvi, southern Finland'. *Finskt Museum* 82, 68–
  105 (1975).
Iversen, J. (1941) 'Land occupation in Denmark's Stone Age'. *Danmarks
  Geologiske Undersøgelse II*, 66, 1–68.
Jaanits, L. (1971) 'Über die Estnischen Bootaxte von Karlova Typus'.
  Finskt Museum 78, 46–76 (1971).
Jacobi, R. M. (1973) 'Aspects of the "Mesolithic Age" in Great Britain',
  in S. K. Kozłowski, ed., *The Mesolithic in Europe*, pp. 237–65,
  Warsaw University Press, Warsaw.
  (1976) 'Britain inside and outside mesolithic Europe'. *Proceedings
  of the Prehistoric Society* 42, 67–84.
  (1982) 'Later hunters in Kent: Tasmania and the earliest neolithic',
  in P. E. Leach, ed., *Archaeology in Kent to AD 1500*, pp. 12–
  24, Council for British Archaeology Research Report 48.
Jacobi, R. M., Tallis, J. H. and Mellars, P. A. (1976) 'The southern
  Pennine mesolithic and the ecological record'. *Journal of
  Archaeological Science* 3, 307–20.
Jennbert, K. (1984) *'Den Produktiva Gåvan'*. [English summary.] *Acta
  Archaeologica Lundensia*, series in 40, 16.
Jones, R. L. (1976) 'The activities of mesolithic man: further palaeobo-
  tanical evidence from north-east Yorkshire', in D. A. Davidson
  and M. L. Shackley, eds., *Geoarchaeology*, pp. 355–67,
  Duckworth, London.
Jørgensen, G., (1976) 'Et kornfund fra Sarup. Bidrag til belysningen af
  traegtbaegerkulturens agerbrug'. [English summary.] *Kuml*,
  47–64.
Khlobistina, M. D. (1978) 'Voprosy socialno-ideologicheskikh inter-

pretatsii drevneishikh form mezoliticheskikh i neoliticheskikh pogrebenii'. *KSIIMK-Kratkie Soobschchenniya Instituta Istorii i Materiyalnoi Kultury* 152, 61–8.

King, T. F. (1978) 'Don't that beat the band? Non-egalitarian political organisation in prehistoric central California', in C. Redman et al., eds., *Social Archaeology: Beyond Subsistence and Dating*, pp. Academic Press, New York.

Kivikoski, E. (1967) *Finland*, Thames and Hudson, London.

Lanting, J. N. and Mook, W. G. (1977) *The Pre- and Protohistory of the Netherlands in Terms of Radiocarbon Dates*, Groningen.

Larsson, L. (1984a) 'The Skateholm project. A late mesolithic settlement and cemetery complex at a southern Swedish bay'. *Meddelånden från Lunds Universitetets Historiska Museum, New Series 5*, 5–38.

   (1984b) 'Gräberfelder und Siedlungen des Spätmesolithikums bei Skateholm, Südschonen, Schweden'. *Archäologisches Korrespondenzblatt* 14, 123–130.

L'Helgouach, J. (1971) 'Les débuts du néolithique en Armorique au quatrième millénaire et son développement au troisième millénaire', in J. Lüning, ed. *Die Anfänge des Neolithikums vom Orient bis Nordeuropa*, Teil VI, pp. 178–200, Fundamenta A3, Bohlau, Köln.

Louwe Kooijmans, L. P. (1974) 'The Rhine/Meuse delta. Four studies on its prehistoric occupation and holocene geology'. *Oudheidkundige Mededelingen* 53/54, 1–421.

   (1976) 'Local developments in a borderland. A survey of the neolithic at the lower Rhine'. *Oudheidkundige Mededelingen* 57, 227–97.

Luho, V. (1976) 'The population and prehistory of Finland', in P. Hajdu, ed., *Ancient Cultures of the Uralian Peoples*, pp. 115–35, Corvina, Budapest.

Lüttschwager, H. (1967) 'Kurzbericht über Tierfunde aus meso- und neolithischen Moorsiedlungen in Schleswig-Holstein'. *Schriften des Naturwissenschaftlichen Vereins für Schleswig-Holstein* 37, 53–64.

Lynch, A. (1981) *Man and Environment in SW Ireland*, BAR British Series, British Archaeological Reports, Oxford.

McLaren, I. (1962) 'Population dynamics and exploitation of seals in the eastern Canadian Arctic', in E. D. Le Cren and M. W. Holdgate, eds., *The Exploitation of Natural Animal Populations*, pp. 168–83, Blackwell, Oxford.

Madsen, T. (1977) 'Toftum ved Horsens, et "befaestet" anlaeag tilhørende Traegtbaegerkulturen'. [English summary.] *Kuml 1977*, 161–84.

   (1982) 'Settlement systems of early agricultural societies in East Jutland, Denmark: a regional study of change'. *Journal of Anthropological Archaeology* 1, 197–236.

Matyushin, G. T. (1976) *Mesolit Yuzhnogo Urala*, Nauka, Moscow.

Meehan, B. (1977) 'Man does not live by bread alone: the role of shellfish in a coastal cuisine', in J. Allen, J. Golston and R. Jones, eds., *Sunda and Sahul*, pp. 493–532, Academic Press, London.

Meinander, C. F. (1954) 'Die Kiukais-Kultur'. *Suomen Muinasimuistoyhdistyksen Aikakavskirja/Finska Förminnes-Foreningens Tidskrift* 53, 1–191.

   (1957) 'Kolsvidja'. *Suomen Muinasimuistoyhdistyksen Aikakavskivja/Finska Förminnes-Foreningens Tidskrift* 58, 185–213.

Mellars, P. (1976) 'Fire ecology, animal populations and man; a study of some ecological relationships in prehistory'. *Proceedings of the Prehistoric Society* 42, 15–45.

   (1978) 'Excavation and economic analysis of mesolithic shell middens on the island of Oronsay (Inner Hebrides)', in P. Mellars, ed., *The Early Postglacial Settlement of Northern Europe*, pp. 371–96, Duckworth, London.

Mellars, P. and Wilkinson, M. R. (1980) 'Fish otoliths as indicators of seasonality in prehistoric shell middens: the evidence from Oronsay (Inner Hebrides)'. *Proceedings of the Prehistoric Society* 46, 19–44.

Meurers-Balke, J. (1983) *Siggeneben-Süd. Ein Fundplatz der frühen Trichterbecherkultur an der holsteinischen Ostseeküste*, Offa Bücher 50, Karl Wachholtz, Neumünster.

Moberg, C. A. (1966) 'Spread of agriculture in the North European periphery'. *Science* 152, 315–19.

Modderman, P. J. R. (1974) 'Die Limburger Keramik von Kesseleyk'. *Archäologisches Korrespondenzblatt* 4, 5–11.

Møhl, U. (1978) 'Aggersund-bopladsen zoologisch belyst. Svanejagt som arsog till bosattelse?' [English Summary.] *Kuml*, 57–76.

Moore, J. (1981) 'The effects of information networks in hunter-gatherer societies', in B. Winterhalder and E. A. Smith eds., *Hunter-Gatherer Foraging Strategies*, pp. 194–217, University of Chicago Press, Chicago.

Morais Arnaud, J. (1982) 'Le Néolithique ancien et le processus de néolithisation au Portugal'. *Archéologie en Languedoc, No. Spéciale 1982*, 29–48.

Morales Muñiz, A. (1977) 'Análisis faunístico de Verdelpino (Cuenca)'. *Trabajos de Pre-historia* 34, 69–81.

Newell, R. R. (1970) 'The flint industry of the Dutch Linearbandkeramik'. *Analecta Praehistorica Leidensia* 3, 144–183.

Newell, R. R., Constandse-Westermann, T. S. and Meiklejohn, C. (1979) 'The skeletal remains of mesolithic man in western Europe: an evaluative catalogue'. *Journal of Human Evolution* 8, 1–228.

Nobis, G. (1962) 'Die Tierreste der prähistorischer Siedlungen aus den Satrupholmer Moor'. *Zeitschrift für Tierzüchtung und Züchtungsbiologie* 77, 16–30.

   (1971) 'Die Tierreste der prähistorischen Siedlung Sussau, Kr. Oldenburg (Schleswig-Holstein)'. *Schriften des Naturwissenschaft Vereins für Schleswig-Holstein* 41, 89–99.

Nuñez, M. G. and Vuorela, I. (1979) 'A tentative evaluation of cultural pollen data in early agrarian development research'. *Suomen Museo* 85 (1978), 5–36.

O'Shea, J. and Zvelebil, M. (1984) 'Oleneostrovski Mogilnik. Reconstructing the social and economic organisation of prehistoric foragers in northern Russia'. *Journal of Anthropological Archaeology* 3, 1–40.

O'Sullivan, P. E. (1976) 'Pollen analysis and radiocarbon dating of a core from Loch Pityoulish, Eastern Highlands of Scotland'. *Journal of Biogeography* 3, 293–302.

Osborn, A. (1977) 'Strandloopers, mermaids and other fairy tales: ecological determinants of marine resource utilisation', in L. Binford, ed., *For Theory Building in Archaeology*, pp. 157–205, Academic Press, New York.

Oshibkina, S. V. (1982) 'Mezoliticheskii mogilnik Popovo na reke Kineme'. *Sovetskaya Arkhaeologiya* 3, 123–31.

Oswalt, W. H. (1976) *An Anthropological Analysis of Food Getting Technology*, Academic Press, New York.

Paaver, K. C. (1965) *Formirovvaniye Teriofaunyi i Izmenchivost Mlekopytayushchikh Pribaltiki v Goltsene*, Akademiya Nauk Estonskoii SSR, Tartu.

Paludan-Müller, C. (1978) 'High Atlantic food gathering in northwestern Zealand, ecological conditions and spatial representation', in K. Kristiansen and C. Paludan-Müller, eds., *New Directions in Scandinavian Archaeology*, pp. 120–57, National Museum, Copenhagen.

Pennington, W. (1975) 'The effect of neolithic man on the environment in north-west England: the use of absolute pollen diagrams?', in J. G. Evans, S. Limbrey and H. Cleere, eds., *The Effect of Man on the Landscape: the Highland Zone*, pp. 74–86, Council for British Archaeology Research Report 11.

Perlman, S. (1980) 'An optimum diet model, coastal variability and nunter-gatherer behaviour', in M. Schiffer, ed., *Advances in Archaeological Method and Theory*, vol. 3, pp. 257–99, Academic Press, New York.

Pilcher, J. R. and Smith, A. G. (1979) 'Palaeoecological investigations at Ballynagilly, a neolithic and bronze age settlement in county Tyrone, Northern Ireland'. *Philosophical Transactions of the Royal Society, London,* series B, 268, 345–69.

Price, T. D. (1981) 'Swifterbant, Oost Flevoland, Netherlands: excavations at the river dune sites S21–S24, 1976. (Final Reports on Swifterbant III)'. *Palaeohistoria* 23, 75–104.

(1985) 'Affluent foragers of mesolithic southern Scandanavia', in T. D. Price and J. A. Brown, eds., *Prehistoric Hunter–Gatherers: The Emergence of Complexity,* pp. 341–65, Academic Press, New York and London.

Price, T. D. and Brown, J. A. (eds.) (1985) *Prehistoric Hunter-Gatherers: The Emergence of Complexity,* Academic Press, New York and London.

Rankine, W. F., Rankine, W. M. and Dimbleby, G. W. (1960) 'Further excavations at a mesolithic site at Oakhanger, Selborne, Hants'. *Proceedings of the Prehistoric Society* 26, 246–62.

Renouf, M. A. P. (1981) Prehistoric coastal economy in Varangerfjord, north Norway. Ph.D. dissertation, University of Cambridge.

(1984) 'Northern coastal hunter–fishers: an archaeological model'. *World Archaeology* 16, 18–27.

Roche, J. (1972a) *Le Gisement Mésolithique de Moita do Sebastião, Muge, Portugal,* second edn, Instituto de Alta Cultura, Lisbon.

(1972b) 'Les amas coquilliers (*concheiros*) mésolithiques de Muge (Portugal)', in J. Lüning, ed. *Die Anfänge des Neolithikums vom Orient bis Nordeuropa,* vol. VII, *Westliches Mittelmeergebiet und Britische Inseln,* pp. 72–107, Fundamenta A/3, Bohlau, Köln.

de Roever, J. P. (1976) 'Excavations at the River Dune sites S21–22. (Swifterbant Contributions 4)'. *Helinium* 16, 209–21.

(1979) 'The pottery from Swifterbant – Dutch Ertebølle? (Swifterbant Contributions 11)'. *Helinium* 19, 13–36.

Roussot-Larroque, J. (1977) 'Néolithisation et Néolithique ancien d'Aquitaine'. *Bulletin de la Société Préhistorique de France* 74, 559–82.

Roussot-Larroque, J. and Thevenin, A . (1981) 'Composantes méridionales et centroeuropéennes dans la dynamique de la néolithisation en France', In *Influences Méridionales dans l'Est et le Centre-est de la France au Néolithique: Le Role du Massif Central,* actes de Colloque Interrégional sur le Néolithique, pp. 109–147, Centre de Recherches et d'Etudes Préhistoriques de l'Auvergne, Cahier no. 1.

Rowley-Conwy, P. A. (1980) Continuity and change in the prehistoric economies of Denmark, 3700–2300 bc. Ph.D. thesis, University of Cambridge.

(1981) 'Mesolithic Danish bacon: permanent and temporary sites in the Danish mesolithic', in A. Sheridan and G. Bailey, eds., *Economic Archaeology,* pp. 51–5, BAR International Series 96, British Archaeological Reports, Oxford.

(1983) 'Sedentary hunters: the Ertebølle example', in G. N. Bailey, ed., *Hunter-Gatherer Economy in Prehistory,* pp. 111–26, Cambridge University Press, Cambridge.

(1984a) 'Postglacial foraging and early farming economies in Japan and Korea: a west European perspective'. *World Archaeology* 16, 28–42.

(1984b) 'The laziness of the short-distance hunter: the origins of agriculture in western Denmark'. *Journal of Anthropological Archaeology* 3, 300–324.

(1985a) 'Middle neolithic economies in Denmark and southern England and the faunal evidence from Fannerup, East Jutland'. *Kuml,* in press.

(1985b) 'The origins of agriculture in Denmark: a review of some theories'. *Journal of Danish Archaeology,* 4, 188–195.

Rowley-Conwy, P. A. and Zvelebil, M. (1987) Saving it for later: storage among high-latitude hunter-gatherers. In O'Shea, J. and Halstead, P., Eds.: *Bad Year Economics; Cultural Responses to Risk and Uncertainty,* Cambridge University Press, Cambridge (in press).

Salo, U. and Lahtiperä, P. (1970) *Metallikautinen Asutus Kokemäenjoen Suussa,* [German summary: Die metallzeitliche Besiedlung und der Mündung des Flusses Kokemäenjoki], pp. 1–219, Satakuntan Museon Kannatusyhdistys Pori.

Scarre, C. (1983) 'The Neolithic of west-central France', in C. Scarre, ed., *Ancient France,* p. 223–270, Edinburgh University Press, Edinburgh.

Schwabedissen, H. (1966) 'Ein horizontier Breitkeil aus Satrup und die Manninfachen Kulturverbindungen des Beginn den Neolitikums im Norden und Nordwesten'. Palaeohistoria 12, 409–68.

(1979a) 'Die 'Rosenhof-Gruppe'. Ein neuer Fund-komplex des Frühneolithikums in Schleswig-Holstein'. *Archäologisches Korrespondenzblatt* 9, 167–72.

(1979b) 'Der Beginn des Neolithikums in nordwestlichen Deutschland' in H. Schirnig, ed., *Grosssteingräber in Niedersachsen,* pp. 202–222, August Lay, Hildesheim.

Serjeantson, D. (1985) Sheep in the mesolithic? The animal bone from mesolithic Farnham reconsidered. unpublished MS.

Siiriäinen, A. (1981) 'On the cultural ecology of the Finnish Stone Age'. *Suomen Museo* 87, 5–40 (1980).

(1982a) 'Jordbruket i Finland under stenäldern: an arkeologisk kommentar', in T. Sjøvold, ed., *Intro. Av Jordbruk i Norden,* pp. 215–28, Oslo.

(1982b) 'Recent studies on the Stone Age economy in Finland'. *Fennoscandia Antiqua* 1, 17–26.

Simmons, I. G. (1969) 'Evidence for vegetation changes associated with mesolithic man in Britain', in P. J. Ucko and G. W. Dimbleby, eds., *The Domestication and Exploitation of Plants and Animals,* pp. 111–19, Duckworth, London.

(1979) 'Late mesolithic societies and the environment of the uplands of England and Wales'. *Institute of Archaeology Bulletin* 16, 111–29.

Sims, R. E. (1973) 'The anthropogenic factor in East Anglian vegetational history: an approach using A. P. F. techniques', in H. J. B. Birks and R. G. West, eds., *Quaternary Plant Ecology,* pp. 223–36, Blackwell, Oxford.

(1978) 'Man and vegetation in Norfolk', in S. Limbrey and J. G. Evans, eds., *The Effect of Man on the Landscape: the Lowland Zone,* pp. 57–62.

Skaarup, J. (1973) *Hesselø – Sølager. Jagdstationen der Südskandinavischen Trichterbecherkultur,* Arkaeologiske Studier 1, Akademisk Forlag, Copenhagen.

(1982) 'Siedlungs- und Wirtschaftsstrukturen der Trichterbecherkulture in Dänemark'. *Offa* 39, 39–52.

Smith, A. G. (1970) 'The influence of mesolithic and neolithic man on British vegetation: a discussion', in D. Walker and R. G. West, eds., *The Vegetational History of the British Isles,* pp. 81–96, Cambridge University Press, Cambrige.

(1981) 'The neolithic', in I. G. Simmons and M. Tooley, eds., *The Environment in British Prehistory,* pp. 125–8, 133–83, 199–209, Duckworth, London.

Spencer, R. F. (1959) *The North Alaskan Eskimo,* Smithsonian Institution/Bureau of American Ethnology, Bulletin 197.

Spratt, D. A. and Simmons I. G. (1976) 'Prehistoric activity and environment on the North York Moors'. *Journal of Archaeological Science* 3, 193–210.

Stark, B. and Voorhies, B. (1978) *Prehistoric Coastal Adaptations,* Academic Press, New York.

Straus, L. (1979) 'Mesolithic adaptations along the northern coast of Spain'. *Quaternaria* 21, 305–27.

Straus, L. and Clark, G. A. (1983) 'Further reflections on adaptive change in Cantabrian prehistory', in G. Bailey, ed., *Hunter-gatherer Economy in Prehistory,* pp. 166–8, Cambridge University Press, Cambridge.

Straus, L., Altuna, J., Clark, G. A., González, M., Laville, H., Leroi-Gourhan, A., Méndez, M. and Ortea, J. (1981) 'Palaeoecology at

La Riera (Asturias, Spain)'. *Current Anthropology* 22, 655–82.

Straus, L., Clark, G. A., Altuna, J. and Ortea, J. (1980) 'Ice-age subsistence in northern Spain'. *Scientific American* 242(6), 142–53.

Switsur, V. R. and Jacobi, R. M. (1979) 'A radiocarbon chronology for the early postglacial stone industries of England and Wales', in R. Berger and H. E. Suess, eds., *Radiocarbon Dating*, pp. 41–68, University of California Press, Berkeley.

Tauber, H., (1972) 'Radiocarbon chronology of the Danish mesolithic and neolithic'. *Antiquity* 46, 106–110.

(1982) 'Carbon-13 evidence for the diet of prehistoric humans in Denmark' *PACT* 7, 235–7.

Testart, A. (1982) *Les Chasseurs-Cueilleurs ou L'Origine des Inégalités*, Société d'Ethnographie, Paris.

Tolonen, K., Siiriäinen, A. and Hirviluoto, A. (1979) 'Iron Age cultivation in S. W. Finland'. *Finskt Museum* 83, 5–66 (1976).

Torrence, R. (1983) 'Time-budgeting and hunter-gatherer technology', in G. Bailey, ed., *Hunter-Gatherer Economy in Prehistory*, pp. 11–22, Cambridge University Press, Cambridge.

van der Waals, J. D. (1972) 'Die durchlochten Rössener Keile und das frühe Neolithikum in Belgien und in den Niederlanden', in J. Lüning, ed., *Die Anfänge des Neolithikums vom Orient bis Nordeuropa. Va, Westliches Mitteleuropa*, pp. 153–84, Fundamenta A/3, Böhlau, Köln.

(1977) 'Excavations at the natural levee sites S2, S3/5 and S4. (Swifterbant Contributions 6)'. *Helinium* 17, 3–27.

Vega del Sella, R. (1914) 'La cueva del Penicial (Asturias)', *Comisión de Investigaciones Paleontólogicas y Prehistóricas, Memoria 4*, Museo Nacional de Ciencias Naturales, Madrid.

(1923) 'El Asturiense, nueva industria Preneolítico'. *Comisión de Investigaciones Paleontológicas y Prehistóricas, Memoria 32*, Museo Nacional de Ciencias Naturales, Madrid.

(1930) 'Las cuevas de La Riera y Balmore'. *Comisión de Investigaciones Paleontológicas y Prehistóricas, Memoria 38*, Museo Nacional de Ciencias Naturales, Madrid.

Vencl, S. (1982) 'K Otázce zániku sberačsko – loveckých kultûr'. *Archeologické Rozhledy* 34, 648–94.

Vuorela, I. (1970) 'The indication of farming in pollen diagrams from S. Finland'. *Acta Botanica Fennica* 87, 1–40.

(1972) 'Human influence on the vegetation of the Katinhanta bog, Vihti, S. Finland'. *Acta Botanica Fennica* 98, 1–21.

(1975) 'Pollen analyses as a means of tracing settlement history in S. W. Finland'. *Acta Botanica Fennica* 104, 1–48.

(1976) 'An instance of slash and burn cultivation in S. Finland investigated by pollen analysis of a mineral soil'. *Mem. Soc. Flora Fauna Fenn.* 52, 29–45.

Walker, D. (1966) 'The late quaternary history of the Cumberland lowland'. *Philosophical Transactions of the Royal Society, Series B*, 251, 1–210.

Welinder, S. (1976) 'The economy of the Pitted Ware Culture in eastern Sweden'. *Meddelanden Fràn Lunds Universitets Historika Museum 1975–76*, new series, 1, 20–30.

(1981) 'The disappearance of a hunting-gathering economy', in B. Gramsch, ed., *Mesolithikum in Europa*, pp. 151–63, Springer Verlag, Berlin.

(1982) 'The hunting-gathering component of the central Swedish neolithic funnel-beaker culture (TRB) economy'. *Fornvännen* 77, 154–66.

(1983) 'Ecosystems change at the neolithic transition'. *Norwegian Archaeological Review* 16, 99–105.

Whallon, R. and Price, T. D. (1976) 'Excavations at the River Dune sites S11–13. (Swifterbant Contributions 5)'. *Helinium* 16, 222–9.

Winge H. (1900) Sections on faunal remains, in A. P. Madsen *et al.*, eds., *Affaldsdynger fra Stenalderen i Danmark*, Reitzel, Copenhagen.

Woodman, P. C. (1978) 'The chronology and economy of the Irish mesolithic: some working hypotheses', in P. Mellars, ed., *The Early Postglacial Settlement of Northern Europe*, pp. 333–70, Duckworth, London.

(1981a) 'The postglacial colonisation of Ireland: the human factors', in D. O'Corrain, ed., *Irish Antiquity*, pp. 93–110, Tara Books, Cork.

(1981b) 'Problems of the mesolithic survival in Ireland', in B. Gramsch, ed., *Mesolithikum in Europa*, pp. 201–10, Veröffentuchungen des Museums für Ur- und Frühgeschichte Potsdam 14/15, Deutscher Verlag, Berlin.

(1985) Settlement and environment in Irish prehistory', in W. Warren and K. Edwards, eds., *The Irish Quaternary*, pp. 251–79, Academic Press, New York.

Yesner, D. R. (1980) 'Maritime hunter-gatherers: ecology and prehistory'. *Current Anthropology* 21, 727–50.

(n.d.) Life in the 'Garden of Eden': causes and consequences of the adoption of marine diets by human societies. Unpublished paper available from the author.

Zagorski, F. (1973) 'Das spätmesolithikum in Lettland', in S. K. Kozlowski, ed., *The Mesolithic in Europe*, pp. 651–69, Warsaw University Press, Warsaw.

van Zeist, W. and Palfenier-Vegter, R. M. (1981) 'Seeds and fruits from the Swifterbant S3 site. (Final Reports on Swifterbant IV)'. *Palaeohistoria* 23, 105–68.

Zvelebil, M. (1978) 'Subsistence and settlement in the north-eastern Baltic' in P. Mellars, ed., *The Early Postglacial Settlement of Northern Europe*, pp. 205–242, Duckworth, London.

(1981) *From Forager to Farmer in the Boreal Zone: Reconstructing Economic Patterns through Catchment Analysis in Prehistoric Finland*, BAR International Series 115 (I and II), British Archaeological Reports, Oxford.

Zvelebil, M. and Rowley-Conwy, P., 1984) 'Transition to farming in northern Europe: a hunter-gatherer perspective'. *Norwegian Archaeological Review* 17, 104–28.

Chapter 7

Foragers of Central Europe and their acculturation

Janusz K. Kozłowski and Stefan K. Kozłowski

Introduction
Objectives
The present work is an attempt at evaluating the process of neolithisation of Central Europe from the perspective of the mid Holocene hunter-gatherer communities. The authors assume that by reconstructing the environmental and demographic conditions in which the mesolithic/epipalaeolithic communities lived, it will be possible to assess the potential for the transition to farming and to the neolithic way of life in general. At the same time we are evaluating the ecological and demographic conditions of the early neolithic peoples. The picture that is emerging from these considerations is that of two reluctantly interacting socio-economic and cultural systems, with the latter of the two, although seemingly superior and certainly more effective, not becoming dominant in Central Europe until a period of extended co-existence between the two cultures has taken place.

In considering the development of postglacial hunter-gatherer adaptations and the transition to farming, three aspects of the process deserve special attention:

(*a*) The survey of those developments among the mid-Holocene hunter-gatherers which were aimed at optimising the traditional system of economic exploitation of the environment.

(*b*) The examination of the potential for the adoption of the food-producing economy by these communities.

(*c*) Analysis of the role of the aboriginal and intrusive factors in this process, and hence of the continuity and discontinuity between the Mesolithic/Epipalaeolithic and the Neolithic.

The Scope
The present study covers the area from the Baltic to the Balkans and from the Elbe to the Dnieper, the reasons for this delimitation being:

(*a*) The considerable ecological and cultural differentiation of the Mesolithic/Epipalaeolithic of this region.

(*b*) The presence in the Early Neolithic of a common trend unifying cultural and economic relations in most of this area and gradually eliminating the previous structures of the hunter-gatherer culture.

(*c*) The existence of communities following their own course of development in the mid Holocene at the periphery of the region ('protoneolithic and para-neolithic' processes).

The lower chronological limit for this study is set at *c.* 6000 bc (the boundary of the boreal and the atlantic periods), a time of serious ecological and cultural changes. The upper chronological limit is set for the southern part of the region at *c.* 4700 bc, and for the north at 3500–3000 bc: the time of the full transition to farming in the western part of the North-European Plain.

In this chapter, only some elements of the natural environment can be reconstructed, such as the vegetational cover and the fauna, the reconstruction of other aspects being precluded by the inadequacy of primary sources. The archaeological evidence is also somewhat limited in the case of the Mesolithic/Epipalaeolithic. The present situation can be characterised as follows:

(i)   Material culture is usually reduced to lithics; the uneven survey of the region hinders the reconstruction of the settlement pattern; a scarcity of radiocarbon dates hampers precise dating of sites; there are few direct archaeological remains enabling the reconstruction of the environment around the separate sites.

(ii) The Neolithic is represented to a slightly greater extent.

(iii) Material culture traces are augmented by ceramics; the distributions of sites in the area are more uniform; radiocarbon dates are also more plentiful; and the faunal remains are far more numerous than for the mesolithic period. However, there are neither palynological nor botanical remains from the sites themselves.

Terminology

Traditional terminology tends to be vague in its meaning of 'Mesolithic', 'Epipalaeolithic' and 'Neolithic', which are often used interchangeably with 'hunter-gatherer economy' or 'food-producing economy'. A brief discussion, which would qualify the most important terms used in this paper, is therefore required (cf. also Kozłowski and Kozłowski 1978).

As Grahame Clark has pointed out (Clark 1962, pp. 109; 1980, pp. 93–104) the Mesolithic cannot be defined on cultural grounds alone, nor can it be seen as a mere 'transition stage' between the Palaeolithic and the Neolithic. Rather, the Mesolithic is defined by several aspects: the chronological (duration from 8000 to 4500–4350 bc), the ecological (postglacial adaptation caused by the replacement of tundra by forest formations), the economical (hunter-fisher-gatherer economy, the share of each specialised activity depending on the type of ecological niche), and the cultural (microlithisation and partly also geometric standardisation of the lithic industry). In our view, this is a period characterised by small-scale changes, as if the mesolithic communities of the early and mid Holocene awaited the major step of the transition to farming. This period of anticipation could have been very long in certain areas, such as Siberia or Canada, or relatively short, as in Europe. The Mesolithic is confined to those regions which saw a drastic environmental change at the turn of the Pleistocene and the Holocene.

The Epipalaeolithic is defined chronologically (as lasting from 8000 to 5000–4500 bc), economically (continuation of the late palaeolithic hunter-gatherer system of Southern Europe), and culturally (continuation of elements typical for the local Late Palaeolithic). It is connected with areas which did not undergo serious ecological changes at the turn of the Pleistocene and the Holocene.

The dividing line between the Mesolithic and Epipalaeolithic is not one of a strictly territorial character. Cultural changes and the oscillation of ecological zones, particularly from the sixth millennium bc, resulted in the integration of both cultural adaptations.

The term 'Paraneolithic' refers to pottery-using hunter-gatherers. The material culture is characterised by a lithic industry nearly identical with that of the Mesolithic or the Epipalaeolithic and by the manufacture of ceramics. This is a phase of more stable settlement. The chipped-stone industry has a more limited range of microliths.

The Neolithic is primarily defined by the preponderance of the food-producing economy: agriculture and animal husbandry. The presence of ceramics and polished tools is not essential. Consequently, we distinguish the aceramic and the ceramic Neolithic.

The Protoneolithic is characterised by certain elements of animal husbandry (less frequently of agriculture) being present within a predominantly food-gathering economy (Benac 1978, pp. 9–19; 1980, pp. 35–48).

Ecology
Vegetation cover

The reconstruction of vegetational cover is based on pollen analyses, much more numerous in the north than in the south, as well as the geomorphological and palaeopedological studies which make it possible to extrapolate palynological results to regions for which such data are not available. Figure 1 presents the generalised floristic situation in the first half of the atlantic period. It is based chiefly on the studies of F. Firbas (1949–51, p. 321), M. Dabrowski (1959, p. 244), M. J. Neushtadt (1957) and P. M. Dolukhanov (1979, Figs. 20, 29, 58).

The area under investigation may be divided into three large phytogeographical provinces: (a) the Mediterranean, characterised by the oak forests of mediterranean type and clear vertical differentiation of vegetational zones (Dinaric Mountains, Adriatic coast, east Balkans); (b) the Carpathian or Danubian basin flanked by the Alps, the Carpathians and the Dinaric Mountains and covered by steppe-forest; (c) the North-European Plain, characterised by a dense forest cover. The last of these provinces is internally differentiated: east of the Polish–Russian border, broadleaf forests of continental type occur, their density decreasing to the southeast, while to the west maritime-type broadleaf forests with *Ulmus*, *Alnus*, *Quercus* and *Pinus* predominated during the Atlantic.

To complete the above description we must mention the woodlands of the river valleys which created environments particularly attractive to holocene hunters and gatherers.

Apart from the climatic and soil conditions responsible for the character of the vegetation, human settlement was an important factor affecting the degree of forestation and biocenose shape. Anthropogenic vegetation changes were first of all results of deforestation connected with man's economic activity. At this point in the Mesolithic, fire might have been employed as an agent of deforestation, although this

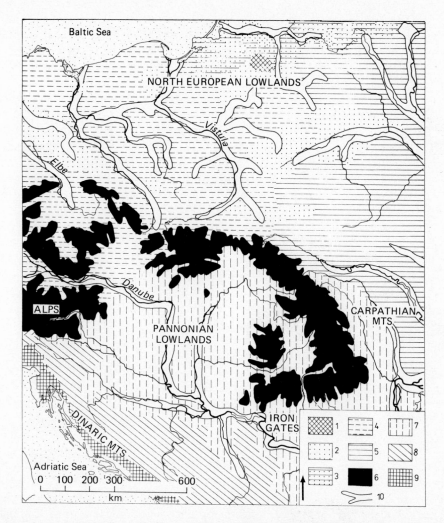

Fig. 1. Principal vegetation zones in the first half of the atlantic period (according to Firbas (1949–51) and Dolukhanov (1979), reviewed by M. Dabrowski personal communication). 1, Taiga; 2, mixed coniferous forest; 3, mixed deciduous forest; 4, deciduous forests of the maritime type 5, continental-type deciduous forests; 6, mountain vegetation; 7, steppe-forest; 8, oak forest in the mountains; 9, mediterranean-type deciduous forests; 10, river valley woods.

phenomenon is usually related to the appearance of plants indicative of land cultivation (cereals and weeds) and pasturing (*Plantago lanceolata*). The environs of settlements are characterised by the presence of synanthropic plants (Chenopodiacae, *Artemisia* and *Rumex*). Clearances by burning were quickly overgrown, particularly by *Pteridium aquilinum* (Mamakowa 1965; Ralska-Jasiewiczowa 1977; Kruk 1980). It is intriguing to speculate whether the mesolithic peoples could have utilised the grain of uncultivated grasses. The presence of Gramineae pollen in coprolites from Vlasac and Icoana proves, according to some researchers, the economic importance of grasses (Carciumaru 1973, 1978); some of the Gramineae pollen are almost as large as the pollen of Cerealia. In the case of Vlasac, however, we are not certain about the connection of the coprolites with the epipalaeolithic layer. In Icoana, on the other hand, the amount of Cerealia pollen is tiny, no more than a 1% fraction of the total. There are no wild ancestors of cereals in holocene phytocenoses of Central Europe, while in the Balkans only *Triticum*

monococcum may have had its progenitor in the locally occurring *Triticum aegilopoides* var. *Thauder*. Other species of wheat and barley occurring with einkorn are of unquestionably Middle-Eastern origin (Lisitsyna and Filipovich 1980).

Fauna

The faunal data come from both mesolithic/epipalaeolithic and early neolithic archaeological sites. To summarise this evidence, the following patterns can be discerned (Figure 2):

(*a*)   In the zone of the western and southern Balkans the most frequently occurring animals are red deer and roe deer, with less numerous wild boar.

(*b*)   In the valleys of the central Balkans and the Pannonian Lowland we find mainly red deer and aurochs, with fewer wild boar and roe deer bones represented.

(*c*)   The sites in the Danube estuary contain large numbers of equines.

(*d*)   Sites in the uplands extending from the Iron Gates,

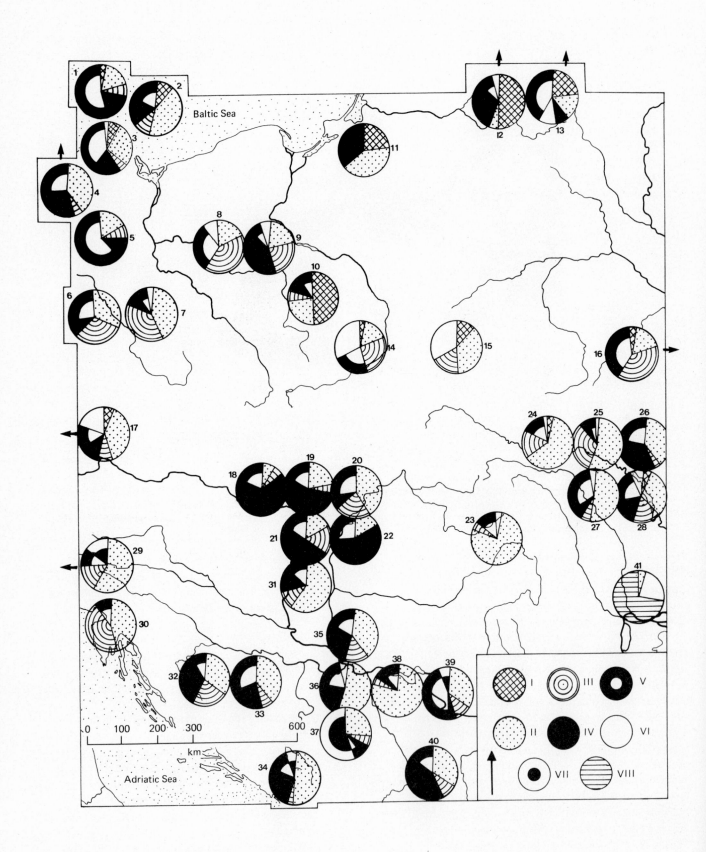

through Transylvania and eastern Carpathians to the east of Moldavia are marked by the dominance of red deer and, to a lesser extent, wild boar and roe deer, the latter less numerous in the foothills.

(*e*) The sites in the northwest part of the North-European Lowland are characterised by the dominance of red deer. wild boar and aurochs with the presence of roe deer;

(*f*) The sites in the northeast part of the lowland are dominated by elk remains, with some presence of red deer and wild boar.

Territories lying between the above-mentioned regions (the river basins of the Elbe, the Oder and the Vistula, Lithuania and Podlasia) had a variable composition of fauna, although wild boar and red deer were always present.

Naturally, other large mammals (wolf, brown bear, lynx) and small mammals were also hunted (Murray 1970, pp. 330–50; Clason 1977, pp. 166–81; Jarman 1972, Figs. 1, 2 and Appendix 1; Brinch Petersen 1973, pp. 106–10), and so were birds; fish (a dozen or so species) and molluscs (*c.* 10 species) were also gathered.

It has been suggested by some scholars (Jarman 1972, pp. 83–96; Barker 1973, pp. 359–70) that early postglacial hunter-gatherers controlled the herds of red deer and practised deliberate selective hunting or even herding. Although some sort of herd control may have been possible, we have no means of verifying this hypothesis. Even if there had been attempts to domesticate the deer, this did not contribute to the subsequent neolithic economy of Central Europe. The local domestication of caprines, on the other hand, can be ruled out in Central Europe with certainty, because of the absence in this area of the ancestors of domesticated sheep and goat.

The easiest to accept is the local domestication of wild boar (David and Markevich 1970). Wild boar is easily domesticated but it also readily reverts to the wild state. Central-European sites (Fig. 2), particularly east of the Carpathians and in the northwest part of the lowland, abound in both wild boar and pig remains. There are, however, taxonomic difficulties in distinguishing between the bones of the wild and the domesticated species. An example of local domestication of wild boar can be observed in layer 3 of Soroki II on the River Dniester, dated to 5570 ± 120 bc (Markevich 1974).

Also possible, but as yet not demonstrated, is the local domestication of aurochs based on local populations of this animal. Their remains are particularly numerous in the Pannonian Lowland and in the valleys of the central Balkans (Fig. 2). Markevich (1974) regards as possible the presence of domesticated aurochs in the preceramic layer 2 of Soroki II (5470 ± 120 bc). These considerations indicate that some mesolithic/epipalaeolithic communities could have engaged in initial domestication relatively early, adopting, on a small scale, elements of pig or cattle husbandry. In such a case their economies would assume a protoneolithic character.

The relief

The relief of the area under investigation features land barriers in the form of uplands and mountains which seriously affect the possibilities of communication and contact. A particularly isolating influence was exerted by the Carpathian and by the Bohemian mountain ranges, both of which acted as an effective barrier to the penetration of the mesolithic 'cultures' from the north to areas south of the mountains. In the case of the eastern Carpathians, this cultural dichotomy continued in the Neolithic (Kozłowski 1974, pp. 5–56).

The situation in the Balkans was also conditioned by the system of intramontane valleys, which in the west (Dinaric Mountains) were arranged roughly meridionally, thus facili-

---

Fig. 2. Shows diagrams of percentages concerning the big game species (number of bones), according to data provided by the archaeological sites (mesolithic, epipalaeolithic, neolithic) dated to the sixth–fifth millennium bc south of the Carpathians and to the sixth–fourth millennium bc in the north (according to S. K. Kozłowski). Each diagram presents the sum of all the bones from the archaeological sites within 100 km² units.

I, *Alces alces*; II, *Cervus elaphus*; III, *Cervus capreolus*; IV, *Bos primigenius*; V, *Sus scrofa*; VI, *Equus caballus*; VII, Capridae (*Rupicapra ibex*); VIII, *Equus hydruntinus*.

1. Norslund, Ringkloster, Dyrholmen (all in Denmark). 2. Ageröd I:B, I:D, V (Sweden). 3. Bodenbrück, Rüde, Pinnberg (all in the German Federal Republic). 4. Ellerbek (Denmark). 5. Ballenstedt, Barleben–Hühnerfarm, Barleben–Schweine Masterei, Barleben–Schweine, Königsaue, Hausneindorf, Gatersleben (all in the German Democratic Republic). 6. Bruchstedt, Schlotheim, Reiser, Körner, Sonderhausen, Hohlstedt, Tröbsdorf, Rossleben (all in the German Democratic Republic). 7. Hainichen, Zorbau, Wulfen, Kóthen–Genz, Halle–Trotha–Brachwitzer Str., Dammendorf, Mücheln, Weimar–Ehringsdorf, Erfurt–Stolzestr, Erfurt–Steiger (all in the German Democratic Republic). 8. Poznań–Debiec (Poland). 9. Koscielec Kujawski, Lojewo, Miechowice, Inowroclaw–Matwy, Strzelce, Broniewice 1/8 i 1/11 + 1/18, Krusza Zamkowa 3/318, 3/400 + 30/1, 2, 3/576, 3/636 (all in Poland). 10. Janisławice (Poland). 11. Pierkunowo (Poland). 12. Zvejnieki (USSR). 13. Osa (USSR). 14. Ćmielów (Poland). 15. Gródek (Poland). 16. Buzki (USSR). 17. Danube sites. 18. Neszmély–Tekeres Patak, Györ–Papai Vam (both in Hungary), Lużianki, Mlynarce (both in Czekoslovakia). 19. Pilismarót–Szobi Rév, Pomáz–Zdravlyák, Jászberény–Cserö–Halom, Békásmegyer–Vörös–Csiliag Tsz (all in Hungary). 20. Tiszaszöllös–Csakanyszeg, Aggtelek–Baradla Barlang, Borsod–Derekegyhazi Dülö, Folias–Szilmeg (all in Hungary). 21. Szagvar–Tuskoves, Maroslele–Pana, Hödmezövásárhely–Bodzaspart (all in Hungary). 22. Lebö (Hungary). 23. Traian–Dealul Viei, Traian–Dealul Fîntinilor (both in Romania). 24. Luka Vrublevetskaya, Bernove, Lenkivici (all in the USSR). 25. Soroki – different sites, Cikinovka (all in the USSR). 26. Floreshty (USSR). 27. Valea Lupului, Pogoresti (both in Romania). 28. Soloncene, Novi Ruseşti (both in the USSR). 29. Vatte di Zambana, Pradestel, Romagnano (all in Italy). 30. Grotta Benussi (Italy). 31. Röszke–Ludvar (Hungary). 32. Ludas-Budzsak (Yugoslavia). 33. Obre (Yugoslavia). 34. Crvena Stijena (Yugoslavia). 35. Sajan-Jaros (Yugoslavia). 36. Starčevo (Yugoslavia). 37. Odmut (Yugoslavia). 38. Divostin, Padina, Lepenski Vir, Vlasac (all in Yugoslavia). 39. Icoana (Yugoslavia). 40. Anza (Yugoslavia). 41. Bolgrad (USSR).

tating north—south contacts; in the rest of the region, however, the east—west orientation of the valleys limited contacts in the north—south direction.

As a result we can observe, in the early postglacial, several lowland zones separated from one another by mountain chains which were difficult to negotiate; within these separate zones the communication was of course relatively simple. It was only in the Early Neolithic that more extensive use was made of the north—south communication routes such as the Vardar, Morava and Struma valleys, the Iron, Moravian and Klodzko Gates, the Carpathian passes, and the Elbe valley.

Hydrography

The transgressions of the atlantic period caused the flooding of the Baltic shelf, forcing the people of the Maglemosian tradition to move to the extensive interior of the North-European Plain. The marine transgression in the Adriatic, on the other hand, cut off the populated coastal islands from the mainland, so that the main area of settlement centred on a narrow sea-coast zone.

It was the river network and the hydrographic regime of the river valleys, however, which played the greatest role in the location of settlement. In our region we may distinguish four provinces from the point of view of hydrography:

(a) The Baltic coastal zone in which the river network is connected with a system of postglacial lakes and often extends to relatively inaccessible and poorly drained moraine hills.

(b) The North-European Lowland zone with a well-developed river system determined by east—west oriented subglacial stream valleys and meridional stretches of medium-sized rivers with numerous small tributaries.

(c) The intra-Carpathian region together with areas to the east of the Carpathians with great rivers separated by interfluvial areas with only a few watercourses.

(d) The west-Balkan Karst area, also relatively dry.

The turn of the boreal and atlantic periods saw a marked increase in river activity with the correspondingly sharp increase of river bed depth. This resulted in the formation of the low river terraces convenient for settlement (Starkel 1977, pp. 223—51).

Lithic sources

The distribution of lithic sources, notably of fine crystalline rocks, is not even throughout our region. Areas north and east of the Carpathians are characterised by numerous deposits of various flints (Cyrek 1981, p. 10; Welinder 1973, p. 592; Ginter and Kozłowski 1975, p. 29), whereas the Carpathian area (not counting the Bükk Mountains, with their obsidian) is rich only in low-quality raw materials such as hornstone, radiolarites and limnoquartzites (Kaczanowska 1984). The nearest area rich in excellent flints and radiolarites can be found in the northern Balkans.

Although in the Mesolithic and the Epipalaeolithic the

share of imported lithic materials is not very large (the exception here being the Janisławician culture), the situation changed in the Early Neolithic. Good-quality raw materials began to be systematically imported, often from fairly distant deposits. The interesting point is that the early neolithic peoples, such as the Linear Pottery culture in Poland, did not always exploit the chipped-stone deposits themselves: they used the flint mined by the mesolithic people (Kozłowski and Kozłowski 1977, p. 263). On the one hand this is shown by the cultural attributes of the flint tools from the Janisławician cultural context, and on the other by the lack of early Linear flint mines of 'chocolate' flint, even though this flint was frequently used by the early Linear Pottery groups in southern Poland.

The archaeology of the postglacial hunter-gatherers

We can now present the basic information on the 'cultural' differentiation (Kozłowski 1975, pp. 39—76) within the ecological zones outlined above, providing data on the origin, chronology, settlement and economy of the separate traditions (Kozłowski and Kozłowski 1975, maps 6 and 16) (Fig. 3).

(a) The Balkans and the Carpathian basin. During the atlantic period, these regions were populated by epi-palaeolithic people with the lithic tradition rooted in the local late glacial Tardigravettian culture. A local modification of this tradition developed in the Iron Gates, known as the Lepenski Vir culture (dated to the turn of the seventh and sixth millennia bc). People of the Lepenski Vir type inhabited large permanent settlements, set up in 30—70 m stretches along large river valleys and consisting of stone, trapeze-shaped houses several dozen in number. The hunting economy was based on the exploitation of red deer, wild boar, small mammals (12 species in all) and birds (13 species); on plant gathering (grasses) and fishing (four species, but very numerous bonds; Bökönyi 1978, p. 36).

(b) The littoral and the mountain region of the Dinaric Alps forms the province of another local tradition: the early postglacial 'Sauveterrian' culture, was succeeded at c. 6000 bc by the Castelnovian, which in turn evolved into the local Impressed Ware culture by adding Cardial ware to the local lithic tradition at c. 5000 bc. Settlement occurred in caves in narrow mountain valleys and later in dense open settlements. The hundreds of artefacts in thick layers contrast with the paucity of solid structures or occupation floors. In our view this would suggest repeated, short-term occupations by a small, mobile population. The broad-based economy included the exploitation of red deer, wild boar, and roe deer, and of caprines in the mountains, shellfish gathering, and fishing.

(c) The area between the Carpathians and the Dniester was occupied by the people of the Grebenikian culture from 6000 bc to the emergence of the protoneolithic phase of

Fig. 3. Mesolithic/epipalaeolithic settlement pattern in the period 8000–3500 bc (according to S. K. Kozłowski). 1, 1–5 sites; 2, 5–50 sites; 3, upwards of 50 sites; 4, mountain areas.

the Bug–Dniester culture around 5500 bc. Small, open camps measuring from several metres to 20 m diameter were located in large river valleys. The camp architecture consisted of oval dug-outs and above-ground huts of up to 6 m diameter. The economy was based on hunting red deer, wild boar, aurochs, roe deer, small mammals and birds (6 species of each), plant gathering and collecting, molluscs (9 species) and freshwater fishing (10 species) (Markevich 1974, faunal tables).

(d)   On the uplands around the western Carpathians, we can record the presence of the Beuron–Coincy culture at the beginning of the atlantic period; but the information is lacking for later times. The remains of red deer, roe deer, wild boar, small mammals and also hazel nuts (cf. Jochim 1976, pp. 148–70; Hahn 1983) suggest a hunting and gathering strategy, typical of the temperate European interior. Other cultural influences were also observed in the region.

(*e*) The western part of the North-European Plain was settled by Maglemosian groups (Jühnsdorf, Chojnice, Pienki) which partly owe their origin to immigration from southern Scandinavia. Further east, the Janisławician culture occupied the area of central and eastern Poland. Radiocarbon dating and the presence of trapezes date these post-maglemosian groups into the atlantic period. Large (more than 30 m in diameter) and small camps were concentrated on sandy terraces in river valleys, and around lakes in the northern part of the lowland. The sites consist of huts occurring singly or in small groups of two or three. As in other parts of temperate Europe, the economy was based on hunting red deer, wild boar, aurochs and roe deer, gathering acorns and hazel nuts, and on freshwater fishing, the latter requiring a specialised toolkit of nets and harpoons (Clark 1975, pp. 99–146). Larsson (1978, pp. 209–13), in his study of post-maglemosian sites in Scania, identified a similar range of food resources.

(*f*) The littoral zone of the western Baltic was occupied at this time by the mesolithic Kongemose culture (*c.* 6000–*c.* 4600 bc) and by its off-spring, the Ertebølle culture. Both cultures are characterised by large, probably permanent settlements on the sea coast, and less frequently, inland. The economy was based on a combination of hunting the usual range of land-based mammals and of sealing. Moreover, the Ertebølle exploited a wider range of smaller resources and small mammals (25 species for Ertebølle, 14 for the Kongemose), birds (45 and 12 species, respectively), fish (14 and 6 species, respectively), plants and molluscs (9 and 1 mollusc species, respectively) than Kongemose or other groups. Hazel nuts, which occur in the cultural deposits of the Danish Late Mesolithic, are also worth noting (Brinch Petersen 1973, pp. 106–10). Although both Kongemose and Ertebølle were heavily oriented towards the marine environment, the Ertebølle groups exploited it more thoroughly than did the Kongemose; in the material culture, this is shown by the finds of bone points, harpoons, fish hooks, basket traps and net floats.

(*g*) In the ease of the European Lowland, deciduous forests of continental type were inhabited by the people of the Janisławician and the Kudlaevka cultures. The chronology of both assemblages is based on the presence of trapezes and a small number of radiocarbon dates. There is some evidence that the Janisławice groups used pottery. Extensive Janisławician settlements are located on river valley terraces, where large camps (20 m in diameter) with multiple artefact concentrations are found alongside small settlements with single occupation layers. The hunting economy is based on the exploitation of elk, red deer and wild boar (Dolukhanov 1979, pp. 174–7).

(*h*) The northeast was occupied by another group, the 'Niemen culture', which had its origins in the Swiderian complexes of Lithuania, Bielorussia and Estonia. These people, too, in the their final stages, used pottery, although the economy was based exclusively on hunting (elk, red deer and wild boar), nut gathering and fishing (Rimantiéne 1971, pp. 165–72). Dense settlement, consisting of moderately large camps, was concentrated mainly in river valleys.

Settlement pattern and density

Figure 3 presents the network of the postglacial hunter-gatherer settlement drawn on the basis of all the sources available to the authors. We can immediately observe that there are large differences in settlement density between the northern and the southern zones. In the latter we have no more than 50–60 inventories, the site density being less than one in 10 000 km^2 (3850 m^2), or 0.007/100 km^2. In Denmark, the comparable figure is 0.516 sites per 100 km^2 and in Lithuania, 0.121/100 km^2. Such differences in settlement density may be only partly explained by the poor research in the southern region. After all, we know from that area numerous early neolithic settlements. The differences are most probably caused by the significant contrasts in the river networks. If, as we argued above, settlement was closely tied to river valleys, with rich woodland, then the total length of rivers, much greater in the north, should correlate with the density of the mesolithic/epipalaeolithic settlement. While in the north, the interfluves are at most 30 km wide, and present no obstacle to the information flow, in the south, such areas can be as much as 100 km wide, thus separating rather than bridging the epipalaeolithic settlement. As a result, the northern system was bound to be more resistant to neolithic acculturation than the southern one, particularly during the progressive reforestation in the atlantic period.

As already stated, settlement was usually confined to a river valley occupying chiefly the lower terraces. Basing their argument on ethnographic parallels, Newell (1973, pp. 399–428) and Price (1981, pp. 217–34) maintain that each mesolithic/epipalaeolithic group practised varied economic activities within its own specific territory, reflected in the settlement pattern by the existence of larger and smaller base-camps, some permanent, which were surrounded by seasonally occupied satellite camps. The latter are supposedly characterised by tool inventories poorer than those of base-camps. In winter the camps could have been connected with big-game hunting and in summer with fishing and gathering. Whatever the case, the mobility of the postglacial food gatherers must have been confined to a strictly defined territorial range, as indicated by the local raw material composition of their flint

industries (Cyrek 1981, p. 10). The shift to a greater permanence of settlement within a given area, on the other hand,
is indicated in the late mesolithic period by the existence of
cemeteries from those times (Vedbaek, Skateholm I and II,
Zvejnieki, Vlasac I–III). These were sometimes situated within
the actual campsites themselves. The cemeteries usually contain the remains of several generations.

As to the population density in the separate ecosystems,
we find that the so-called net dry biomass yield in northern
deciduous and mixed forests is on the average higher (*c*. 1300
g/m^2 per year; cf. E. R. Pianka 1981) than the corresponding
yield of the steppe-forest (over 700 g/m^2 per year). The
situation in the animal world is the reverse – the steppe-forest
is certainly the more affluent environment. On the other hand,
ethnological data obtained from the Canadian Indians indicate
a population density for the boreal forest of 0.2–0.8 people
per km^2, and that of the mixed deciduous forest as 1–2
people per km^2 (Stoczkowski 1983). Other authors (Kroeber
1963, tables 7–8) give higher figures: 0.75–2 for the boreal
forest and 5–12 for the temperate forest, and 2–5 for the
steppe-forest, respectively. Whichever of these estimates is
true, we can see that the population density in the zone of
deciduous and mixed deciduous forest is clearly greater than in
the steppe-forest. Hence we can justifiably believe that the
epipalaeolithic populations south of the Carpathians were
considerably less numerous than the population of the North-
European Lowland and thus certainly less resistant to the
process of neolithisation.

They probably also had no need for economic and social
intensification because they never experienced overpopulation.
The situation of the northern mesolithic communities was a
little different. Although more numerous, they were nevertheless free of population pressure because of their skilful
utilisation of a wide range of resources. This situation lasted
practically up to the emergence of local Funnel Beaker-like
lowland cultures. Given these conditions, the neighbouring
neolithic food producers in southern and central Poland would
not present a socio-economic model attractive to the
hunting and fishing communities, until the North-European
Lowland become overpopulated, probably through the decline
in natural resources at the beginning of the sub-boreal period.

The optimisation of the hunter-gatherer economy
From what we have said so far it seems that three
separate systems, based on a different degree of organisation
of the food-gathering economy emerged in the atlantic period:
first, in the south, one based on the more traditional strategy,
connected with the still active palaeolithic tradition, and
relatively vulnerable to disintegration. The second, a highly
organised, specialised, economically diversified system of
mesolithic economy, was developed locally in the northern
lowlands. This latter system was very well adapted to the
various ecological niches. It reached its full development in the
fifth millennium bc. The third system is that of epipalaeolithic
cultures of the Black Sea coast and western Balkans. As the

presence of trapezes, notched blades and, later, Impressed ware
suggest, Mediterranean and Middle Eastern cultures contributed to its development (Kozłowski 1976, 135–60). It is
possible, though not certain, that these outside elements are
connected with the beginnings of ovicaprid husbandry, which,
along with the trapezes (Clark 1980, pp. 52–6) could have
spread westwards via the mediterranean corridor (Guilaine
1978; pp. 81–92).

On the one hand, it seems that the mesolithic system
was highly organised and that it facilitated information flow
through a well-developed network of settlement. On the other,
it could be divided into separate territorial units, identifiable
on the basis of variation in the material culture. These units
probably corresponded to tribal territories (Stoczkowski
1983). One could find some support for this idea in the sizes
of these territories, which correspond very well with the sizes
of inland (150 000–300 000 km^2) and coastal (40 000 km^2)
territories of North American tribal groups.

The mobility of mesolithic populations was likely to
have been confined to restricted areas, always a good deal
smaller than the tribal area, inside of which their alleged
'owners' possessed a number of large and small (at the level of
the regional group and the nuclear family) maintenance camps
and a larger number of temporary extraction camps.

In summary, we may say that the epipaleolithic communities in the southern zone of our area were rather
vulnerable to the introduction of the neolithic way of life and
perhaps indeed anticipated it by adopting elements of early
animal husbandry through the continuous intensification of
man–animal relationships. The northern zone, on the other
hand, was entirely self-sufficient, well organised and secluded
from the centres of early farming. There is no reason to
suppose that it would profit from the adoption of farming at
an early date.

Archaeology of the Early Neolithic
Cultural–ecological zones
As in the Mesolithic, the ecological zones distinguished
above form a framework for the regional differentiation of
culture as in the Mesolithic, making it possible to recognise the
following units (Fig. 4):

(*a*)   The Balkans, consisting of three subunits: the pre-
ceramic phase of the Anatolian–Balkan complex
(Thessaly), the ceramic phase of this complex with the
Protosesklo, Anzabegovo–Vršnik, Karanovo I and
Starčevo groups, and the Impressed–Cardial complex
(Garašanin 1980, pp. 57–72) in Dalmatia.

The Anatolian–Balkan complex in both of its
phases represents a fully formed neolithic economy
complete with the cultivation of the four cereals and of
other plants (e.g. *Vicia, Lens, Pisum*) and with the
dominant role of animal husbandry, ovicaprids being
the most important animal group (70–85%). A lesser
role is played by the rearing of cattle and pigs, and by
hunting: wild animals amount to only 1–7%. Despite

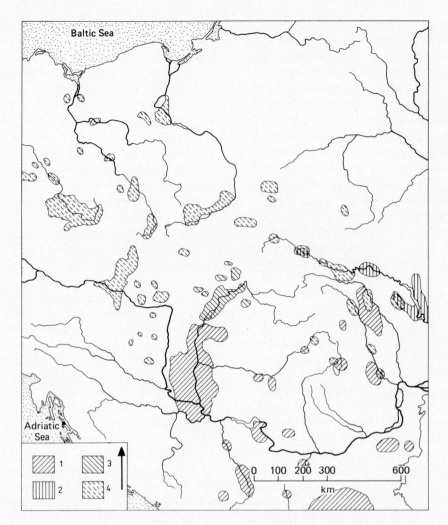

Fig. 4. Early neolithic settlement pattern. Site concentrations of three or more sites are represented graphically. 1, Barbotino complex; 2, Bug-Dniester culture; 3, eastern Linear complex; 4, western Linear complex.

the economic similarities with Anatolia there are no analogies in lithic industries. Rather, in the preceramic phase they are related to the local Epipalaeolithic, while in the ceramic phase they evolve into a characteristic and homogeneous blade industry; the ceramics, on the other hand, reflect the Anatolian style (Kozłowski 1982, pp. 131–67). This complex develops mainly in the sixth millennium bc.

The Impressed–Cardial complex, appearing towards the end of the sixth millennium on the Adriatic coast, is characterised by the smaller contribution of the food-producing economy. The stone industry is related to the local Epipalaeolithic. The ceramics belong to the broadly defined Mediterranean complex of Cardial wares.

(*b*)   In the region between the Carpathians and the Dniester/ southern Bug, the protoneolithic phase of the Bug– Dniester culture takes on a fully neolithic character with the introduction of pottery and the adoption of further elements of farming. At the beginning of the fifth

millennium bc contacts are evident with the Criş culture in Moldavia, through which the elements of the traditional neolithic economy – cereal cultivation, rearing of ovicaprids – were introduced. In the second half of the fifth millennium, subsequent contacts were made with the Linear Band Pottery groups to the north (Danilenko 1969, pp. 206–9).

(*c*)   The Carpathian basin is the scene of very early expansion of the Anatolian–Balkan complex, manifested by the presence of monochrome ceramics (Vlassa 1972; Makkay 1981, pp. 95–101) and by the traditional neolithic economy: cultivation of several cereals and almost 90% of the animals domesticated. It is only later, at the turn of the sixth and fifth millennia that the middle and lower Danube areas of the Carpathian basin see the emergence of the Körös–Criş complex with features specific to the barbotino-type, but only rarely to the painted, ceramics (Tringham 1971, Fig. 41). The stone industry is of divergent character: on the one hand it is a continuation of the Anatolian–Balkan/Starčevo tradition, and on the other it is enriched by microlithic and geometrical elements (Kozłowski and Kaczanowska 1985). The economy also reflects this divergence: there are sites with a relatively small share of game (up to 30%) while on other sites, game exceeds 50% (Bökönyi 1974, pp. 52–5). The share of cattle increases (up to 45%) although there are still sites with a high share of ovicaprids (up to 70%). These changes may be explained either by the adaptation to the ecological conditions of the intra-Carpathian zone or by contacts with the local hunter-gatherers. .

(d) In the zone of *circum*-Carpathian loess uplands, the early neolithic communities undergo further changes with the development of the Linear Pottery culture. In terms of lithic industry, the eastern Linear Pottery complex is a direct continuation of the Körös culture, while the western complex is probably a result of contacts with the Vinča complex in the middle of the fifth millennium bc. The western Linear complex is better adapted to the ecological conditions of the loess uplands, which is evidenced by the further reduced role of hunting in the economy (less than 10% of game, except for the area east of the Carpathians where wild animals constitute up to 35%) and by the absolute dominance of cattle (with the exception of sites between the Elbe and the Saale) (Kruk 1980a, figs. 33 and 40; Murray 1970, pp. 238–64). Agricultural practices are also modified with the addition of rye, although the exact date for its transition from weed of cultivation to cultigen is subject to dispute. The western Linear complex takes up the entire area of loess uplands and also extends to the North-European Plain, where the Linear-bandkeramik groups co-existed with the local mesolithic population. The development of the eastern and western Linear complexes continued until the beginning of the fourth millennium bc.

(e) As already mentioned, the western Lowland was inhabited only sporadically by the Linear Pottery groups, who selected clayey soils for their settlements (Czerniak 1980, pp. 1–202). At first these enclaves maintained their contacts with the south, a fact which can be deduced from the movement of lithic materials between the two areas. By the middle of the fourth millennium bc, Linear settlement extends to more marginal zones, shedding, in the process, some 'southern' features, and becoming better adapted to the sandy lowland soils. It is probably in this way that the first groups of the Funnel Beaker culture emerged. The Funnel Beaker can be regarded as the first local Neolithic, fully adapted to the ecological conditions of the lowland and facilitating the subsequent transition to farming by almost the entire western lowland population (Kosko 1980, pp. 123–36). The economy of this cultural tradition is based on the extensive cultivation of cereals, which, as pollen analysis indicates, necessitates

large forest clearings (Wiślanski 1969, pp. 218–61; Ralska-Jasiewiczowa 1977, pp. 75–89). The role of hunting remains considerable (34–60% of wild animals), however, and among the domesticated animals, cattle and pigs predominate. Ceramics bear some resemblance to Linear pottery, but the flint industry of the early phase is related to the local Mesolithic.

The course of the neolithisation process is somewhat different in the littoral zone where, by the first half of the fourth millennium, the productive economy has still not been adopted, and the only innovations is pottery occurring in fully mesolithic contexts.

(f) Similarly, the area of the eastern Lowland has been inhabited by ceramic mesolithic (or paraneolithic) communities. In northeast Poland and Lithuania, settlements dated to the second half of the fourth millennium bear some traces of influence from the Dnieper–Don and other cultures of the steppe-forest zone, but these do not cause a change in the economy towards agriculture and animal husbandry (Kempisty 1983, pp. 175–203).

Settlement structure

The neolithic settlement patterns reflect the adaptation of the neolithic economy to the regional environmental conditions. In the earliest stage, in Thessaly, *tells* with several layers of occupation indicate that the settlement network of the Anatolian–Balkan tradition consisted of widely spaced stable communities, lasting for several centuries. The *tells* were set up on fairly prominent peninsular-shaped elevation in the valleys of rivers flowing into the Aegean Sea. The epipalaeolithic settlements occur primarily in the mountainous part of Thessaly, in the Rhodope, and in the south in littoral caves.

In the following stage, small population groups penetrated the Balkans as far as the intra-Carpathian zone, following the river valleys. The earliest settlements were relatively small, set up in areas with no signs of previous settlement, usually on fairly low river terraces and, particularly, on peninsulas created by meandering rivers. This would indicate that the flood plains of river valleys were being used for intensive cultivation. Houses in the entire zone were constructed using a mixture of clay and daub or wooden uprights. As the early neolithic settlement advanced into the Danube basin, the density of settlements increased considerably: in the Körös valley alone, 350 sites were recorded on a 70 km stretch. This reflects not only the increase in population density, but also the frequently shifting settlement, probably related to the system of settlement rotation determined by the rapid turnover of fields along river valleys (the mesolithic/epipalaeolithic system probably made use of the rotation method as well). This is suggested not only by the ethnological evidence, but also by the small size of the sites. The choice of site location was dictated by the intense flooding activity of the rivers, and resulted in the occupation of areas with a lower water table (Nandris 1970).

Further changes in the settlement system are connected with the loess uplands adjoining the Carpathians and with the Linear Pottery complex. In this zone only loess-covered territories, cut by large and medium-sized rivers, were exploited (Kruk 1978, p. 75; 1980*b*, pp. 139–49). Regions with other soils were scrupulously avoided and remained free of settlement by neolithic groups up to the end of the fourth millennium bc, serving in some areas (such as Lower Silesia), at least, as settlement areas for the mesolithic people. The edges of terraces and plateaus in river valleys were settled first of all. Godlowska (1976, pp. 7–37) observed frequent changes of settlement localities, caused by the exhaustion of soil fertility and by the increase of settlement density.

By the end of the Neolithic and the beginning of the Eneolithic, neolithic settlement had expanded to plateaus and interfluvial areas. This extension of settlement was aided by the development of extensive agriculture and by the adoption of a more flexible system of farming (see above p. 105). The assimilation of the remaining hunter–gatherers took place probably at this time.

Conclusion: neolithic acculturation and mesolithic continuity

As we have indicated, the opportunities for local domestication were limited by the unsuitability of local plants and animals for domestication (see also Rowley-Conwy, Chapter 2). If, however, there were elements of the food-producing economy in some local mesolithic or epipalaeolithic communities, these phenomena remained without significant influence on the final shape of the Central-European Neolithic. An exception to this is the zone east of the Carpathians where the mesolithic communities between the southern Bug and the Dniester apparently developed an independent system of animal husbandry (chiefly pig rearing).

The eventual form of the neolithic transition in Central Europe was thus determined by the progress of the traditional neolithic economy, introduced from Anatolia to the Balkans and subsequently modified to suit Central-European conditions. Despite these modifications, the Central-European Neolithic remained independent of the hunter-gatherers throughout the Early Neolithic. This would suggest that the introduction of farming to Central Europe was brought about by the actual movement of the neolithic farmers northwards. It was only during the second stage of the expansion of the neolithic economy that the transition to farming by the local neolithic groups took place. These later neolithic formations differed strongly from their early neolithic predecessors. The integration of mesolithic and neolithic systems occurred in the western part of the North-European Lowland only in the second half of the fourth millennium bc, by which time the south of Europe was already in the stage of the developed Eneolithic.

In conclusion, we would like to emphasise the basic distinction between the two non-identical systems – the Mesolithic in the north and the Epipalaeolithic in the south.

Their final development took different paths during the atlantic period. The former system represented a successful adaptation to the differentiated environmental zones, attaining considerable autonomy and economic equilibrium. As a result, it became more impervious to external influences, and more vigorous demographically. The second system is characterised by a lower degree of adaptive fitness and by a reduced demographic potential. The susceptibility to external influences was correspondingly greater although, even here, the development of 'affluent' foragers took place in exceptional situations (i.e. the Iron Gates).

The two systems of mid Holocene hunter-gatherer adaptations experience, at different points in time, the disturbing influence of external factors. The reason for this is the northward movement of groups with a complete system of highly efficient neolithic economy of Anatolian–Balkan origin. Initially, the mesolithic/epipalaeolithic and neolithic systems co-exist, occupying mutually exclusive territories for at least several hundred years – even longer in the north – and maintaining little contact (with the exception of an exchange of raw materials and some artefacts). The hunting–gathering–fishing systems are at this stage fully autonomous.

Only after an extended period of co-existence can we observe the actual integration of areas hitherto occupied by mesolithic/epipalaeolithic peoples into the neolithic settlement pattern. This is accompanied by a further modification of the Anatolian–Balkan tradition of farming to fit the local Central-European conditions. While the independent development of hunter-gatherer communities ends in acculturation, they influence the neolithic populations. This is mainly the case in the north. Finally, in the northeast the transition to farming is not completed until a much later period.

Thus, gradually vanish the 'last Indians' of Central Europe.

Acknowledgement
This paper has been supported by the Polish research project R-III-6. The assistance of Dr M. Dabrowski in the interpretation of the palynological evidence is gratefully acknowledged.

References
Barker, G. W. (1973) 'Cultural and economic change in the prehistory of central Italy', in C. Renfrew, ed., *The Explanation of Culture Change. Models in Prehistory*, pp. 359–70, Duckworth, London.
Benac, A. (1978) 'Les thèses fondamentales sur l'origine du Néolithique dans les Balkans et les regions avoisinantes'. *Godišnjak – Centar za Balkanološka Ispitivanja* 14, 9–20.
(1980) 'Conditions géographiques du processus de néolithisation dans certaines régions de l'Europe', in J. K. Kozłowski, ed., *Problèmes de la néolithisation dans certaines regions de l'Europe*, pp. 35–48, Ossolineum, Kraków.
Bökönyi, S. (1974) *History of Domestic Mammals in Central and Eastern Europe*, Akademiai Kiado, Budapest.
(1978) 'The vertebrate fauna of Vlasac', in M. Garašanin, ed., *Vlasac, Mezolitsko naselje u Djerdapu*, vol. 2, pp. 35–65, Serbian Academy of Science, Beograd.
Brinch Petersen, E. (1973) 'A survey of the late palaeolithic and the

mesolithic of Denmark', in S. K. Kozłowski, ed., *The Mesolithic in Europe*, pp. 77–128, University Press, Warsaw.

Carciumaru, M. (1973) 'Compte rendu de l'analyse pollinique des coprolithes d'Icoana – Portes de Fer'. *Actes du 4. Congrès International des Sciences Préhistoriques et Protohistoriques, Beograd* 2, 172–3.

(1978) 'L'analyse pollinique des coprolithes de la station archéologique de Vlasac', in M. Garašanin, ed., *Vlasac-Mesolitsko naselje u Djerdapu*, vol. 2, pp. 31–4, Serbian Academy of Sciences, Beograd.

Clark, J. G. D. (1962) 'Survey of the mesolithic phase in the prehistory of Europe and South-West Asia'. *Atti del VI Congresso Internazionale delle Scienze Preistoriche e Protoistoriche* 1, 97–117.

(1975) *The Earlier Stone Age Settlement of Scandinavia*, Cambridge University Press, Cambridge.

(1980) *Mesolithic Prelude. The Palaeolithic–Neolithic Transition in Old World Prehistory*, Edinburgh University Press, Edinburgh.

Clason, A. T. (1977) *Jacht en veeteelt van prehistorie tot middleenwen*, Fibula-Van Dishoeck, Haarlem.

Cyrek, K. (1981) 'Uzyskiwanie i uzytkowanie surowców krzemiennych w mezolicie dorzeczy Wisly i górnej Warty'. *Prace i Materiały Muzeum Archeologicznego i Etnograficznego w Łodzi*, pp. 5–107, Seria Archeologiczna 28.

Czerniak, L. (1980) *Rozwój społeczeństw późnej ceramiki wstęgowej na Kujawach*, Poznań University Press, Poznań.

Dabrowski, M. (1959) 'Późnoglacjalna i holoceńska historia lasów Puszczy Białowieskiej'. *Acta Societatis Botanicorum Poloniae* 28 (2), 197–248.

Danilenko, V. N. (1969) *Neolit Ukrainy*, Naukova Dumka, Kiev.

David, A. J. and Markevich, V. J. (1970) 'Khozaystvo i fauna neoliticheskikh poselenyi Sredniego Podniestrovia', in K. N. Negodayev-Nikonov ed., *Fauna Kainozoya Moldavii*, p. 3 *passim*, Shtintsa, Kishinev.

Dolukhanov, P. M. (1979) *Ecology and Eonomy in Neolithic Eastern Europe*, Duckworth, London.

Firbas, F. (1949–51) *Spät- und nacheiszeitliche waldgeschichte Mitteleuropas nördlich der Alpen*, Fischer, Jena.

Garašanin, M. (1980) 'Les origines du néolithique dans le bassin de la Méditerranée et dans le Sud-est européen', in J. K. Kozłowski, ed., *Problèmes de la néolithisation dans certaines régions de l'Europe*, pp. 57–72, Ossolineum, Kraków.

Ginter, B. and Kozłowski, J. K. (1975) *Technika obróbki i typologia narzedzi kamiennych paleolitu i mezolitu*, PWN, Warsaw.

Godlowska, M. (1976) 'Proba rekonstrukcji rozwoju osadnictwa neolitycznego w rejonie Nowej Huty'. *Materialy Archeologiczne Nowej Huty* 5, 7–179.

Guilaine, J. (1978) 'La néolithisation du Languedoc et de la Catalogene'. *Godišnjak – Centar za Balkanološka Ispitivanja* 14, 81–92.

Hahn, J. (1983) 'Die frühe mittelsteinzeit', in H. J. Müller-Beck, ed., *Urgeschichte in Baden-Württemberg*, pp. 363–92. Konrad Theiss.

Jarman, M. R. (1972) 'European deer economies and the advent of the neolithic', in E. S. Higgs, ed., *Papers in Economic Prehistory*, pp. 125–48, Cambridge University Press, Cambridge.

Jochim, M. A. (1976) *Hunter-Gatherer Subsistence and Settlement, a Predictive Model*, Academic Press, New York.

Kaczanowska, M. (1984) *Rohstoffe, Technik und Typologie der neolithischen Feuerstein industrien in Nordteil des Flussgebietes der Mitteldonau*, PWN, Warsaw.

Kempisty, E. (1983) 'Neolityczne kultury strefy leśnej w północnej polsce', in T. Malinkowski, ed., *Problemy epoki kamienia na Pomorzu*, pp. 175–200, Wyzsza Szkoła Pedagogiczna, Słupsk.

Kośko, A. (1980) 'The position of Funnel Beaker Culture in the Lowland model of neolithization', in J. K. Kozłowski, ed., *Problèmes de la Néolithisation dans certaines Regions de l'Europe*, pp. 123–38, Ossolineum, Kraków.

Kozłowski, J. K. (1974) 'Über die Untersuchungen der ostlichen Peripherien der Linien-Bandkeramik-Kultur'. *Acta Archaeologica Carpathica* 14, 5–56.

(1982) 'La néolithisation de le zone balkano-danubienne du point de vue des industries lithiques'. *Prace Archeologiczne* 33, 131–70.

Kozłowski, J. K. and Kaczanowska, M. (1985) 'Barbotino and Linear Complex – continuation or discontinuation?' *Arheološki Radove i Rasprave IAZU*, in press.

Kozłowski, J. K. and Kozłowski, S. K. (1975) *Pradzieje Europy od XL do IV tysiaclecia, p.n.e.*, PWN, Warsaw.

(1977) *Epoka kamienia na ziemiach polskich*, PWN, Warsaw.

(1978) 'Le rôle de substrat mésolithique dans la néolithisation de la partie nord de l'Europe central'. *Godišnjak – Centar za Balkanološka Ispitivanja* 14, 93–104.

Kozłowski, S. K. (1975) *Cultural Differentiation of Europe Between 10th and 5th Millennium BC*, Warsaw University Press, Warsaw.

(1976) 'Les courants interculturels dans le mésolithique de L'Europe occidentale', in S. K. Kozłowski, ed., *Les civilisations du 8e au 5e millénaire avant notre ère en Europe*, IXe Congrès International des Sciences Préhistoriques et Protohistoriques, Nice, Colloque XIX.

Kroeber, A. L. (1963) *Cultural and Natural Areas of Native North Americans*, University of California Press, Berkley.

Kruk, J. (1978) 'The distribution of Linear Pottery Culture. Proposed model'. *Godišnjak – Centar za Balkanološka Ispitivanja* 14, 125–38.

(1980a) *Gospodarka w Polsce pd.-wsch. w V-III tysiacleciach p.n.e.* Ossolineum, Wrocław.

(1980b) 'Einige Fragen der Ökonomik des Frühen Neolithikums des Lösskochbenwen', in J. K. Kozłowski, ed., *Problèmes de la néolithisation dans certaines regions de l'Europe*, pp. 139–50, Ossolineum, Kraków.

Larsson, L. (1978) 'Ageröd I: B-I:D. A study of early Atlantic settlement in Scania'. *Acta Archaeologica Lundensia* 4 (4), 1–258.

Lisitsyna, G. N. and Filipovich, L. A. (1980) 'Paleoetnobotnicheskiye nakhodki na Balkanskom poluostrovu'. *Studia Praehistorica* 4, 5–90.

Makkay, J. (1981) 'Painted pottery of the Körös–Starčevo Culture from Szarvas site No 23'. *Acta Archaeologica Carpathica* 21, 95–104.

Mamakowa, K. (1965) 'Postep badań nad wplywem osadnictwa prahistorycznego na szatę roślinną Polski'. *Archeologia Polski* 11 (1), 107–17.

Markevich, V. I. (1974) *Bugodnestrovskaya kultura na territorii Moldavii*, Shtintsa, Kishinev.

Murray, J. (1970) *The First European Agriculture, a Study of the Osteological and Botanical Evidence until Two Thousand BC*, Edinburgh University Press, Edinburgh.

Nandris, J. (1970) 'Ground water as a factor of the first temperate neolithic settlement of the Körös region'. *Sbornik Narodnog Muzeja* 6, 59–72.

Neushtadt, M. J. (1957) *Istoria lesov i palaeogeografia SSSR v golotsene*, Akademia Nauk SSSR, Moskva.

Newell, R. R. (1973) 'The post-glacial adaptations of the indigenous population of the Northwest European Plain', in S. K. Kozłowski, ed., *The Mesolithic in Europe*, pp. 399–440. Warsaw University Press, Warsaw.

Pianka, E. R. (1981) *Ekologia ewolucyjna*, PWN, Warsaw.

Price, D. T. (1981) 'Regional approaches to human adaptation in the mesolithic of the North European Plain', in B. Gramsch, ed., *Mesolithikum in Europa*, pp. 117–234, Veröffentlichungen des Museums für Ur- und Frühgeschichte Potsdam 14–15, Deutscher Verlag, Berlin.

Ralska-Jasiewiczowa, M. (1977) 'Impact of prehistoric man on natural vegetations recorded in pollen diagrams from different regions of Poland'. *Folia Quaternaria* 49, 75–92.

Rimantiéne, R. (1971) *Paleolit i mezolit Litvy*, Mintis, Vilinus.

Starkel, L. (1977) *Paleogeografia holocenu*, PWN, Kraków.

Stoczkowski, W. (1983) Rozmiary; społeczeństw pierwotnych myśliwych. Manuscript at the Archaeological Institute, Warsaw. University, Warsaw.

Tringham, R. (1971) *Hunters, Fishers and Farmers of Eastern Europe 6000–3000 BC*, Hutchinson University Library, London.

Vlassa, N. (1972) 'Cea mai veche faza a complexului cultural Starčevo-Criş in Romania'. *Acta Muzei Napocensis* 9, 7–28.

Welinder, S. (1973) 'Mesolithic sites with flint in Eastern Middle Sweden', in S. K. Kozłowski, ed., *Mesolithic in Europe*, pp. 583–594, Warsaw University Press, Warsaw.

Wislanski, T. (1969) *Podstawy gospodarcze plemion neolitycznych w Polsce polnocno-zachodniej*, Ossolineum, Wroclaw.

Chapter 8

The Late Mesolithic and the transition to food production in Eastern Europe

P. M. Dolukhanov

The gradual expansion of the farming economy in the steppe and forest-steppe zones of Eastern Europe during the fourth and third millennia bc took the form of an integration of foraging strategies into the predominantly food-producing subsistence strategies (the substitution phase). The consolidation of the farming economy was reached during the middle stage of the Tripolye culture (fourth to third millennium bc). After a period of crisis in the economy, predominantly stock-breeding communities spread in the area. In the boreal zone of Eastern Europe, hunter-gatherer communities flourished during the early and mid Holocene. A substantial population increase in this zone was attained by the late third millennium bc. During the second and first millennia bc, elements of farming were integrated into a predominantly foraging economy. The consolidation of the farming economy occurred in the course of the sixth to tenth centuries AD.

Introduction

One of the most difficult, and one of the most fascinating tasks in modern archaeology consists of the reconstruction of the *socio-economic dynamics* of prehistoric societies from the archaeological record. The most obvious difficulties in achieving this aim arise from the inadequacy or, more precisely, the discontinuous nature of archaeological data. Archaeological remains tend to reflect the static stages in the evolutionary processes, while the periods of transition are either poorly represented or omitted altogether. Hence, models relating to the evolutionary processes are often built on a fallacious body of facts. The missing links (which usually correspond to periods of rapid change) are being replaced by

the evidence referring mostly to static phenomena. Such an approach results in a bias towards speculative hypotheses and mentalist conceptions which increasingly contradict the observed data.

The debate which has developed around the problem of the origin and spread of the farming economy, and its relation to alternative strategies of the food quest presents an illuminating example to this effect. According to the model proposed by Ammerman and Cavalli-Sforza (1973, pp. 343–57), the spread of early farming in Europe can be seen as a linear wave of advance of logistically increasing neolithic population 'forcing out or exterminating' the mesolithic one. Such a model falls well within the generally accepted paradigm, upheld, however unintentionally, in the ethnographic work of Sahlins (1974), Service (1966) and Lee and DeVore (1968), by the assumption that hunting communities always consisted of small nomadic groups.

Following Grahame Clark's early lead (Clark 1952, 1953, 1957), I have put forward a model of a dynamic *eco-social system* based on the interactions between the prehistoric society and its natural environment (Dolukhanov 1979*a, b*). This model stressed the importance of the information about the availability of resources and the cultural experience and traditions of a given community in selecting economic strategies.

Examination of the processes related to socio-economic

development should be based on the whole body of evidence regarding economic and social patterns and the ideological superstructure of prehistoric societies. Particular attention should be given to the functioning of the system as a whole. An important element of this approach consists in the evaluation of the system's stability, its capacity to resist environmental or social pressure and its adaptive success. This approach requires sophisticated information, such as the duration of a site or of an archaeological culture, the degree of sedentism, the size and dynamics of the population, socio-cultural symbolism, and the interactions with neighbouring cultural and economic units, all of which can only be obtained at a level of extrapolation beyond the primary description of the archaeological data. In the present paper, an attempt is made to interpret, in the light of the above remarks, some socio-economic processes which occurred in the Russian (East European) Plain during the Late Pleistocene and Holocene.

As the latest palaeoenvironmental evidence indicates, the maximum period of cool and arid climate in the northern hemisphere occurred between 25 000 and 15 000 years bp. Considerable areas in the northern latitudes were covered by glaciers. In the ice-free regions of Eastern Europe the landscape at that time was dominated by periglacial forest-steppes and steppes. The woodland vegetation is thought to have survived only in river valleys and in piedmont areas. Around 15 000 years bp, the late glacial amelioration of climate began. During the Bölling/Alleröd interval (*c.* 11 000–10 000 years

bp) mean July temperature reached the present-day value (Shotton 1978). After the short-lived but intensive cold spell of the Younger Dryas, an abrupt rise in the temperature followed. According to Mörner (1980), in the short time-span between 9700 and 9000 years bp, mean annual temperatures rose to 15 °C, exceeding the present values. The maximum extension of forest formations, rich in thermophilous species, occurred in the Russian Plain during the atlantic period between *c.* 8000 and 5000 years bp. Forests penetrated along river valleys far to the south, the true steppe being restricted to the southernmost area of the Pontic Lowland. Following this period of the Climatic Optimum, between 4600 and 3400 years bp, a temperature drop, accompanied by a decrease in precipitation in the Russian Plain, led to the establishment of an arid climate in Eastern Europe in the course of the second and first millennia bc. At around the seventh to sixth century bc, an increase in both temperature and precipitation occurred, reaching a maximum value in the tenth to twelfth century AD, a period known as the 'Little Climatic Optimum' (Gribbin 1978).

The late pleistocene and holocene hunter-gatherers of the Russian Plain
The south (Fig. 1)
Judging from the number of sites, the upper palaeolithic population of the Russian Plain was considerable. The optimal population density seems to have been attained during the

---

Fig. 1. The Neolithic in the European part of the USSR, Caucasus and Central Asia (*c.* 6000–5000 bp). ▲, foraging economy; △, mixed farming/foraging economy; ○, farming economy; –, boundaries of archaeological cultures, – – –, less certain boundaries.

Archaeological cultures: I, Narvian; II, Early Neolithic of Polessye; III, Dnieper–Donetsk; IV, Bug–Dniester; V, Linear Pottery; VI, Crimean Early Neolithic; VII, West Caucasian Neolithic; VIII, Transcaucasian Eneolithic; IX, Kel'teminar; X, Djeitun; XI, Ghissar; XII, Early Neolithic of Kola peninsula; XIII, Sperrings; XIV, Early Neolithic of northeastern Russia; XV, Upper Volga culture; XVI, Volga–Kama culture; XVII, Rakushechnyi Yar culture; XVIII, Seroglazovka culture.

Sites: 1, Narva–Riigiküla; 2, Kroodi; 3, Akali; 4, Kääpa; 5, Osa; 6, Dubicijai; 7, Zatsen'e; 8, Kamen'; 9, Sienchitsy; 10, Borisovshchina; 11, Strumel', Gastiatin; 12, Grini; 13, Vita Litovskaya; 14, Nikol'skaya Slobodka; 15, Buz'ki; 16, Sobachki; 17, Vovchok; 18, Sandraki–Khmel'nik; 19, Samchintsi, Sokol'tsy; 20, Mikolina Broyarka; 21, Shimanovskoye, Zan'kovtsy; 22, Mel'nichna Krucha; 23, Skibentsy, Baz'kov Island, Mit'kov Island, Sokol'tsy; 24, Gard; 25, Probuz'ki; 26, Vladimirovka; 27, Kotovany; 28, Kolodnitsa; 29, Torskoye; 30, Bukovina; 31, Nezvizko; 32, Goloskov; 33, Burach, Popovtsy; 34, Zvienyachin; 35, Bel'che–Zolotoie; 36, Sin'kov; 37, Kamennaya Mogila; 38, Izyum; 39, Bondarikha; 40, Ust'e Oskola; 41, Dolinka; 42, Kukrek; Tash–Air; 43, Kaya–Arasi, Zamil–Koba; 44, Fatima–Koba, Shan-Koba; 45, Balin-kosh, At-bash; 46, Karasu-bashi, Alachuk, Adji–Koba; 47, Frontovoye, Chernaya Balka; 48, Tasunovo, Alekseyevka; 49, Soroki sites; 50, Slobodezya–Voronkovo, Puteneshty; 51, Floreshty, Gura Kamenka; 52, Novye Ruseshty; 53, Tsyra, Rogozhany; 54, Nizhne-Shlivskaya; 55, Odishi; 56, Asenauli; 57, Belaya; 58, Amiranis–Gora; 59, Natsar–Gora; 60, Tetri–Tzkaro; 61, Arkhulo; 62, Tsopi, Abelia, 63, Yanik, Geoi, 64, Khatunarkh; 65, Kyul-tepe; 66, Djebel, Dam–Dam-Cheshma; 67, Djatruk; Adji-kuyu, Togolok; 68, Kurtysh-baba; 70, Tugupek, Peshke-kuyu, Zangi-baba; 71, Taryshly; 72, Khatyb, Gyaur; 73, Djanbas; 74, Darbazakyr; 75, Utembai, Bolayuk; 76, Toskenbai; 77, Sam; 78, Beleuli, Churuk; 79, Bulak; 80, Kosbulak; 81, Ak-Tan'ga; 82, Tepai–Gazien; 83, Tutkaul; 84, Sai–Sayed; 85, Kui Bulen; 86, Bami, Naiza; 87, Djeitun, Chopan, Togollok, Pesedjik; 88, Novaia Nisa; 89, Monzhukly; 90, Chagylly; 91, Chavan'ga; 92, Navolok; 93, Ust'–Drogodovka; 94, Lovozero; 95, Zasheyek; 96, Segozero; 97, Medvezh'egorsk; 98, Sunskaya; 99, Semozero; 100, Solomennoie; 101, Derevyannoie; 102, Muromskaia; 103, Prilukskaia; 104, En'-ty; 105, Chernoborskaia; 106, Yazykovo; 107, Spasskoie; 108, Glivistenka; 109, Barskaia Ledka; 110, Ilovets; 111, Koptishche; 112, Romanova; 113, Baranova Gora; 114, Riabinova Relka; 115, Glebovshchina; 116, Mikulino Gorodishche; 117, Nikolo–Perevoz; 118, Davydkovo; 119, Patietskaia; 120, Ust'–Poksha; 121, Ozimienki; 122, Krasnoborskaia; 123, Gavrilovskaia; 124, Parizhskaia Kommuna; 125, Penzenskaia; 126, Dubrovskaia; 127, Voroniy Kust; 126, Kartashihkinskie; 129, Kuz'kinskaia, Balachikhinskaia; 130, Nizhnemar'yanovskaia, Boziakovskaia; 131, Aga–Bazerskaia, Novomordovskaia; 132, Moiechnoie Ozero; 133, Barnoshinskaia Poliana; 134, Universitetskaia; 135, Dermodekhinskaia; 136, Orlovka; 139, Rakushechnyi Yar; 138, Tsymlianskaia; 139, Mu–Buzu–Khudlakh; 140, Koshelok.

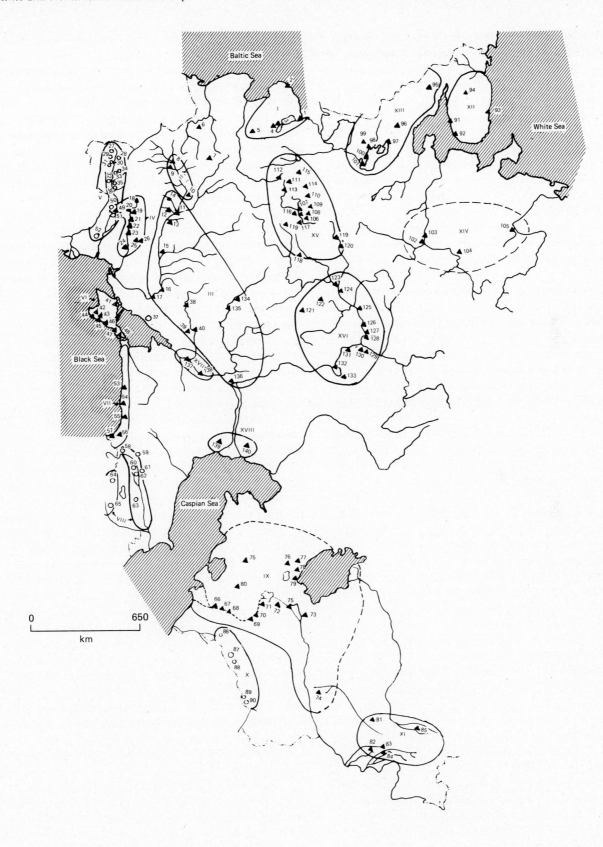

coldest stage, between c. 25 000 and 15 000 years bp. The majority of sites are found in the periglacial forest-steppe zone. The sites are usually situated on high river terraces or on promontories penetrating deep into lacustrine widenings of the valleys. Such a situation enabled palaeolithic hunters to exploit to the full the resources of the river flood plains. The woodland environments were feeding grounds for numerous herds of herbivores, which formed the principal game of palaeolithic men. The question remains open as to whether the mammoth was actually the prey hunted, or whether the sites were located at the points of naturally induced mass extinctions of this animal (Vereshchagin 1979).

At present, the state of our knowledge remains incomplete about the nature of mammoth bone structures, a common feature of upper palaeolithic sites in Eastern Europe. Were these dwellings or ceremonial emplacements? Ecological analysis of the faunal remains from the site of Mezhirich in the middle Dnieper valley (Korneits et al. 1981, pp. 117–18) provides evidence that at least this site was inhabited the whole year round. It is gradually becoming clear that we are dealing with a complicated network of upper palaeolithic sites of various ranks which embraced the river valleys of the middle Dniester basin and of the middle Don.

During the Late Würm, palaeolithic sites have appeared in the Pontic Lowland (Bol'shaya Akkarzha, Sagaidak), in the lower Dnieper valley (Kaistrova Balka I–IV) and in the littoral zone of the Azov Sea (Amvrosievka, Muralovka). The faunal remains of these sites include bison, wild horse and aurochs. No remains of dwellings have been recorded.

Viewing the Russian Plain as a whole, it seems that the network of large campsites was restricted to the periglacial forest-steppe zone. As for the periglacial steppe zone in the south, its upper palaeolithic population consisted of comparatively small nomadic groups.

During the Late Glacial (15 000–10 000 years bp), the basin of the middle Dnieper and the middle Don area appear to have been all but deserted by palaeolithic people. A shift in population seems to have taken place northwards: to the upper Dnieper and its tributaries; to the basins of the Niemen and to the upper Volga. Judging from the remains of the contemporaneous sites in the lowlands of Central Europe, nomadic reindeer hunting was the principal strategy adopted by the hunters. By contrast, no changes in the economy and in the way of life can be observed in the southern regions of the Russian Plain.

The settlement remained concentrated in river valleys during the early postglacial period. Bison, horse and elk constituted the principal hunted resources in the middle Dniester area. Aurochs were the most common prey in the Pontic Lowland (Telegin 1982, p. 40). Aurochs and tarpan (Equus caballus gmelini) were hunted in the northwest Pontus (Bibikova 1982, pp. 139–64).

In most cases no remains of permanent dwellings have been found at mesolithic sites. Remains of light semi-subterranean dwellings have been uncovered at the site of Igren' 8 (Telegin 1982, pp. 110–12) and Bielolessie (Stanko 1982, pp. 126–7); Stanko (1982, pp. 127–9) suggested that Mirnoye and Ghirzhevo in the northwest Pontic were base-camps surrounded by satellite sites stretching along river valleys at distances ranging from 0.5 to 10 km.

Cemeteries, tentatively attributed to the Mesolithic, have been uncovered on the lower Dnieper. The prevalence of males among the buried and the presence of individuals who met a violent death led Stolyar (1959, p. 119) and Dvorianinov (1978, pp. 13–16) to postulate the existence of 'male military units' and of patrilocality.

Telegin (1982) and Stanko (1982) have distinguished at least two archaeological cultures in the Mesolithic of the steppe: the Kukrekian and the Grebenikian. The fact that at Mirnoye (Stanko 1982, pp. 58–81) both Kukrekian and Grebenikian inventories are present at various contemporary loci of the same site suggests that these units represent functionally distinct assemblages rather than ethnically separate groups.

Viewed as a whole, both the subsistence and the settlement patterns of the mesolithic populations in the south Russian Plain were direct continuations of those of the Late Palaeolithic. The population consisted of small social groups seasonally migrating over vast territories.

The beginning of the atlantic period, at around 5500 bc, heralded a considerable change in the economy of the mesolithic population, marked by a shift to the exploitation of a wider range of resources, including red deer, roe deer, wild pig, elk, fish and molluscs. The production of pottery begins at about 5500 bc in the context of a purely hunting and gathering economy. Pottery-bearing sites in the Dniester and southern Bug valleys are considered to belong to the Bug–Dniester Early Neolithic [ceramic mesolithic, ed. note] (Danilenko 1969; Markevich 1974). Both the stratigraphy of the sites and the faunal remains indicate that we are dealing with the remains of temporary hunting camps. The location of the sites on the flood plains, far away from arable lands, makes it extremely improbable that these communities could have subsisted by farming (Dolukhanov 1979a, p. 95). The occurrence of isolated bones of domesticates (pig and cattle) as well as impressions of grain on pottery sherds (emmer, einkorn, spelt, millet, barley) are best explained in terms of economic contacts with farming communities of the Criş/Körös culture, which occupied the neighbouring region of southern Moldavia (Comşa 1974, p. 6). The existence of such contacts is substantiated by the remarkable similarities in the ornamentation of pottery.

In this way, a mosaic of economic patterns seems to have emerged in southeast Europe between 6000 and 4500 bc. The areas most suitable for farming, such as intermontane depressions, were settled by agricultural populations on the one hand, while communities based on the stable foraging economy exploited the resources of river valleys on the other. The settlements along the Bug and the Dniester, and further south, the Lepenski Vir culture, can be seen as good examples of the latter. The stability of both systems was enhanced by economic exchanges between these communities which included both raw materials and products.

During the next stage at around 4500–4000 bc, Linear Pottery sites occur in Moldavia and the Ukraine. (Fig. 2) The sites were situated predominantly on the high terraces of the Prut, Dniester, Reut and their tributaries. Agriculture played an important role in the economy; among the cultivated plants einkorn, emmer, spelt, millet, and oats were predominant (Yanushevich 1976). Stockbreeding provided the best part of the meat consumed; none the less the proportion of wild animals in the faunal remains reached 26% (Tsalkin 1970).

At the same time the Bug–Dniester occupation continued on the flood plains of the Dniester, Reut and Prut, still relying on the predominantly foraging economy. In the Reut valley, the Bug–Dniester sites have been found in the proximity of the Linear Pottery settlement (Fig. 2); archaeological remains indicate the existence of close ties between the Linear Pottery and the Bug–Dniester communities. For example, the pottery belonging to the Bug–Dniester Neolithic has been found at the Linear site of Novye Ruseshty (Markevich 1974, p. 159), while sherds of Linear pottery with *notenkopf* ornamentation have been reported from the Baz'kov Island site on the southern Bug (Danilenko 1969, p. 68). One may logically assume that the objects of exchange included food as well. Hence, the situation remained essentially unchanged: while retaining their separate identities, both economic systems continued to co-exist and complement one another in their use of the environment.

The maximum expansion of the farming economy throughout the steppe and forest-steppe zones coincides with the emergence of the Gumelniţa and Tripolye cultures, the ultimate roots of which lie in the Dudeşti and Boian cultures of southeast Europe (Comşa 1974, pp. 25–6).

The Gumelniţa culture appeared on the territory of the northeast Pontic area in a developed form. Gumelniţa sites are usually situated on the loess plains flanking limans or lakes, or in river valleys. Farming constituted the basis of the economy. The cultivated plants included einkorn, emmer, spelt, six-row barley, oats and broom-corn millet (Yanushevich 1976). Stockbreeding formed an equally important part of the economy. Sheep and goat prevailed in the faunal remains of the early stage; cattle became predominant at a later stage. The importance of hunting diminished simultaneously.

The Tripolye culture, a hybrid of the Boian and Linear Pottery cultures (Comşa 1974, p. 19), appeared in the forest-steppe zone as a result of an eastward expansion into the Bug–Dniester area. According to Bibikov (1953, p. 280), this led to a conflict between the farming and foraging settlements, which resulted in the end of the foraging communities. Local foraging traditions can be observed in the initial stages of Tripolye, namely, in the importance of hunting (in some cases wild species amounted to more than 50% of the faunal assemblage), in the construction of semi-subterranean dwellings and in the stone industry. The Early Tripolye sites were usually situated within the river valleys.

The Tripolye economy acquired a fully food-producing character by its middle stages. Ethnobotanical finds included emmer, einkorn, spelt, club wheat, naked and hulled six-row barley, millet and oats as well as various fruits and pulses (Yanushevich 1976). Cattle formed the most important element of animal husbandry, pigs and ovicaprids being of secondary importance. The settlements, some of which were of considerable size (the site of Kolomyishchina had *c.* 500 inhabitants, according to Bibikov (1965, p. 58) occupied the margins of loess plains adjoining the river valleys. By the mid-fourth millennium bc, therefore, the substitution of foraging by farming can be considered to have been completed in the region.

Following the end of the Middle Tripolye period, the further development of the settlement and economy in the south Russian Plain was marked by the shift to pastoralism and by the colonisation on interfluvial areas (Zbenovich 1974; Dergachev 1980; Telegin 1973).

The zone of farmer–forager contact moved further north, to the valleys of the Dnieper, Severski Donetsk and their tributaries. The economy and the settlement pattern of the earliest ceramic mesolithic culture, the Dnieper–Donetsk (4200–2500 bc; Dolukhanov 1983, pp. 481–2), was essentially the same as that of the Bug–Dniester groups. Although it was based on hunting, fishing and food-collecting were also extremely important. The occurrence of domesticated animals, predominantly the bones of cattle, in the faunal remains as well as the rare impressions of grain on the pottery sherds (e.g. the impression of *Hordeum sativum* at Vita Litovskaya) seem to indicate trade links with the agricultural communities, rather than farming economy. The remains of material culture point in the same direction: The Dnieper–Donetsk pottery assemblages included imported Tripolye ware (Telegin 1968). Dolukhanov (1979a), p. 149) noted the similarities of ornamental patterns of the Dnieper–Donetsk pottery with those of the funnel beakers in Central Europe. By the end of the second millennium bc the sites of the Middle Dnieper culture appeared along the stretches of the middle and upper Dnieper and its tributaries (Artemenko 1967). The economy of this culture was of a predominantly stockbreeding character, while hunting remained important. The material culture and the burial rites of the Middle Dnieper culture is markedly different from either Tripolye or the Dnieper–Donetsk and shows strong affinities with the Corded Ware tradition.

In summary, the above evidence indicates that farming was adopted in the southern part of the Russian Plain gradually, only after an extended transitional period of farmer–forager contacts, during which elements of the neolithic economy and technology were selectively adopted, presumably in response to the socio-economic needs of the local mesolithic population. Aided by favourable climatic conditions, the gradual adoption of farming progressed in a northeastern direction during the atlantic period. Farming attained its greatest extent with the spread of Tripolye and Gumelniţa

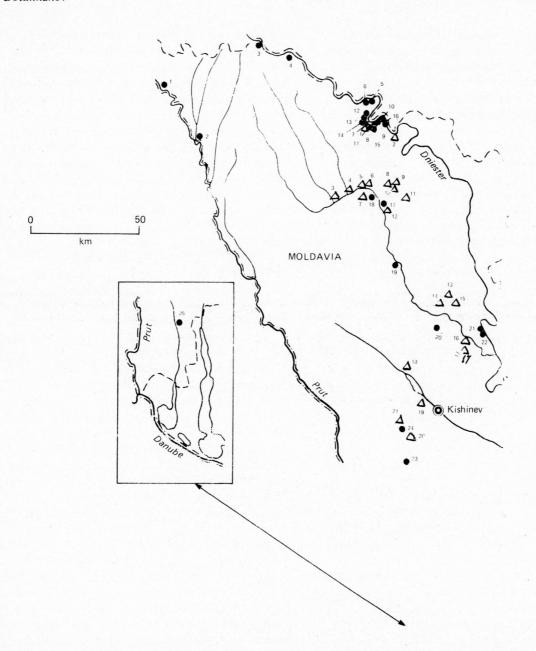

Fig. 2. Sites of the Bug–Dniester (●) and Linear Pottery culture (△) on the territory of the Moldavian SSR (after Markevich 1974, pp. 11, 29).
    Sites of the Bug–Dniester culture: 1, Pereryta I; 2, Korpach VII; 3, Naslavcha I; 4, Kalarshovka I; 5, Kosoutsy III, Kosoutsy IV; 7–15, Soroki I–IX; 16, Trifautsy V; 17, Tsyra; 18, Strycheny I; 19, Sarateny; 20, Selishte; 21, Golerkany I; 22, Gorlekany VII; 23, Khanska V; 24, Novye Ruseshty; 25, Gavanos I.
    Sites of the Linear Pottery culture: 1, Soroki V; 2, Slobodzeya–Voronkovo I; 3, Putineshty I; 4, Markuleshty II; 5, Floreshty I; 6, Floreshty II: 7, Varvarovka VIII; 8, Gura Kamenka VI; 9, Gura Kamenka VII; 10, Gura Kamenka X; 11, Rogozhany II; 12, Tsyra II; 13, Izvory I; 14, Kipercheny I; 15, Kipercheny II; 16, Braneshty I; 17, Braneshty XIII; 18, Panasheshty I; 19, Dancheny I; 20, Novye Ruseshty I; 21, Novye Ruseshty II. —·—·—, ————, Present day state boundaries.

settlement, 6000–5000 years ago. At all the stages of its expansion the farming economy was accompanied and supplemented by foraging.

    The breakdown of the Tripolye was largely due to a decrease in the agro-climatic potential that occurred in the early sub-boreal. The subsequent development in the plains of southern Russia was marked by the emergence of balanced economies relying on nomadic stockbreeding in the steppe and farming in the forest-steppe. This dichotomy and its social, economic and ethnic implications were to play a major role in the historic development of Eastern Europe in the centuries that followed.

The northwest (Fig. 3)

The initial settlement of the northwestern part of the Russian Plain occurred about 10 000 to 9000 bc, soon after the retreat of the glacier. Lithic inventories with similarities to the Swiderian and other final palaeolithic cultural groups in North-central Europe have been found on sites in Lithuania, Latvia, Bielorussia and in the region south of Pskov. These sites were usually located on the dunes developed on the shores of huge 'ice-dammed' lakes. During the preboreal, boreal and early atlantic periods, a typical early mesolithic assemblage, bearing similarities to the Maglemosian of Northern Europe, characterised sites situated on the shores of the Baltic lagoons and small lakes and on the flood plains of rivers. The economy was based on the hunting of elk, wild pig, red deer, water fowl, and, in coastal areas, on sealing. It is worth noting that fishing and collecting edible plants and molluscs provided considerable parts of the diet. Permanent dwellings are unknown and the sites are generally small, coastal sites such as Narva or Kunda being the exceptions.

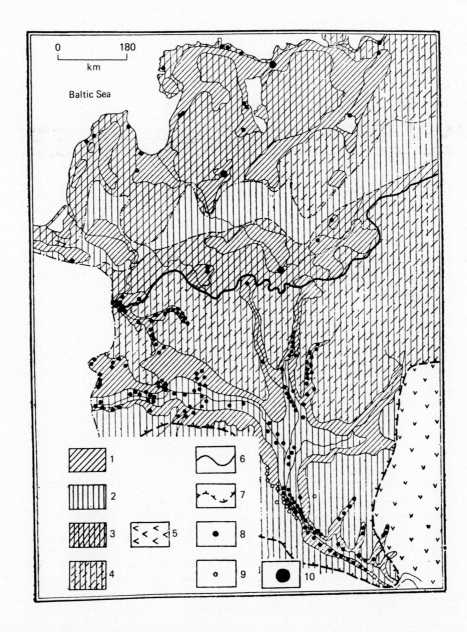

Fig. 3. Northwestern part of the European USSR 6000–4500 years bp.

1, Pine forests; 2, broadleaved forests; 3, coniferous forests with broadleaved elements; 4, broadleaved forests with coniferous elements; 5, steppes and forest-steppes; 6, limits of the Valdai (Wechselian) glaciation; 7, limits of the Dnieprian (Riss) glaciation; 8, sites with foraging economy; 9, sites with farming economy; 10, cluster of sites.

Apart from the coastal areas, these mesolithic remains, generally known as the Kunda culture, were most probably produced by small nomadic groups.

Pottery production began in the northwest c. 4000–3700 years bc. The economy of the 'forest' Neolithic, however, continued to be based on an effective exploitation of the wild resources of the forest: on hunting, fishing and food-collecting. Judging from the number of sites, the 'forest' neolithic population had increased as compared with the earlier period. There was also an important shift in the settlement pattern: the forest neolithic sites are concentrated in the coastal areas, and within the lake country shaped by the last glaciation; while in the main morainic zone, which is devoid of lakes, these sites are practically absent.

Vereshchagin, Dolukhanov and Miklyaev (1979, p. 364) have noted that the catchment area of the sites included the offshore areas of shallow lakes (usually remnants of ice-dammed lakes), parts of sand-covered glacio-lacustrine plains and of clay morainic hills. The forest neolithic lake side dwellings were of considerable size; some of them were inhabited by no less than 100 persons. From the seasonal indicators in the faunal remains from Naumovo south of Pskov (Vereshchagin et al. 1979, pp. 366–8), it is clear that the settlement was occupied the whole year round. Numerous radiocarbon dates, pollen and palaeolimnological data indicate that at least several large sites (e.g. Usvyaty, Naumovo) existed at the same place for no less than 1500 years, from about 3000 to 1500 bc. Hence, by the end of the atlantic and at the beginning of the sub-boreal, a highly effective adaptation, based on foraging, flourished in the forest zone of Eastern Europe.

By the end of the third millennium, cultures containing Corded Ware pottery made their appearance in the northwest of Eastern Europe. Following the drop in temperature and precipitation in the early subboreal period, the agricultural potential of many areas in Eastern Europe declined. This encouraged a shift to alternative forms of subsistence, particularly animal husbandry, and occasioned movements of population. The Corded Ware can be seen as a part of this process.

The detailed analysis of the material culture from the lakeside dwelling sites south of Pskov (Dolukhanov and Miklyaev 1979, pp. 73–81; Dolukhanov, Miklyaev and Fonyakov 1981, pp. 65–6) show that the Corded Ware intrusion had only a limited impact on the foraging communities of the forest zone. The most significant changes occurred in the stone inventory, in the ceramic technology and in the pottery ornamentation patterns. A small proportion of domesticated animals (pig, cattle) has been reported in the faunal assemblages. All this seems to indicate that the Corded Ware groups had been absorbed into the local population, without affecting significantly the local culture and subsistence patterns. In its turn, the newcomers transmitted to the local groups some ceramic traditions as well as the knowl-edge of stockbreeding.

Nevertheless the economy of the forest neolithic groups continued to rely on strategies which were essentially hunting and gathering until the first millennium bc. Only with the appearance of the fortified sites in the early Iron Age do we get a decisive shift in settlement from the lacustrine or littoral environments to the end-morainic zone where no sites had existed previously.

As the faunal records show, the significance of this shift was that stockbreeding and agriculture, rather than the distribution of wild resources, now determined the location of the settlement. Hunting, however, retained its economic importance, particularly during the early stages (Zvelebil 1978, 1985). Finds of grain (wheat, barley) as well as of agricultural implements (mortars, iron axes, sickles) indicate the existence of cultivation, in all probability of the slash-and-burn type. The majority of Iron Age sites investigated have revealed traces of metallurgy (Sedov 1970, p. 28).

We have every reason to believe that the transition to farming and the increase in agricultural activities resulted mainly from indigenous development, within the same cultural tradition, even though the contacts with the developed farming communities in the west (Lausitzian) and in the south (Milogradian, the agricultural Scythians) must have been very important.

Foraging strategies retained a great importance in the Iron Age economy of the forest zone, based, as it was, on the combination of animal husbandry, foraging and slash-and-burn cultivation. This system persisted into the second half of the first millennium AD, forming the economic basis of the Long Barrow culture, the people of which occupied the sandy glacio-lacustrine plains of the northwest during the sixth to tenth century AD. The shift to the more intensive plough agriculture occurred only in the tenth to eleventh century AD, marked archaeologically by the appearance of conical barrows (Sedov 1982). The extension of arable farming to the north coincided with the onset of the conditions known as the 'Little Climatic Optimum'.

To summarise, the hunting–gathering communities in the northwestern Russian Plain attained a noteworthy success in their effective exploitation of the wild resources of the arboreal ecotones. This is shown by the remarkable stability and long persistence of the foraging adaptations, and by the extended resistance to the adoption of farming. During the late atlantic/early sub-boreal periods, the hunter–gatherer culture reached an advanced stage with a complex network of large, permanent settlements evolving in the littoral zones of the glacial lakes and Baltic lagoons. The initial spread of some elements of farming occurred on the threshold of the third to second millennium bc and was primarily due to the penetration of the Corded Ware groups from North-central Europe. In the course of the second to early first millennium bc there was a gradual increase in farming activity, while hunting and gathering remained the dominant factor in the subsistence pattern. Significant changes in the settlement patterns and economy — the widespread adoption of swidden farming and of stockbreeding — have taken place only in the middle of the first millennium bc. These changes were primarily due to indigenous development as the local population was becoming a part of the cultural and economic exchange network of the Halstatt period. The final shift to farming as the sole subsistence strategy in northwestern Russia occurred in the course of the tenth to eleventh century AD in the conditions of the 'Little Climatic Optimum'.

The mechanisms responsible for these changes are not altogether clear as the economy of the Iron Age has not yet been sufficiently studied. One may assert, however, that they were due primarily to indigenous developments. In some areas (such as the south Pskov district), an uninterrupted cultural development accompanied a steady increase in the percentage of domesticated animals in the faunal remains. On the other hand, the change in the settlement pattern, appearance of 'hillforts' and the emergence of metallurgy indicate important modifications in the organisation of the society. Some of these changes are common to the whole Halstatt area, of which northwest Russia was a part. Among the most important of these developments one can list the increase in the intensity of trade, a rise in political tension resulting in warfare, and a rapid development of metallurgy. Their social implications included an accelerated social stratification and the crystallisation of a military elite, merchants and craftsmen, all groups not directly concerned with food production. The need to feed these important social groups, on the one hand, and the availability of imports traded against local commodities, were among the factors continuously accelerating the transition to farming in this area.

Conclusions

The archaeological evidence cited above and its palaeoeconomic interpretation convincingly show that the transition to farming in Eastern Europe was a complicated and lengthy process, which does not fit into the 'wave of advance' model by Ammerman and Cavalli-Sforza (1973). In Eastern Europe, we are dealing with foraging communities much more sophisticated than those outlined by Sahlins (1974), Service (1966) and Lee and DeVore (1968). An attempt to apply the 'Frontier' concept to the study of agricultural diffusion in Europe (Alexander 1978) is of a certain interest. The East-European records indicate the existence of both static and moving frontiers between farmers and hunter-gatherers—fishers. But the implication of farmer—forager contacts which follow from our analysis are quite different from those postulated by Alexander (*ibid.*).

Zvelebil and Rowley-Conwy (1984, and Chapters 1 and 6, this volume) distinguish three transitional phases between the farming and non-farming communities: (1) availability, (2) substitution, (3) consolidation. The availability phase, defined as 'a situation, where farming is known and familiar to the foraging group in question, and some exchange of

materials and information goes on between farming and foraging settlements, yet farming is not adopted by the hunter-gatherer societies', may be easily traced in the East European evidence (Fig. 4). The settlements of the Bug—Dniester, Dnieper—Donetsk and the north Bielorussian Corded Ware cultures fit well into this phase.

The substitution phase is less clearly marked. We have failed to find any indications of 'competition between two mutually incompatible ways of life' or 'competition for space and access information', the concepts crucial to the substitution phase (Zvelebil and Rowley-Conwy 1984). Our evidence speaks in favour rather of the integration of the two subsistence patterns. Two patterns of integration may be distinguished: (*a*) a trading integration of two cultural and economic entities occupying neighbouring territories, in the course of which these entities are engaged in the multifaceted exchange, while retaining their own identities (examples: Bug—Dniester plus Criş, plus Linear Pottery; Dnieper—Donetsk plus Funnel Beakers); (*b*) an economic integration where a shift to farming takes place but where foraging strategies retain their economic significance in a predominantly food-producing subsistence pattern (examples: Early Tripolye; Early Iron Age cultures in the northwest; probably, the culture of 'long barrows').

Finally, let us consider the consolidation phase, which is seen as 'the final stage in the transition to farming, marked by both the extensive and the intensive growth of food production' (Zvelebil and Rowley-Conwy 1984). The notion of 'stability' outlined in the Introduction to this chapter can be considered as pivotal for the identification of this phase. In this expanded sense, the consolidation phase may be distinguished not only in relation to the farming economy, but to the foraging one as well. Thus a period of stability occurred in the Upper Palaeolithic in the periglacial forest-steppe (25 000—15 000 years bp), but also during the forest neolithic phase in the northwest (5000—3500 years bp). In relation to farming communities, this phase may be applied to the Middle Tripolye, to the Iron Age communities in the forest-steppe and to the agricultural communities of the northwest in the tenth to eleventh century AD.

Hence, one may conclude that contacts between farming and foraging communities were in most cases of a peaceful nature, guaranteeing a constant exchange of goods and ideas across often ephemeral boundaries. These contacts were responsible for the appearance of common ornamental patterns in the pottery, such as Criş elements in the Bug—Dniester culture or the Corded Ware in the Late Neolithic of northwestern Russia, and for the directly imported goods, such as the Linear pottery in the Bug—Dniester Mesolithic. The trade in food stuffs is indicated by the finds of cereals and of bones belonging to domesticated animals in the sites left by foraging communities. Even though such finds imply the existence of a more or less systematic exchange, it should be stressed that contacts of this kind did not affect the basic subsistence pattern of the communities involved.

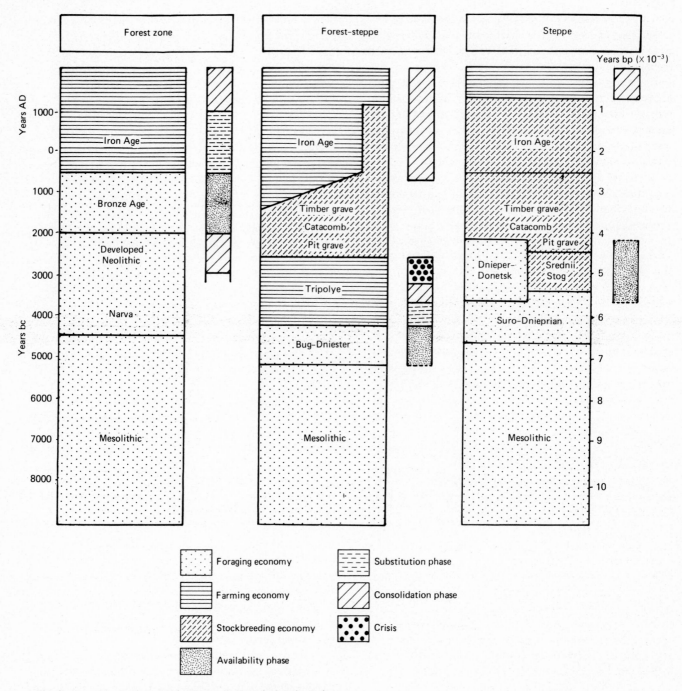

Fig. 4. Economic development in Eastern Europe during the Holocene.

In some cases one may distinguish a period of crisis. The critical conditons may be caused either by ecological factors (e.g. by a decrease in the agro-climatic potential) or by inner social contradictions. The most obvious example of such a critical situation may be seen in the final Palaeolithic or in the Late Tripolye developments.

Finally, the problem of the transition to a farming economy should be dealt with in a more general way. In the preceding paragraphs at least three cases of important changes in the subsistence pattern were established. They coincided (1) with the appearance of the Early Tripolye, (2) with the appearance of the Middle Dnieper culture, and (3) with the Iron Age in northwest Russia. The first two cases coincided with the introduction of alien cultural entities. Nonetheless, in each case the underlying processes were totally different. The appearance of the Early Tripolye must have taken the form of an extensive migration of a large agricultural community from an overpopulated area in the southwest. Remnants of the local foraging communities were either absorbed or evicted. One may only speculate about the competition between the two populations: archaeology retains no trace of it. The appearance of predominantly stockbreeding Middle Dnieprian communities arose mainly from the crisis of the Late Tripolye agricultural economy. This was largely due to the growing aridity of climate and to the inability of the Tripolyan economy to cope with the ecological crisis. On the contrary, the gradual transition to farming in northwest Russia in the course of the Iron Age was basically caused by inner socio-economic development. The outer factors were acting indirectly, accelerating this process.

In all cases, the fundamental changes in the subsistence pattern follow directly the critical situation arising from (1) overpopulation in areas adjacent to the zone of transition (as in the Early Tripolye), (2) and ecologically induced economic crisis (as in the Late Tripolye/Middle Dnieprian), and (3) a social crisis resulting mainly from domestic development (as in the Iron Age of northwest Russia). Thus despite the similarities in the process itself, the concrete trajectory of the transiton to farming and its social implications was dependent on a variety of conditions — the ecological setting, and the social, economic and cultural experience of the communities involved — which in each case combined in a particular way to bring about the shift to food production.

References

Alexander, J. (1978) 'Frontier studies and the earliest farmers in Europe', in D. Green, C. Hazelgrove and M. Spriggs, eds., *Social Organisation and Settlement*, pp. 13–29, BAR International Series 47, British Archaeological Reports, Oxford.

Ammerman, A. J. and Cavalli-Sforza, L. L. (1973) 'A population model for the diffusion of early farming in Europe', in C. Renfrew, ed., *The Explanation of Culture Change*, pp. 343–57, Duckworth, London.

Artemenko, I. I. (1967) *Plemena Verkhnego I Srednego Podneprovya V Epokhu Bronzy*, Nauka, Moscow.

Bibikov, S. N. (1953) 'Poselenie Luka-Vrubleveckaya'. *Materialy i Issledovaniya Po Arkheologii SSSR* 38.

(1965) 'Khozaistvenno-ekonomicheskii kompleks razvitogo Tripoliya (Opyt izucheniya pervobytnoi ekonomiki)'. *Sovetskaya Arkheologiya* 1, 48–62.

Bibikova, V. N. (1982) 'Teriofauna poseleniya Mirnoe', in V. N. Stanko, ed., *Mirnoe*, pp. 139–64.

Clark, J. G. D. (1952) *Prehistoric Europe; The Economic Basis*, Duckworth, London.

(1953) *The Economic Approach to Prehistory*, Albert Reckitt Archaeological Lecture, British Academy, London.

(1957) *Archaeology and Society*, Methuen, London.

Comşa, E. (1974) 'Die Entwicklung, Periodisierung und relative Chronologie der jungsteinzeitlichen Kulturen Rumäniens'. *Zeitschrift für Archäologie* 8, 1–44.

Danilenko, V. N. (1969) *Neolit Ukrainy*, Naukova Dumka, Kiev.

Dergachev, V. A. (1980) *Pamyatniki Pozdnego Tripolya*, Shtiintsa, Kishinev.

Dolukhanov, P. M. (1979a) *Ecology and Economy in Neolithic Eastern Europe*, Duckworth, London.

(1979b) *Geografiya Kamennogo Veka*, Nauka, Moscow.

(1983) 'The Neolithic of S.W. Asia and S.E. Europe as seen through the radiocarbon chronology', in H. G. Mook, ed., *^{14}C and Archaeology*, Journal of the European Study Group on Physical, Chemical and Biological Techniques applied to Archaeology 8, 469–90.

Dolukhanov, P. M. and Miklyaev, A. M. (1979) 'Kulturno-istoricheskie osnovy khronologii neolita i rannei bronzy v basseine zapadnoi Dviny'. *Kratkie Soobshchenia Instituta Arkheologii An SSSR* 157, 73–81.

Dolukhanov, P. M., Miklyaev, A. M. and Fonyakov, D. I. (1981) 'Smena kultur epokhi neolita-bronzy v basseine zapadnoi Dviny', in V. M. Masson and V. N. Boriaz, eds., *Preemstvennost i Innovatsii V Razvitii Kultur*, pp. 65–6, Nauka, Leningrad.

Dvorianinov, S. A. (1978) 'O dneprovskikh mogilnikakh kamennogo veka', in P. O. Kryshkovskiy, ed., *Arkheologicheskiye Issledovaniya Severo-Zapadnogo Prichernomoriya*, pp. 5–16, Naukova Dumka, Kiev.

Gribbin, J. (ed.) (1978) *Climatic Change*, Cambridge University Press, Cambridge.

Korneits, N. L., Gladkikh, M. I. and Velichko, A. A. (1981) 'Mezherich', in A. A. Velichko, ed., *Arkheologiya I Paleogeografiya Poznego Paleolita Russkoi Ravniny*, pp. 107–18.

Lee, R. B. and DeVore, I. (1968) *Man the Hunter*, Aldine, Chicago.

Markevich, V. I. (1974) *Bugo-Dnestrovskaya Kultura Na Territorii Moldavii*, Shtiintsa, Kishinev.

Mörner, N. A. (1980) 'A 10,000 years palaeotemperature record from Gotland and Pleistocene–Holocene boundary events in Sweden'. *Boreas* 9(4), 283–7.

Sahlins, M. (1974) *Stone Age Economics*, Aldine, Chicago.

Sedov, V. V. (1970) 'Slavyane Verkhnego Podneproviya i Podviniya'. *Materialy i Issledovaniya Po Arkheologii SSSR* 163.

(1982) *Vostochnye Slavyane v VI–XIII Vekhakh*. *Arkheologiya SSSR*, Nauka, Moscow.

Service, E. R. (1966) *The Hunters*, Prentice-Hall, Englewood Cliffs, New Jersey.

Shotton, F. M. (ed.) (1978) *British Quaternary Studies*, Clarendon Press, Oxford.

Stanko, V. N. (1982) *Mirnoe: Problema Mezolita Stepei Severnogo Prichernomoriya*, Naukova Dumka, Kiev.

Stolyar, A. D. (1959) 'Pervyi Vasil'evskii Mogilnik'. *Arkheologicheskii Sbornik Gosudarstvennogo Ermitazha* 1, 78–165.

Telegin, D. Ya. (1968) *Dniepro-Donetska Kultura*, Naukova Dumka, Kiev.

(1973) *Srednyo-Stogivska Kultura Epokhi Midi*, Naukova Dumka, Kiev.

(1982) *Mezolitichni Pamyatki Ukraini IX–VI Tisyacholittya Do Nashei Epokhi*, Naukova Dumka, Kiev.

Tsalkin, V. I. (1970) 'Drevneishie Domashnie Zhivotnye Vostochnoi Evropy'. *Materialy i Issledovaniya Po Arkheologii SSSR* 161.

Vereshchagin, N. K. (1979) *Pochemu vymerli Mamonty*, Nauka, Moscow.

Vereshchagin, N. K., Dolukhanov, P. M. and Miklyaev, A. M. (1979) 'Khozaistvo i ekologiya svainogo poseleniya Naumova v Pskovskoi oblasti'. *Izvestiya Vsesoyuznogo Geograficheskogo obshchestva* 4, 363–8.

Yanushevich, Z. V. (1976) *Kulturnye Rasteniya Yugo-Zapada SSR Po Paleobotanicheskim Dannym*, Shtiintsa, Kishinev.

Zbenovich, V. G. (1974) *Pozdnetripolskie Plemena Severnogo Prichernomorya*, Naukova Dumka, Kiev.

Zvelebil, M. (1978) 'Subsistence and settlement in the northeastern Baltic', in P. Mellars, ed., *The Early Postglacial Settlement of Northern Europe*, pp. 205–41, Duckworth, London.

(1985) 'Iron Age transformations in northern Russia and northeast Baltic', in G. Barker and C. Gamble, eds., *Beyond Domestication*, pp. 147–80, Academic Press, London.

Zvelebil, M. and Rowley-Conwy, O. (1984) 'Transition to farming in northern Europe: a hunter-gatherer perspective'. *Norwegian Archaeological Review* 17, 104–28.

Chapter 9

Foragers and farmers in west-Central Asia

P. M. Dolukhanov

The spread of economy in the Kopet Dagh piedmont occurred in the mid seventh millennium bc as a result of an integration of agricultural traditions originating in the Zagros with the local long-standing food-collecting traditions (the substitution phase). The social and economic development in the course of the sixth to third millennium bc resulted in the emergence of a network of proto-urban settlements in the late third millennium bc (consolidation phase). At the same time, groups of neolithic hunters, fishers and gatherers continued to exist in the Turanian lowland, maintaining intensive contacts with the agricultural communities to the south (the availability phase).

Introduction

Nowhere else in the USSR is the emergence and development of early farming and its interaction with foraging economies as evident as in Soviet Central Asia. The contrasting character of the natural environment, marked by sharp transitions from mountains to plains and by rapid changes from areas relatively rich in water to bare deserts, was a least partly responsible for this situation. Moreover, the region forms a part of the Central-Asian centre of origin of cultigens and is situated close to the Near-Eastern one (Vavilov 1960). As Vavilov (1960, p. 24) pointed out, the importance of the Turkmeno-Khorasan centre of origin of major domesticated plants, which provided the basis for settling the piedmonts of the Elburz and the Kopet Dagh, has often been overlooked. Similarly, Lisitsyna (1978) has distinguished another centre of early farming in Central Asia, located along the southeastern shores of the Caspian Sea.

Ecology

Tectonically, Central Asia lies within the border zone between two major structural units: the folded zone, a part of the alpine geosyncline belt, on the one hand, and the Turanian platform, on the other. An evenly folded arc of the Kopet Dagh, situated in the south of Turkmenia, constitutes the northernmost extension of the Turkmeno-Khorasan mountain system. An evenly tilted aggradation plain (or 'the piedmont strip') flanks the mountains to the north (Fig. 1).

The Turanian lowland takes up large areas in the north. Its folded basement is covered with thick deposits from the Mesozoic and Cenozoic. Huge plains are formed predominantly by the sands deposited by the two greatest central-Asian rivers, Amu-Darya and Syr-Darya, the Oxus and Jaxartes of antiquity. Large tablelands (Ust–Urt and Krasnovodsk plateaus) are situated in the northeast; they are formed by the exposures of the mesozoic structural basement of the Turanian plate.

The climate of the area is continental and extremely arid. The precipitation is insufficient. The Kopet Dagh mountains and the piedmont strip are the moistest areas: the annual precipitation there exceeds 250 mm. For the rest of the territory, the annual rainfall varies between 80 and 150 mm.

The mountain vegetation is of the steppe and forest-shrub types. Grass ephemeral vegetation prevails in the uncultivated areas of the piedmont strip. Wormwood ephemeral vegetation and saltwort formations cover the tablelands. The

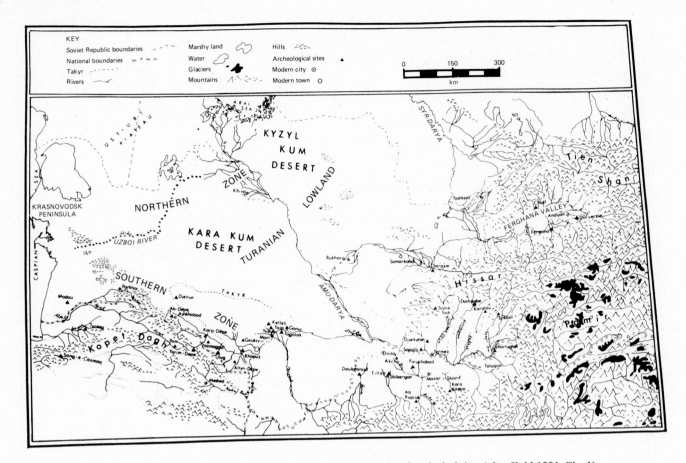

Fig. 1. Soviet Central Asia and surrounding territories: landscape features and archaeological sites (after Kohl 1981, Fig. 1).

tugai[1] exist in the flood plains of large rivers. The desert and semi-desert types of vegetation prevail in the rest of the territory.

Central Asia is a region of inner drainage. The Caspian and Aral Seas are lakes which have no outlet to the ocean. The greatest rivers, the Amu-Darya and Syr-Darya are fed mostly by meltwater of high mountain glaciers. Their discharge pattern depends on the general glaciological situation in the mountain area. Two other large rivers, Tedjen and Murghab, are fed predominantly by rainfall; consequently, the discharge values of these rivers vary enormously, depending on the weather conditions. About 50 rivers and numerous small streams flow across the northeastern slopes of the Kopet Dagh and the piedmont strip. Discharges of these rivers are relatively small but stable, groundwater making a major contribution to them. In the areas where the mountain river valleys open onto the piedmont strip, numerous terminal fans are formed. Due to a powerful underground artery which flows along the mountain range, the Kopet Dagh piedmont is well supplied with fresh groundwater.

Ecologically, therefore, the region under consideration can be subdivided into two zones: the southern, which includes the mountains, the aggradation plain, the delta plains of Tedjen and Murghab, all relatively rich in water, and the northern, which includes the desert/steppe lowlands and

tablelands with scarce water resources (Fig. 1). The distinctions in the natural resources of these two zones have greatly influenced the social and economic development of the local population in prehistory.

The environmental changes that occurred in Central Asia in the course of the late Pleistocene and Holocene are far from being clear. An insufficient amount of evidence (among other things due to the poor preservation of organic matter) has resulted in a great divergence of palaeoclimatic interpretations.

The natural environment of the western areas of Central Asia has been closely linked to the evolution of the Caspian Sea. In the Late Pleistocene there occurred at least two major Caspian transgressions referred to as the Lower and the Upper Khvalynian. There are three explanatory hypotheses as to the cause of the fluctuations of the Caspian Sea. Several researchers tend to correlate this process with tectonic movements. Others believe that these fluctuations are caused by the changes in the temperature and precipitation (Zubakov and Borzenkova 1983, pp. 118–19). According to the third hypothesis, put forward by Fedorov (1978) and Kvasov (1975), and which the present writer shares, the fluctuations in the level of the Caspian Sea have primarily been due to the changes in the catchment areas in conjunction with the development of glaciation. The absolute datings of the Caspian marine sediments seem to substantiate this view. The dates of

the Lower Khvalynian deposits lie in the time-span 65 000 to
35 000 years bp, thus closely coinciding with the age of the
Early Valdai (Wurm, Weichselian) glaciation, whereas the age
of the Upper Khvalynian (*c.* 20 000 to 10 000 bp) is roughly
similar to that of the Late Valdai glaciation (Kaplin *et al.*
1977).

At its maximal stage, the Lower Khvalynian transgression reached the levels of 47–50 m above the mean ocean
level; that is to say, about 78 m above the present level of the
Caspian Sea (which is now *c.* 28–29 metres below the ocean).
In the course of this transgression, the sea submerged the low-
lying areas in western Turkmenia, creating an extensive
estuarine and lagoon environment.

There is, at present, a considerable controversy about
the climatic conditions of the Late Pleistocene. On the basis
of the palynological records from the Caspian marine sediments, Abramova (1972) claims that the climate of the area
at that time was moister and colder than that of today.
Detailed palynological investigations of the sediments from
Lake Zeribar in the Zagros Mountains (west Iran) have convincingly shown that the climate in that area during the
'Pleniglacial' (*c.* 22 000–16 000 bp) was both dryer and colder
than at present (van Zeist and Bottema 1977). A considerable
dryness is indicated by the palynological evidence secured for
the late pleistocene deposits in eastern Georgia (Gogichaishvili
1973, pp. 46–8). Extreme aridity is also indicated at *c.*
10 000–8000 bp when the Caspian sea level dropped down
to 58–50 m below the ocean level (Maev and Maeva 1977;
Fedorov 1978, pp. 120–1) during the Mangyshlak regression.
Widespread eolian processes, recorded in the Caspian deposits
and the palynological data, which have revealed the prevalence
of desert and semi-desert vegetation (Fedorov 1978, p. 121;
Abramova 1980, p. 71), lend further support to this
interpretation.

A new rise in the sea-level began *c.* 8000–7000 bp, with
a series of transgressions known collectively as Neo-Caspian.
The highest transgressive levels have been dated to 6700–6400
and to 3400–3000 bp (Maev and Maeva 1977; Kaplin *et al.*
1977). At approximately the same time, an increase in the
discharge of both the Amu- and Syr-Darya resulted in the
formation of a huge Aralian-Sarykamysh basin (Fig. 2). The
overflowing of this basin has led to the formation of the Uzboi
river, through which the overflowing water has been dis-
charged into the Caspian Sea. The functioning of the Uzboi is
estimated to have lasted from 9000 to 3000 bp (Kes 1969; Kes
et al. 1980; Kvasov 1980). (See Figs. 1 and 2.)

The majority of researchers share the opinon that during
the Neo-Caspian transgression (which corresponded in time to
the atlantic period or hypsithermal in the northern latitudes),
the climate in Central Asia was both moister and less continental than now. An increase in precipitation is indicated by
the geochemical composition of the Neo-Caspian sediments
(Fedorov 1978, p. 121). The palynological spectra of these
deposits contain tree species indicative of forest-type ecotopes
(Abramova 1980, p. 72) and species which are either non-

existent at present or are restricted to the most humid microenvironments (Samsonov 1963).

Palaeogeographical and archaeological investigations
carried out in the inner areas of the Kyzyl Kum Desert by
Vinogradov and Mamedov (1975; Vinogradov 1981) have
made it possible to distinguish in that area a so-called
'Lyavlyakan pluvial phase'. The occurrence of this phase is
substantiated by the fossil carbonate soil established in the
area of the Lyavlyakan lake. Judging from the number of
neolithic–eneolithic sites, the large population which had
existed there required the presence of either fresh or slightly
brackish water in lakes that now consist of salt water.
Vinogradov and Mamedov (1975, p. 253) imply that the
climate of the central Kyzyl Kum Desert at that time had been
similar to that of the present day steppe zone, with the annual
rainfall ranging from 250 to between 400 and 500 mm, and
the mean July temperature being above 21–23 °C.

The occurrence of an extensive drainage network was
one of the main features of the humid phase in Central Asia.
Apart from the Uzboi river, numerous streams and lakes, both
perennial and seasonal, supplied the area with water. The
tugai forests grew in the flood plains, providing food for many
animals. Dense vegetation is thought to have existed in low
and medium high mountains.

Summing up the existing palaeogeographical and
archaeological evidence for Soviet Central Asia and neighbouring regions, one may conclude that there are good reasons to
accept the occurrence of a lengthy humid phase in the course
of the Holocene. During this phase there was an increase in
the precipitation and a decrease in the continentality of the
climate; woodland vegetation expanded considerably, mostly
in the mountain areas; and the area was drained by a well-
developed hydrological network. This humid phase occurred
from *c.* 8000 to 3000 bp (6000 to 1000 bc).

The Mesolithic
The onset of the Holocene coincided with a marked
increase in the population. The number of mesolithic sites is
much greater than that of Upper Palaeolithic; some writers
(Davis 1980, p. 41) suggest that considerable parts of Central
Asia were deserted during the last glaciation, between 30 000
and 14 000 bc. After that time epipalaeolithic sites occur in
the region. The epipalaeolithic layer I at the site of Shugnou in
the Tadjik depression has a radiocarbon date of 10 700 ± 500
bp (Pakhomov, Nikonov and Ranov 1977). At present about
20 stratified mesolithic sites are known from Central Asia
(Korobkova 1977, p. 109). These sites are unequally distributed over the whole area. The majority of sites are located in
the mountain areas: in canyons and within the intermontane
depressions in eastern Central Asia. The cave site of Machai,
radiocarbon dated to 7550 ± 110 bp, is situated in the
Machaidarya valley, in the mountain area of southern
Uzbekistan (Islamov 1975). The mesolithic cave sites,
Obishir 1 and Obishir 5, were found in the southern part of
the Ferghana valley, on the bank of a stream, which crossed a

plateau flanking a high mountain ridge (Islamov 1980). *Capra ibex sibirica* prevailed in the faunal remains at all these sites. Apart from that, the faunal lists included argali, gazelle and Tartarian roe deer. In all these sites the occurrence of domesticated animals has been reported. Vinogradov (1981, p.138) has expressed doubts about the stratigraphical authenticity of these finds. In his opinion, the bones of domesticated animals have penetrated the cave deposits in post-mesolithic times.

The co-existence of an advanced blade technique with archaic pebble-tools is the main feature of the mesolithic cave sites in southern Uzbekistan (Korobkova 1977, p. 112). Islamov (1975, p. 121) has stressed the resemblance between the stone inventories of the Machai cave, on the one hand, and those of the Upper Palaeolithic Samarkand site on the other (notched blades, end-scrapers, cores).

Mesolithic sites have been found on wind-blown dunes surrounding the extinct lakes in the central regions of the Ferghana valley (Zadneprovskii 1966, pp. 134—42). Korobkova (1969, pp. 127—41; 1977, p. 112) has remarked that, with the exception of pebble tools, the stone inventory of these sites is similar to that of the cave sites.

Numerous mesolithic sites (e.g. Tutkaul: layers 2a and 3; Sai—Sayod layer 3; Oshkhona; Obi—Kiik) are situated within the high mountains of the western Pamir and surrounding areas of eastern Central Asia. These are predominantly open-air sites located on the terraces of mountain rivers. The radio-carbon dates of these sites range from the twelfth to the tenth millennium bp. As indicated by the pollen data (Pakhomov *et al.* 1977, pp. 61—4), vegetation of mountain desert type prevailed in the neighbourhood of these sites. The economy was based on nomadic hunting (Masson 1966, pp. 145—8; Ranov and Korobkova 1971, pp. 133—47). Korobkova (1977, p. 113) has recognised several local variants of the blade and pebble-tool industries. In some cases, (layer 3 at Tutkaul) geometric microliths, consisting mainly of trapezes and rectangular pieces, formed a part of the industry. Between 10 000 and 6000 years bp a neolithic Hissar culture developed in the same area on the basis of the local Mesolithic. The occurrence of stockbreeding and agriculture has been attested for the later stages of the Hissarian Neolithic (Ranov 1982, pp. 22—41).

The lower layers of several cave sites in western Turkmenia have been attributed to the Mesolithic. These are: Kailyu on the Krasnovodsk peninsula; Dam-Dam-Cheshma 1 and 2; the Djebel Cave on the slopes of the Greater Balkan ridge (Okladnikov 1966, pp. 59—66; Korobkova 1969, pp. 193—5). All these sites were also occupied in neolithic times.

The lithic assemblages of the mesolithic sites in that area consisted of various cores and core-like implements, blades, borers, end-scrapers, discoid scrapers, as well as microlithic tools (trapezes and crescents) (Okladnikov 1966, pp. 59—63). Korobkova (1970, pp. 21—5; 1977, pp. 109—12) distinguished two types of industries there: the first one being related to the

cave sites in northern Iran (Belt, Hotu), the second to the Zarzian.

The available evidence is insufficient for the chronological division of the Mesolithic in Central Asia. None the less, from the typology of stone tools (appearance of trapezes and of symmetrical crescents), Okladnikov (1966, pp. 60—2) was able to distinguish an early and a late stage in the Mesolithic of the Caspian region.

The evidence related to the settlement pattern of the Mesolithic is equally insufficient. Islamov (1975, p. 111) considers that the large cave site of Machai was a base-camp. If so, the culturally related open-air sites of the Ferghana Mesolithic may be viewed as seasonal sites of the same cultural group. In summary, one may assume that the majority of the mesolithic sites in Central Asia were seasonal camps which belonged to small groups of hunters exploiting migratory ungulates. These sites were deposited during the gradual expansion of the population, previously restricted during the glacial epoch. Long-range migration (from the Zagros range) does not seem probable.

The Neolithic

Korobkova and Masson (1978, p. 103) consider the Neolithic as a final stage of the Stone Age. In their view, the Neolithic in Central Asia can be defined by the exclusive utilisation of stone and bone tools (survival of the mesolithic traditions supplemented by new technical methods, such as polishing, sharpening of cutting edges etc.; emergence of completely new tools, e.g. sickle blades, polished axes, adzes etc.) and an extensive use of ceramics.

As noted above, ecologically the territory of Central Asia may be divided into two zones, which are clearly distinct in terms of the scope of the natural resources. In the course of the Neolithic, distinct social and economic patterns developed within each zone, thus providing a basis for the rise of two separate cultural traditions (Korobkova 1969, p. 7).

Northern zone (Fig. 2)

According to Korobkova and Masson (1978, pp. 103—8), neolithic industries occur in the northern zone in the late sixth to early fifth millennium bc. New evidence secured in the course of control excavations of the Djebel Cave seems to support an earlier date for the 'northern' Neolithic. A charcoal sample taken from the layer corresponding to layer 4 as distinguished by Okladnikov (1956) has yielded an age of 6140 ± 80 bp (P-3081) or *c.* 4100 bc. Thus, the earliest Neolithic as represented by the layers 5 and 5a of the Djebel Cave cannot be more recent than the sixth millennium bc.

Western Turkmenia has come to be seen as one of the centres of early neolithic settlement. The sites include the Djebel and the Kailyu Caves (Okladnikov 1966, pp. 59—60) and the cave sites of Dam-Dam-Cheshma 1 and 2. The Djebel Cave (*ibid.* 1956) was found on the northern slope of a canyon

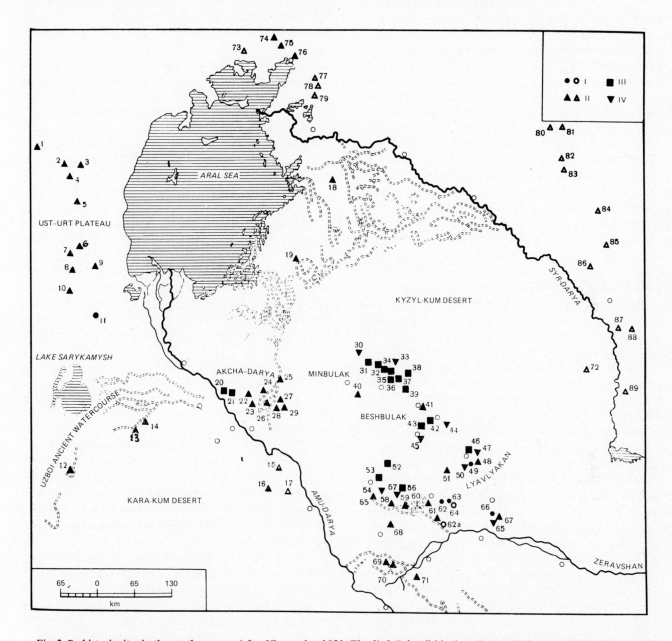

Fig. 2. Prehistoric sites in the northern zone (after Vinogradov 1981, Fig. 4). I, Palaeolithic sites; II, mesolithic and neolithic sites; III, rock painting; IV, turquoise mines.

1, Sam; 2, Karakuduk; 3, Aidabol; 4, Churuk; 5, Beleuli; 6, Kosbulak; 7, Aktailak; 8, Isatai; 9, Bulak; 10, Alan; 11, Yesen; 12, Upper Uzboi; 13, Gyaur; 14, Tumekkichidjik cemetery; 15, Sultansahdjar; 16, Transunguz Kara Kumy sites; 17, Kosbulak I; 18, Kosmola; 19, Zhalpak; 20, Tebinbulak; 21, Sultanuizdag; 22, Burly workshop; 23, Kavat; 24, Kurgashin; 25, Tadjikazgan; 26, Djanbas; 27, Jingeldy; 28, Bairamkazgan; 29, Mamur; 30, Burkantau rock-paintings; 31, Irlir; 32, Ayakashchi; 33, Bukantau rock paintings; 34, Turbai I; 35, Jaman-Kaskyr; 36, Karatau; 37, Derbez; 38, Kuniya; 39, Tasgazgan; 44, Tadymtau rock-paintings; 45, Sugraly; 46, Ayakudak; 47, Kazakhtau; 48, Lyavlyakan; 49, Lyavlyakan (palaeolithic finds); 50, Kazakhtau; 51, Karakata; 52, Uireltytau; 53, Taskazgan; 54, Tasbulak; 55, low Daryasai sites; 56, Taushan; 57, Taushan (cluster of rock-paintings); 58, middle Daryasai sites; 60 eastern Ayakagitma delta sites; 62a, Echkiliksai (palaeolithic, neolithic); 62, palaeolithic sites on the eastern edge of Ayakagitma; 63, palaeolithic finds in Karasygyr depression; 64, Kyzylnura I; 65, Sarmichsai; 66–67, Uchtut and Idjont workshops (palaeolithic–neolithic); 68, sites along ancient waterways between Daryasai and Makhandarya; 69, Great Tuzkan; 70, Little Tuzkan; 71, Paikent; 72, Karaktau; 73, Agispe; 74, Saksaul'skaya; 75, Kontu; 76, Aralsk; 77, Tampi; 78, Shulkum; 79, Baskuduk; 80, Sarysubulak; 81, Boktykatyn; 82, Aktuzbulak; 83, Ashchisorsu; 84, Segiz; 85, Engels; 86, Besaryk; 87, Mayatas; 88, Aktobe; 89, Taskotan.

cutting into a monocline fold. An aggradation plain lies at its base, while the terraced Uzboi valley is situated below. In the course of his excavations, Okladnikov (*ibid*.) distinguished in Djebel 10 archaeological layers, the five lower ones of which he has attributed to the Mesolithic, and the five upper to the Neolithic.

The osteological investigations performed by Tsalkin (1956, pp. 220–2) failed to establish any changes in the faunal composition, remains of gazelle, sheep and goat being dominant in all the layers. It is worth noting that Tsalkin (1956, p. 221) a zoologist, reserved his judgement on whether the sheep and goats had been domesticated or not. Fishing played an important role in the economy of the site, situated close to a major river. Numerous fish bones have been identified, sterlet and carp being the most common. Among the small animals typical of the desert and steppe ecotones (tortoise, agama), species of lizards at present existing far to the north have been identified. A pomegranate skin and apricot stones have been found in the uppermost layers.

A great number of neolithic sites has been established in the Uzboi valley. Some 550 km in length, the valley extends from the southern bay of the Sarykamysh depression up to the Balkhan gulf of the Caspian Sea. The slopes of the valley are terraced, the width of the terrace varies from 0.5 up to 1.5 km. Relics of numerous small lakes and pools are visible within the valley. Neolithic sites have been found mostly in the upper stretches of the Uzboi. The sites are usually located between the sand ridges developed on the margins of terraces, or on the shores of pools and lakes in the valley (Tolstov and Kes 1960, pp. 267–343). The bulk of the sites date to the fourth to third millennium bc (Itina 1958). Pollen records indicate a rich *tugai* vegetation, which included numerous trees: fir, pine, birch, alder, oak, hornbeam, hazel (Kes 1952, p. 21), covering the valley in neolithic times. Judging by the age of the archaeological sites, the Uzboi river ceased to exist at the beginning of the first millennium bc (Tolstov and Kes 1960, p. 310).

The huge oval-shaped depression of Sarykamysh is now situated at a depth of about 40 m below the ocean level. Earlier in the Holocene it contained a lake, which reached a maximum depth of 98 m, judging from the heights of corresponding terraces, beach ridges and cliffs. The neolithic sites, dated mainly to the fourth and third millennia bc, have been found mostly on the southern shores, usually on sand terraces of small bays (Tolstov and Kes 1960, pp. 226–32).

The greatest cluster of neolithic sites is situated along the southern course of the Amu-Darya, the Akcha-Darya delta. Vinogradov (1968, p. 10) has noted that the sites are usually situated in the marginal zone of the delta. The oldest sites lie on the inner delta uplands, on cut-off lobes of pre-quaternary sediments. The Djanbas upland is a typical example; on its northwestern margin the bulk of sites belonging to 'the Djanbas cluster' was established (Tolstov 1948; Vinogradov 1968, pp. 25–65). According to the geomorphological data obtained by Kes, Vinogradov and Itina (1968, pp. 163–4), only small streams and seasonal pools had been

present in the area during the initial settlement (Djanbas 4). The *tugai* vegetation was well developed. Thus, the settlement pattern was entirely dependent on the evolution of the Amu-Darya and the surrounding basins.

Several clusters of neolithic sites have been uncovered in the lower Zeravshan valley, dating from the sixth to the late third millennium bc (Vinogradov 1981, pp. 132–3). The sites are located on sand ridges situated on the banks of lakes or in dry valleys (Darbazakyr 1, 2, Tuzkan sites; Gulyamov, Islamov and Askarov 1966), or along the streams in the northern section of the delta plain (Vinogradov 1981, pp. 64–77). The economy of these sites was based mostly on gazelle hunting, fishing (pike, catfish) and on food collecting (including the harvesting of wild cereals).

Recent investigations have also resulted in the discovery of many neolithic sites in the inner areas of the Kyzyl Kum (Fig. 2). It has been established (Vinogradov and Mamedov 1975; Vinogradov 1981) that the majority of these sites is located in the depressions of inner drainages, the origin of which is largely due to wind erosion: Lyavlyakan, Karakata, Beshbulak, Minbulak. The sites are usually situated in the blow-outs within huge sandy plains flanking the lakes from the south.

Numerous neolithic sites have also been discovered on the Ust–Urt plateau. The sites are located on the shores of dry lakes and in dry valleys. Vinogradov (1981, p. 29) has noted that the sites cluster on heights around 100 m and between 120 and 130 m above sea level.

Let us have a close look at what is definitely known about the subsistence pattern of the Neolithic in the northern zone. The number of sites which contain organic remains is relatively small. In his synopsis, which includes the existing evidence for the sites in the Akcha-Darya delta, the lower Zeravshan valley and the Lyavlyakan, Vinogradov (1981, pp. 139–41) has distinguished the two faunal groups which constituted the principal hunted resources: (1) red deer, fallow deer, wild pig; (2) kulan, saiga, gazelle, aurochs, moufflon, camel (Tables 1 and 2). Judging from the ecology of these animals, the hunting territory included the *tugai* forests, open steppes and mountain ridge. There is some evidence that the hunting of waterfowl played a major role in the economy. Bird bones found at the Tolstov site in the Akcha-Darya delta belong exclusively to waterfowl; these include mallard, pochard, teal, golden eye, grebe and cormorant (Vinogradov 1981, p. 142).

Trace-wear analysis provides additional information relating to the importance of hunting in the neolithic economy of the northern zone. According to Korobkova (1969, pp. 182–3), 70–80% of the implements from neolithic sites in the Caspian area, in the Akcha-Darya delta, the lower Zeravshan and the Ferghana valley revealed traces of use either directly related to hunting or connected to the processing of products secured by hunting.

Fish remains indicate the importance of fishing in the neolithic economy. Apart from the records from the Djebel

Table 1. *Bones remains from the Tolstov site*

Species	Number of bones
Large bovines	49
Red deer	287
Camel	1
Onager	1
Gazelle	9
Wild pig	35
Hare	2
Fox	42
Dog	16
Dog/jackal/wolf(?)	1
Badger	2
Polecat	1
Bobak marmot	2
Large ungulates	189
Small ungulates	4
Undetermined	1603
Birds	45
Total	2289
	Fish (%)
Pike	86
Carp	9
Catfish	3
Pike-perch	2

After Vinogradov 1981, p. 140.

Table 2. *Bone remains from Uchashchi 131 site*

Species	No. of bones	No. of individuals
Bison	65	6
Onager	4	2
Gazelle	20	3
Wild pig	20	3
Corsac fox	1	1
Badger	1	1
Suslik	1	1
Rodents	1	1
Undetermined (mainly ungulates)	170	?
Total	283	

After Vinogradov 1981, p. 140.

most striking differences occur in the pottery assemblages. On the basis of the analysis of ceramics, Vinogradov (1968) distinguished the following cultures in the Kyzyl Kum area: Lower Uzboi, Upper Uzboi, Kelteminar proper (or Akcha-Darya) with local variants: Lyavlyakan and Lower Zeravshan.

The remains of dwellings have been found on several sites in the northern neolithic province. Summing up the existing evidence, Vinogradov (1981, pp. 148–54) noted that the most common type of dwelling in the northern zone was a rectangular house, the roof of which was supported by posts; the size of these houses varied from 80 to between 120 and 150 m^2. The second type of dwelling was a semi-subterranean hut, presumably of rectangular shape but of a smaller size than the other type. At the Tolstov site, both types of dwelling existed simultaneously.

In the delta areas the neolithic settlements were of a considerable size. Three dwellings have been established at the sites of Uchashchi 131 in the Zeravshan valley and at Tolstov. A great number of dwellings have been unearthed at the site of Uchashchi 159.

At least several sites in the delta area were of a permanent or semi-permanent character. According to Vinogradov (1981, p. 155) the population of such sites might have reached up to 150–200 persons (these appear to be the maximum estimates). A fixed number of hearths within the dwelling and their regular setting are seen as an indication of the existence of the basic social unit, the nuclear family.

The emergence and development of the neolithic in the northern zone may be seen as an adaptation by the local population to an increase in precipitation during the mid Holocene. This resulted in the appearance of a complicated hydrological network, which included the Amu-Darya–Sarykamysh–Uzboi system, with countless freshwater streams and lakes. Biotopes rich in wild plant and animal resources evolved along these watercourses. Under these conditions, a rapid population growth occurred as the expanding population was moving along the watercourses colonising new areas rich in

Cave mentioned above, fish remains have been found at two sites in the Akcha-Darya delta: Djanbas 4 and Tolstov (Vinogradov 1981, p. 143). At both sites the bulk of fish fauna belonged to pike, which together with carp made up more than 90% of the entire sample of fish (Table 1).

There is extensive evidence for food gathering. This includes pomegranate and apricots found at Djebel, wild olive stones, egg shells and edible freshwater molluscs from the Tolstov and Djanbas 4 (Vinogradov 1981, p. 146), and tortoise shells, reported from a number of sites. Numerous finds of grinding stones, mortars, pestles and sickle blades provide additional evidence concerning the importance of food collecting. The sickle blades are present in small numbers at the sites in the lower Zeravshan valley; at Kyzylryk, however, they make up more than 10% of the entire toolkit (Korobkova 1969, p. 186). From the occurrence of Linear Wear patterns identified microscopically on the sickles, Korobkova (1969, p. 186; 1978, pp. 42–4) has assumed that the implements were used for cutting domesticated grains. Vinogradov (1981, p. 139) on the other hand, argues that the whole tool assemblage reflected the harvesting of wild plants.

The stone industry of the northern zone is reasonably uniform. Korobkova (1969) distinguishes several local assemblages (Caspian, Kelteminar, Ferghana, Hissar) while stressing the common elements existing in all of them. The

---

natural resources. The economy remained, however, based on the exploitation of wild resources. In the deltas, a pattern of permanent or semi-permanent settlement seems to have evolved. These sites were surrounded by special-purpose, seasonal camps in the interfluves. Due to the lack of evidence, one cannot reconstruct this pattern in more detail.

The neolithic population of the northern zone maintained extensive economic and cultural contacts with its agricultural neighbours in the south. Thus, the spread of pottery manufacture in the north may be satisfactorily explained as the adoption of a technological innovation which originated in the south. The adoption of pottery, even though it did not change the general subsistence pattern, has contributed to the sedentism of the local population.

As the duration of its existence indicates, the subsistence pattern which evolved in the northern zone was a stable one, albeit dependent on the abundance of wild resources. The decline in the number of sites at the end of the third and the beginning of the second millennium bc corresponds to the general aridisation of climate and the attendant decrease in the wild resources. The demographic pressure from the south,

where overpopulation was more acute, was an important factor too. In these conditions, a gradual spread of stock-breeding became a widely accepted alternative to both foraging and farming. Stockbreeding became the dominant form of economy in the course of the second millennium bc.

Southern zone (Fig. 3)

The sites of the sedentary food-producing Djeitun culture, dated to the final seventh and sixth millennia bc, correspond to the initial settlement of the Kopet Dagh aggradation plain (Korobkova and Masson 1978, p. 106). The Djeitun settlements are usually situated on the terminal fans of small Kopet Dagh rivers entering the piedmont strip. The sites tend to cluster along the watercourses. The largest cluster of these sites can be observed in the central Kopet Dagh oasis, Ahala. The largest Djeitunian settlement of Bami (c. 4 ha), however, is situated at the western margin of Djeitun settlement, on an evenly tilted plain dissected by numerous dry valleys (Berdyev 1969, pp. 28–9). Archaeological investigations in northern Iran extend the area of the Djeitun culture to the intermontane valleys and the southern piedmont of the

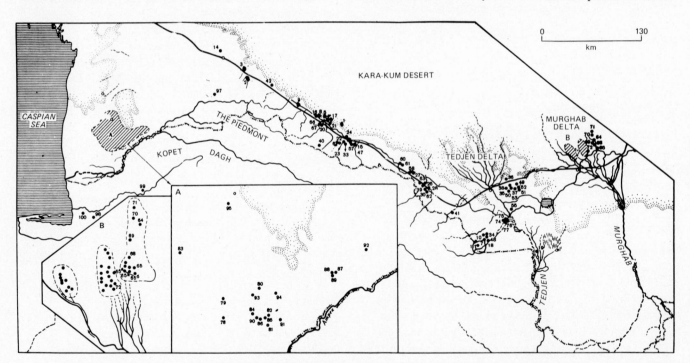

Fig. 3. Prehistoric sites (sixth to first millennium bc) in the southern zone (after Lisitsyna 1978, Fig. 3).

1, Djeitun; 2, Bami; 3, Naiza-tepe; 4, Chopan-depe; 5, Togollok-depe; 6, Novaia Nisa; 7, Chagylly-depe; 8, Pessedjik-depe; 9, Kelyata; 10, Monzhukly-depe; 11, Gadymi-depe; 12, Kepele; 13, Kantar; 14, Kizyl–Arvat; 15, Yarty–Gumbez; 16, Geok-tepe; 17, Geok-depe II; 18, Ilgynly-depe; 19, Serakhs; 20, Tilkin-depe; 21, Dashly-depe; 22, Bagir; 23, Ekin-depe; 24, Ovadan-depe; 25, Kaushut; 26, Anau, northern hill; 27, Kara-depe; 28, Yassy-depe; 29, Sermancha-depe; 30, Namazga-depe; 31, Beurme; 32, Karntki-depe; 33, Ak-depe; 34, Altyn-depe; 35, Geoksyur I; 36, Dashlydji-depe; 37, Geoksyur 7; 38, Akcha-depe; 37, Gara-depe; 40, Chulinskoie; 41, Ulug-depe; 42, Suncha-depe; 43, Suncha-depe; 44, Chinghiz-depe; 45, Gavych-depe; 46, 102 km; 47, Govuch-depe; 48, Chakmakly-depe; 49, Yalangach-depe; 50, Geoksyer 9; 51, Chong-depe; 52, Mullali-depe; 53, Aina-depe; 54, Telken-depe; 55, Khapuz-depe; 56, Kosha-depe; 57, Anau, southern hill; 58, Taichanak-depe; 59, Shor-depe; 60–61, Baba Durmaz hills; 62, Tekkem-depe; 63 Yelken-depe; 64, Auchin-depe; 65, Takhirbai 3; 66, Yangi–Kalin cemetry; 72, Yaz-depe; 73, Togollok; 74, Saryk-depe; 75, Chemche-depe; 76, Kush-depe; 77, Khairak-depe; 78, Tanksikyldja; 79, Chialyk-depe; 80, Madau-depe; 81, Chopan-depe; 82–96, sites of archaic Dahistan culture; 97, Parkhai-depe; 98, Tureng Tepe; 99, Yarim-Tepe; 100, Shah Tepe.

Turkmeno-Khorasan mountains where these sites have been dated to the mid seventh millennium bc (Kohl 1981, p. xiv).

Judging from the available evidence, the earliest Djeitunian sites were situated in areas comparatively distant from the mountain chains, a fact already observed by Bukinich (1924). The eponymous site of Djeitun, is typical in that respect (Masson 1971): it is located within the southernmost sand ridge of the Kara Kum Desert. Geomorphological investigations have shown that the settlement lay on the alluvial fan of the Kara-su river (Lisitsyna 1965, pp. 24–5). A perennial stream was situated in the vicinity; the *tugai* vegetation grew on its banks.

The economy of the Djeitun settlements was based on agriculture. The palaeobotanical remains include the following cereals: two-row barley, bread wheat and club wheat (Masson 1971, p. 79). From the beginning of the period, stockbreeding (predominantly sheep/goat) was an important element in the Djeitunian economy (Table 3). At later stages the existence of cattle breeding is attested (Masson 1971, p. 86). At the same time hunting remained economically important, providing no less than 25% of the meat diet. Gazelle and onager seem to have been the most common wild resources. The continuing importance of hunting is also attested by the trace-wear analysis. According to Korobkova (1969, pp. 70–2), implements related to hunting (geometric microliths, knives) and to the processing of skins (side-scrapers) held a significant position in the toolkit of the Djeitunian sites.

Judging from the size of the completely excavated sites, an average Djeitunian settlement included 150–180 persons. It consisted of small houses, taken to indicate that the nuclear family was the basic social unit (Masson 1971, pp. 103–4). Large dwellings or 'communal houses', thought to have had a specialised economic function, have been uncovered at a number of sites, as well. At the same time, no evidence of either exogamic phratries or of any kind of social stratification have been found.

Several hypotheses have been put forward to explain the origins of the Djeitun culture. The notion, held by some, of a local origin, presumes the existence of a hypothetical 'Protodjeitunian site' in the Kopet Dagh mountains. Since no such site has been found so far, this suggestion remains purely speculative. Noting the similarity between the Djeitunian lithic industry on the one hand, and that of the Caspian Mesolithic, on the other, Korobkova (1969, pp. 195–6) sees the emergence of the Djeitun culture as being due to the migration of the mesolithic population from the Caspian area on to the Kopet Dagh piedmont. Masson (1971, p. 77), examining the Djeitunian against the background of the early farming civilisations in the vast area of the Near and Middle East, considers the Djeitunian as one of the elements in the emergence of agricultural civilisation throughout this territory as a whole.

In the present writer's view, any discussion of the origin of early farming in Central Asia should take into account the following considerations: (1) the long-standing traditions of a foraging economy dating back to the Mesolithic; (2) the ecological prerequisites for the development of early farming in the Kopet Dagh piedmont, brought about by the increase in precipitation and a decrease in the continentality of climate; (3) the demographic instability of early farming (Dolukhanov 1981*b*, pp. 141–8), often resulting in emigration. The last process might have been responsible for the initial spread of the farming economy in the intermontane valleys and in the piedmont of the Turkmeno-Khorasan mountains. In all probability, a comparatively small population of farmers and stockbreeders from the Zagros dispersed among the communities of hunters, fishers and food collectors, introducing agricultural practices, architectural traditions and ceramics. Farming became established, however, only in the ecologically favourable zone and even there only as a part of a mixed economy, where foraging strategies have retained their position. The mesolithic element in the Djeitunian culture is demonstrated in the stone and bone inventory, related to the foraging activity.

During the Eneolithic period (fifth to third millennium bc), a further consolidation of the agricultural settlements occurred. This is marked by the increase in population density and the development of large settlements such as Namazga-depe and Kara-depe. The pattern of settlement shifted to the middle stretches of the piedmont rivers. This is shown, for example, by the siting of Namazga-depe, located in the Kaakhka section of the proluvial–alluvial zone of the piedmont strip (Dolukhanov 1981*a*, pp. 365–76).

The penetration of agricultural settlement onto the delta plain of the Tedjen by the end of the Namazga 1 stage (*c.* 3700 bc) marks the expansion of the farming economy beyond the piedmont to a new and different niche, characterised by seasonal fluctuations in the volume of the watercourses in the Tedjen plain. In response to these changes in environmental conditions, a complicated system of irrigation came into being at Geoksyur oasis and elsewhere in the Tedjen (Lisitsyna 1965).

Intensive cultivation in the Tedjen continued until the end of the fourth millennium bc, when life in the Geoksyur oasis gradually faded away. In my opinion one main factor for this was the instability of agriculture in the Tedjen delta.

Table 3. *Faunal remains from the Djeitun site*

Species	No. of Ind.	Weight (kg)	(%)
Bezoar goat	58	3135	41
Wild goat	18	900	11.7
Sheep and goat	23	1196	15.6
Gazelle	27	675	8.6
Ungulates	51	1351.5	18.9
Wild pig	2	300	4

After Masson 1971, p. 86.

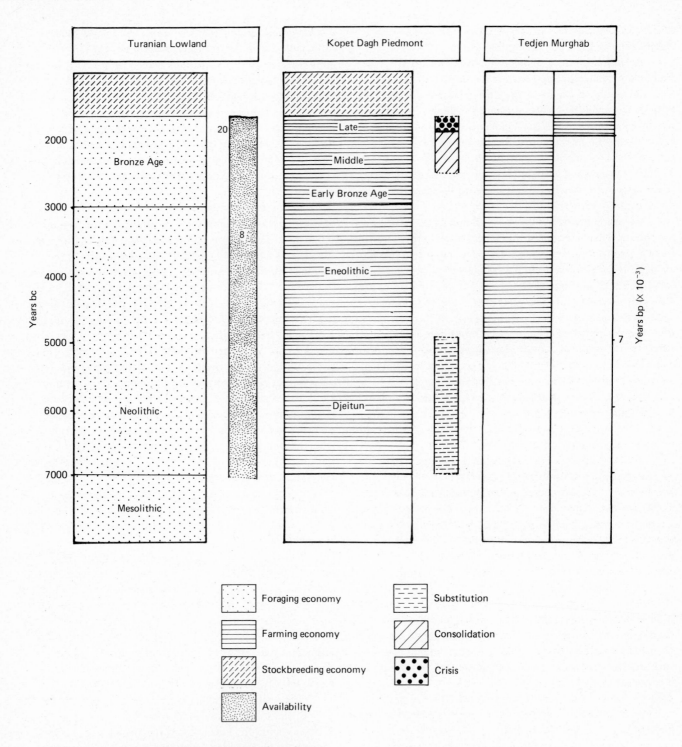

Fig. 4. Economic development in Central Asia in the Holocene.

Several droughts in succession causing severe famines could have forced the population to abandon the area.

Another period of agricultural expansion occurred in the Bronze Age. Although the spatial pattern of agricultural settlements remained basically the same as in the previous stages, the size and the complexity of the major settlements increased to a proto-urban level (Masson 1981). The Altyn-depe, for example, a settlement housing 6000–7000 people, possessed such classic attributes of proto-urban society as monumental religious architecture and seals with inscriptions similar to those found in the Indus valley.

By this time we are dealing with fully agricultural communities in the southern zone, consolidating their position by increasing the sophistication of the farming system, which included irrigation and the use of beasts for traction. Nevertheless, hunting retained some of its economic importance:

onager, gazelle, wild pig, saiga and wild goat continued to be hunted.

During all the stages discussed above, the south continued to maintain contacts with communities less committed to farming in the northern zone. Vinogradov (1968, pp. 146–8) observed similarities in the ornamentation of pottery of the Khorezmian Neolithic, on the one hand, and that of the agricultural settlements in the south, on the other, which seem too extensive to be merely coincidental. Korobkova (1969, pp. 178–9) noted a similarity in the sickle blades between the Djeitunian and neolithic sites in the lower Zeravshan valley. The contacts between agricultural and 'northern' neolithic sites were made easier by the close proximity of the sites in the contact zone. Thus, the site of Kyrk–Kyly, with lithic industries similar to those of Djebel Cave, was situated only 20 km northeast of the Djeitunian settlement (Korobkova 1969, p. 196).

Summarising the evidence related to the Neolithic, Eneolithic and Bronze age of the 'southern zone' one may draw the following conclusions. The emergence of agriculture in this zone was primarily due to a process common to Central Asia as a whole: a gradual increase in precipitation and a subsequent population growth. A part of the expanding population which had penetrated the Kopet Dagh piedmont found itself in an environment highly suitable for farming.

The combination of the farming practices with the local foraging strategies during the humid phase of the mid Holocene resulted in the emergence of highly effective socioeconomic adaptations in the Kopet Dagh piedmont. In the course of the fifth to third millennium bc, the gradual development of a complex social structure and a concomitant increase in population density took place. During this period contacts were maintained with the neighbouring civilisations to the south and also with the 'neolithic' groups to the north. The contacts with the latter included exchanges of raw material, food, and tools related to agriculture and gathering. Similarities in the ornamentation of pottery imply some form of relationship in the social and ideological sphere. It seems certain, however, that no major population displacements from the south to the north, or in the opposite direction, occurred in the Neolithic. Surplus population resulting from the excess population growth of the Kopet Dagh piedmont migrated either to the Tedjen and Murghab deltas and further to the east, or to the south, e.g. to the Hilmand valley in Sistan (Tosi 1979, pp. 152–3).

The development of economic and social patterns in the southern zone reached its apex during the Middle Bronze Age, with the development of proto-urban centres. In the following centuries, with the increasing aridity of the climate and a shift to desert conditions, the agricultural settlements in the south of Central Asia gradually disappeared.

Conclusions

Let us try to evaluate the transition to farming of the prehistoric groups in Central Asia in the terms suggested by Zvelebil and Rowley-Conwy (1984, pp. 104–6; Chapter 6,

this volume) (Fig. 4). As in Eastern Europe, the availability phase can be clearly traced. In the northern zone, where foraging strategies remained for a long time the most effective and often the only possible form of food quest, all neolithic groups passed through this stage. Agriculture in the greater part of this zone was impossible without complicated irrigation schemes, which were unattainable in neolithic times. By the end of the neolithic epoch, in conditions of growing aridity, a gradual transition to stockbreeding occurred.

As in the case of Eastern Europe, the Central-Asian evidence suggests a 'substitution phase' slightly different from that described by Zvelebil and Rowley-Conwy for Northern Europe. In the former area, we fail to see any indications of 'competition between two mutually incompatible ways of life' (Zvelebil and Rowley-Conwy 1984, p. 105). In both Eastern Europe and south-central Asia, the evidence seems to indicate a successful integration of two subsistence patterns within the framework of a predominantly food-producing economy.

As for the 'consolidation phase', it fully corresponds to the proto-urban period of the Middle Bronze Age in the southern zone. Finally, as in the case of Late Tripolye culture in Eastern Europe, we can detect an economic crisis in the Late Bronze Age of the Kopet Dagh, associated with the disappearance of the proto-urban centres and with a return to a less complex economic organisation, which entailed a temporary increase in hunting and gathering.

Notes

[1] *Tugia* is a bottomland geobotanic complex consisting of mature woodland, thicket and meadow in river valleys in Central Asia.

References

Abramova, T. A. (1972) 'Rezultaty paleobotanicheskogo izucheniya chetvertichnykh otlozhenii zapadnogo poberezhya kaspiiskogo morya', in *Kompleksnye izuchniya Kaspiiskogo Morya*, vol. 3, pp. 24–32, Moscow State University, Moscow.

(1980) 'Izmenenie uvlazhennosti kaspiiskogo regiona v golotsene po palinologicheskim dannym', in B. V. Andrianov, ed., *Kolebaniya Uvlazhnennosti Aralo-Kaspiiskogo Regiona v Golotsene*, pp. 61–71, Nauka, Moscow.

Berdyev, O. (1969) *Drevniye Zemledeltsy Yuzhnogo Turkmenistana*, Ylym, Ashkhabad.

Bukinich, D. O. (1924) 'Istoriya pervobytnogo orosheniya v zakaspiiskoi oblasti v svyazi s problemoi proiskhozhdeniya zemledeliya i skotovodstva'. *Khlopkovoe Delo* 3–4, 92–134.

Davis, R. S. (1980) 'Pleistocene archaeology in the southern Afghan–Tajik depression', in K. V. Nikiforova and A. Y. Dodonov, eds., *Granitsa neogena i chetvertichnoi sistemy*, pp. 32–56, Nauka, Moscow.

Dolukhanov, P. M. (1981*a*) 'The ecological prerequisites for early farming in southern Turkmenia', in P. Kohl, ed., *The Bronze Age Civilisation of Central Asia. Recent Soviet Discoveries*, pp. 359–85, M. E. Sharpe, Armonk, NY.

(1981*b*) 'Příčiny migrací', in J. Malina, ed., *Archeologie včera a dnes*, pp. 141–9, Jihočeské Muzeum, České Budějovice.

Fedorov, P. V. (1978) *Pleistotsen Ponto-Kaspia*, Nauka, Moscow.

Gogichaishvili, L. K. (1973) 'K istorii nizmennykh lesov Gruzii v golotsene'. in M. I. Neistadt, ed., *Palinologiya Golotsena i Marinopalinologiya*, pp. 46–8, Nauka, Moscow.

Gulyamov, A. G., Islamov, U. and Askarov, A. (1966) *Pervobytnye*

Kultury i Proiskhozhdenie Oroshaemogo Zemledeliya v Nizoviakh Zeravshana, Fan, Tashkent.

Islamov, U. I. (1975) *Peshchera Machai*, Fan, Tashkent.

(1980) *Obishirskaya Kultura*, Fan, Tashkent.

Itina, M. A. (1958) 'Pamyatniki pervobytnoi kultury Verkhnego Uzboya'. *Trudy Khorezmskoi Arkheologo-Etnograficheskoi Ekspeditsii*, vol. 2, pp. 259–310.

Kaplin, P. A., Leontev, O. K., Rychagov, G. I., Parunin, O. B., Svitoch, A. A. and Shlokov, A. I. (1977) 'Khronologia i paleogeografiya pleistotsena Pontokaspiya (Po dannym absolotnogo datirovaniya)', in P. A. Kaplin and F. A. Shcherbakov, eds., *Paleogeofrafiya i Otlozheniya Pleistotsena Yuzhnykh Morei SSSR*, pp. 33–42, Nauka, Moscow.

Kes, A. C. (1952) 'Proiskhozhdeniye Uzboya'. *Izvestiya An SSSR, seriya geograficheskaya* 1, 20–31.

(1969) 'Osnovnye etapy razvitiya Aralskogo morya', in A. S. Kes, ed., *Problemy Aralskogo Morya*, pp. 21–9, Nauka, Moscow.

Kes, A. C., Andrianov, B. V. and Itina, M. A. (1980) 'Dinamika Gidrograficheskoi seti i izmeneniya yrovnya Aralskogo morya', in B. V. Andrianov ed., *Kolebanyiya Uvlazhnennosti Aralo-Kaspiiskogo Regiona v Golotsene*, pp. 185–98, Nauka, Moscow.

Kes, A. C., Vinogradov, A. V. and Itina, M. A. (1968) 'Paleogeografiya raiona vozvyshennosti Dzhanbas i istoriya ee drevneishego osnoveniya', in S. P. Tolstov and B. V. Andrianov, eds., *Zemli Drevnego Orosheniya i Problemy ikh Khozyaistvennogo Izpolzovaniya*, pp. 150–67, Nauka, Moscow.

Kohl, Ph. L. (1981) 'Introduction: the Namazga Civilisation', in Ph. Kohl ed., *The Bronze Age Civilisation of Central Asia. Recent Soviet Discoveries*, pp. 7–34, M. E. Sharpe, Arnonk, N.Y.

Korobkova, G. F. (1969) 'Orudiya Truda i Khozyaistvo Neoliticheskikh Plemen Srednei Azii', *Materialy i Issledovanya Po Arkheologii SSSR*, 158, Nauka, Moscow.

(1970) 'Problema kultur imlokalnykh variantov v mezolite i neolite Srednei Azii'. *Kratkie Soobshchenia Instituta Arkheologii AN SSSR* 122, 21–6.

(1977) 'Mezolit Srednei Azii i ego osobennosti'. *Kratkie Soobshchenia Instituta Arkheologii AN SSSR* 149, 108–14.

(1978) 'Drevneishie zhatvennye orudiya i ikh proizvoditelonost'. *Sovetskaya Arkheologiya* 4, 36–52.

Korobkova, G. F. and Masson, V. M. (1978) 'Ponyatie neolit i voprosy khronologii neolita srednei Azii'. *Kratkie Soobshchenia Instituta Arkheologii AN SSSR* 153, 103–8.

Kvasov, D. D. (1975) *Pozdnechetvertichnaya istoriya krupnykh ozer i vnutrennich morei vostochnoi Evropy*, Nauka, Leningrad.

(1980) 'Paleogidrologia Arala', in B. V. Andrianov, ed., *Kolebaniya Uvlazhnennosti Aralo-Kaspiiskogo Regiona v Golotsene*, pp. 181–5, Nauka, Moscow.

Lisitsyna, G. N. (1965) *Oroshaemoe Zemledeliye Epokhi Eneolita Na Yuge Turkmenii*, Nauka, Moscow.

(1978) *Stanovlenie i Razvitie Oroshaemogo Zemledeliya v Yuzhnoi Turkmenii*, Nauka, Moscow.

Maev, E. G. and Maeva, S. A. (1977) 'Paleogeograficheskii analiz izmenchivosti urovnya Kaspiiskogo i Aralskogo morei', in P. A. Kaplin, ed., *Paleogeografiya i Otlozheniya Pleistotsena Yuzhnykh Morei SSSR*, pp. 69–74.

Masson, V. M. (1966) 'Gissarskaya Kultura v zapandnom Tadzhikistane'. *Srednyaya Aziya v Epokhu Kamnya i Bronzy*, pp. 145–7, Nauka, Moscow.

Masson, V. M. (1971) 'Poselenie Dzheitun'. *Materialy i Issledovaniya Po Arkheologii SSSR* 180, Nauka, Moscow.

(1981) *Altyn-Depe. Trudy Yuzhnoturkhenistanskoi Kompleksnoi Arkheologischeskoi Ekspeditsii* 18, Nauka, Moscow.

Okladnikov, A. P. (1956) 'Peshchera Dzhebel-pamyatnik drevnei kultury prikaspiiskikh plemen Turkmenii'. *Trudy Yuzhnoturkhenistanskoi Kompleksnoi Arhkeologicheskoi Ekspeditsii* 7, 11–219.

(1966) 'Srednii paleolit – musterskoe vremya v srednei Azii; verkhnepaleliticheskoe i mezoliticheskoe vremya', in V. M. Masson, ed., *Srednyaya Aziya v Epokhu Kamnya i Bronzy*, pp. 23–75, Nauka, Moscow.

Pakhomov, M. M., Nikonov, A. A. and Ranov, V. A. (1977) 'O Paleogeograficheskikh usloviyakh severnogo Pamira v rannem golotsene po rezultatam izucheniya mezoliticheskoi stoianki Oshkhona'. *Doklady Akademii Nauk Tadzhikskoi SSR* 20(5), 61–4.

Ranov, V. A. (1982) 'Gissarskaya kultura: Rasprostranenie, khronologiya, ekonomika', in V. A. Ranov, ed., *Kultury Pervobytnoi Epokhi Tadzhikistana*, pp. 22–41, Donish, Dushanbe.

Ranov, V. A. and Korobkova, G. F. (1971) 'Tutkaul – mnogosloinoe poselenie gissarskoi kultury v yuzhnom Tadzhikistane'. *Sovetskaya Arkheologiya* 2, 133–47.

Samsonov, S. K. (1963) *Paleogeografia Zapadnoi Turkmenii v novokaspiiskoe vremia (po dannym floristicheskogo analiza)*, Nauka, Moscow.

Tolstov, S. P. (1948) *Drevnii Khkorezm: Opyt Istoriko-Arkheologicheskogo Issledovaniya*, Izdatelstvo MGU, Moscow.

Tolstov, S. P. and Kes, A. S. (eds.) (1960) *Nizoviya Amudari, Sarykamysh, Uzboi. Istoria Formirovaniya i Zaseleniya*, Materialy Khorezmskoi Ekspeditsii, vol. 3, Nauka, Moscow.

Tosi, M. (1979) 'The proto-urban cultures of Eastern Iran and the Indus Civilisation', in M. Taddei. ed., *South Asian Archaeology 1977*, pp. 149–71, Istituto Universitario Orientale, Seminario di Studi Asiatici Series Minor VI, Naples.

Tsalkin, V. I. (1956) 'Predvaritelnye dannye izucheniya fauny iz raskopok Dzhebela'. *Trudy Yuzhnoturkhemenestanskoi Kompleksnoi Arkheologisheskoi Expeditsii* 7, 120–4.

van Zeist, W. and Bottema, S. (1977) 'Palynological investigations in western Iran'. *Palaeohistoria* 19, 19–85.

Vavilov, N. I. (1960) *Botaniko-geograficheskie osnovy selektsii*, Izbrannye Trudy, vol. 5, Nauka, Moscow.

Vinogradov, A. V. (1968) *Neoliticheskie Pamyatniki Khorezma*, Materialy Khorezmskoi Ekspeditsii, vol. 8, Nauka, Moscow.

(1981) *Drevnie Okhotniki i Rybolovy Sredneaziatskogo Mezhdorechya*. Trudy Khorezmskoi Arkheologo-Etnograficheskoi Ekspeditsii, vol. 13, Nauka, Moscow.

Vinogradov, A. V. and Mamedov, L. D. (1975) *Pervobytnyi Lyavlyakan*. Materialy Khorezmskoi Ekspeditsii, vol. 10, Nauka, Moscow.

Zadneprovskii, Yu. A. (1966) 'Neolit tsentralnoi Fergany'. *Kratkie Soobshchenia Instituta Arkheologii AN SSSR* 108, 134–42.

Zubakov, V. A. and Borzenkova, I. I. (1983) *Paleoklimaty pozdnego Kainozoia*, Gidrometeoizdat, Leningrad.

Zvelebil, M and Rowley-Conwy, P. (1984) 'Transition to farming in northern Europe: a hunter-gatherer perspective'. *Norwegian Archaeological Review* 17, 104–28.

Chapter 10

**The Mesolithic and Neolithic in the southern
Urals and Central Asia**

G. Matyushin

Introduction

The development of food production in the temperate
zone of Eurasia can be divided into three stages corresponding
to the three main ecological changes of the Postglacial. It can
be assumed that the changes in material culture and essential
shifts in the economy of the postglacial period are the outcome of cultural responses to the considerable drop in
humidity and the decrease in precipitation. It was in the
steppes, forest-steppes, and semi-deserts that the process of
desiccation was progressing most rapidly. This process was less
pronounced in the forest zone, where the population
experienced only the indirect influence of the ecological crisis.
In the area between the Volga and the Yenisei we can distinguish two main regions: (1) the Ural–East Caspian region,
and (2) the Tobol–Yenisei. In the former, agriculture had
been in existence since the Early Neolithic. In the latter, it did
not occur until the Metal Age.

It seems that the process of transition to productive
agriculture was not simultaneous in all areas: in the steppes of
the east Caspian basin and in the southern Urals, domestic
animals appeared earlier than in the steppes of northeastern
Kazakhstan. Evidently, the earlier appearance of domestication in the southwestern foothills of the Urals and the
eastern Caspian basin, was influenced to a great extent by the
existence of contacts between the local cultures and those in
the Middle East known for their early plant and animal

husbandry. The existence of contacts throughout this vast
area has been clearly demonstrated by the successive diffusions
of various microlithic elements, such as obliquely blunted
points with concave bases (Fig. 1) (Clark 1936). Such contacts
were less characteristic of the Kazakhstan uplands and of the
upper Ob and Irtysh; consequently, food production was
introduced later. Ecological changes brought about large
reductions of population in these areas. Thus, by the end of
the Mesolithic and in the Early Neolithic, the upland regions
of Kazakhstan as well as the Ob–Irtysh basin apparently
experienced a major depopulation, while in the southern Urals,
Central Asia and the eastern Caspian basin, cultural development continued uninterrupted, and the population was slowly
growing. The existence of early cultural ties between these
areas and the southern shores of the Caspian, as well as other
areas of early domestication, enabled the population of these
areas to cope with the marked ecological changes, such as the
Mangyshlak regression, by adopting elements of the farming
economy.

The southern Urals

Neolithic sites have been known in the Kama region of
the Urals since the last century (Malakhov 1887; Teploukhov
1892). However, until recently, their origin, periodisation, and
chronology were far from certain (Gimbutas 1958; Matyushin
1959). The absence of reliable research into the stratification

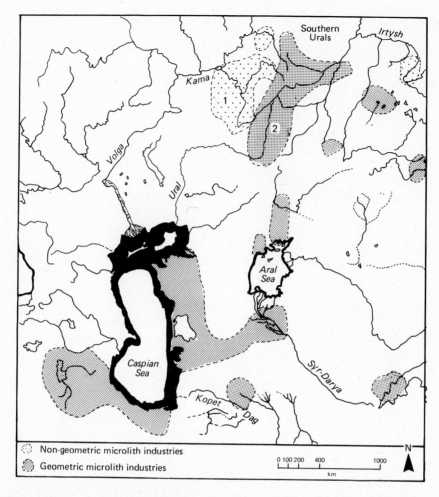

Fig. 1. Principal lithic traditions in the Caspian Sea basin and in the southern Urals during the early postglacial period. 1, Romanovsk–Ilmursin culture; 2, Yangelskaya culture. Dagestan Transgression of the Caspian shown in black; Mangyshlak regression, no shading. The current level is intermediate between these two extreme situations.

of various Stone Age settlements, and the poor preservation of the faunal and pollen remains on most Stone Age sites in the Urals and the neighbouring regions have all been hindering our understanding of the prehistory of the area.

Radiocarbon dates (uncalibrated) obtained in various laboratories for the Mesolithic and Neolithic in the southern Urals show the following picture. The most complete sequence comes from the site of Mullino (Fig. 5), where the date of the earliest mesolithic layer was established as follows: 6370 ± 110 bc (Bash GI 58), 6510 ± 130 bc (Bash GI 37) and 6550 ± 180 bc (Bash GI 59). From the domestic animal bones found in the neolithic layers (Mullino II), the following date was obtained: 6100 ± 160 bc (IGAN 383). The mesolithic layer (Mullino I) is separated from the neolithic one by a thin layer corresponding to an interval of 300–500 years. Another site, Berezki I, gave a radiocarbon date of 5650 ± 200 bc (IGAN 218). It follows, therefore, that the date of the first appearance of domesticated animals in the southern Urals dates back to no later than the end of the seventh/beginning of the sixth millennium bc.

A further date was obtained for Mullino III: 4500 ± 80

bc (IGAN 382). From human bones found in the Khvalinskii mound, three dates were obtained for the various stages of Mullino III and IV: 3848 ± 79, 3071 ± 75, and 4130 ± 193 bc (Vasilev 1981). Mullino IV contained Srednii Stog pottery, identical with the Derievka ware found in the Ukraine (Telegin 1973, ill. 67, 24). Radiocarbon dates obtained from Derievka (3450 ± 100 bc (KI 2193); 3280 ± 100 (KI 2197)) place this phase of settlement into the end of the fourth and the beginning of the third millennium bc. These early radiocarbon dates are fully supported by the analysis of the shoreline displacement of the Caspian Sea and correspond to the location of settlement on the high terraces during marine transgressions (i.e. Staraya Mushta I, Kaga I during the Dagestan transgression) and in the flood plain during the regression (i.e. the different occupation layers at Mullino, see Figs. 2 and 5).

The transition to the Neolithic, therefore, is mainly related to the atlantic period. However, the length and the gradual nature of changes implied by the pollen-based zonation mask the existence of shorter term fluctuations in the palaeogeographical conditions. It was these, rather than the long-term changes, which were likely to elicit cultural responses from the prehistoric communities. Many scientists have tried recently to divide the Atlantic into several stages. Khotinskii (1977) recognised three stages in the Atlantic (AT1, AT2, AT3), while Bergelund (1966), divided it into the Early (6200–4600 bc) and the Late (4600–3300 bc) Atlantic. Wendland and Brighson (Starkel 1977) divide the Atlantic into four stages: AT 1, 6540–5790 bc; AT 2, 5790–4960 bc; AT 3, 4960–4100 bc; and AT 4, 4100–3100 bc. Starkel has also distinguished four stages in the Atlantic: 6450–5750 bc, 5750–4650 bc, 4650–4050 bc, and 4050–3150 bc. It is worth noting that most authors place the beginning of the Atlantic in the seventh millennium bc and subdivide it into four stages which correspond to the periods of transgression and regression noted in the deposits of the Caspian Sea. These periods also coincide with the stages of development in the Stone Age of the south Urals during the Holocene. It must be observed that the chronological determinations based on palynology can serve only as delayed indications of climatic conditions, as vegetational changes respond to, and follow, changes in climate. To determine the precise boundaries of the arid and humid phases, better results can be obtained by observing the fluctuations in the levels of closed internal drainage basins.

The Stone Age sites of the southern Urals lie in the Caspian Sea basin, the largest of the basins without an outlet to the ocean (Fig. 1). The fluctuations in its water level have been extensively investigated (Fedorov 1957; Leontev, Mayev and Rychagov 1977; Vronskii 1983; Varushchenko, Varushchenko and Klige 1980). This work was based on the examination of submerged terraces, raised beaches and more than 30 radiocarbon dates. The results correlate with the changes in the altitude of prehistoric settlements at the end of the Pleistocene and during the Holocene (Figs. 2 and 3).

At present, the level of the Caspian Sea is 28.5 m lower than that of the world oceans. In the Holocene it fell four

times: in the first, the Begdash regression, it was 58 m lower than the present level of the world oceans; then, in the Sartass transgression it rose by 11 m. In the second, Mangyshlak, regression, at the end of the eighth and the beginning of the seventh millennium bc, the level of the sea fell again to 50.5 m lower than that of the contemporary world oceans. The Mangyshlak regression was followed by the Dagestan transgression, during the course of which the level of the Caspian Sea rose by 20 m. In the second half of the fifth millennium bc, the Jilaldin regression began, with the level of the sea falling to 44.5 m below present sea-level. In the latter half of the fifth millennium bc, the level of the sea rose by 18 to 21 m. By the end of the fourth millennium bc, the last important regression, the Makhachkalinsk regression, had begun, and continued to the middle of the second millennium bc. The sea level fell to 40.5 m below present sea level.

In the catchment area of the rivers in the southern Urals and along its western foothills, three kinds of river terraces can be traced: (1) the high flood plain, (2) the first above the flood plain (the lower terrace), and (3) the second above the flood plain (the higher terrace). Stone Age sites in the southern Urals occupy all three terraces. Although at first it appeared that the earliest sites were located on the highest terraces, with the later ones below, and, consequently, that the water level in the catchment of the Caspian Sea was falling, it is now clear that the location of the settlement was changing in response to the rise and fall in the level of the Caspian Sea, and, consequently, the river water levels (Fig. 2), producing a situation where the early mesolithic and middle neolithic sites (Staraya Mushta I) are located on the higher terraces, and the early neolithic (Mullino II), the late mesolithic and late neolithic sites (characterised by the early Collared ceramics, Mullino III) are located on the flood plain (Fig. 2).

Sites with the later Collared ceramics (Davlekanovo III, Belskaya II, Ust Yuzyuanskaya, Sauz IIIb) are again located on

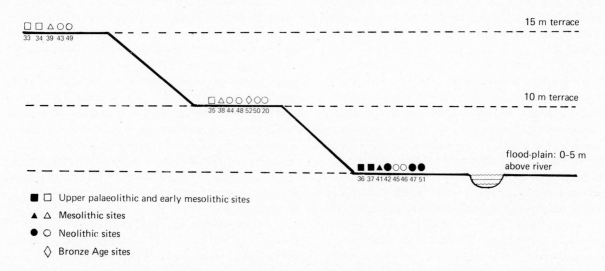

Fig. 2. The location of mesolithic and neolithic sites in the southern Urals on river terraces. For names of sites, see caption to Fig. 3. Settlements containing major cultural innovations are solid black symbols.

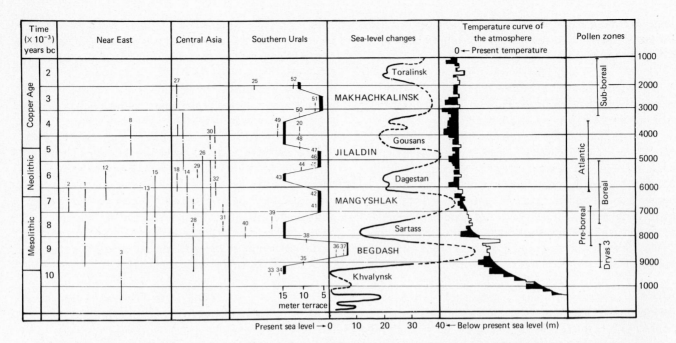

Fig. 3. Cultural developments related to the climatic changes of the Holocene and to the fluctuations in water level of the Caspian Sea. 1, Jericho; 2, Beidha; 3, Shanidar; 4, Cayönü; 5, Bouqras; 6, Zawi Chemi Shanidar; 7, Um Dabagian; 8, Ubaid culture; 9, Tell Ramad; 10, Erbaba; 11, Ganj Dareh; 12, Çatal Huyuk; 13, Ali Kosh; 14, Mergara; 15, Jarmo; 16, Guran Tepe; 17, Caspian sites; 18, Djeitun, 19, Berezki; 20, Khvalynskii Burial; 21, Mullino II; 22, Mullino III; 23, Hacilar; 24, Hassuna; 25, Botay; 26, Djeitun; 27, Namazga; 28, Kara Comar; 29, Machai; 30, Djebel; 31, Osh Khona; 32, Tutkaul; 33, Milovka I–III; 34, Romanovka II, III, VIII; 35, Ilmursino; 36, Staryi Tchekmak; 37, Mikhailovka; 38, Ilmursino III; 39, Staraya Mushta II; 40, Yangelka; 41, Mullino I; 42, Mullino IIa; 43, Staraya Mushta I; 44, Davlekanovo II; 45, Mullino IIb; 46, Mullino IIc; 47, Mullino III; 48, Davlekanovo III; 49, Belskaya II; 50, Ust–Yuryuzanskaya; 51, Mullino IV; 52, Davlekanovo IV.

Transgressions are in lower-case letters; regressions in CAPITALS. Sites in the southern Urals are shown in relation to river terraces.

the terraces. The late Agidelsk culture sites, of Mullino IV type, are back on the flood plains, while the following Bronze Age sites return to the lower terraces (Fig. 2).

It seems that new elements appeared in the economy and culture towards the end of the settlement on the flood plains. Thus arrowheads made on blades, as well as trapezes and triangles, appeared towards the end of the occupation of the flood plain and at the beginning of the shift to the high terraces. The next phase of settlement on the flood plains saw the introduction of ceramics and of some elements of farming (Mullino II). In the third stage of the shift to the lower terraces, traces of the Collared ceramics appear, while the Comb ceramic tradition expands far to the north, to the forested area of Prikamiye and Povolzhie (the Kama–Volga region; Denisov 1960; Khalikov 1973). During the last descent of the settlement to the flood lands, the population living in the forest-steppe of the foothills of the Urals moved to the steppes of the Volga and to the circum-Caspian steppes where large cattle-breeding communities were forming. In the eastern Urals (the Asian slopes of the mountains), there was similarly a decline in lake-shore settlement, coinciding, perhaps, with a population shift to the steppes of northern Kazakhstan.

As noted above, the stages of the descent of the settlements to the flood plains correspond to the regressions of the Caspian Sea and its catchment. This suggests that the changes in the altitude of the settlements are linked with the fall of the water level in the Caspian basin. It would appear that the lowering of precipitation in the area had an unfavourable impact on the flora and fauna. This, in turn, was likely to cause a shortage of food resources, with the result that the population had to find a way out of the critical situation either by economic intensification or by migration.

Certainly the high terraces could have been occupied independently of the regressions and transgressions. However, the low-lying terraces which form the flood plain today could have been inhabited only during the regressions because, now, even a small rise in precipitation would cause their flooding, rendering settlement on these terraces impossible. Consequently, the study of successive settlements on the terraces immediately adjacent to the flood plain, as well as on the flood plain itself, can determine the date of regressions, and, accordingly, the dating of ecological change in the region. Especially good results for the study of the development of various cultures can be obtained from settlements consisting of multiple, clearly stratified layers, such as Davlekanovo and Mullino.

On the southeastern flanks of the Urals at Murat, Berezki, Karabalykty VII–IX, and other sites, numerous artefactual and faunal remains have been preserved which enable us to reconstruct the development of the various cultures and their economy during the transition from food gathering to food production. The study of these remains and their comparison with the palaeogeographical data reveal three stages in the transition to food production in the southern Urals and neighbouring regions.

The development of the conditions for domestication and the question of the transition to a food-producing economy

In the Palaeolithic, the Urals were sparsely inhabited, although, in addition to Peshcherny Log (Talitskii 1946) a number of other sites dating back to the Early and Late Palaeolithic have been discovered in recent years (Matyushin 1973). However, settlements of greater permanence, with dwellings made of mammoth bones, which are so characteristic of the Russian Plain, have not been discovered in the south

Urals. According to the drawings from Kapovaya Peshchera (Bader 1965) and the surviving faunal remains, hunting herbivorous animals, including horse, was typical of the economy.

Sudden ecological changes at the end of the Pleistocene led to the penetration of the southern Urals by South Caspian populations, with the result that a unique culture (Yangelskaya), characterised by obliquely blunted points, including some with concave bases, developed in the area. At the same time, in the southwest Urals, the Romanovsk–Ilmursin culture, characterised by arrowheads made on blades, emerged (Fig. 4). There is evidence for fishing with large nets, up to 45 m long, which probably played a role in the development of more permanent settlement. Unfortunately, none of

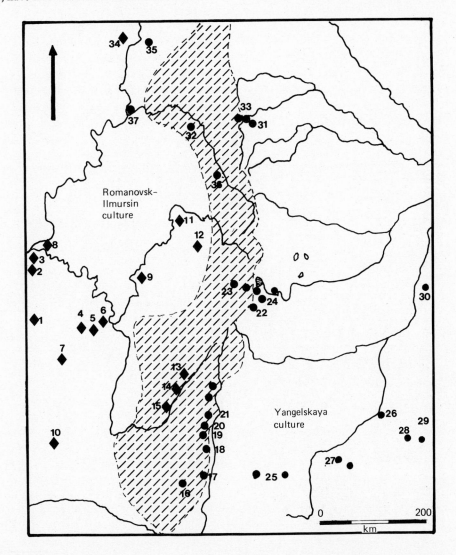

Fig. 4. Cultures and settlement in the southern Urals. Hatching, Ural Mountains; circles, Yangelskaya culture; diamonds, Romanovsk–Ilmursin culture.

1, Mullino; 2, Syun II; 3, Kholodnyi Klyuch (Syum I); 4, Ilmursino; 5, Romanovka II–VIII; 6, Milovka; 7, Davlevanovo; 8, Staraya Mushta; 9, Aydos; 10, Starotokskaya; 11, Ustie Urusanskaya; 12, Kosirbakovo; 13, Asopkino; 14, Kapovaya Peshchera (Cave); 15, Akbuta; 16, Talcas lake sites; 17, Yangelka; 18, Yakty-Kul; 19, Kusimovskoe; 20, Murat; 21, Mindiak sites; 22, Dolgii Elnik; 23, Mys Bezymyanni; 24, Chebarkul; 25, Sintasha sites; 26, Eugenievka; 27, Solenoe Ozero sites, Tersek; 28, Amangeldi; 29, Alkau; 30, Shikaevka II; 31, Poludenka I–II; 32, Penki; 33, Krutiaki, Vyyka etc.; 34, Ogurdino; 35, Novozhilovskaya; 36, Shumkovskaya; 37, Nizhnee Adishchevo.

the mesolithic sites in the Urals provides sufficient numbers of animal remains to enable us to make a precise reconstruction of the economy. However, on the basis of the material found in the neighbouring territories, we can suppose that the population also engaged in hunting. Deukovo II, Barinka (Petrenko 1984), Veretie (Oshibkina 1983) and other mesolithic sites of the surrounding regions yielded animal bones, stressing the economic importance of elk, wild boar, bear, beaver and other fauna typical of the temperate and boreal forests of Eurasia.

The elk, beaver, and the horse are the most numerous animal remains of the Early Neolithic in the southern Urals. The mosaic of forest and steppe ecozones in the area seems to be responsible for the odd co-occurrence of various types of forest and steppe fauna. This would explain the co-occurrence of elk and horse in the sites of the southern Urals and the piedmont. It is possible that, owing to this unusual faunal composition, it was here that early horse breeding began. The domestic horse appeared in this area as early as the end of the seventh millennium bc (Mullino II) (Fig. 5; Table 1).

The assumption that various elements of cattle breeding were known in the southern Urals as early as the Mesolithic is supported in an indirect way by the fact that the bones of the animals which have evidently long been domesticated, such as the horse, sheep, goat and cow can be found in early neolithic layers at Mullino II. The presence of a complete set of domesticated animals (with the exception of the pig), dating to the very beginning of the Neolithic, suggests an earlier phase of their gradual domestication in the southern Urals. The alternative explanation, that the domesticates were introduced as a package from outside the region, may be rejected because of the local cultural continuity and the absence of new traits in material culture, except pottery: the Mesolithic–Neolithic transition is mainly one of subsistence. Thus it seems that there is good reason to relate the beginning of food production to the Late Mesolithic.

It must further be noted that the geometric microliths and points found in the mesolithic sites of the southern Urals are identical with the inventory of the remains found in Belt Cave, Hotu, Shanidar B, Karim Shahir, Zawi Chemi Shanidar, Jarmo (Braidwood *et al.* 1983) and other sites in southwestern Asia – the area of the origin of domestication during the tenth to eighth millennium bc. Trapezes, triangles and quadrangular

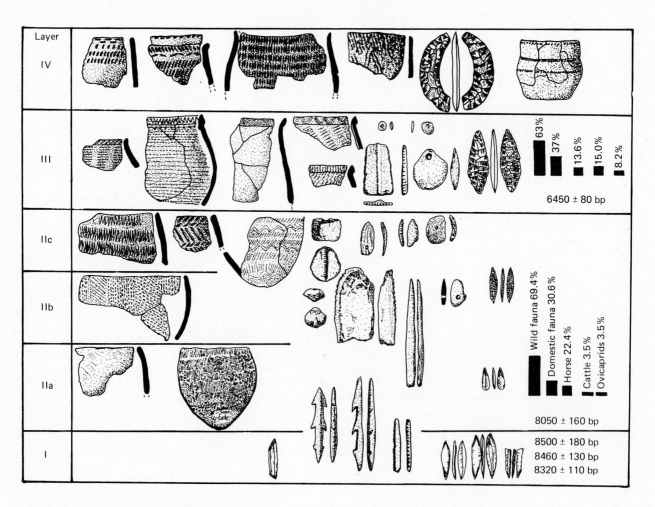

Fig. 5. Cultural sequence from Mullino.

Table 1. *Animal remains from Mullino II, Mullino III, Davlekanovo II, Davlekanovo III, and Belskaya II*

Animal species	Mullino II, neolithic layers		Mullino III, eneolithic layers		Davlekanovo II, neolithic layers		Davlekanovo III, eneolithic layer		Belskaya II	
	No.	%	No.	%	No.	%	No.	%	No.	%
Domestic										
Cattle										
A	3	3.53	11	15	12	20	7	15.2	4	27
B	10	0.93	118	8.36	52	16	43	12.39	20	36
Sheep/Goat										
A	3	3.53	6	8.21	6	10	9	19.5	–	–
B	4	0.37	17	1.2	17	5.44	30	8.64	–	–
Horse										
A	19	22.35	10	13.69	15	25	9	19.5	2	13
B	82	7.63	50	3.54	132	42.3	130	37.4	16	29
Dog										
A	1	1.17	–	–	–	–	1	2.17	–	–
B	1	0.093	–	–	–	–	1	0.28	–	–
Wild										
Beaver										
A	13	15.29	12	16.4	8	13.3	4	8.69	–	–
B	93	8.65	50	3.54	15	4.8	12	3.45	–	–
Hare										
A	1	1.17	–	–	1	1.66	3	6.52	–	–
B	1	0.093	–	–	1	0.32	3	0.86	–	–
European vole										
A	3	3.53	1	1.36	–	–	–	–	–	–
B	17	1.53	1	0.07	–	–	–	–	–	–
Gopher										
A	1	1.17	1	1.36	–	–	–	–	–	–
B	1	0.09	1	0.07	–	–	–	–	–	–
Marmot										
A	–	–	–	–	2	3.3	–	–	–	–
B	–	–	–	–	2	0.64	–	–	–	–
Badger										
A	1	1.17	1	1.36	–	–	1	2.17	–	–
B	2	0.18	7	0.49	–	–	1	0.28	–	–
Marten										
A	1	1.17	1	1.36	–	–	1	2.17	–	–
B	1	0.09	1	0.07	–	–	1	0.28	–	–
Fox										
A	1	1.17	–	–	–	–	–	–	–	–
B	2	0.18	–	–	–	–	–	–	–	–
Bear										
A	5	5.88	2	2.73	–	–	1	2.17	–	–
B	16	1.48	3	0.21	–	–	1	0.28	–	–
Elk										
A	30	35.29	27	36.98	15	25	9	19.5	2	13
B	768	71.5	1153	81.77	79	25.3	120	34.5	3	5
Reindeer										
A	2	2.35	–	–	–	–	–	–	7	47
B	4	0.37	–	–	–	–	–	–	16	29

Table 1. (*cont.*)

Animal species	Mullino II, neolithic layers		Mullino III, eneolithic layers		Davlekanovo II, neolithic layers		Davlekanovo III, eneolithic layer		Belskaya II	
	No.	%	No.	%	No.	%	No.	%	No.	%
Roe										
A	1	1.17	1	1.36	1	1.66	1	2.17	–	–
B	2	0.18	2	0.14	1	0.32	1	0.28	–	–
Turtle B	6	0.55	–	–	–	–	–	–	–	–
Fowl B	60	5.58	5	0.35	5	1.6	1	0.28	–	–
Fish B	4	0.37	2	0.14	8	2.56	3	0.86	–	–
Totals										
A.	85	100	73	100	60	100	46	100	15	100
B.	1074	100	1410	100	312	100	347	100	55	99
Total domesticates										
A	26	30.60	27	37.00	33	55.00	26	56.50	6	40
B	97	9.03	185	13.12	201	64.40	204	58.80	36	65
Total wild										
A	59	69.40	46	63.00	27	45.00	20	43.50	9	60
B	977	90.97	1225	86.87	111	35.60	143	41.20	19	35

A: indiviudal animals; B: bones.

forms are so similar in their shape and technique of production (Fig. 6), that they strongly imply a penetration of the population in the early Holocene, from the southern flanks of the Caspian Sea along its eastern shore to the southern Urals. Admittedly, it is difficult to find the reasons for such a migration. We must remember, however, that, especially with the Begdash regression (ninth millennium bc), the gradual falling of the water level in the Caspian Sea began. The changes in the climatic conditions can perhaps be held responsible for the northward drift of the population.

Assuming that the bearers of the microlithic cultures of the Belt Cave, Zawi Chemi Shanidar and Jarmo types already had domesticated animals, it may be perhaps the case that they introduced some form of animal husbandry to the north. At this early date (ninth to eighth millennium bc), however, the severe and alien climatic conditions in the northern Caspian region and in the southern Urals were hardly conducive to the assimilation of domesticated animals to a new environment. According to the pollen diagrams from Romanovka II and other similar sites, the plains of the southern Urals were covered essentially by a cold steppe of a periglacial type (Yakhimovitch 1978, p. 81).

The mesolithic communities shared another feature usually associated with a farming way of life. Owing to the development of lake and river fishing, settled communites appeared in the southern Urals (Fig. 4). Settlements such as Yangelka or Romanovka II, yielded remains of large dwellings and thousands of blades and other artefacts. Smaller sites, such as Romanovka III, VIII, Milovka I, III, which surrounded the larger sites, could be seen as temporary hunting and fishing localities or dwelling sites of individual families. The character of their artefacts, identical with those found in the base camps, suggests a link between them. According to the present-day fishermen, the large sinkers found in mesolithic sites of the southern Urals belonged to nets whose length was as great as 45 m. Obviously intensive fishing of this kind played an important role in facilitating a settled way of life.

It seems that the Begdash regression which started in the ninth millennium bc not only coincided with the transition to fishing but also served as an impulse to improve hunting implements. At the end of this stage, mesolithic sites shifted location to the high terraces and at the same time their inventory expanded to include both microliths and arrow-heads made on broad blades (Staraya Mushta II, Staro-kainlykovo, Ilmursino III), suggesting the transition to bows and arrows for hunting. Similar technological developments also took place east of the Urals (Matyushin 1976).

In the latter half of the eighth millennium bc, further climatic shifts caused a decrease in the humidity of the area. The Mangyshlak regression was more than twice as long as the preceding Begdash regression (Fig. 3). Such a long period of marine regression must have reflected a longer, and consequently more significant, ecological crisis. It is at the end of this period that the bones of domesticated animals and the earliest pottery appeared in the south Urals, a co-occurrence that could hardly have been accidental. This marks the beginning of the next phase in the transition to farming.

The substitution phase (in term. *Zvelebil and Rowley-Conwy 1984*): the appearance of elements of a food-producing economy

Large faunal assemblages are available in the Urals only from the beginning of the Neolithic. Animal bones have been found on 21 neolithic and eneolithic sites in the southern

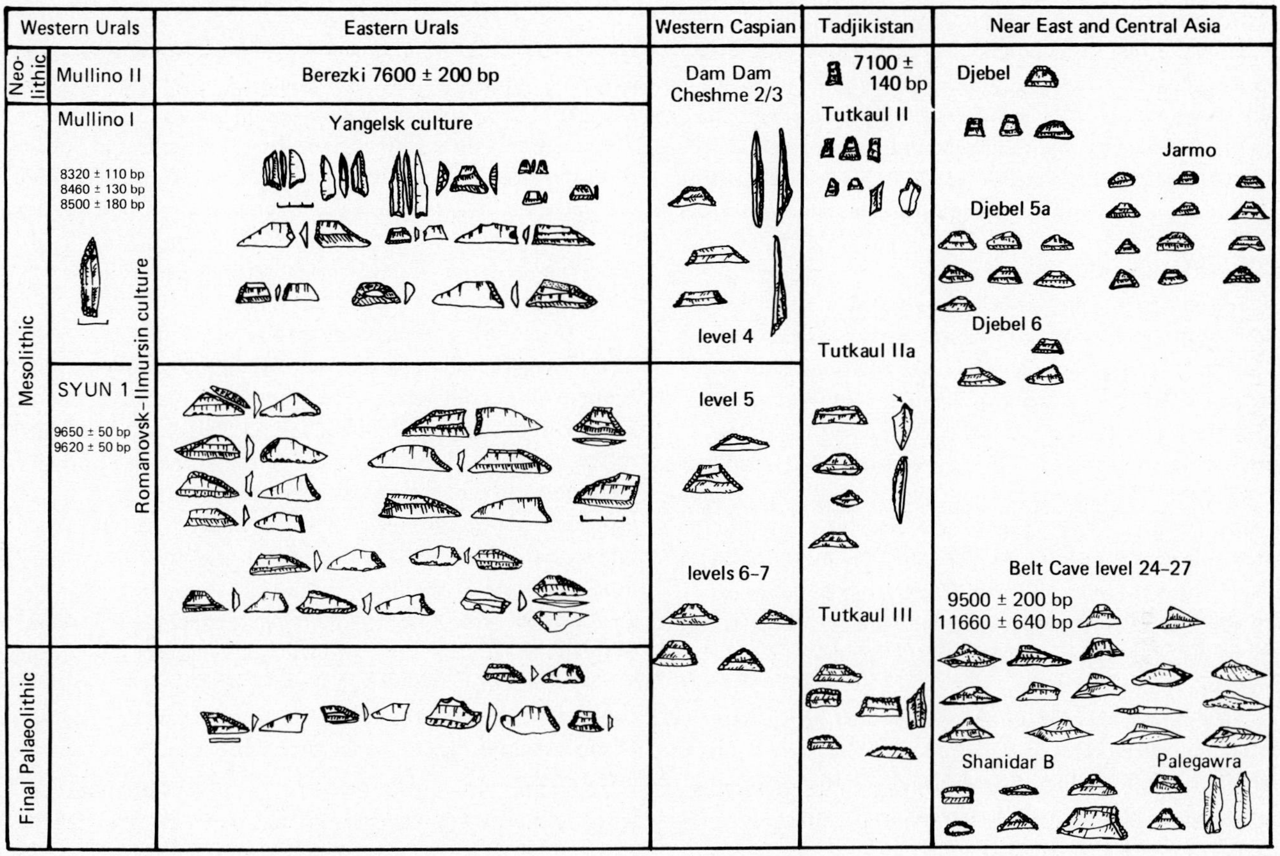

Western Urals	Eastern Urals	Western Caspian	Tadjikistan	Near East and Central Asia

Neolithic

| Mullino II | Berezki 7600 ± 200 bp | Dam Dam Cheshme 2/3 | 7100 ± 140 bp | Djebel |

Mesolithic

Mullino I	Yangelsk culture		Tutkaul II	
8320 ± 110 bp				Jarmo
8460 ± 130 bp				Djebel 5a
8500 ± 180 bp				
				Djebel 6
SYUN 1		level 4	Tutkaul IIa	
9650 ± 50 bp		level 5		
9620 ± 50 bp				
Romanovsk–Ilmursin culture		levels 6-7	Tutkaul III	Belt Cave level 24-27
				9500 ± 200 bp
				11660 ± 640 bp

Final Palaeolithic

| | | | | Shanidar B   Palegawra |

Fig. 6. Microlithic forms prevalent in the Caspian basin, Central Asia and the southern Urals.

Urals and in their eastern foothills (Matyushin 1982). Almost all of them contained the bones of horse, cattle and sheep. Taking into account that wild sheep are absent from the Urals and the surrounding areas, and that their region of origin was northern Mesopotamia and northern Iran (Vorontsov *et al.* 1972), it can be assumed that stockbreeding was introduced to the Urals from Iran and the southern shores of the Caspian. The introduction of the 'southern' stockbreeding elements may date well back into the Mesolithic, possibly to the date of the appearance of the geometric microliths (ninth to seventh millennia bc). However, analysis of the faunal remains and their early appearance suggests that in the steppes and forest-steppes of the southern Urals certain animal species were domesticated independently.

On the southwestern slopes of the Ural Mountains, animal bones were found on 12 sites; two of these (Mullino and Davlekanovo) are multilayered settlements and their investigation has made it possible to trace the development of a food-producing economy in the southern Urals (Table 1).

Mullino II and Davlekanovo II pottery consists mostly of vessels of an egg-shape with a conical bottom, decorated with comb ornamentation. Flint artefacts contain many blades and bifacial tools. According to the pollen data which can be dated to the Mesolithic and Early Neolithic, these sites were surrounded by birch, pine and spruce forests. Treeless associations – steppes and meadowlands – created extensive open areas within the forest cover.

The excavation at Davlekanovo covers 506 m^2. From this area, Tsalkin (see Table 1) and Petrenko (1984) have identified 2304 bones from 280 individuals, including both wild and domestic species. Table 1 summarises the faunal material recovered from neolithic (Mullino II, Davlenkanovo II) and eneolithic (Mullino III, Davlenkanovo III) layers. Mesolithic layers (Mullino I, Davlenkanovo I) contained only sparse and fragmented bone material and were not included in the analysis. The evidence, as it stands at present, shows only a slow increase in the percentage of domestic animals during the neolithic and eneolithic periods. Bones of wild species form as much as 90% of the total in the neolithic layers at Mullino, this figure decreases only slightly during the eneolithic. At Davlenkanovo, the percentage of wild fauna remains within the 35–45% range. Among domesticates, horse is the most important species. Pig is absent from both neolithic and eneolithic layers, its bones first appearing in the area in the Late Bronze Age.

The settlement of Belskoe II is located in the wooded mountain regions in the upper reaches of the river Belaya. Its artefacts, however, suggest a close link with the Agidelsk culture of the steppes southeast of the Urals. It is characterised by Comb and Collared ceramics, as well as flint blades. The site is not very large and was, obviously, temporary. Nevertheless about a half of the faunal assemblage consisted of bones of wild animals, while the remainder was composed of the bones of cattle (26%) and horse (29%). This would indicate that animal husbandry penetrated the more remote areas of the south Urals during the mid Neolithic (dated to the sixth to fifth millennium bc).

Faunal assemblages from other settlements of the south Urals and adjacent regions are not as extensive as those at Mullino and Davlekanovo. However, the osteological material from the neolithic and eneolithic layers has established quite reliably the presence of the major domesticates within the region: cattle, ovicaprids and horse (Petrenko 1982) (Table 2).

In recent years, bones of domestic animals were found in the steppes of the Volga, a region neighbouring on the southwestern slopes of the Ureas. At Vilovatoe, for instance, layers dating to the Neolithic and Eneolithic contained bones of sheep and goat (107 bones from 10 individuals), of cattle (34 bones from 7 individuals), and of horse (156 bones from 12 individuals) (Petrenko, 1984).

Faunal remains have also been preserved on the neolithic and eneolithic sites of the southern and eastern slopes of the southern Urals (Table 2). As elsewhere in the region, the early neolithic layers date to no later than the first half of the sixth millennium bc and contain bones of both wild and domestic animals. For example, in the settlement of Berezki, in the neolithic layer dated according to ^{14}C to the sixth millennium bc (5650 ± 200 bc) bones of the horse prevail. However, bones of domestic sheep and of cattle are also present. A similar picture is to be found in the eneolithic layer of Berezki (Surtanda culture). A similar situation can be observed on the neolithic and eneolithic sites of Yubileinoe, Bannoe II, Surtandy VIII, Karabalykty VIII, Murat, Surtandy III, Surtandy VII, and others.

A new group of sites has recently been excavated in the area of the River Tobol in western Siberia. Numerous bones of domestic animals were found. However, in contrast to the southern Urals, bones of the horse dominated the faunal assemblages. Taking into account that these sites can be dated to a later period than can the eneolithic sites located around the lakes of the southern region of the eastern Urals, the Tobol sites probably represent the further development of a food-producing economy and its specialisation towards horse breeding.

In analysing the economic patterns of the Urals in the Stone Age, the unique character of the food-producing economy and the contrast with that of the Black Sea and the Balkans should be emphasised (Fig. 7). Perhaps the principal difference is the absence of swine in the Stone Age of the Urals and adjacent regions, as compared with its great economic importance in areas further west. A further difference can be observed in the much larger presence of the domestic horse of the Stone Age of the southern Urals, analogies for which can be found in the subsequent, *circum*-Caspian and Central Asian Bronze Age, but certainly not in the Ukraine or the Balkans. Taking into account the early connection between the south Urals and the east and south Caspian regions, the following propositions merit further investigation:

(1) Food production in the south Urals arose independently of the introduction of farming to southeast Europe and western Russia.

(2) In all probability, the first domesticates and stock-breeding traditions were obtained at an early date (certainly prior to the sixth millennium bc) from northern Iran and the southern shores of the Caspian. This opens up the possibility of another, eastern, route of penetration of farming into Europe (as opposed to the western route through the Balkans).

(3) Familiar with the idea of animal husbandry, the popu-

Table 2. *Percentage of faunal remains at neolithic and eneolithic sites in the Urals*

Site	Totals[a]	Horse	Cattle	Goats and sheep	Dog	Elk	Reindeer	Red deer	Roe deer
Murat	15/5	66.7	26.6	—	—	—	—	—	6.7
Surtandy VII	8/3	33.3	33.3	—	—	33.3	—	—	—
Surtandy III	5/2	60	—	—	—	40	—	—	—
Surtandy VIII	5/2	80	—	—	—	20	—	—	—
Surtandy I	1/1	—	—	—	—	100	—	—	—
Karabalykty VIII	1/1	—	100	—	—	—	—	—	—
Bannoe II	10/2	90	—	—	—	—	10	—	—
Yubileinoe	6/2	—	66.6	33.4	—	—	—	—	—
Berezki	32	68.5	9.3	12.5	—	9.3	—	—	—

[a]In this column, the numerator designates the number of bones, and the denominator the number of specimens; figures in other columns designate percentage of bones

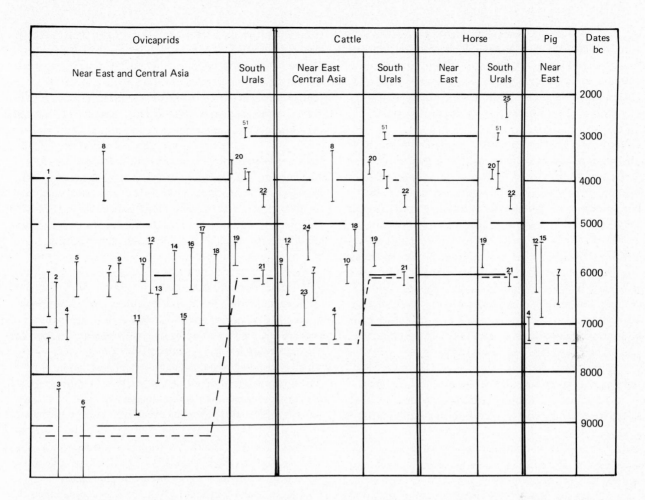

Fig. 7. Appearance of domesticates in the Near East, Central Asia and the southern Urals. For names of sites, see caption to Fig. 3.

lation of the western Urals domesticated the horse on its own. The roots of this process lie in the mesolithic period.

Anthropological data provide further evidence for an arrival of population from the south to the Urals, in the Mesolithic. For example a burial has been uncovered under a hearth containing ceramics of Mullino II type in Davlekanovo. The bones were partially burned by the hearth. A reconstruction of the buried man's features by M. M. Gerasimov revealed clear mediterranoid characteristics (Matyushin 1970). Anthropologists have also traced mediterranoid/Middle-Eastern features among the recent native population of the Urals (Mansy and Khanty) which are thought to have been connected with the arrival of the population from the southern shores of the Caspian (Davidova 1976).

The causes of the transition to food production

It seems that the first definite signs of a food-producing economy in the south Urals were connected with the long-lasting Mangyshlak regression of the Caspian Sea. The prolonged period of arid climate associated with the regression was bound to reduce food resources on the steppes and

forest-steppes of the southern Urals and on their eastern flank, to such an extent that it became necessary to supplement the old way of life by new methods of obtaining food: stockbreeding and hoe-farming.

Significantly, the increasing aridity of the climate in the seventh millennium bc has been noted not only from the low levels of large inland lakes such as the Caspian or Aral seas, but also from the disappearance of settlement from areas sensitive to desiccation throughout the Middle East. Thus, the occupation of Jericho ceased around 6000 bc, evidently because of an increase in the aridity of the climate (Legge 1977). After 6000 bc, large settlements such as those of the pre-pottery Neolithic A and B never reappeared at Jericho. Evidence of desiccation and of contemporary economic intensification was also found at Ali Kosh (Flannery 1969; Hole, Flannery and Neeley 1969; Hole 1977). It seems that change of climate in the seventh millennium bc was more significant than the climatic fluctuations of preceding or succeeding periods. It apparently influenced not only the Caspian Sea and its catchment but also a considerable part of Eurasia. It probably provided the impulse for the intensification of a food-gathering economy and for the transition to food production in the Caspian basin.

In the area of the southern Urals and the neighbouring steppes and forest-steppes, the transition from foraging to food production was a gradual process. Thus, at Mullino II, domestic animals represented 31% of MNI or 9% of bone counts, while in the Mullino III layers the corresponding figures were not much higher (Table 1).

Obviously the percentage of animal bones, even when coupled with the minimum number of individual counts does not give a realistic picture of the relative importance of the actual subsistence strategies. The amount of meat obtained from individual animals has to be taken into account. According to Petrenko (1984), 17 cattle provided as much meat as 34 elk or 476 sheep; or 72 horses, found in the Neolithic of the southern Urals, could replace 122 elk and almost 1500 beaver. Significantly, most of the horses at Mullino were younger than five years. From this it would appear that the importance of wild animals has been overemphasised by the bone counts; on the other hand there is bias of another kind introduced into faunal samples which favours the representation of domestic animals (Zvelebil 1985).

It would seem, therefore, that the role of hunting and fishing was no less significant than that of stockbreeding and hoe-farming during the neolithic period in the southern Urals.

During the following Jilaldin regression (Mullino III), the production of the Collared ceramics, which had hitherto been confined to the northern shores of the Caspian Sea basin, must have extended to the southern Urals, replacing Combed ware, characteristic of the previous period (Mullino II). This change in the ceramic style, possibly indicating a shift in population northwards, coincides once again (as did the previous cultural changes) with the regression of the Caspian Sea.

The Jilaldin regression occurred at the end of the sixth

millennium and the beginning of the fifth millennium bc. During this time the water level in the Caspian Sea fell to 44.5 m below sea level, that is 24 m below the present level. Correspondingly, the remains of Mullino III and other contemporaneous settlements are located in the present day flood plain, confirming that the waters of the Caspian Sea must have been lower than at present.

The change in ceramics is associated with possibly significant shifts in the composition of domestic fauna. Although at Mullino III the proportion of domestic animals increased only slightly to 37%, within the domesticated sector, the percentage of horse bones fell dramatically from 66.6% at Mullino II to 38.1% at Mullino III. Cattle, on the other hand, almost trebled its representation from 16.7 to 42.8%.

Consolidation phase: the Surtanda and Pit Grave cultures
From the end of the fourth millennium bc, the population of the forest-steppe and steppe regions gradually adopted the practice of nomadic stockbreeding. This was also the date of the last major Caspian (Makhachkalinsk) regression, which began at the end of the fourth millennium bc and continued through to the first half of the second millennium bc. During this period, the population gradually shifted to the steppes, where cattle breeding eventually became the principal means of subsistence. By about 2000 bc, an extensive cultural tradition, the Andronovo, had formed in the eastern Urals (Fig. 8), while in the western Urals, the Timber Grave culture emerged. The origin of these major traditions dates to the Eneolithic of the southern Urals and neighbouring territories.

It would be difficult to pinpoint the cultural tradition, or a population ultimately responsible for the transition to nomadism. However, at the beginning of the third millennium

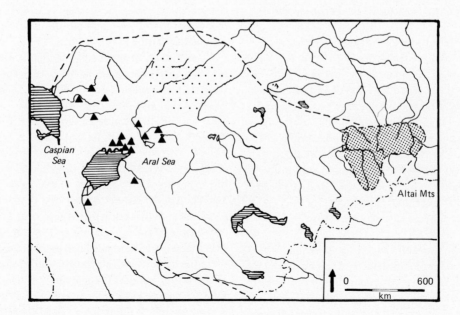

Fig. 8. The extent of Surtanda (stippled), Kelteminar (▲), Afanasievo (densely stippled) and Andronovo (broken line) cultures in Central Asia.

bc, the lakeside settlements of the eastern Urals (the eastern slopes of the mountains and adjacent foothills) ceased to be inhabited, with the population adopting a more nomadic way of life. The shift in residential mobility is associated with the increased reliance on horse breeding. The cultural context of these developments is known as the Surtanda culture. During the course of the third millennium bc, Surtanda pottery appeared over an extensive area, which included the steppes of northern Kazakhstan, the western and southern foothills of the Urals and even as far north as the forest zone along the Kama river (the site of Bor I) (Fig. 8). In the southwest Urals, sites which previously had served as base camps were also by now becoming deserted. At a few sites, such as Mullino IV, where occupation does continue, the cultural layers are very thin and contain relatively few finds. Porous ceramics, typical of the local forest groups, become quite scarce. The indigenous population — the bearers of the Collared ceramic tradition — also seem to have shifted in their resource-use patterns to nomadic pastoralism and to the exploitation of the steppes to the south.

Both the bearers of the Surtanda culture and the local groups from the southwest Urals contributed to the formation of the Pit Grave culture in the Volga–Ural interfluve during the third millennium bc (Merpert 1974; Telegin 1973; Shilov 1975). The economy of the Pit Grave culture was characterised by ovicaprid pastoralism, to the extent that ritual burials of sheep and goats were found among the funerary equipment, as in the Khvalinskii burial (Petrenko 1984). Subsequently the nomadic form of ovicaprid and bovine husbandry extended over the steppes north of the Black Sea across Eastern Europe.

During the same period, groups inhabiting the eastern Urals and the north Kazakhstan steppes also increased their commitment to pastoralism. The late Surtanda settlements have been found to abound with the remains of domestic animal bones, principally the horse, but also some cattle. At the late Surtanda settlement of Botai, horse bones constituted almost 99% of all bone remains. In comparison with the Neolithic, the size of the Surtanda settlements increased by 10–20 fold, reaching 10–15 hectares at Botai. Although some zoologists question the domestic status of some of the horse remains, this may be due more to the problems of establishing morphological criteria of horse domestication than to the absence of horse husbanding practices which would constitute a *de facto* domestication. Petrenko (1984) has carried out extensive research on the skeletal morphology of domestic animals from the Volga and Ural regions, spanning the periods from the Neolithic to the seventeenth century AD. According to her, horse bones from neolithic sites do not differ from those found in medieval East European towns. There is, consequently, every reason to assume that the steppe inhabitants of the eastern Ural region and northern Kazakhstan adopted specialised horse and cattle pastoralism not later than the third millennium bc.

In developing specialised nomadic pastoralism, the steppe population of Eurasia completed the transition to a food-producing economy. The bearers of the Surtanda–Botai culture in the east, and the descendants of the Pit Grave culture to the west of the Ural Mountains have subsequently become major elements contributing to the formation of the later pastoral tradition, namely the Abashevo/Timber Grave culture in the west and the Andronovo in the east.

Central Asia

Many sites containing geometric microliths and extending over a large area between the southern Urals and southern shores of the Caspian have been uncovered in the last few years. They were especially numerous on the Ust–Urt plateau (Bizhanov 1982) and along the banks of the Ural and Emba rivers (Melentev, 1977, 1981). They have also been located in the southern part of Central Asia (Masson 1964, 1971, 1981).

Virtually the entire territory from Ali Kosh and Shanidar (Fig. 1) to the Urals is very rich in obliquely blunted points with concave bases (the Belt type; Matyushin 1964). Nevertheless, out of the many microlithic sites found along the eastern shores of the Caspian and in the inland regions of Central Asia, only three multi-layered settlements, showing clear stratification, have been investigated: Dam-Dam-Cheshma II, in the east Caspian region (Markov 1966), Tutkaul in Tadjikistan (Ranov 1982) and Djebel (Okladnikov 1956).

All three sites revealed similar typological developments in the microlithic industry. Microlithic forms in the earliest layers are characterised by the abundance of obliquely blunted points with concave bases. In the later layers, a tendency towards diminution in size and elongation of forms can be observed, so that in the late mesolithic layers very narrow and extended points or high and symmetrical trapezes predominate. For instance, Tutkaul layer III, characterised by triangles reminiscent of the Shanidar microliths, has been assigned a date of the tenth to eleventh millennium bc. The succeeding layer IIA, which contained narrow trapezoidal and triangular forms, was dated to the eighth to seventh millennium bc. Finally, a more definite date was provided by ^{14}C from layer II, which contained a variety of trapezoidal forms (A8, B8, C8). The layer has been dated to 6070 ± 170 bc (Le 772) (Ranov 1982).

Similar tendencies can be observed in the southern Urals in the late Yangelskaya culture. Microliths develop either into pointed rods (Dolgii Elnik II) or into small, symmetrical trapezes (Dolgii Elnik II, Yakty-Kul I, Kusimovskoe). The similarity is apparent not only in the form, but also in the method of manufacture.

The highly standardised shape of the microliths and the uniform way in which they were processed throughout the area under discussion is of great interest. The geometric microliths found in the region of the Urals and in the Caspian basin are the most standardised. This applies not only to individual items but to the whole series of artefacts, whether found on the same site or in a group of sites which are often located far from each other. The sides of the trapezes and triangles, whether found on one site or over a wider area, show strictly standardised edge angles. The precision and limited variability suggest that there had been an intentional effort towards standardisation, a fact which suggests certain links among various communities. The polygonal objects found in early sites show two varieties of edge angles. Although each side of the microlith, as a rule, has a different angle, both sides show a minimal range of variation. The blunter side of the microlith is almost always at an angle within the range of 20° to 30°, the steeper one within the range of 45° to 55°.

It seems that the existence of such overwhelming standardisation could be explained only functionally. Assuming that the microliths served as insets for harvesting knives, then the effort to increase the sharpness of the knives would result in the reduction of the size of the insets and the introduction of more of them into each tool. The more numerous the insets became, the more difficult it was to fix them into the handle. This problem could have been solved only by standardisation. A strict standardisation of the edge angle permitted them to be inserted securely into the holder, the edge of one insert overlapping with another, thus preventing them from slipping out during use. The effectiveness of these tools could be ensured only by a strict correspondence of the angles of individual insets. A similar precision in adjusting the insets was not necessary for the tools used in fishing and hunting. There is no sign of it in the production of arrowheads, or in the fixing of inset blades into daggers, where the insets were often only unprocessed blades, flakes, or bifaces.

Only the need for short-term intensification could have required such a high level of standardisation. Such maximisation of labour output must have been conditioned by the growing importance of seasonal work; such as the harvesting of cereals and other grasses. It may be more than an accident that standardised geometric forms occurred mostly in societies which were on the threshold of food production.

An interesting fact is that the origin of geometric forms coincides with an increase in the world's temperature (Fig. 3) (Dansgaard and Tauber 1969). It could be argued that the rise of temperature between the eleventh and ninth millennium bc, which occurred all over the planet, resulted in an increase in the aridity of the steppe and other semi-arid zones of the Near and Middle East and other regions of Eurasia. This in turn generated the need for a more controlled collection of cereals and for higher productivity within the more restricted areas of natural occurrence.

Other later sites, where plants and animals changed morphologically as a result of continuing domestication, flat, low forms of microliths do not appear; generally, only microliths with 'steep' sides retained their significance. Even so, in the majority of cases the angle remains within the range of 45°–55°. As examples one may quote Jarmo, Mergara and Djeitun. At the end of the Neolithic and in the Eneolithic, geometrical forms can still be found, but only as individual types, rather than as a series of forms. They too tend to be symmetrical, with steep sides (45°–55°). It would seem that after the introduction of the sickle, standardisation became less compelling.

The earliest culture with geometric microliths to appear in the southern Urals and the north-eastern Caspian basin was the Yangelskaya, dated to 9000 to 6000 years bc. The shape, angles and the retouch of the Yangelskaya microliths are virtually identical with the south Caspian microliths from the lower layers of Belt Cave (Coon 1951), both areas being characterised by the prevalence of obliquely blunted points with concave bases. Towards the end of this period, the number of high, steep symmetrical forms increased throughout the area (Fig. 6).

The contacts between the southern Urals and the southern Caspian basin can be clearly traced not only in the Mesolithic, but also during the Neolithic and Eneolithic. For the latter two periods, elements of Middle Eastern influence can be detected in clay figurines (Karabalykty VII), in the collared ceramics and, perhaps, in the geometrical ornament of the Surtanda pottery. The persistence of connections with the south gives us good reason to believe that the southern Caspian and perhaps even Mesopotamian populations obtained, from the southern Urals, precious stones and coloured metals. The southern Urals are richer than any other mountain range in Eurasia in the variety of precious and semi-precious rocks and metals (Matyushin 1977). A small mountain range, the 'Ilmenskiy', for example, has presented a challenge to mineralogists for more than 150 years: of more than 180 minerals found, about 30 were the first to be recognised in the world. The southern Urals are the only region north of Mesopotamia to have such an abundance of minerals and may have been the legendary 'Arattu' (Kramer 1965), lying 'six or seven ridges to the north of Uruk', from where the first King of Uruk, Emmericer, obtained sapphire, carnelian and lazurite in exchange for grain. Fersman (1961, pp. 34–7) noted the presence of Ural stone in Mesopotamian cities, as, for instance, at Mama in Syria. One of the special features of mineral layers in the southern Urals is their availability. Jasper, flint and other kinds of valuable stone can often be found on the surface.

Gems were first processed in the southern Urals during the Palaeolithic (Mysovaya); metal mining began in the context of the Surtanda culture at about 3000 bc (Chernykh 1970).

The whole question of the nature and intensity of contacts between the south Urals and the south Caspian region merits further investigation. Attempts at a more accurate reconstruction of these contacts are hampered by the eustatic movements of the Caspian Sea. During the periods of regression, the eastern shore of the Caspian – the natural zone of settlement and a route of contact – was located further to the west and would now be flooded, due to currently higher water levels. However, even the sketchy picture presented above provides convincing evidence for a long-lasting relationship between the south and north Caspian as well as the explanation for the existence of such contacts. The Caspian

Sea, with the territories adjacent to the north (south Urals) and the south (Mesopotamia) can be viewed as one extensive zone of trading connections and cultural contact, where movement was facilitated by aquatic routes (see Herodotus 1972, for later periods). Within this context, it is only reasonable to assume that the knowledge of agriculture and stockbreeding was obtained from the south, which in the material culture might be reflected by the diffusion of standardised geometric microliths.

The earliest remains of domesticated animals in Central Asia due to the eighth and seventh millennia bc. These include domestic goat found in layer 4 at Dam-Dam-Cheshma (Markov 1966; Masson 1971), and goat, sheep and cattle in Tutkaul, Saed (Ranov 1982). Domestic animals were therefore known in this area in the context of geometric microlithic assemblages, usually assigned to the Mesolithic. Further elements of farming — intensive agriculture and cattle breeding — appeared in the area with the Djeitun culture, during the seventh millennium bc (Fig. 7).

The population responsible for the Djeitun culture and the practice of agriculture had inhabited Central Asia since the seventh millennium bc (Masson, 1982). Various agricultural tools and the remains of barley and wheat provide unmistakable evidence of the existence of food production. Flint tools include trapezes and other geometric microliths demonstrating the connection between the Djeitun population and mesolithic cultures which had previously inhabited the area.

However, in contrast to the more northerly cultures of Central Asia, the food-producing economy relied on arable farming rather than cattle breeding. The material culture of the South-central-Asian Neolithic, as demonstrated by the mud-brick architecture and ceramics, had more in common with the Middle-Eastern traditions than with the northern margins of the steppes or with the Urals. The early evidence for farming within this region has compelled many authors to argue that the southern margins of Central Asia formed one of the 'nuclear areas' of plant cultivation and animal domestication (see also Dolukhanov, Chapter 9, this volume).

From the survey presented above, we can conclude that major settlements with reasonably extensive remains of neolithic economy, showing the transition from food-gathering to food production, occur, so far, in the foothills of the mountains which flank the margins of Central Asia: in the north, it was the southern Urals, in the south, the Kopet Dagh, which supported most of the settlement. The intervening territory consisted mainly of arid and semi-arid lands which were likely to have been utilised only periodically.

Coping with sudden and rather substantial increases in aridity, evident in archaeological layers at sites such as Mullino or in the regressions of the Caspian Sea, must have been far easier in the foothills, where changes in altitude offered a range of rapidly alternating habitats, than in the vast expanse of desiccated lowland, where any migration to more favourable areas at times of increased aridity must have involved a journey of thousands of kilometres. As modern

parallels, such as the case of Sahel show, even a slight change in atmospheric moisture can set off a sudden transformation of a semi-desert area into a death trap. There is good reason to believe, therefore, that the arid areas of Central Asia were occupied only periodically, during the moister climatic phases.

Although the arid lands of Central Asia yielded cultural remains, their internal periodisation is very difficult due to their temporary character, lack of datable stratigraphic context and the disruptive effect of wind-blown sand deposits. Such so-called 'desert complexes' must be treated with utmost caution when one attempts to reconstruct diachronically the culture history and socio-economic changes of the area.

This note of caution takes on an added emphasis when dealing with the 'Kelteminar', 'Seroglazovskaya' and other so-called cultures. It is no accident that these cultures are often redefined without the rationale of new evidence. Since the 1940s, the Kelteminar culture for instance, was redefined three times, using almost the same set of finds. According to the current interpretation, Kelteminar is now dated from the seventh to third millennium bc (Vinogradov 1981, pp. 119–35), in contrast to the original date of the fourth to second millennium.

Our confidence in this latest date is further eroded by Vinogradov's contradictory remarks about the depth of the cultural layer of the principal site of the early Kelteminar phase, Uchashchi 131: said to be buried at the depth of 90 cm, on p. 131 of the article, it reached a depth of 2 m by p. 132, while the profile photograph shows it just under the topsoil (Vinogradov 1981). Dating of the middle and late Kelteminar phases is based on equally implausible stratigraphic evidence. Typologically, arrowheads made of blades and typical of the Eneolithic and the early mesolithic geometric forms are both assigned to Kelteminar. In neighbouring regions, such finds are separated, in stratigraphically controlled situations, by thousands of years. This chronological confusion means that faunal remains, which were found in 'Kelteminar' contexts and which contained bones of both domesticated and wild animals, cannot be dated with any precision. It may be significant, however, that most of the domesticated bones were recovered from the site of Tolstov, which also contained Bronze Age and later materials. (See also Chapter 9, this volume.)

In summary, it seems that we are dealing with a desert adaptation of long standing, a chronological agglomerate of cultural remains which extended from the Mesolithic to the Metal Age, reflecting perhaps the repeated but discontinuous use of the marginal arid areas during the periods of climatic amelioration. In the circumstances, however, it would be prudent to refrain from suggesting any conclusions until sites with better stratigraphical control are found.

The region between the Urals and the Yenisei
The Ural–Irtysh interfluve
During the Mesolithic, the catchment area of the Tobol, and also, quite possibly, the Ishim river were occupied by the Yangelskaya culture. There is no evidence of neolithic

occupation in the area; in the Eneolithic the area between the Urals and the Irtysh belonged to the zone of the Surtanda culture.

With obliquely blunted points as the principal type-fossils (Zaibert 1979), mesolithic sites in the area between the Ishim and the Irtysh are very similar to those in the Urals and the Caspian region. The mesolithic sites are followed in time by the large settlements of the Surtanda culture. The most famous site of the third millennium bc – Botai – is known to have covered 15 ha and archaeological investigations are still continuing. On the whole, this region can be seen as an outlier of the Stone Age traditions which were centred in the southern Urals.

The eastern margins of the Eurasian steppe

In the upper reaches of the Yenisei, sites dating back to the Mesolithic and Early Neolithic are almost unknown. It may be the case that the area was not inhabited at that time. It was only in the Eneolithic, during the third millennium bc, that a large ethno-cultural group colonised the area, leaving behind various relics of the Afanasievo culture (Fig. 8).

The knowledge of the Afanasievo culture is based on the examination of the burial sites (Teploukhov 1927; Kiselev 1951). More than 200 mounds have been excavated in the Minusinsk steppes alone, and several more have been uncovered in the Altai Mountains. The mounds often contain metal objects made of copper, gold, silver and iron, whose function was decorative rather than functional. No metal tools have been found. The majority of the tools continued to be made of stone.

The remains of domestic animals found in the burial grounds are a clear sign of food production. Among them are bones of sheep, cow, and horse. On the whole, the structure of animal remains seems to be similar to that of the Neolithic in the southern Urals. It is possible that the practice of cattle breeding had been brought to the area from the eastern Ural steppes. The wild animals most frequently exploited seem to have been bison, fox and aurochs. Fish remains have been found as well.

In contrast to the predominantly mongoloid population settled around the shores of the Baikal, the Afanasievo groups were clearly europoid/caucasoid and probably related, in physical characteristics, to their western neighbours, the bearers of the Surtanda culture. Indeed, in terms of physical characteristics, an argument could be put forward in favour of an aboriginal europoid population inhabiting the steppes of Eurasia, over the vast area from the Volga to the Yenisei. The similarities apparent in the skeletal populations throughout the Eurasian steppes is not in contradiction with the cultural uniformity characteristic for the area in the Eneolithic, providing additional evidence of their common origin.

The Angaro-Baikal region

The inhabitants of the forest zone between the River Angara and the Baikal continued the hunting and gathering way of life until the end of the third millennium bc, despite their proximity to the Altai–Siberian steppes, which sup-

ported pastoral economies throughout the third millennium bc (Okladnikov 1974).

Until recently, the preneolithic sites of the Angara–Yenisei region were thought to belong to the Palaeolithic. It was argued that there was no Mesolithic in the area but rather a transition from the Palaeolithic directly to the Neolithic. However, a thorough study of the holocene sites in the area showed that, despite certain resemblances to the Palaeolithic in the stone assemblage, such as the continued use of bifaces and flake implements, other aspects of the material culture reflected technological and economic adaptations associated with the Mesolithic.

The distribution of the sites and animal remains found in them suggests that the economy had changed considerably since the Palaeolithic. Thus the majority of the bones found at the site of Ust–Belaya on the Angara belonged to roe deer and fish, 50% of the latter remains belonging to the sturgeon (Medvedev 1971, 1980).

Many tools for fishing were also found at the site: harpoons made of bone and antler, bone fishing hooks, fish spears and other fishing gear. In the Late Mesolithic, large sinkers appeared, suggesting the introduction of net-fishing. Similar sinkers appeared earlier in the southern Urals.

The transition from hunting large pleistocene mammals to the fishing and hunting of small mammals observed in the region between the Yenisei and the Angara can be taken as a hallmark of the mesolithic period in general.

Conclusions

Within an area as vast as the southern Urals and the steppes of Central Asia, differences in the socio-economic development of mesolithic communities and in their adaptation to the postglacial conditions were bound to occur. Throughout the area, however, major changes coincide with the periods of increased aridity, conditions which can be best detected from the fluctuations in the level of the Caspian Sea.

During the first of the Caspian Holocene regressions, the Begdash, dated to the ninth millennium bc, plant cultivation and animal husbandry appeared in the Near East and in the south Caspian region, while further to north the groups inhabiting the Central-Asian plains and southern Urals adopted more intensive forms of food procurement, with the development of fishing and the use of the bow and arrow. Although this remains speculation for the present, some elements of animal husbandry might have been introduced along with the new range of microliths at this date. During the second regression, the Magyshlak, in the late seventh and early sixth millennia bc, domestication occurred in the steppe and forest-steppe of the southern Urals, presumably as a response to the shortages in food supply provided by hunting and fishing. However, foraging remained the principal means of subsistence, while stockbreeding probably played no more than a subordinate role. In South-Central Asia, on the other hand, we can observe a marked shift to food production, which included not only stockbreeding but also intensive arable cultivation (the Djeitun culture). During the period of increased aridity, marked by the third regression, the Jilaldin (late sixth to early fifth millennium bc), cultural changes took place in Central Asia that were associated with the Eneolithic. In the southern Urals, Collared ware replaced earlier pottery styles (Pitted and Combed wares), while at the same time the overall zone of pottery-producing forest cultures expanded further to the north, into the basin of the River Kama.

During the last major regression, the Makhachkalinsk (late fourth to early second millennium bc), Bronze Age cultures came into existence in the arid regions of Central Asia. The steppe margins in northern Kazakhstan and the forest-steppe regions of the southern Urals experienced depopulation, or, at any rate, a decline in the density of settlement. These shifts in the settlement pattern are associated with the transition to the nomadic pastoral economy. From its probable centre of origin within the cultural context of the Surtanda culture in the southeast Urals, nomadic pastoralism gradually extended to cover the Ural–Volga interfluve (Pit Grave culture), northern Kazakhstan (Surtanda culture), the eastern margins of the Eurasian steppe (the Angara–Altai region, Afanasievo culture) and, at the other extreme, the steppes of Eastern Europe. By the end of the Makhachkalinsk regression, in the mid-second millennium bc, most of the area east of the Urals was integrated into a uniform cultural horizon, known as the Andronovo Bronze Age, while west of the Urals, in the East-European steppes, the Timber Grave culture emerged. The economy of these nomadic cultures continued to develop towards more specialised nomadic pastoralism, with a corresponding decrease in the importance of other economic pursuits; by the second millennium bc this process was consolidated with the establishment of specialised cattle and horse nomadism.

Of the four major periods of aridity, recorded in archaeological and geological deposits, the Mangyshlak and Makhachkalinsk phases were probably the most pronounced. During the first phase, food production penetrated to the southern Urals and Eastern Europe, during the second, a widespread shift to the nomadic mode of existence took place.

The transition to food production involved not only animal husbandry, but also cultivation. Pollen samples from at least one site, Kaga I, located near the neolithic settlements of Belskaya I and II, show that non-arboreal pollen formed 60–70% of pollen counts and Cerealia formed up to 50% of non-arboreal pollen remains already in layers dated to the Neolithic (Khotinskii 1985).

The agricultural transition was accomplished by the indigenous hunter-gatherers in the course of adaptation to the postglacial conditions. This process involved not only the adoption of cultigens and domesticates from the south, but also the local domestication of native species, such as the horse and possibly cattle. The significance of equine domestication cannot be overestimated: horse remains predominate on all neolithic and eneolithic settlements of the southern Urals. It could be argued that the contribution of the aboriginal population to the process of transition to food production was of importance equal to the earlier domestication of plants and

animals in the Near East. Needless to say, this proposition requires further investigation and further evidence.

References

Bader, O. N. (1965) *Kapovaya Peshchera*, Nauka, Moscow.

Bergelund, B. E. (1966) 'Late Quaternary Vegetation in Eastern Blekinge, South-Eastern Sweden. A Pollen Analytical Study'. *Opera Botanica* 12, parts 1 and 2.

Bizhanov, E. V. (1982) 'Mezoliticheskie i neoliticheskie pamyatniki Severo-Zapadnogo Ustyurta', in S. K. Kamalov, V. N. Jagodin and J. F. Buriakov, eds., *Arkhaeologiya Priaralya*, pp. 14–39, Fan, Tashkhent.

Brainwood, S., Braidwood, R. J., Howe, B., Reed, C. and Watson, P. (1983) *Prehistoric Archaeology Along the Zagros Flanks*. Oriental Institute Publications, vol. 105, University of Chicago Press, Chicago.

Chernykh, E. N. (1970) *Drevneishaya Metallurgiya Urala i Povolzhiya*, Nauka, Moscow.

Clark, J. D. G. (1936) *The Mesolithic Settlement of Northern Europe*, Cambridge University Press, Cambridge.

Coon, C. (1951) *Cave Explorations in Iran 1949*, Philadelphia University Press, Philadelphia.

Dansgaard, W. S. J. and Tauber, H. (1969) 'Glacier oxygen-18 content and Pleistocene ocean temperatures'. *Science* 166, 499–502.

Davidova, G. M. (1976) Antropologicheskie issledovaniya severnykh Mansy i nekotorye voprosy ikh raso-i ethnogenesa. Summary of Ph.D. thesis, Moscow.

Denisov, V. P. (1960) 'Khutorskaya neoliticheskaya stoyanka. Uchenie zapiski', Vol. 12, publ. 1. *Trudy Kamskoi arkheologicheskoi exspeditsii* 3, 34–70.

Fedorov, P. V. (1957) 'Stratigrafiya chetvertichnih otlozhenii i istria razvitia Kaspiiskogo morya.' *Trudy Geologia Instituta* 10.

Fersman A. E. (1961) *Ocherki po Istorii Kamnya*, Nauka, Moscow.

Flannery, K. V. (1969) 'Origins and ecological effects of early domestication in Iran and the Near East', in J. J. Ucko and G. W. Dimbleby, eds., *The Domestication and Exploitation of Plants and Animals*, pp. 73–100, Aldine, Chicago.

Gimbutas, M. (1958) 'Middle Ural sites and the chronology of northern Eurasia'. *Peabody Prehistoric Society* 24 (8), 120–57.

Herodotus (1972) *Istoria*, transl. G. A. Stratanovsky, Nauka, Leningrad.

Hole, F. (1977) *Studies in the Archaeological History of the Deh Luran Plain. The excavation of Chagha Sefid*, Ann Arbor, Michigan.

Hole, F., Flannery, K. V. and Neeley, J. A. (1969) *Prehistory and Human Ecology of the Deh Luran Plain*, Ann Arbor, Michigan.

Khalikov, A. K. (1973) 'Neoliticheskie plemena srednego Povolzhiya'. *Materialy i Issledovaniya Po Arkheologii SSSR* 172, 102–21.

Khotinskii, N. A. (1977) *Holocene of Northern Eurasia*, Nauka, Moscow.

(1985) Report on the conference held at the Institute of Archaeology on the 17th of January on the Neolithic and Bronze Age, Moscow.

Kiselev, S. V. (1951) *Drevnya Istoria Yuzhnoi Sibiri*, Moscow.

Kramer, S. N. (1965). *History begins at Sumer*, transl. K. D. Mendelson, ed. V. V. Struve Publ., Nauka, Moscow.

Legge, A. J. (1977) 'The origins of agriculture in the Near East', in J. V. S. Megaw, ed., *Hunters, Gatherers and First Farmers Beyond Europe*, pp. 51–68, Leicester University Press, Leicester.

Leontev, O. K., Mayev, E. G. and Rychagov, G. I. (1977) *Geomorfologia beregov i dna Kaspiiskogo Moria*, Moskovskii Universitet, Moscow.

Malakhov, M. V. (1887) 'O doistoricheskikh epokhakh na Urale'. *Zapiski Uralskogo Obschestva Lyubitelei Estestvoznaniya* 11 (1), 3–10.

Markov, G. E. (1966) 'Razkopki grota Dam-Dam Cheshme'. *Sovetskaya Arkheologiya* 2, 104–25.

Masson, V. M. (1964) *Srednaya Aziya i Drevnii Vostok,* Nauka, Moscow, Leningrad.

(1971) 'Poseleniye Djeitun'. *Materialy i Issledovaniya Po Arkheologii SSSR* 180, 5–207.

(1982) 'Eneolit Srednei Azii' in B. M. Masson and N. V. Merpert, eds., *Eneolit SSSR,* pp. 9–92, Nauka, Moscow.

Matyushin, G. N., (1959) 'Pamyatniki kamennogo veka na territorii BASSR', in A. P. Smirnov and R. G. Kuseev, eds., *Bashkirskii Arkheologicheskii Sbornik*, pp. 17–29, Academy of Sciences, Ufa.

(1964) 'Novye neolitischeskie Stoyanik Bashkirii'. *Kratkie Soobshchenia Instituta Arkheologii AN SSSR* 92, 91–6.

(1970) 'Neoliticheskoye poselenie i pogrebenie u goroda Davlekanovo na Yuzhnom Urale'. *Sovetskaya Arkheologiya* 4, 160–8.

(1973) 'Mnogosloinoe poseleniye Mysovoe na ozere Karabalykty'. *Kratkie Soobshchenia Instituta Arkheologii AN SSSR* 136, 67–76.

(1976) *Mezolit Yuzhnogo Urala,* Nauka, Moscow.

(1977) *Jasshmovoy Poyas Urala*, Iskusstvo, Moscow.

(1979) 'Nekotoryie voprosy perevonachalnogo zaseleniya Urala i Sibiri'. *Kratkie Soobshchenia Instituta Arkheologii AN SSSR* 157, 6–43.

(1982) *Eneolit Yuzhnogo Urala,* Nauka, Moscow.

Medvedev, G. I. (ed.) (1971) *Mezolit Verkhnego Priangarya,* Part 1, Irkutskii Universitet, Irkutsk.

(ed.) (1980) *Mezolit Verkhnego Priangarya,* Part 2, Irkutskii Universitet, Irkutsk.

Melentev, A. N. (1977) 'Pamyatniki seroglazovskoi kultury'. *Kratkie Soobshchenia Instituta Arkheologii* AN SSSR 149, 100–8.

(1981) 'O vozniknovenii skotovodstva v evraziiskikh stepyakh', in L. I. Futoranskii, N. J. Saygin and N. Hozoyukova, eds., *Problemy Epokkhi Eneolita Stepnoi i Lesostepnoi Polosy Vostochnoi Evropy*, p. 13, Orenburg, Tezisi.

Merpert, N. Y. (1974) *Drevneishie skotovody Volzhsko-Uralskogo mezhdurechiya,* Nauka, Moscow.

Okladnikov, A. P. (1956) 'Peschera Dzhebel pamyatnik drevneishey cultury prikaspiiskih plemen Turkmenii', in M. E. Masson, ed., *Trudy Yuzhnoturkmenistanskoi Archeologicheskoi Kompleksnoi Ekspeditsii* 7, 11–214.

(1974) *Neoliticheskiye Pamyatniki Angary,* Nauka, Novosibirsk.

Oshibkina, S. B. (1983) *Mezolit basseina Sukhonmy i vostochnogo Prionezhiya,* Nauka, Moscow.

Petrenko, A. G. (1982) 'Kostyanye ostatki zhivotnykh s poseleniya Mullino', in G. N. Matyushin, ed., *Eneolit Yuzhnogo Urala* pp. 301–7, Nauka, Moscow.

(1984) *Drevnee i srednevekovoe zhivotnovodstvo Srednego Povolzhiya i Preduraliya,* Nauka, Moscow.

Ranov, V. A. (1982) 'Gissarskaya kultūra: rasprostranenie, khrono-

logiya, ekonomika', in N. N. Negmatov and V. A. Ranov, eds., *Kultura Pervobytnoy Epokhi Tadzhikistana*, pp. 22–41, Donish, Dushanbe.

Shilov, V. P. (1975) *Ocherki po Istorii Drevnikh plement Nizhnego Povolzhiya,* Nauka, Leningrad.

Starkel, L. (1977) *Paleogeografia holocenu*, Wrolawnietwo Polskiej Akademii Nauk, Warsaw.

Talitskii, M. V. (1946) 'Paleoliticheskaya stoyanka. Pesherny log'. *Ksiimk-Kratkie Soobshchenniya Instituta istorii i Materiyalnoi Kultury* 12, 9–14.

Telegin, D. Y (1973) *Seredni-stogivska kultura epokhi midi*, Naukova Dumka, Kiev.

(1978) 'Voprosy khronologi i periodizatsii neolita Ukrainy'. *Kratkie Soobshchenia Instituta Arkheologii AN SSSR* 153, 46–8.

Teploukhov, S. A. (1892) 'Veshestvennii pamyatniki kamennogo i bronzovogo periodov v zapadnoi chasti Permskoi gubernii'. *Trudy Permskoi Uchenoi Archivnoi Komissii* 1, 4–19.

(1927) 'Drevnie pogrebeniya v Minusinskom krae'. *Materialy po Etnographii* 3 (2), 57–112.

Varushchenko, A. N., Varushchenko, S. I. and Klige, R. K. (1980). 'Izmenenie urovnya Kaspiiskogo morya v pozdnem pleistotsene-golotsene', in B. V. Andrianov, L. V. Sorin, R. V. Nikolaeva, eds., *Kolebaniya uvlazhnennosti Aralo-Kaspiiskogo regiona v golotsene*, pp. 79–90, Nauka, Moscow.

Vasilev, I. B. (1981) *Eneolit Povolzhiya*, Pedagogicheski Institut, Kuibyshev.

Vinogradov, A. V. (1981) *Drevnie Okhotniki i Ribolovy Sredneasiatskogo Mezhdorechya,* Trudy Khorezmskoi Arkheologo-Etnograficheskoi Ekspeditsii, vol. 13, Nauka, Moscow.

Vorontsov, N. N., Korobtsina, K. B., Nadler, C. F., Hoffman, R., Sapozhnikov G. N. and Golerov Y. K. (1972) 'Chromosomy dikikh baranov i proiskhozhdeniye domashnikh ovets'. *Priroda* 3, 74–82.

Vronskii V. A. (1983) Mariopalinologiya i paleogeografiya yuzhnykh morie SSSR v golotsene. D. Sc. thesis, Baku.

Yakhimovich, V. L. (ed.) (1978) *K Istorii Pozdnego Pleistotsena i Golotsena Yuzhnogo Urala i Preduraliya*, Baskirskii filial akademii nauk SSSR, Ufa.

Zaibert, V. F. (1979) 'Pamyatniki kamennogo veka Petropavlovskogo Priishimya'. *Sovetskaya Arkheologiya* 1, 89–110.

Zvelebil, M. (1985) 'Iron Age transformations in northern Russia and north-east Baltic', in G. Barker and C. Gamble, eds., *Beyond Domestication*, pp. 147–80, Academic Press, London.

Zvelebil, M. and Rowley-Conwy, P. (1984) 'Transition to farming: a hunter-gatherer perspective'. *Norwegian Archaeological Review* 17, 104–28.

Chapter 11

**Hunter-gatherer adaptations and the transition
to food production in Japan**

Takeru Akazawa

Introduction

The objective of this chapter is to show regional
diversity in Jomon hunter-gatherer adaptations, and to
explain this phenomenon with reference to the economic basis
of the different Jomon groups. It is also hoped that a better
understanding of the different procurement systems of various
Jomon groups will give us a reliable perspective from which to
explain the cultural change from a hunting—gathering subsistence system to one based on rice cultivation.

In the light of recent research, it has been concluded
that the beginning of rice cultivation was stimulated by
influences from the continent during the Jomon period (e.g.
Yamazaki 1979, 1982; Nakajima 1982). However, the problem
of whether the transition to a rice culture occurred as a result
of immigration or as a result of adoption by local Jomon
groups is still a controversial subject in Japanese prehistory.

A number of scholars in the field of physical anthropology have supported a hybridisation theory (e.g. Kiyono
1938, 1949; Kohama 1960; Turner 1976; Kanaseki 1976;
Omoto 1978; Yamaguchi 1982; Brace and Nagai 1982;
Hanihara 1983). These studies all proposed, with some
differences in the analytical data, that the Japanese population was formed by an admixture of two major populations:
the indigenous Jomon and immigrants from the continent.

For example, Kanaseki (1976) concluded from the
analysis of human skeletal remains found in the Kyushu and
Chugoku districts that the Yayoi population in western Japan
was composed of descendants of the indigenous Jomon people
and immigrants from the continent who brought rice culture
to the Japanese archipelago. Hanihara (1983) has recently
put forward a similar view, that in western Japan an admixture
of immigrants with the Jomon people took place during the
Yayoi period. Moreover, he concluded, from the multivariate
analysis of human skeletal measurements of Jomon, Yayoi and
other relevant Asian populations, that the immigrants were
originally Siberians from the Amur river area.

Another plausible hypothesis, a transformation theory,
has been formulated by H. Suzuki (e.g. 1956, 1969, 1981,
1983). He based his conclusions on extensive studies of a long
series of Japanese skeletal remains dating from the Pleistocene
to the present. His view is that, if repeated waves of immigration occurred during the Yayoi and subsequent periods, the
immigrants were not numerous enough to affect significantly
the then-existing Japanese gene pool. In conclusion, he states
that the physical change over time and regional differentiation
in physical characteristics observed among the Japanese
occurred mainly as a result of the man—environment relationship, especially through diversity in nutritional and dietary
patterns, and not because of interbreeding with immigrants.

Suzuki's hypothesis is supported by recent work by
Kouchi (1983, 1986). Kouchi discusses reasons for changes
over time in physical traits which took place in only 20 years,

or one generation, with reference to her work on somato-metric data from modern Japan. She concludes that some of the physical traits represented by the cephalic index, which had been considered reliable racial characteristics, are highly unstable in certain circumstances. She also states that dietary patterns are one of the most important factors responsible for changes of these physical traits over time.

In order to evaluate Suzuki's transformation theory from an archaeological viewpoint, evidence concerning Jomon subsistence activities is needed. In this chapter, I discuss regional diversity in the Jomon hunter-gatherer response to rice cultivation by proposing a hypothetical model of the distribution of differing Jomon procurement systems. I show that there is a strong possibility for the transition from hunting and gathering to rice agriculture, while an innovational and dramatic event in Japanese history can be explained as a series of adaptive processes on the part of Jomon hunter-gatherers, with no consideration of large immigrant groups from the continent.

The Jomon period

There can be no doubt that Japanese history began in the Pleistocene epoch, but the question of when the earliest immigrants came, remains unanswered. Almost all the materials discovered in the Pleistocene deposits so far are dated to between 30 000 and 10 000 years ago.

During the closing phases of the terminal Pleistocene, pottery first appeared in several areas of Japan. This marks the start of the Jomon tradition, which dominated the Japanese archipelago for approximately 10 000 years. Although the question of whether the pottery-making technology originated in Japan or developed as a result of diffusion from elsewhere in eastern Asia remains unsolved, it is clear that the pottery complex persisted throughout the long Jomon period with stylistic and incremental changes.

The term 'Jomon' means cord marked. Though this style of decoration developed in prehistoric Japan several millennia ago and gave its name to the period, it was not the earliest type of pottery to enter Japan. This initial Jomon pottery is generally characterised by linear-relief, appliqué, and nail-impressed decoration. The earliest pottery of this kind first appeared in the context of microlithic and large biface-point industries that were not significantly different from the final palaeolithic industries in Japan. One site where an assemblage was recovered, with a good stratigraphic context, is the Fukui cave in Kyushu (Kamaki and Serizawa 1965). The earliest Jomon pottery appears in stratum 3 in association with micro-blades, and is radiocarbon dated to 12 400 ± 350 bp (Gak-949), and 12 700 ± 500 bp (Gak-950) — the earliest date for pottery anywhere in the world.

The Jomon period is usually divided into several sub-periods based upon ceramic stylistic changes, as discussed by Yamanouchi (1967). These subperiods are well documented by a large number of radiocarbon datings (see Fig. 1). However, there is still some discussion among Japanese archaeologists concerning the span of the Initial Jomon subperiod.

Ikawa-Smith (1980), for instance, separates the Initial Jomon subperiods into two further subperiods: the Incipient and the Initial (see Table 1).

There is also some controversy regarding the regional and temporal differences in the Jomon subsistence economy suggested by their artefact assemblages and settlement patterns. Here, I summarise the Jomon period by focusing on the major changes over time in the Jomon culture.

During the early phases of the Jomon period, a number of new elements indicating radical technological innovations were found together with pottery. These new components include: chipped-stone projectile points, stone drills, various types of flake scrapers, chipped and polished stone axes, stone querns, grinding stones, and various types of stone sinkers. These components characterise the toolkits of Jomon hunter-gatherers, and were all present during the Initial Jomon. The same period witnessed a change in settlement pattern — a shift to sedentism. This new settlement style is characterised by clusters of subterranean pit-houses.

Another change occurring in the early phases of the Jomon period is the increased number of shell midden sites. This coincides with the maximum stage of the early Holocene Jomon transgression in Japan (e.g. Toki 1926a, b; Iseki 1975, 1978; Sakaguchi 1983). At this time, the sea encroached far into the coastal lowlands of the Japanese archipelago, and, as the transgression spread, estuarine/lagoon conditions were formed in many areas along the coast. This made it highly possible for a former cultural tradition of terrestrial hunting-gathering to be replaced by one with a maritime orientation. The Jomon people now occupied a region with a much longer coastline.

Fishing and shellfish gathering became a well-established subsistence activity during the Middle and Late Jomon times. This is evidenced by the marked increase in the extent of shell middens, composed of a great variety of aquatic species and fishing equipment. The following characteristics together indicate the radical change in subsistence stability and speciali-sation that could have taken place during the Middle and Late Jomon periods: large-scale settlement sites, possibly with large populations, numerous chipped axes, adzes, stone querns and grinding stones, an increased variety of ceramics, some of which may have had ritual and storage functions, numerous clay figurines, and a variety of pottery-made objects which also may have had ritual functions (see Pearson and Pearson 1978).

Much debate concerns primarily the premise that these new developments could not have occurred without dietary supplementation, in the form of cultivated and/or intensively collected plants. Recent research on plant remains strengthens the possibility that some kind of incipient cultivation might have been practised by the Jomon people (e.g. Nishida 1980, 1983; see also Rowley-Conwy 1984). There still remain some theoretical problems, though, particularly concerning the proportion of the nutritional contribution of cultivated plants to the overall diet of the Jomon people.

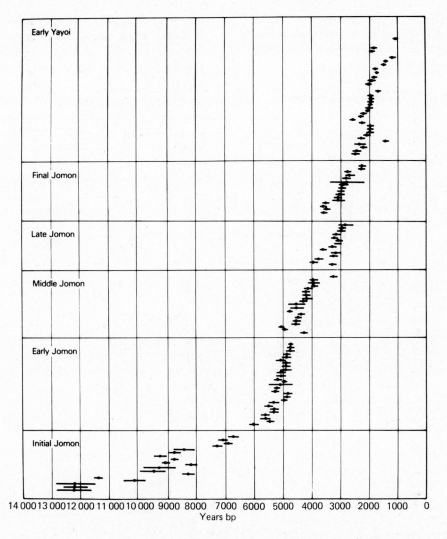

Fig. 1. Radiocarbon dates pertaining to Japanese prehistory (Jomon to Yayoi), based upon the pottery-type stage (from Aikens and Higuchi 1982, Fig. 3.2).

Table 1. *Chronology of Japanese cultural periods*

Historic	AD 600—present
Kofun	AD 300—AD 600
Yayoi	
Late	AD 100—AD 300
Middle	100 BC—AD 100
Early	300 BC—100 BC
Jomon	
Final	1000 BC—300 BC
Late	2500 BC—1000 BC
Middle	3600 BC—2500 BC
Early	5300 BC—3600 BC
Initial	7500 BC—5300 BC
Incipient	11 000 BC—7500 BC
Palaeolithic	Before 11 000 BC

Modified from Ikawa-Smith 1980, Table 1.

In conclusion, the available data suggest that the majority of Jomon subsistence was primarily provided by wild resources, even though it was regionally diversified, as will be discussed in the following section. Since the Jomon period saw the development of extremely sophisticated pottery techniques and various polished stone tools, it is called Neolithic. But unlike the neolithic subsistence patterns in Europe and Western Asia, the Jomon people should be defined as foraging hunter-gatherers who practised an intensive collection of a wide variety of natural resources, with a possible use of cultivated plants in some areas in later periods (see also Koyama and Thomas 1981).

The succeeding Yayoi period witnessed the appearance of a settled life of rice agriculture. However, the initial appearance of the rice cultivation in Japan is regarded as the product of diffusion from the continent during the final stage of the Jomon period, around 3000 bp. In this study, I intend to demonstrate that there was a differential preadjustment for receptivity to rice agriculture among Jomon societies, spanning the period from about 2500 to 300 bc, the time immediately preceding the transition from Jomon hunting–gathering to Yayoi rice cultivation.

Regional differences in Jomon hunter-gatherer adaptation

A number of different approaches have been taken to explain regional differences in hunter-gatherer adaptation. The most popular method to date in the field of Japanese pre-history has been to study the distribution of local pottery-making traditions. In this study, however, stone and bone tools are defined through discriminant function analysis, and the adaptation patterns at various localities are postulated from the inferred functions of the artefacts.

Toolkits of Jomon hunter-gatherers

First, it is necessary to summarise the results of site clustering by discriminant function analyses of two kinds of Jomon toolkits, lithic (Akazawa 1982a; Akazawa and Maeyama 1986a) and fishing (Akazawa 1986b). Approximately 200 sites representing the later Jomon period, c. 2500 to 300 bc, can be discriminated into four homo-

geneous groups, using weighted combinations of the original variables. Each group of sites, discriminated by the same pattern of gathering–hunting–fishing equipment, also displays a similar geographical distribution, i.e. a geographical clustering (Table 2; Fig. 2).

Toolkit of western Jomon site cluster

Western Jomon sites are distinguished from other site groups by a weighted combination of six artefact types: stone querns, grinding slabs, grinding stones, chipped-stone axes, and two types of stone sinkers. The analysis particularly stressed the discriminatory power of the chipped-stone axe and the stone sinkers. The frequency of these tools shows a high positive correlation within this site group, while a set of fishing equipment made from bone and antler material shows a high negative correlation.

Toolkits of eastern Jomon site clusters

Eastern Jomon sites are divided into three geographical clusters, on the basis of the well-defined discriminations that may be seen in Table 2. The most distinctive characteristic of the coastal site cluster from northern Japan – i.e. from the Pacific coast of the Tohoku district – is a toolkit composed of

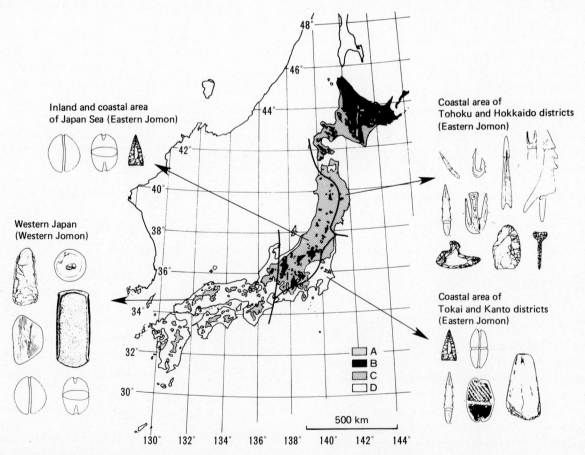

Fig. 2. Synoptic chart illustrating the major geographical boundary of the later Jomon sites and the combination of artefacts showing the results of the two discriminant function analyses (compiled from Table 2). A, above timber line; B, coniferous forest zone; C, deciduous forest zone; D, laurel forest zone.

Table 2. *Area-specific interassemblage variabilities derived from the discriminant function analysis of later Jomon sites, c. 2500 to 300 bc*

	Western Jomon	Eastern Jomon		
		Inland and coastal area of Japan Sea	Coastal area Tokai and Kanto Districts	Coastal area Tohoku and Hokkaido Districts
Lithic assemblage				
Projectile point	+	++	++	+
Stemmed scraper	−	+	+	++
Awl	−	+	+	++
Flake scraper	+	+	+	++
Stone quern	++	+	+	+
Grinding stone	++	+	+	+
Grinding slab	++	+	+	+
Chipped stone axe	++	+	+	+
Polished stone axe	+	+	++	+
Fishing gear assemblage				
Toggle harpoon head of open socket type	−	−	−	++
Toggle harpoon head of closed socket type	−	−	−	++
One-piece fishhook	−	−	+	++
Fishhook of anchor type	−	−	−	++
Composite fishhook	−	−	−	++
Spear point	+	+	++	++
Reused potsherd sinker	−	−	++	+
Grooved pottery sinker	+	+	++	−
Grooved stone sinker	++	++	−	−
Notched stone sinker	++	++	−	−

++, Positively significant, discriminating variable; +, frequent, but less significant discriminating variable; −, negligible.
Data compiled from Akazawa (1982a), Akazawa and Maeyama (1986a) for lithic assemblages, and from Akazawa (1986b) for fishing gear assemblages. The data concerning spear points is empirical, since it is not included in the variable for the discriminant analysis.

a great variety of artefact types. The site cluster is separated from the others by the discriminatory power of stemmed scrapers, stone awls, flake scrapers, open and closed socket toggle harpoon heads, and one-piece, anchor and composite fishhooks. In particular, the analysis stressed the discriminating variable of the toggle harpoon heads.

A second cluster of eastern Jomon sites is distributed in the coastal lowlands of the Kanto and Tokai districts of central Japan. It is separated from the other clusters by the discriminatory power of stone projectile points, polished stone axes, and reused potsherd and grooved pottery sinkers. The frequencies of reused potsherd sinkers and projectile points show a particularly positive correlation in this site cluster. In addition, the toolkit of this site grouping, as inferred from archaeological research to date (e.g. Kaneko 1971; Watanabe 1973), includes bone and antler spearheads in significant proportions.

The final cluster of eastern Jomon sites, which is distributed in the interior and along the sea coast of eastern Japan, is distinguished by an intermediate combination of variables from the western and eastern clusters. Indeed, this site group is discriminated by projectile points and two types of stone sinkers, which are discriminants for the eastern coastal sites of the Kanto and Tokai districts, and the western sites, respectively.

Exploitation territories of Jomon hunter-gatherers

On the basis of the well-defined discriminants outlined above, we can postulate a strong possibility that specific toolkits composed of a certain set of artefact types were developed at the sites of certain groups in different areas. Furthermore, if the working model that intersite variability displayed by artefact assemblages was due to differences in activity in different environments is correct, it may be that a site cluster (so defined because of identical toolkits showing the same pattern of gathering—hunting—fishing) was composed of a group of sites which underwent a similar process of adaptation to environmental conditions.

In order to evaluate this postulate about the significance of area-specific interassemblage variabilities in Jomon societies, it is necessary to learn more about the environmental conditions of the exploited areas in which these toolkits were utilised. In delineating different territorial models of these four site clusters, it should be noted that geographical analysis of most of the Jomon shell midden sites discussed here shows that they were located in transitional zones between two or more diverse environments, e.g. between mountainous forest and maritime settings. Location patterns of this kind, as well as constituent deposits at the sites, suggest the following three types of exploitation territories: a combined forest—freshwater ecosystem, a combined forest—estuary ecosystem, and a combined forest—Pacific shelf littoral ecosystem (Fig. 3; see also Akazawa 1982b, 1984, 1986b).

The combined forest—freshwater ecosystem

Exploitation territories utilising this type of ecosystem are characteristic of the site clusters of western and inland eastern Japan. In western Japan, these sites are situated in transitional zones between freshwater rivers or streams, marshes or lakes, and mountainous laurel forests. In eastern Japan they occupy similar settings within the deciduous forests. Figure 3a shows the primary productive zones of the two major areas.

The toolkits found in the western cluster stress the exploitation of plant resources and freshwater fish species from the two ecosystems mentioned above. Chipped-stone axes, the most significant variable discriminating this site cluster, are generally considered to have been used as tools for harvesting plant resources such as roots, bulbs and tubers (e.g. M. Suzuki 1981; Kobayashi 1983). It is noteworthy that this tool is significantly connected with stone querns and grinding stones in this cluster's toolkit, because they are also described as processing tools for plant resources (e.g. Watanabe 1969; M. Suzuki 1981; Kogayashi 1983). Stone sinkers, the other significant constituent in the toolkit of this cluster, were possibly used for net-fishing of freshwater species (Watanabe 1968).

The toolkit found in the inland site cluster of eastern Japan is different from that found in the western cluster, although the ecosystems of the two areas were similar: the eastern site cluster does not exhibit as high a positive weighting of chipped-stone axes and other stone tools related to plant resource exploitation as does the western cluster. Projectile points, which are the most significant discriminant variable of the eastern inland cluster, were a hunting tool for terrestrial game in deciduous forests and/or equipment for freshwater fishing. Stone sinkers, also a significant variable, were possibly used during net-fishing in freshwater conditions.

The combined forest—estuary ecosystem

Exploitation territories characterised by this type of ecosystem occurred in the coastal regions of the Kanto and Tokai districts of eastern Japan. This region has diluvial uplands which are flat in land form, with alluvial lowlands

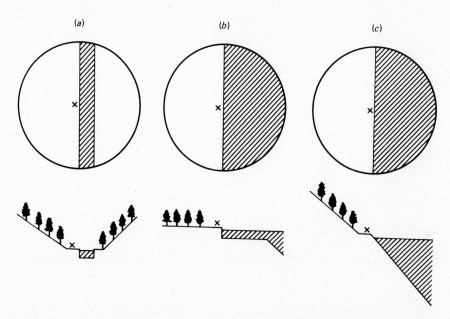

Fig. 3. Schematic representation of three types of exploitation territories of the Jomon hunter-gatherers, showing their settlements in transitional zones between two specific ecosystems. (a) Combined forest—freshwater ecosystem; (b) combined forest—estuary ecosystem; (c) combined forest—Pacific shelf littoral ecosystem. Site clusters represented by types (b) and (c) are characterized by a high density of extensive shell middens, though the components of the deposits vary.

along the coast (Fig. 3*b*). In particular, it should be pointed out that a great many shell middens and other types of occupation sites were formed during the Holocene marine transgression in these coastal regions. At this time great lagoons, surrounded by much longer coastlines, existed. These generally extended far inland, with no direct influence from oceanic currents. Rivers also flowed into the bays, contributing to the creation of estuarine ecosystems (Akazawa 1980, 1982*b*, 1986*b*).

The toolkit of this site cluster is closely related to fishing activities in estuarine conditions. Pottery sinkers, which are most significantly correlated with this site cluster, were possibly developed through net-fishing for estuarine species, and maritime species which migrated seasonally into the bays. Projectile points and spearheads, which are also significantly positive discriminants for this site cluster, were primary tools utilised to exploit maritime species as well as terrestrial game.

The discovery of a broken spear point embedded in the head bone of a red snapper (*Chrysophrys major*) in the stratified deposits of the Shiizuka shell midden gives us an example of how spear points were used (see Fig. 4). This fish was approximately 1 m in length (Tsuboi 1938). Other dominant species such as the black snapper (*Acanthropagrus schlegelii*), sea bass (*Lateolabrax japonicus*), and grey mullet (*Mugil cephalus*), found in midden deposits in this site cluster, as well as the red snapper, are usually larger sized or adult fish (Akazawa 1969, 1980). From this evidence, in addition to the toolkit of this site cluster, we can postulate that a fishing method using spear points and projectile points was developed in the shallow waters of the bays.

Fig. 4. Spear point removed from the skull of a red snapper (*Chrysophrys major*) (shown next to where it was imbedded) found in a Jomon midden deposit at Shiizuka, Kanto district.

Thus, occupational specialisation for a forest—estuary ecosystem was well developed under the special environmental conditions occurring during the Jomon transgression. In the regions of eastern Japan from Tokai to Kanto, the coastal lowlands were encroached on by the sea. As the transgression spread, the coastal lowlands became widespread, and specific exploitation territories, composed of forest and estuarine conditions characterised by having the potential marine resources conducive to an estuarine—oriented subsistence economy, were formed.

The combined forest—Pacific shelf littoral ecosystem

Exploitation territories combining forest and littoral ecological sectors were inhabited by the northern Jomon people in Hokkaido and the Tohoku coastal district. This site cluster, like that of the Kanto and Tokai districts, is characterised by a high density of extensive shell middens. However, estuarine conditions were not included in the exploitation territory as a major ecological niche (Fig. 3c). Geomorphological evidence from site surroundings, as well as the marine species assemblages found in the midden deposits, have contributed to this conclusion (e.g. Watanabe 1973; Akazawa 1982b, 1986). The marine territory of this site is characterised by rocky to sandy flats of ria type, directly facing the open sea. These flats are strongly washed by the oceanic currents which run along the Pacific coast of eastern Japan; they are not influenced by fresh water. The marine territory in this region was only slightly affected by the Jomon transgression, and, as a result, the marine environment (i.e. its proportion to the total territory, salinity, depth and bottom sediments) has not been changed since the time the site was occupied. The process of adaptation to a marine environment within this site cluster was not significantly affected by the Holocene transgression, which elsewhere created extensive estuarine conditions.

This group was well adapted to the open ocean environment and its resource potential (e.g. Watanabe 1973; Akazawa 1982b, 1986). Its most important resource was the various large-scale migratory species of fish, such as tuna (*Thunnus* sp.) and bonito (*Katsuwonus* sp.), that migrate seasonally to the coastal area of this region. Other major marine resources were a number of sea mammals in Hokkaido and a variety of coastal fish species which widely inhabit the rocky-shore zones of this region.

Under these circumstances, a great variety of fishing equipment developed as illustrated in the results of the discriminant function analyses. Toggle harpoon heads, with a highly significant intragroup correlation, are considered to have been used in the fishing of migratory species and for hunting sea mammals on the continental shelf littoral. Other equipment, including various fishhooks, suggests that different fishing methods were used in taking the rocky-shore species of this region, which constitute the largest proportion of faunal remains in the deposits.

Stemmed scrapers, awls, and flake scrapers, which are significant variables discriminating this site cluster, are all non-primary tools (e.g. Kusumoto 1973; M. Suzuki 1981; Kobayashi 1983). It can also reasonably be inferred from the archaeological context and ethnographic data that these tools were associated with scraping, slicing, and chopping actions, as well as piercing and sharpening. This site cluster, therefore, is discriminated by a toolkit characterised by a weighted combination of different kinds of fishing equipment and secondary tools for food resource processing and tool making.

The three types of ecosystems (subsistence—settlement patterns) can be discerned among occupational specialisations of the Jomon hunter-gatherers. Obviously, there can be some criticism of the results, on the basis of the broad criteria presented here. It is assumed that in reality, the same group of people exploited different ecosystems, i.e. forest—estuary on the coast and forest—freshwater inland. However, for further evaluation of this kind, it is necessary to have more descriptive information on exploitative patterns (including seasonality). The evidence presented here gives one fuel for further discussions on the significant differences in the major procurement systems from area to area in Japan.

So we find, in comparing regional differences in the adaptation of hunter-gatherers from an ecological viewpoint, that area-specific interassemblage variability is due to activity differences adapted to different environmental conditons. Western Jomon hunter-gatherers developed a procurement system which relied more on plant resources from a laurel forest ecosystem, and so prepared on appropriate toolkit adapted to their environmental milieu. Other Jomon groups, at least the two different groups of coastal hunter-gatherers from eastern Japan, developed more specialised fishing—hunting procurement systems, with less specialised plant-collecting activities, and this was reflected in the contents of their toolkit.

In other words, terrestrial productivity, diversity, and biomass (particularly of edible plants) played a more critical role in the west and in the eastern interior, whereas the coastal subsistence procurement system in the east stressed the marine component, as developed in the transitional zones between two major ecosystems: forest, and estuarine—Pacific shelf littoral.

Hunter-gatherers adaptations and their relation to the Jomon population

It is well known that Jomon sites are concentrated in eastern Japan, and that sites are scarcer in western Japan. Jomon sites in the coastal regions are often characterised by shell middens. The largest and densest of these deposits are also found in eastern Japan, especially along the Pacific coast. According to Kaneko's (1980) recent calculation, over 90% of the approximately 1000 shell midden sites from the Jomon period are distributed in eastern japan. Furthermore, 90% of the shell middens in eastern Japan are concentrated along the Pacific coast.

Koyama (1978, p. 60) concluded from palaeodemographic studies based on the differential distribution of Jomon sites that, 'The Jomon population was densest in deciduous and evergreen-deciduous mixed forests in eastern Japan' (Fig. 5). He proposed, therefore, that the differing distribution and density of Jomon sites between western and eastern Japan should be attributed to differences between the two major forest zones in the amount and nature of available foods. However, an equally plausible hypothesis can be proposed by

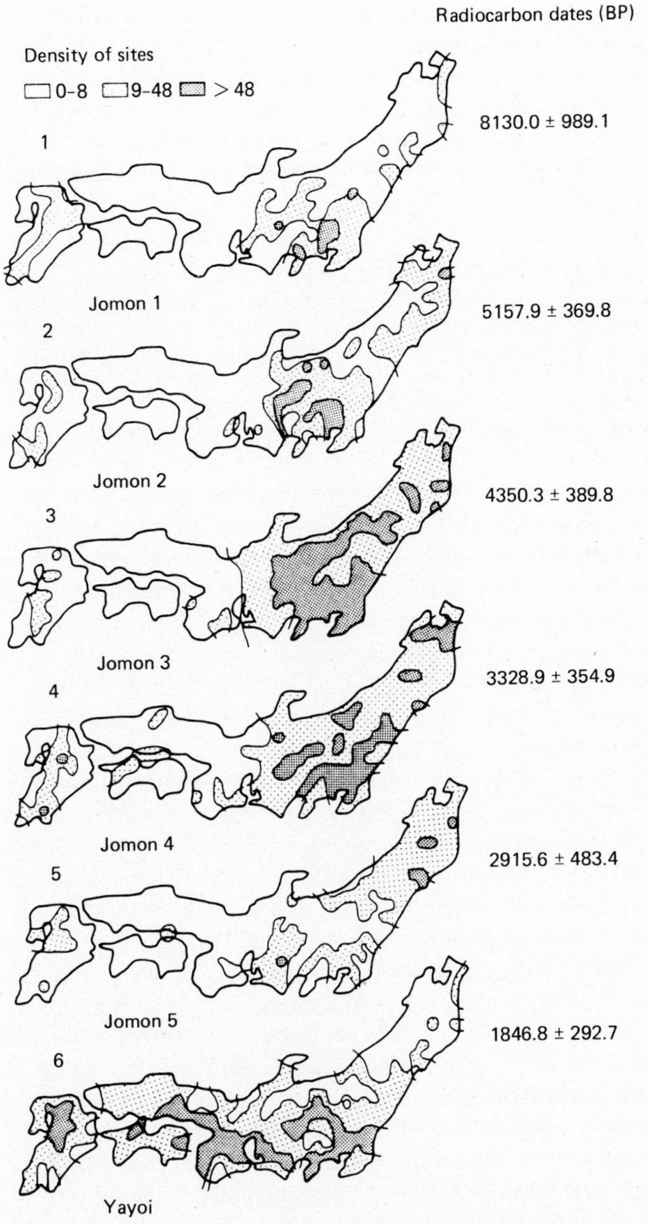

comparing Koyama's conclusion about Jomon population with the regional diversity in adaptations just described, as discussed below.

Prehistoric population density has often been discussed from an ecological viewpoint (e.g. Clarke 1976; Yesner 1980; Perlman 1980; Hassan 1981). According to these arguments, regional differences in population size and density are closely related to the productivity and diversity of the procurement systems of hunter–gatherer societies. Comparing the differences in environmental productivity obtaining among major ecosystems calculated by ecologists (e.g. Odum 1971; Whittaker and Likens 1975), we find that discrete productive potentials are characteristic for each ecosystem (Fig. 6).

Among the major ecosystems of the Japanese archipelago, estuarine systems, including coastal marshes and swamps, have the highest gross productivity in average values, and forests have the second highest productivity. Moreover, these ecosystems generate much higher productivity than do continental shelf aquatic and inland freshwater systems, including lakes and streams.

If we compare this ranking of environmental productivities with the three specific types of Jomon exploitation territories described earlier, we see an interesting phenomenon. First, the exploitation territories consisting of a combined forest–estuarine ecosystem generate the highest productivity, whereas the exploitation territories composed of forest–freshwater or forest–Pacific shelf littoral ecosystems have lower productivities. This can explain the regional differences in Jomon population reasonably well, at least the difference between the western and the eastern Pacific coastal regions, as compared with the Kanto and Tokai districts of eastern Japan. However, the phenomenon that western Japan was less populated than the eastern Pacific coastal region cannot be explained only by productivity potentials. These two exploitation territories generate approximately the same level of environmental productivity (see Fig. 6). This kind of discrepancy can only be examined from a functional understanding based upon the seasonal rounds of resource potentials as discussed below.

The difference in productivity between east and west was probably restricted to periods when estuarine conditions existed in the eastern coastal lowlands during the Holocene transgression. A combined forest–estuarine ecosystem developed in the Pacific-coastal lowlands at around 6000 to 5000 bp, when the Holocene transgression reached its highest level. During the subsequent period, i.e. the post-maximum sea regression postulated by most geomorphologists, the highest density of Jomon sites in eastern Japan is thought to have occurred (*c.* 4000 to 3500 bp). Although there has been much discussion over why this phenomenon took place, the Late Jomon re-transgression theory, as discussed in Sakaguchi's (1982, 1983) work, can adequately explain it. Given this scenario, we can see that the previously noted difference in Jomon population density between the east and the west continued throughout the entire period mentioned above, from about 6000 to 3000 bp as seen in Jomon 2 to 4 of Fig. 5.

Fig. 5. Distribution of Jomon and Yayoi sites which form the basis of the evidence for regional differences in population density in prehistoric Japan, excluding Hokkaido, and the means and standard deviations of radiocarbon datings for the main divisions of the Jomon (1 to 5 are Initial, Early, Middle, Late and Final Jomon) and Yayoi periods (adapted from Koyama 1978 Table 7 and Fig. 9).

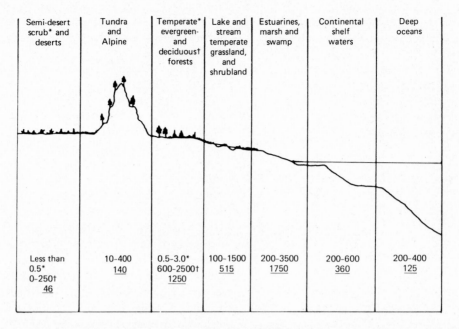

Fig. 6. A transect from the open ocean to interior regions providing comparative information on net primary productivity ranges and averages for specific ecosystems (Perlman 1980, Fig. 6.5). Jomon settlements, at least large-scale ones, were located in transitional zones between two or more ecosystems, such as forest and lake/stream, forest and estuarine, forest and continental shelf, and so on. Environmental productivity varied greatly between these combinations. The figures show ranges of values and mean values (underlined) of net primary productivity unit are (g dry wt/m² per year) (after Whittaker 1975).

One important factor is that maritime conditions provided a wide range of resource potentials on which coastal Jomon groups could develop a variety of seasonal procurement systems. Under Japanese forest conditions, plant productivity provided the most stable primary food supply for the Jomon hunter-gatherers. The view, inferred from archaeological evidence, based on plant remains and storage pits (e.g. Watanabe 1975; Suzuki 1979; Nishida 1980), and the ethno-archaeological approach to Japanese forest edible-plant productivities (Koyama 1981; Matsuyama 1981), has often been endorsed. All these studies emphasise the greatly superior edible-plant productivity of various nuts and acorns in forest ecosystems, as opposed to maritime productivity.

However, the actual importance of wild food resources in a hunting–gathering economy should be measured in terms of a seasonal productivity covering all the major parts of the ecosystem within the exploitation territory. If the Jomon people exploited all the edible parts of about 300 available wild plant species (Akazawa 1984, 1986a), a year-round continuum of plant-collecting activities could be practised in the forest ecosystem, although some seasonal fluctuations in intensity are also clearly recognisable (Fig. 7). Nevertheless, the most highly productive season must have been concentrated in autumn, around October, when various fruits and seeds, the most important plant products nutritionally, were obtained. These resources were also stored for the following lean seasons, as indicated by storage pits containing plant remains such as nuts and acorns (Makabe 1979; Otomasu 1984). On the other hand, the other edible parts of plant resources were not a major food source, although they may

have been a resource to fill up the lean seasons.

In examining the seasonal round of maritime productivity among the coastal Jomon peoples of eastern Japan, we find that the most common fish from midden deposits were of species which migrate within the estuarine zone, coming close inshore during their breeding and feeding activities in early spring and summer (Table 3). Thus the majority of these fish species were probably caught from spring through summer, during the season with the least plant food productivity. A similar pattern has been detected by Koike (1979, p. 267) from her extensive studies of the dominant species of shellfish in midden deposits in the Kanto district: about 70% of the total shells dated from spring and summer, then this percentage decreasing gradually in late summer and autumn, reaching almost zero in winter.

Comparing the procurement rounds of different Jomon groups based on seasonal fluctuations in the productivity of major food sources, we find that the forest–estuarine and forest–Pacific shelf littoral ecosystems could supply a much more stable seasonal procurement round for Jomon hunter-gatherers than could the forest–freshwater ecosystems. A higher population density in Pacific coast Jomon societies was thus maintained by this kind of procurement system, characterised by the year-round continuation of two major productivities, the maritime from spring to summer, and the forest, especially in autumn.

The Jomon sites in the Kanto district drastically decreased in number and size at around 3000 bp, during the final Jomon period (Fig. 5). This phenomenon has long been a controversial point in Japanese prehistory. In the context

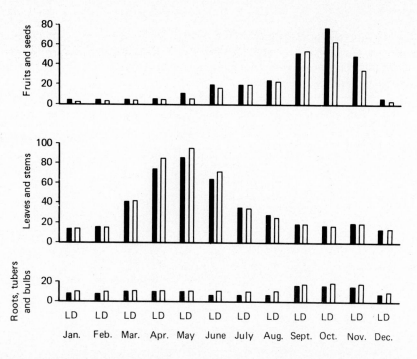

Fig. 7. The monthly change of edible-plant resources available in Japanese forest zones: L, Laurel forest; D, deciduous forest. On the basis of contribution to the diet, with fruits and seeds having the greatest nutritional value, the most productive season is in autumn, around October, when fruits and seeds become ripe, although a year-round continuation of plant resources seems to have been probable.

of the present study, it can be adequately explained by the evidence that, after the retransgression, estuarine conditions were reduced in scale in this region, and moved away from the exploitation territories (Sakaguchi 1982, 1983). This local environmental change quite possibly brought about changes in productivities in the combined forest—estuarine ecosystem of the region. Thus, the Jomon hunter-gatherers had to reduce their birth rate and/or emigrate to adjacent areas, since they could not continue their previous procurement system. However, drastic changes of this kind did not occur in other coastal Jomon societies of the Tohoku district, because the continental shelf littoral ecosystem there was neither originally formed by changes in sea level, nor greatly affected by them.

Procurement systems and their relation to technological specialisation of the Jomon hunter-gatherers

In examining the regional specialisations of exploitative patterns and associated toolkits, we find that the procurement systems in the west and in the eastern interior were equipped with a rather simple and generalised toolkit. This differs from the coastal subsistence procurement system in the east, which was maintained by a specialised toolkit. With regard to this kind of differentiation, special notice should be taken that non-primary tools, and not weapons, most positively correlate with toolkits of the Pacific coastal sites in eastern Japan (as mentioned earlier in the combined forest—Pacific shelf littoral ecosystem section) (see also Table 2; Fig. 2).

Recent studies (Dennell 1983; Torrence 1983; Zvelebil 1984) discuss the diversity and complexity of toolkits among hunter-gatherers from the perspective of 'time budgeting'. Zvelebil (1984, p. 314) summarises as follows:

> foragers (exploiting seasonal and mobile resources) can increase the reliability and productivity of their subsistence strategy: by budgeting their time and by preparing in advance more specialised but also more complicated tools . . . In societies dependent on stationary ubiquitous resources, time is not so important and the use of a complex and specialised technology would not bring benefits that would justify the time and effort spent in its development [*parenthesis added*].

These ideas are derived mostly from ethnographic data. Further research using the archaeological record must be made to show the effects of time budgeting among hunting—gathering societies. But the present study is very encouraging.

Regional variations in the diversity and complexity of the Jomon people are probably due to shifts in subsistence strategies. Where the procurement system was characterised by the year-round continuation of different major productivities, as in the Pacific coast Jomon sites, highly specialised complex assemblages are found that require specialised skills and secondary tools to produce. In contrast, the use of simple general-purpose tools is associated with the western Jomon societies that live in a forest—freshwater ecosystem where most of the food comes from reliable plant sources.

The transition to rice farming in Japan

As the recent advances in Japanese prehistory indicate, there can be no doubt that the Jomon societies in northern Kyushu had accepted the rice cultivation diffused from the

Table 3. *Spawning seasons and grounds of commonly identified fish species (symbol *) in Jomon midden deposits and unidentified species potentially available to coastal Jomon people. The commonly identified species are all characterised by migration to bays and/or coming close to littoral zones during their breeding and feeding activities from spring to autumn when edible-plant productivities for Jomon coastal groups were more limited*

Species	Jan.	Feb.	Mar.	Apr.	May	June	July	Aug.	Sep.	Oct.	Nov.	Dec.	A	B	C	D
Clupanodon punctatus			+	+	+	+								+	+	
Etrumeus teres				+	+	+									+	
Clupea pallasi			+	+	+	+								+	+	
Sardinops melanosticta*		+	+	+	+	+								+	+	
Engraulis japonica*		+	+	+	+	+	+		+	+				+	+	
Oncorhynchus keta	+								+	+	+	+	+			
Oncorhynchus masou								+	+	+			+			
Salmo gairdnerii irideus	+	+	+							+	+	+	+			
Salvelinus pluvinus	+	+								+	+	+	+			
Plecoglossus altivelis										+	+	+	+			
Spirinchus lanceolatus										+	+	+	+			
Hypomesus olidus	+	+	+	+	+	+							+			
Salangichthys microdon			+	+	+	+							+			
Salangichthys ishikawai		+	+	+	+	+									+	
Zacco platypus					+	+	+	+						+	+	
Cyprinus carpio*					+	+	+							+	+	
Carassius carassius cuvieri					+	+	+							+	+	
Anguilla japonica*[1]																+
Mugil cephalus*[1]	+	+								+	+	+				+
Sphyraena pinguis						+	+									+
Sphyraena japonica			+	+	+	+	+									+
Thunnus thynnus[2]																+
Scomber japonicus*			+	+	+	+	+							+	+	
Trachurus japonicus*					+	+	+								+	+
Seriola quinqueradiata			+	+	+	+				+	+				+	+
Arctoscopus japonicus										+	+				+	
Lateolabrax japonicus*[1]	+										+				+	
Sillago japonica						+	+	+	+					+	+	
Girella punctata				+	+	+								+	+	
Chrysophrys major*			+	+	+	+	+							+	+	
Evynnis japonica						+	+	+	+	+				+	+	
Acanthopagrus schlegelii*			+	+	+									+	+	
Parapristipoma trilineatum						+	+	+	+					+	+	
Ammodytes personatus	+	+	+	+	+		+				+			+	+	
Acanthogobius flavimanus			+	+	+								+			
Navodon modestus					+	+	+	+	+						+	+
Sebastes inermis	+	+	+								+				+	
Sebastiscus marmoratus	+	+	+	+							+	+		+	+	
Hexagrammos otakii	+									+	+	+	+		+	

A, Riverine freshwater zone; B, embayment, estuarine zone; C, open sea littoral zone; D, offshore zone.
1, These species live in an embayment, estuarine zone from spring to autumn; 2, these species live close to the littoral zone from spring to autumn.
Data compiled from Japanese Association of Aquatic Resource Preserves (1980, 1983).

continent by 3000 bp. Shortly after this new agricultural technology became established in Kyushu, the rice culture complex spread eastward and southward through the Japanese archipelago. Comparisons among various Jomon groups reveal, however, a number of significant differences both in the process and the results of their acceptance of the rice culture complex.

Among these, the difference in the regional receptivity to rice is the most significant, as discussed in various studies (Kondo 1962; Kanaseki and Sahara 1978; Akazawa 1981, 1982*a*, *b*). Different groups of Jomon hunter-gatherers followed divergent paths at variable rates in their transition to a settled life of agriculture: the western Jomon groups accepted rice quite readily, whereas the eastern Jomon groups, especially the coastal groups, resisted accepting the rice culture complex. In order to explain these differences of regional change, a number of working hypotheses have been offered.

Kondo (1962, pp. 150—2) propose that the western Jomon societies readily accepted rice cultivation because they depended on a relatively simple, rather than a specialised, mode of subsistence, Western Japan was sparsely populated due to the paucity of natural resources. Therefore, the Jomon people there developed a simple mode of subsistence, and did not become specialised hunter-gatherers. For these western hunter-gatherers to settle down to a new way of life, a revolutionary readjustment of their sociocultural habits was not needed, thus making the transition easier. On the other hand, the eastern Jomon were specialised hunter-gatherers in an environment that was rich in natural resources and, as a result, had a higher population density. Thus, the eastern societies could not readily adopt a new way of life; and even after their eventual shift to rice cultivation, the regional traditions of the Jomon period survived on into the new Yayoi culture.

Another diffusion pattern point of view has been proposed by Sasaki (1971, 1982). The two major areas (west and east) are characterised by different forest zones. Western Japan is situated at the northern end of the laurel forest zone which covers central Southeast Asia, where a swidden type of agriculture developed. Therefore, it is possible that the same type of agriculture could have been diffused to western Japan during the Jomon period, and been pursued by the inhabitants of this region. Sasaki has suggested that an appropriate cultural milieu, resulting from dependence on a swidden subsistence economy, played a crucial role in mediating the transition to rice cultivation in western Japan.

It is quite apparent that these functional interpretations have succeeded in increasing our understanding of the transition to agriculture in Japan, but these suggestions have not been verified in the archaeological record. They also tend to focus too much on a generalised description of the cultural dichotomy between these two major areas. Another view that sedentism and increased social complexity in later Jomon society might have encouraged the transition to farming is proposed by K. Suzuki's (1984) recent work. He feels that almost all Jomon people, regardless of western and eastern habitation, were able to react to rice cultivation positively. Why was rice farming adopted by the western Jomon people more readily than by the eastern Jomon people? Could the adoption of rice farming be the result of some weakness in the procurement system of the eastern Jomon hunter-gatherers?

It is easy to argue that the western Jomon people gained a greater degree of botanical experience in following their terrestrial procurement system. They relied more heavily on plant productivities in laurel forest zones and therefore developed an appropriate cultural milieu that increased their receptivity to adopting a rice culture. These circumstances are supported by the composition of the western Jomon toolkit, which shows the potential for adaptation to agriculture. In addition, this change could be smoothly incorporated into their procurement system because the development of rice agriculture did not conflict with the already established seasonal round. One of the most regulated seasons in rice agriculture, the rice planting season, takes place in spring, when forest productivity is low, as discussed above. The adoption of rice agriculture may also have been reinforced by western Japan's proximity to the continent and its biophysical similarities to the areas providing the stimulus for rice cultivation.

Conversely, where the procurement system was more rigidly regulated by the seasonal scheduling demands of two or more major productivities, as in the case of the eastern coastal Jomon societies, where maritime resources were well incorporated into terrestrial resource exploitation systems, then such agricultural innovation would have been resisted. Special attention should be paid to the fact that the rice planting season overlapped with the eastern coastal Jomon people's fishing season. Fish constituted a major food supply for them, and they had developed a specific toolkit composed of a large variety of fishing equipment to facilitate their procurement.

Conclusion

The transition to rice farming in Japan can be adequately explained from the Jomon hunter-gatherer point of view in terms of advantages and disadvantages. This particularly concerns the regional differences in time budgeting/ curation relating to the scheduling of procurement, manufacture and maintenance activities. Rice cultivation would seem redundant to those Jomon societies whose procurement system was regulated by the year-round demands of different major food-gathering activities, whereas it would seem attractive to those Jomon societies characterised by a rather simple procurement system, supported by a single major food-gathering activity. In sum, the most crucial point in mediating the transition to food production was the extent of the cultural re-adjustment that was needed. Had there been enough time to develop a hunting-gathering efficiency, the adoption of food production might have threatened not only the already established procurement system, but the overall socio-cultural system as well.

Acknowledgements
I would like to thank particularly Marek Zvelebil, who read this study and presented thoughtful and careful comments. I am also grateful for the cooperation and advice of Tokiharu Abe (Department of Zoology) and Hideaki Ohba (Department of Botany), of the Tokyo University Museum, and Toshio Hamaya (Department of Forest Botany, Faculty of Agriculture) of Tokyo University, for the ecological interpretation of the plant and fish species presented in Table 2 and Figure 7 in the text. Also I would like to thank Nicole Coolidge, visiting Research Associate of the Tokyo University Museum, who read and criticised this study.

References

Aikens, C. M. and Higuchi, T. (1982) *Prehistory of Japan*, Academic Press, New York.

Akazawa, T. (1969) 'Body size composition of the fish from the Jomon shellmound in Japan and its implications in studies on the fishing activities of the Jomon people'. *Journal of the Anthropological Society of Nippon* 77, 154–78.

(1980) 'Fishing adaptation of prehistoric hunter-gatherers at the Nittano site, Japan'. *Journal of Archaeological Science* 7, 325–44.

(1981) 'Maritime adaptation of prehistoric hunter-gatherers and their transition to agriculture in Japan', in S. Koyama and D. H. Thomas, eds., *Affluent Foragers*, pp. 213–60, National Museum of Ethnology, Osaka.

(1982a) 'Jomon people: subsistence and settlements: discriminatory analysis of the later Jomon settlements'. *Journal of the Anthropological Society of Nippon* 90 (suppl.), 55–76.

(1982b) 'Cultural change in prehistoric Japan: receptivity of rice agriculture in the Japanese archipelago', in F. Wendorf and A. F. Close, eds., *Advances in World Archaeology*, vol. 1, pp. 151–212, Academic Press, New York and London.

(1984) 'Japanese environment and regional diversity in Jomon culture', in Anthropological Society of Nippon ed., *Japanese Anthropology*, pp. 14–29 Nippon Keizai Shinbunsha, Tokyo.

(1986a) 'Regional variation in seasonal procurement systems of Jomon hunter-gatherers', in T. Akazawa and C. M. Aikens, eds., *Prehistoric Hunter-Gatherers in Japan: New Research Methods*, Bulletin No. 27, pp. 73–89, The University Museum, The University of Tokyo, Tokyo.

(1986b) 'Variability in the types of fishing adaptation of the later Jomon people, ca. 2500 to 300 BC', in G. N. Bailey and J. E. Parkington, eds., *The Archaeology of Hunter–Gatherers Subsistence Economies in Coastal Environments*, Cambridge University Press, Cambridge, in press.

Akazawa, T. and Maeyama, K. (1986) 'Discriminant function analysis of the later Jomon settlements', in R. J. Pearson, ed., *Studies in Japanese Archaeology*, Michigan University Press, in press.

Brace, L. and Nagai, M. (1982) 'Japanese tooth size: past and present'. *American Journal of Physical Anthropology* 59, 399–411.

Clarke, D. (1976) 'Mesolithic Europe: the economic basis', in G. de G. Sieveking, I. H. Longworth and K. E. Wilson, eds., *Problems in Economic and Social Archaeology*, pp. 449–81, Duckworth, London.

Dennell, R. (1983) *European Economic Prehistory*, Academic Press, London.

Hanihara, K. (1983) 'Formation of the Japanese'. *Saiensu* (Scientific American, Japanese version) 13 (1), 92–4.

Hassan, F. A. (1981) *Demographic Archaeology*, Academic Press, New York and London.

Ikawa-Smith, F. (1980) 'Current issues in Japanese archaeology'. *American Scientist* 68, 134–45.

Iseki, H. (1975) 'The sea-level changes in the late Holocene and the topographical environment of archaeological sites in Japan'. *Archaeology and Physical Science* 8, 39–52.

(1978) 'Review of studies on sea-level changes in Japan'. *Geographical Review of Japan* 51, 188–96.

Japanese Association of Aquatic Resource Preserves (ed.) (1980) *Ecological Data of Japanese Aquatic Species* 1, NUS Press, Tokyo.

(ed) (1983) *Ecological Data of Japanese Aquatic Species* 2, NUS Press, Tokyo.

Kamaki, Y. and Serizawa, C. (1965) 'The rockshelter of Fukui, Nagasaki Prefecture'. *Memoirs of the Tokyo Archaeological Society* 3 (1), 1–14.

Kanaseki, H. and Sahara, M. (1978) 'The Yayoi period'. *Asian Perspectives* 19, 15–26.

Kanaseki, T. (1976) *Origins of the Japanese*, Hosei University Press, Tokyo.

Kaneko, H. (1971) 'Fishing activities in lower reaches of the Tone River during Jomon period', in Joint Expedition to the Tone River ed. *The Tone River: Environment, Culture and Society*, pp. 113–32, Kobundo, Tokyo.

(1980) 'Jomon fishing from midden deposits'. *Shizen* 2, 38–46.

Kiyono, K. (1938) 'Anthropological study of the Kofun people', in K. Nagasaka, ed., *Jinruigaku-Senshigaku Koza*, vol. 2, pp. 1–20, Yuzankaku, Tokyo.

(1949) *Study of the Japanese on the Basis of Human Skeletal Remains*, Iwanami-Shoten, Tokyo.

Kobayashi, Y. (1983) 'Lithic assemblage of Jomon Period', in S. Kato, Y. Kobayashi, and T. Fujimoto, eds., *Study of the Jomon Culture*, vol. 7, pp. 16–27, Yuzankaku, Tokyo.

Kohama, M. (1960) 'Origins and structure of the Japanese viewed from somatometric studies'. *Jinruigaku-Kenkyu* 7, 56–65.

Koike, H. (1979) 'Seasonality of shell collecting activity and accumulation speed of shell midden sites in Kanto, Japan'. *Quaternary Research* 17, 267–78.

Kondo, Y. (1962) 'Yayoi culture'. *Japanese History*, vol. 1, pp. 139–88, Iwanami-Shoten, Tokyo.

Kouchi, M. (1983) *Geographic Variation in Modern Japanese Somatometric Data and its Interpretation*, Bulletin No. 22, The University Museum, The University of Tokyo, Tokyo.

(1986) 'Geographical variations in modern Japansese somatometric data', in T. Akazawa and C. M. Aikens, eds., *Prehistoric Hunter-Gatherers in Japan: New Research Methods*, Bulletin No. 27, pp. 93–106, The University Museum, The University of Tokyo, Tokyo.

Koyama, S. (1978) 'Jomon subsistence and population'. *Senri Ethnological Studies* 2, 1–65.

(1981) 'A quantitative study of wild food resources', in S. Koyama and D. H. Thomas, eds., *Affluent Foragers*, pp. 91–115, National Museum of Ethnology, Osaka.

Koyama, S. and Thomas, D. H. (eds.) (1981) *Affluent Foragers: Pacific Coasts East and West*, Senri Ethnological Studies 9, National Museum of Ethnology, Osaka.

Kusumoto, M. (1973) 'Prehistoric hunting–gathering culture in Sendai Bay, Tohoku district'. *Yamotochoshi*, vol. 1, pp. 47–264 Yamoto, Tokyo.

Makabe, Y. (1979) 'Prehistoric diet', in H. Otsuka, M. Tozawa, and M. Sahara, eds., *Japanese Archaeology*, vol. 2, pp. 231–53, Yuhikaku, Tokyo.

Matsuyama, T. (1981) 'Nut gathering and processing methods in traditional Japanese villages', in S. Koyama and D. H. Thomas, eds., *Affluent Foragers*, pp. 117–39, National Museum of Ethnology, Osaka.

Nakajima, N. (1982) 'Paddy fields and agricultural tools from the Nabatake site, Karatsu City'. *Rekishi Koron* 74, 40–50.

Nishida, M. (1980) 'Natural resources and Jomon subsistence activities'. *Quarterly Anthropology* 11 (3), 3–56.

(1983) 'The emergence of food production in Neolithic Japan'. *Journal of Anthropological Archaeology* 2, 305–22.

Odum, E. P. (1971) *Fundamentals of Ecology*, Saunders, London.

Omoto, K. (1978) 'Genetic polymorphism in the Japanese', in J. Ikeda, ed., *The Japanese*, pp. 217–63, Yuzankaku, Tokyo.

Otomasu, S. (1984) 'Use and function of Pits', in Kokugakuin University (ed.) *Nippon Shigaku Ronshu*, vol. 1, pp. 32–67, Yoshikawa-Kobunkan, Tokyo.

Pearson, R. and Pearson, K. (1978) 'Some problems in the study of Jomon subsistence'. *Antiquity* 52, 21–7.

Perlman, S. M. (1980) 'An optimum diet model, coastal variability, and hunter–gatherer behaviour', in F. Wendorf and A. F. Close, eds., *Advances in Archaeological Method and Theory*, vol. 3, pp. 257–310, Academic Press, New York.

Rowley-Conwy, P. (1984) 'Postglacial foraging and early farming economies in Japan and Korea: a west European perspective'. *World Archaeology* 16(1), 28–42.

Sakaguchi, Y. (1982) 'Climatic variability during the Holocene epoch in Japan and its causes'. *Bulletin of the Department of Geography, University of Tokyo* 14, 1–27.

(1983) 'Warm and cold stages in the past 7600 years in Japan and their global correlation'. *Bulletin of the Department of Geography, University of Tokyo* 15, 1–31.

Sasaki, K. (1971) *Before Rice Agriculture*, Nippon Hoso Shuppan Kyokai, Tokyo.

(1982) *Laurel Forest Culture in Japan*, Nippon Hoso Shuppan Kyokai, Tokyo.

Suzuki, H. (1956) 'Changes in the skull features of the Japanese people from ancient to modern times', in A. F. C. Wallace, ed., *Men and Culture*, pp. 717–24, University of Pennsylvania Press, Philadelphia.

(1969) 'Microevolutional changes in the Japanese population from the prehistoric age to present-day'. *Journal of Faculty of Science, University of Tokyo*, Sect. V, 3 (4), 279–309.

(1981) 'Racial history of the Japanese', in I. Schwidetzky, ed., *Rassengeschichte der Menschheit* 8, 7–69.

(1983) *Origins of the Japanese*, Iwanami-Shoten, Tokyo.

Suzuki, K. (1979) 'Jomon culture', in H. Ohtsuka, M. Tozawa, and M. Sahara, ed., *Japanese Archaeology*, vol. 3, pp. 178–202, Yuhikaku, Tokyo.

(1984) 'Neolithic period of Japan', in H. Hara and M. Sato, eds., *Japanese History*, vol. 1, pp. 75–116, University of Tokyo Press, Tokyo.

Suzuki, M. (1981) *Fundamentals of Jomon Lithic Tools*, Kashiwa-Shobo, Tokyo.

Toki, R. (1926a) 'Geomorphological study of the distribution of shell middens'. *Journal of Anthropological Society of Nippon* 41, 746–73.

(1926b) 'The ancient shoreline in the lowlands of the Kanto districts, estimated from the distribution of shell middens'. *Geographical Review of Japan* 2, 597–607.

Torrence, R. (1983) 'Time budgeting and hunter–gatherer technology', in G. Bailey, ed., *Hunter-gatherer Economy in Prehistory*, pp. 11–22, Cambridge University Press, Cambridge.

Tsuboi, S. (1938) 'On use and function of spear points from Jomon midden deposit'. *Toyo Gakugei Zasshi* 168, 446–50.

Turner, C. G. II (1976) 'Dental evidence on the origins of the Ainu and the Japanese'. *Science* 193, 911–13.

Watanabe, M. (1968) 'Net fishing of the Jomon period in western Japan'. *Material Culture* 12, 14–19.

(1969) 'Early Jomon culture of eastern Japan', in I. Ohba, M. Naito, and I. Yahata, eds., *Japanese Archaeology*, vol. 3, pp. 69–83, Yuzankaku, Tokyo.

(1973) *Fishing of the Jomon Period*, Yuzankaku, Tokyo.

(1975) *Edible-Plant Resources of the Jomon Period*, Yuzankaku, Tokyo.

Whittaker, R. and Likens, G. E. (1975) 'Biosphere of man', in R. Whittaker and H. Leith, eds., *Primary Productivity of the Biosphere*, pp. 305–28, Springer-Verlag, New York.

Yamaguchi, B. (1982) ' A review of the osteological characteristics of the Jomon population in prehistoric Japan'. *Journal of the Anthropological Society of Nippon* 90 (suppl.), 77–90.

Yamanouchi, S. (1967) *Pottery Types of Prehistoric Japan*, Senshi Kokogakkai, Tokyo.

Yamazaki, S. (1979) *Preliminary Excavation Report of the Itazuke Site, 1977–1978*, Report of the Cultural Properties, Fukuoka City 49.

(1982) 'Establishment and development of the Itazuke site, Fukuoka City'. *Rekishi Koron* 74, 51–8.

Yesner, D. R. (1980) 'Maritime hunter-gatherers: ecology and pre-history'. *Current Anthropology* 21, 727–50.

Zvelebil, M. (1984) 'Clues to recent human evolution from specialised technologies?' *Nature* 307, 314–515.

Chapter 12

Mesolithic societies and the transition to farming: problems of time, scale and organisation

Marek Zvelebil

Introduction

The principal aim of this volume has been to examine the transition to farming from the hunter-gatherer perspective. The foregoing contributions have brought to light a number of general observations which place the transition to farming in the temperate zone firmly in the regional hunter-gatherer context. First, the variability and flexibility of postglacial hunter-gatherers has been underlined. Rowley-Conwy's call for recognition of variability in hunter-gatherer behaviour (Chapter 2, p. 25) receives a good deal of support from the regional case studies that follow. No longer can the Mesolithic be regarded as 'a pregnant pause in European prehistory', nor can it be interpreted as an age of ubiquitous affluence.

Second, it has become clear that the transition to farming took a long time to complete, considerably longer than is usually acknowledged. Hunter-gatherer societies did not adopt farming indiscriminately, but selectively, to fit the local needs. These needs varied from region to region, and so did the factors which combined to bring about the shift to food production. It follows, therefore, that there is no single cause for the transition which would fit all situations.

Third, the preceding contributions have raised the question of the nature and the significance of the Mesolithic itself. Several contributors (Zvelebil, Chapter 1; Rowley-Conwy, Chapter 2; Gamble, Chapter 3; Vencl, Chapter 4; Kozłowski and Kozłowski, Chapter 7) refer to problems

encountered when trying to define the Mesolithic and assess its significance. Beneath this discussion lurks an important question, which goes beyond the dissent about the terminology appropriate for postglacial hunter-gatherers in Europe: are we dealing with a period of fundamental innovations which resulted in the development of farming, or, as Gamble (Chapter 3) argues, does the Mesolithic represent a continuation of upper palaeolithic traditions, elaborated in some areas, such as the Atlantic margins of northern Europe, but, as Vencl implies (Chapter 4), remaining undeveloped in others, such as Central Europe?

Fourth, contributions in this book have also called into question the nature of the agricultural transition: its causes, its method of a dispersal and the very meaning of the phenomenon. As some authors have shown (Lewthwaite, Chapter 5; Akazawa, Chapter 11), the transition to farming must be seen as a complex process resulting from several forces operating simultaneously at different chronological and spatial scales of resolution.

Any attempt at understanding the transition to farming has to take into account the method of its dispersal. Lewthwaite, in Chapter 5, has shown how important it is to move away from entrenched positions, favouring, often in the face of evidence, but with a great amount of personal conviction, 'indigenous development only' or 'farmer colonisation only' explanations, and how to develop more sophisticated models of the dispersal of farming, such as the filter model. This does not mean, however, that the role of the farmer colonisation should be ignored, especially, as Vencl (Chapter 4) suggests, if it is perceived as occurring regionally, rather than as a long-distance phenomenon.

Moreover, the very meaning of the transition has been called into question. On one hand, the initial occurrence of isolated cultigens and domesticates in otherwise hunting and gathering contexts does not necessarily represent a transition to farming (Barker 1975; Dennell 1985; Zvelebil and Rowley-Conwy 1984 and Chapter 6, this volume; Dolukhanov 1979 and Chapter 8, this volume). It may indicate forager–farmer contact and exchange, or it may indicate an *addition* of a new and initially subordinate strategy within a hunting–gathering economy. As shown in Chapter 6, such a situation may continue for hundreds of years before food production replaces foraging as the principal means of subsistence. On the other hand, the evidence for sedentism, and social and technological complexity among the postglacial hunter-gatherers, described in the present volume (Chapters 2 and 5–11) and other recent works (Koyama and Thomas 1981; Price and Brown 1985), obscures the non-economic signatures which conventionally separate the mesolithic and neolithic periods. If the postglacial hunter-gatherers of the temperate zone can really be characterised by logistic, rather than residential mobility, storage, intensive resource-use strategies, non-egalitarian social organisation and the use of pottery, polished stone and other technological innovations traditionally associated with the Neolithic, what is left of the difference between the Mesolithic and the Neolithic?

These are the main issues which featured implicitly or emerged outright in most contributions. An overview and evaluation of these issues is presented in this concluding chapter of the volume.

Mesolithic innovations

Chronologically, the first issue concerns the status and organisation of the postglacial hunter-gatherers. Are we dealing with qualitative or quantitative change? Gamble (Chapter 3) and others (Dennell 1983) have minimised the difference between late glacial and postglacial foraging societies, arguing that the socio-economic developments during the postglacial period represent no more than an elaboration of patterns already emerging with the advent of modern man in the Upper Palaeolithic. Grahame Clark (1980), Hayden (1981), Testart (1982a) and Newell (1984), on the other hand, see the postglacial period as one of fundamental innovations which led to the development of farming. If the former view is correct, then the 'restructuring of human societies' (Gamble, Chapter 3) is related, at least implicitly, to the biological evolution of human species, rather than to cultural dynamics; if the latter view prevails, then these changes in the organisation of human society can be related more specifically to the development of temperate conditions.

From recent literature it would appear that continuity,

rather than contrast, is the fashion of the day. Just as many previously 'neolithic' traits were found to exist in the Mesolithic, so too have many features, hitherto considered 'mesolithic' been found to occur in the late glacial period. These include: technological traits, such as the bow and arrow, harpoon, or ground-stone tools; resource use, such as the evidence for fishing, shellfish collection and even, possibly, the domestication of the dog (Musil 1970); organisational complexity, such as logistic mobility and social stratification and storage; and sedentism (Gamble, Chapter 3; Dennell 1983; Mellars 1985; Soffer 1985). On the other hand, Newell (1984), Testart (1982a, b) and Hayden (1981) list technological, social and economic innovations which do not occur in the Upper Palaeolithic. These include: new flint-working techniques, and new flint, bone and antler tool types, such as antler axes, sickles, fishhooks, etc; nets, fish traps and other sophisticated capture facilities; ceramics; transport equipment such as sledges and skis; most of the mesolithic decorative ornaments; new mortuary rituals, and so on.

Do these amount to qualitative change? Newell (1984, p. 71) argues that postglacial hunter-gatherers articulated and mobilised these elements to produce a qualitatively different adaptation. I will try to show that, at least, they entered into a new set of relationships, both in terms of ecology of the postglacial environment and of the organisation of the society.

Ecological transition at the end of the ice age has been thoroughly discussed by many researchers (for a recent review, see Dennell 1983); Gamble (Chapter 3) and Rowley-Conwy (Chapter 2) discuss the subject. To summarise the main implications of this discussion: (1) in general, the available biomass increased with the transition from late glacial to post-glacial conditions, but the concentration of resources at the herbivore trophic level was replaced by a variety of species occupying different positions within the food-web and creating new food chains. This has contributed to the restructuring of the whole ecosystem and inevitably involved a redefinition of the human position within it. (2) From the point of view of human food resources, their range expanded by the colonisation of new habitats by smaller, more opportunistic species, while some of the glacial fauna (mammoth, woolly rhino, reindeer) was not replaced by the corresponding temperate forms. As Flannery (1969), Hayden (1981) and others have noted, a corresponding change in subsistence strategies took place by adding the smaller, more opportunistic species (the *r* strategists) to the existing range. Even though the origins of this trend can be traced to the Upper Palaeolithic (Gamble, Chapter 3), this shift was accelerated in the early postglacial period (Hayden 1981; Dolukhanov, Chapters 8 and 9; Matyushin, Chapter 10; Azakawa, Chapter 11). The preponderance of opportunist species tends to cause unpredictable and extreme fluctuations in resources, marked by periodic population crashes. Hayden notes that while dramatic fluctuations 'characterise many *r*-selected resources, in comparison with *K*-selected species they are very brief (one or two years) and can be usually compensated for by other resources (*providing the options are diverse enough*)' (Hayden 1981, p. 544, italics mine). Hayden's afterthought actually marks out one of the major differences between the late glacial and postglacial ecosystems. If the late glacial ecosystems are, in their essentials, comparable to subarctic environments today, the diversity of resources would have been too low to provide a sufficient range of alternatives for the development of broad-based resource-use strategies. With the addition of new opportunistic species, migratory fauna and plant food, strategies based on periodically fluctuating resources became far more feasible.

Postglacial conditions also altered the spatial and temporal context of potential food resources. Resources in temperate and boreal habitats are characterised by relatively low stability and high patchiness (Winterhalder and Smith 1981; Watt 1973; Colinvaux 1973) with many potential sources of food clustered along rivers, lakes and sea coasts. Higher latitudes are also strongly seasonal (Fig. 1) and show marked variation in resource availability from season to season. These variations, combined with the inherent instability of *r*-selected populations, render food resources of the temperate and boreal habitats in Eurasia prone to seasonal peaks in availability and to fluctuations at several scales of resolution (Rowley-Conwy and Zvelebil, 1987). For human societies, the implications are two-fold: on the one hand, seasonality introduces elements of risk in that dietary requirements have to be continuously met from resources that are unevenly distributed in time and space; on the other hand, an effective exploitation of the seasonally abundant food could raise the carrying capacity of the area above the natural minimum set by Liebig's law.

It has been generally recognised in recent literature on hunter-gatherers that risk and stress are important if not the crucial factors in determining the organisation of hunter-gatherer social and economic strategies (Winterhalder and Smith 1981; Jochim 1976; Torrence 1983; Price and Brown

1985; O'Shea and Halstead, 1987). At least two models of the postglacial development of hunter-gatherers explicitly refer to risk and stress as principal variables in generating culture change (Hayden 1981; Harris 1977). Similarly, risk and stress would appear to be a crucial factor in the development of postglacial hunter-gatherers in the temperate zone, in that the evolution of postglacial habitats favoured the retention and development of procurement strategies, technological innovations and of social adaptations which minimised the spatial and temporal incongruity of resources inherent in such environments.

When faced with the dilemma of securing a continuous food supply from resources which are unevenly distributed in time and space, people have two basic choices. They can either move around a landscape from one source of food to another, or they have to develop technological, economic and social means of coping with a periodic absence of resources (Fig. 2).

At the beginning of the postglacial period, hunter-gatherer communities in many parts of the temperate zone invested in the development of the latter option. This was especially the case in areas with seasonal resource aggregations (Rowley-Conwy 1983). In such areas, one or two seasonally abundant resources may be relied on to produce the critical storable surplus for the lean seasons. This would require short periods of intensive harvest and precise scheduling during those times of the year when these resources were available (Torrence 1983; Zvelebil 1984; Henry 1985). In such 'time-stressed environments' (Torrence 1983), time was at a premium and hunter-gatherer societies responded by developing time-saving devices: by budgeting their time and by preparing in advance more sophisticated, but also more complicated tools designed for the specific tasks involved (Fig. 3). The development of capture facilities, such as pits, traps, weirs and nets can be also seen as time-saving devices (Torrence 1983). Another technological requirement for effective

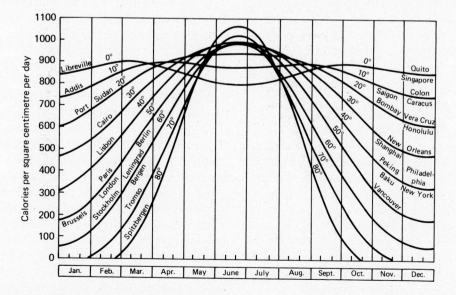

Fig. 1. Variation in solar radiation at different latitudes as a broad index of seasonality (after Watt 1973).

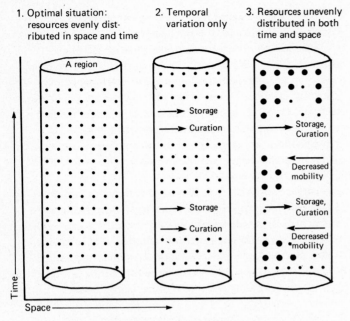

Fig. 2. Spatial and temporal incongruity of resources and the organisation of foraging resource-use strategies.

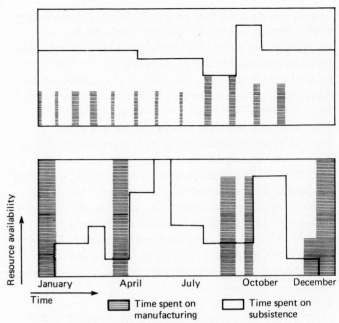

Fig. 3. Tool manufacture and seasonal variation in the level of resources (after Zvelebil 1984).

exploitation of seasonal resources consists of storage. Several authors in the present volume (Rowley-Conwy, Chapter 2; Kozłowski and Kozłowski, Chapter 7; Akazawa, Chapter 11) as well as other workers (Testart 1982*a, b*; Price 1985, pp. 354–55) point to the accelerated development of specialised toolkits, curated technology, storage and capture facilities in many areas of the temperate zone.

These technological developments, combined with the development of the microlithic industry, could be called, with some justification, the original industrial revolution. Composite tools, using microliths as insets in wooden or bone shafts, have several important advantages over the monolithic long-bladed technology prevalent in the Upper Palaeolithic. Semenov (1964), Clarke (1976), Korobkova (Semenov and Korobkova 1983) and others have argued that composite tools with microlith insets are more flexible, more easily repaired, less fragile and more economical in terms of lithic sources. Moreover, as component tools, they can be more easily modified by replacing individual components (Clarke 1976; Bleed 1986). This makes such industries suitable for the performance of a wide variety of tasks with little need for extensive modification or specialist care. Therefore, in addition to being versatile, microlithic tools are also particularly suited for use in the context of time-stressed activities. The increase in the incidence of use of microlith tools should coincide, therefore, with activities which require complex time-scheduling and with executing highly seasonal tasks, such as the wild cereal harvests. This is a point elaborated by Matyushin in Chapter 10, where he links the development of standardised geometric microliths to seasonal intensification and increased labour investment in the harvesting of wild cereals.

In this way, the microlithic industry provides an alter-

native and an insurance to the specialised technology. Both can be said to have been developed to meet scheduling problems caused by the seasonal use of a wide range of resources. But rather than being purpose-made in advance, microlithic component tools would be dedicated to their specific tasks in the field in response to the foraging opportunities as they arise. Even though not all postglacial hunter-gatherers developed both kinds of technology to the same degree, it is tempting to see the dual technology – one designed for flexibility and a broad range of resources, the other dedicated to specialist tasks – as the hallmark of the Mesolithic.

The dual nature of the technology is matched by the dual organisation of food procurement. Throughout the Mesolithic, we can detect the development of specialised patterns of food procurement (Jarman 1972; Fitzhugh 1975; Zvelebil 1980, 1981). Several authors in the present volume draw attention to specialisation on a wide range of resources, including marine species (Zvelebil and Rowley-Conwy, Chapter 6; Akazawa, Chapter 11); terrestrial game (Lewthwaite, Chapter 5; Dolukhanov, Chapter 8; Matyushin, Chapter 10); plant food (Lewthwaite, Chapter 5; Matyushin, Chapter 10); fish and waterfowl (Dolukhanov, Chapter 9). At the same time, the increase in the total breadth of food resources, used by postglacial as opposed to late glacial hunter-gatherers has been noted by many workers, most notably Flannery (1969), who termed this trend 'broad spectrum revolution'. While Gamble (Chapter 3) and other workers (Mellars 1985) see the trend towards the 'broad spectrum' already developing in the Upper Palaeolithic, others have pointed out that the maximum range of resource use was reached during the postglacial period (Cohen 1977; Clark and

Yi 1983; Henry 1985; Binford 1968). As noted above, Hayden (1981) has linked these trends to the greater reliance on *r*-strategists in the postglacial period. However, there is no need to regard specialisation and diversification as developing separately in different environments, as Hayden does (1981). Rather than being regarded as mutually exclusive, these strategies should be seen as complementary, developing together as a part of the same regional economic pattern.

These technological and economic developments were likely to initiate or expand the already established trend towards greater sedentism. Testart (1982*a*, p. 524) noted that storage inhibits the possibility of, and the need for, moving. Bender (1985*a*, p. 26) sees sedentism as 'a response to delays on technological investment', brought about by the development of curated technology and storage, while Rowley-Conwy (1983) elaborates the point that areas with seasonal aggregations of migratory resources were particularly favourable for

the development of sedentary communities, because their exploitation would not be density dependent.

Most contributors to the present volume, as well as other workers (Newell 1984; Testart 1982*a, b*; Price 1985) have suggested that, with the development of postglacial conditions, sedentary existence became more widespread in the temperate zone. In northwest Russia, for example, dwellings and other structures found on hunter-gatherer settlements during the later Mesolithic appear as permanent as any found in farming communities in Europe. On some of these sites, year-round occupation was inferred from seasonal indicators of occupation (Vankina 1970; Rowley-Conwy 1983; Zvelebil 1986*a*; Dolukhanov, Chapter 8). The use of pottery, far more widespread among the mesolithic hunter-gatherers than was hitherto realised (Fig. 4), has been also interpreted as indicative of greater sedentism (Testart 1982*a*). On closer examination, however, we have no certain measures of residential

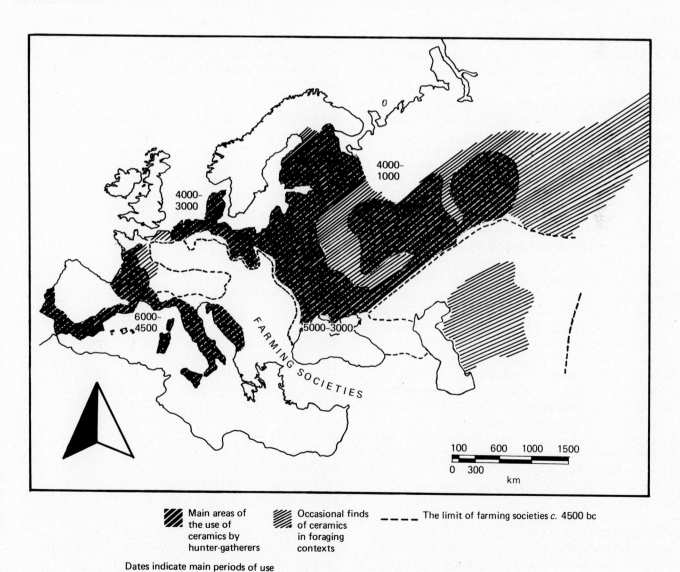

Main areas of the use of ceramics by hunter-gatherers

Occasional finds of ceramics in foraging contexts

The limit of farming societies *c.* 4500 bc

Dates indicate main periods of use

Fig. 4. Pottery-using hunter-gatherers in Europe and temperate Asia, 6000–1000 bc.

permanence in the archaeological record of the Stone Age. All of the standard indicators of sedentism may also reflect the operation of other variables, such as group size, site function, or re-occupation at short time intervals (Woodman 1985; Price 1985). On the one hand, we may be confusing the quality of the archaeological record with residential permanence; on the other, the old dichotomy of mobile mesolithic versus the sedentary neolithic still influences our interpretation of often very similar sets of data.

Tool curation, storage and greater residential permanence – if we accept the present evidence – were also bound to encourage logistic patterns of resource use, marked by the existence of specialised task groups. This in turn would lead to task specialisation and possibly craft specialisation within hunting–gathering communities. Sheehan (1985) presents an excellent ethnographic example of this process among the Alaskan Eskimos, it would be more difficult to identify such a course of events in the archaeological record. Nevertheless, the widespread distribution of specialised sites during the postglacial period (Dolukhanov, Chapter 8; Akazawa, Chapter 11; Kozłowski and Kozłowski, Chapter 7; Woodman 1985; Price 1985; Rowley-Conwy 1983; Zvelebil 1980, 1981, 1986a) implies the logistic pattern of resource use. Task and craft specialisation can be suggested only in few areas: thus specialisation may be perhaps suggested by special status positions held by different groups in the community buried at Oleneostrovskii Mogilnik (O'Shea and Zvelebil 1984), while specialised production of high quality tools has been suggested for the Jomon culture in Japan (Akazawa, Chapter 11).

Ames (1985), Watanabe (1983), Woodburn (1982) and Testart (1982a, b), as well as other workers, link logistic strategies and storage techniques to the concepts of investment and delayed return and note the incipient organisational complexity and social stratification which are likely to arise from them. Testart (1982a, b) goes further to postulate 'accumulation ideology', differential access to resources and the development of individual ownership. 'Accumulation ideology' is likely to be enhanced by contact and exchange (Testart 1982a, p. 526) and through the use of social mechanisms as systems of insurance against economic failure (Suttles 1960; O'Shea 1981; Cohen 1985). This is particularly the case among storage-using hunter-gatherers, who are likely to overproduce as a part of their normal subsistence strategy ('the normal surplus', see O'Shea and Halstead 1987). Within a wider redistribution system, such surplus food can be readily converted into either prestige or value tokens, both of which can be later reclaimed for food ('social storage', see Halstead and O'Shea 1982).

This brings us to the organisation of social relations in mesolithic society. As noted in Chapter 1, a wide range of models have been advanced to account for the emergence of social stratification; some consider social stratification as almost an automatic consequence of human development and the attendant social competition. Within the context of temperate hunter-gatherers, developments such as the differential access to resources, 'accumulation ideology', asymmetrical reciprocity, differential ownership of the means of production (such as food capture technology) and the need in a more sedentary society for alternatives to mobility as the mechanism of conflict resolution, can all be used as an explanation for development of social stratification.

How far can we advance our claims, however, for social stratification in the Mesolithic? The evidence for social ranking comes mainly from cemeteries and from the wide distribution of status objects. Although burials do occur in the Late Pleistocene in Eurasia, actual cemeteries, containing internments of a large number of people, which must have included more than one (extended) family occur only in North Africa, moreover in contexts which in many respects (including the temperate climate) resemble the Mesolithic (Phillipson 1985). The European evidence, as it stands (see Chapter 6, Fig. 9) indicates the following patterns: (1) cemeteries occur exclusively in coastal areas, in lake districts and along major watercourses; (2) settlement patterns in these areas are usually regarded as sedentary or semi-sedentary (i.e. Lepenski Vir in the Danube Gorges, Abora, Sarnate, Sventoji and other sites in the east Baltic; sites on the middle and lower Dnieper and in southern Scandanavia); (3) most, if not all, of the cemeteries revealed variation in mortuary equipment, method of burial and funerary architecture. In most cases, this has been interpreted as indicating status differentiation. At the largest of these cemeteries, Oleneostrovskii Mogilnik, in northern Russia, several status ranks have been identified, and at least two of these represent inherited social positions within the Oleneostrovskii society (O'Shea and Zvelebil 1984).

While these observations offer only glimpses of the organisation of mesolithic society, they indicate a development towards social complexity, formalised in the mortuary context, for which there is no real evidence in the Upper Palaeolithic of temperate Eurasia.

Finally, one has to consider the role of population growth. Like social competition, population growth can act at any stage to accelerate cultural development. Cohen (1985, p. 112) has explicitly linked increasing societal complexity to a rise in population density, patchiness of resources and storage. Population growth might, of course, have been a factor in generating cultural changes which characterise the Mesolithic. Although the debate on the demographic implications of sedentism continues to defy resolution (Hayden 1981, with comments; Hassan 1981; Cohen 1977), it as at least likely that the reduced residential mobility of mesolithic hunter-gatherers increased their reproductive potential. Ethnographic sources show beyond a doubt that those hunting–gathering groups who rely to a large extent on aquatic resources, employ storage and practice a degree of sedentism maintain population densities which are within the range of simple farming societies, both of which are far higher than those common among the more mobile, generalised foragers (Lee and DeVore

1968; Hassan 1981; Testart 1982*a*).

A critical survey of the evidence pertaining to the Mesolithic, however, reveals little convincing evidence for an overall increase in population density. Although Newell (1984) and Constandse-Westerman (Constandse-Westerman, Newell and Meiklejohn 1984) have noted an increase in the number and size of sites in the Mesolithic as compared to the Palaeolithic, Hassan (1981, p. 199) failed to observe any substantial increase in the overall population density during the early postglacial period, while the population growth rate is thought to have actually dropped below that of the upper palaeolithic period (Hassan 1981, p. 200). Given the present distribution of mesolithic remains and the multiple biases which distort the archaeological record at every stage of its retrieval and interpretation (for specific reference to the Mesolithic, see Clarke 1976; Woodman 1983, 1985; Clark 1983), the reconstruction of the overall pattern of population growth cannot but be little more than inspired guesswork. A good case can be made for an increase in population density at a regional level, however, and here it would appear that, while in the interior of Europe and in the interfluvial areas of southern Russia and Central Asia there is little evidence for population increase during the early Holocene (Vencl, Chapter 4; Kozłowski and Kozłowski, Chapter 7; Dolukhanov, Chapter 8; Matyushin, Chapter 10); coastal zones, riparian habitats and lacustrine regions experienced quite a remarkable growth in the density of population (Constandse-Westermann *et al.* 1984). This is indicated by the increase in size, density and duration of settlements in areas where the influence of biasing factors can be assessed over time. The existence of cemeteries and the establishment of a cultural (anthropogenic) landscape on the European periphery also lends indirect support to the idea of increased population density (Rowley-Conwy, Chapter 2; Lewthwaite, Chapter 5; Zvelebil and Rowley-Conwy, Chapter 6, Kozłowski and Kozłowski, Chapter 7; Dolukhanov, Chapter 8; Matyushin, Chapter 10; also Mellars 1976; Simmons 1979; Dennell 1985). Even though the increase in the population density of coastal areas may be at least in part a function of loss of land, submerged by the postglacial rise in the sea level, rather than merely of population growth, this evidence supports the model postulated by Clarke (1976) of a saucer-like distribution of dense mesolithic settlement along the 'coastal and glaciated rim' of Europe (*ibid.*, p. 468) and extends this pattern beyond Europe into temperate Asia. Constandse-Westermann *et al.* (1984), drawing on their northwest European data, suggest an important distinction between the upper palaeolithic and mesolithic patterns of population dynamics: during the Upper Palaeolithic, population growth was checked by strong oscillations at both the regional and local levels, but during the Mesolithic it was replaced by 'a more stable population growth process, characterised by only a limited amount of stochasticity' (*ibid.*, p. 164).

To summarise the contrasts between the late glacial and postglacial periods, mesolithic resource-use strategies appear to have been inherently unstable, yet offered scope for improvement with techno-economic intensification in the

situation of decreasing mobility. With the increasing technological and organisational competence of foragers, a steady supply of food could be obtained from fluctuating resources. In the Upper Palaeolithic, on the other hand, resources, though seasonal, were larger in size and probably more abundant in relation to their human predators; they belonged to the same trophic level of herbivorous ungulates, with similar patterns of behaviour, and similar niches; and were therefore easier to exploit in terms of organisation and technology. As Binford noted (1983), since these larger resources had larger ranges, groups depending on them must have had larger territories and therefore a greater scope for mobility and a greater 'natural store' of back-up resources. This does not mean that none of the upper palaeolithic groups used logistic mobility and practised sedentism, merely that mobility was a more feasible solution to social and economic problems. In a sense, it could be suggested perhaps that, whatever complexity arose among the upper palaeolithic groups in Eurasia (Price and Brown 1985), it did so out of relative affluence. In the case of the Mesolithic, more complex forms of social and economic organisation arose out of need: without the recourse to nomadism, mesolithic strategies for survival depended on organisational complexity for success and were locked into pursuing the course, outlined above, towards increasing economic intensification and social complexity.

Alternative pathways of intensification

Recent studies of postglacial hunter-gatherers have emphasised the development of complex (Rowley-Conwy 1983; Price 1981; Price and Brown 1985) or affluent foraging societies (Koyama and Thomas 1981). These societies are said to be characterised by (1) the intensified use of resources, (2) the shift from residential to logistic mobility and towards more permanent settlement, and (3) an increase in the complexity of social organisation. Although there is no general agreement on the meaning of complexity among hunter-gatherers (e.g. Price and Brown 1985; Gamble, Chapter 3), it is clear from the preceding section that most of the mesolithic societies in temperate Eurasia could be regarded as complex in terms of mobility, resource-use patterns and social organisation.

If the meaning of complexity is a subject of debate, the origin of complexity is much more so. I have tried to argue here that, in the case of the Mesolithic, the development of social and economic complexity can be seen as a process designed to secure a steady supply of food from unpredictable resources. I have further argued that this process involved an increase in labour investment and, in most cases, an increase in food procurement. The mesolithic economy can then be seen as one among several patterns of development, all of which proceed in the same general direction, towards greater intensification.[1]

Development of agriculture has been traditionally regarded as almost a unique process, fundamentally different from socio-economic developments in other non-farming societies (Childe 1928, 1957; Braidwood 1958; Reed 1977). Harris (1977) has shed new light on an old problem by considering the emergence of farming as one of several specialised resource-use systems, developing in response to stress. In agreement with this view, I would argue that the evolution of temperate foraging represented, both in time and in function, a parallel development with the evolution of agro-pastoral farming in the Near East. Both processes occurred during the early postglacial period, and both were essentially concerned with increasing the productivity of their environments. The difference rests in the fact that the Near-Eastern pathway resulted in genetic domestication of a mutually complementary set of species; the temperate pathway continued in the direction of technological specialisation and intensive resource management, which did not, by and large, result in genetic domestication. This can be at least partly accounted for in terms of different sets of resources which were initially used in the process.

Plants and animals must possess special characteristics to facilitate complete (i.e. genetic) domestication and very few, in fact, are fit to become major domesticated food resources (McCullough 1970). In the Near East, both wild cereals and social ungulates permitted initial domestication and responded to genetic selection which resulted in the establishment of desired characteristics — above all, the increased productivity of these species. Such species could become fully domesticated, and, moreover, the agro-pastoral combination of farming proved highly adaptable to other environments (Harris 1977).

In the temperate forest zone, on the other hand, food resources cannot be easily domesticated. Most, if not all of the ungulates available lack one or more of the characteristics which would make their manipulation, close herding and complete domestication possible. These characteristics include high productivity, non-specialist feeding patterns, gregariousness, polygamy and hierarchical group structure (Garrard 1984). As Rowley-Conwy shows in Chapter 2, roe and red deer would be unsuitable as early domesticates because of their territorial behaviour (for the opposite view, see Jarman 1972; Barker 1985). Other ungulates such as fallow deer, elk and gazelle are territorial at least part of the year, usually during the rut (Garrard 1984; for elk, see Zvelebil 1981) and moreover they have fairly narrow dietary requirements. This leaves wild pig, aurochs and the caprines as potentially domesticable temperate species. Local domestication of caprines has been postulated in both the western and the eastern Mediterranean (Dennell 1983; Barker 1985), but, at least for the west Mediterranean, the idea of local caprine domestication has been convincingly refuted by Geddes (1985, pp. 27–31) on genetic, palaeontological and zoological evidence. Cattle (Rowley-Conwy, Chapter 2; Matyushin, Chapter 10) and pig (Dolukhanov, Chapter 8) on the other hand, may well have been domesticated locally in Eastern Europe and along the northern fringes of Central Asia. However, their domestication did not alone cause a shift from hunting and gathering to a farming economy.

The absence in temperate Eurasia of the indigenous development of farming as an integrated economic strategy can be explained by the absence of other potential domesticates and by the relative strength and productivity of the temperate foraging. Perlman (1980, pp. 270–1), for instance, noted the low aquatic productivity of Mediterranean and Near-Eastern coastal zones in comparison to those of Atlantic Europe. On the other hand, domestication of pig or cattle in the temperate zone would not be compatible with other resources, as in the Near East, where an agro-pastoral system emerged out of plural domestication of cereals, pulses and ungulates, mutually reinforcing and complementing one another.

With the possible exception of its southern margins (Dennell 1983), the temperate zone lacked the potential cultigens which contributed to the formation of the Near-Eastern agro-pastoral system (Kozłowski and Kozłowski, Chapter 7). While other plant resources occurred in abundance and while there is some indication that they were intensively harvested, indeed perhaps cultivated (Clarke 1976; Zvelebil 1981; Lewthwaite, Chapter 5), the consideration of these non-cereal resources shows that because of low productivity (roots and tubers), long maturation period (nut and fruit trees), specific habitat requirements (water chestnut), high processing costs and/or restricted possibilities for genetic domestication (nuts), they could not have become a basic element of the food-producing system in temperate Eurasia (Rowley-Conwy, Chapter 2; Harris 1977).

Other major sources of food in the temperate zone would be unsuitable as early domesticates for similar reasons. Aquatic species, including seal, waterbirds, fish and beaver would be difficult to domesticate owing to the restricted nature of their habitat and, in some cases, to the migratory nature of their life cycle. Fish, moreover, have a cumulative, rather than sigmoid, rate of growth (McCullough 1970). As a consequence, various forms of selective cull which would effectively increase production among mammals, would not be effective on fish. As almost every contributor to the present volume shows, fishing and specialised marine hunting formed a very important element of mesolithic economies; yet it could not develop into a form of management which would result in domestication.

In summary, the scope for domestication in the temperate forest zone was limited by the range of resources. The development of farming economy was unlikely to take place using indigenous resources alone, and the domestication of individual species such as cattle or pig, or the tending of nut trees, remained within the context of a hunting–gathering economy until the introduction of a more productive and balanced range of cultigens and domesticates.

Transition to farming
The question of the transition to farming can be approached from two perspectives: from the Near-Eastern, which presumes the colonisation of much of Europe by farming populations from the Near East; and from the European,

which postulates the adoption, and/or the development, of farming locally by the indigenous hunter-gatherers. The difference between these two approaches goes far beyond the geographical emphasis. The theoretical and philosophical background to the two approaches (see Chapter 1) appears in fact so different and mutually exclusive that, within each approach, different terminology has been developed to describe the same phenomena. So, within the colonisation model, farmers 'migrated' and 'colonised'; farming was 'introduced' and 'diffused'; hunter-gatherers are cast in the role of 'survivals' which were 'absorbed' (e.g. Vencl, Chapter 4). Within the indigenous model, farmers and foragers are the same people, so farming emerged through 'transition' from one state of economy to another, or was 'adopted' by the local foragers, who are regarded as initiators, or at least active contributors to the 'process of transition'. Within the first approach, all the important developments took place in the Near East, and, in order to understand the spread of farming in Europe, we really have to understand the conditions surrounding its origin in the Fertile Crescent. Early postglacial societies in temperate Europe and Asia are held to have contributed little to their own Neolithic; they are at best regarded as props against which the inexorable advance of Neolithic civilisation unfolds through the processes of migration and colonisation. Within the second approach, local hunting and gathering societies are held to be primarily responsible for the transition to farming, accomplished through a 'do-it-yourself kit' of intensifying husbandry practices, dating back to the Upper Palaeolithic and tried on anything from snails to sheep (Bahn 1984). It follows that it is the local hunter-gatherers which should be the proper object of study of the agricultural transition. The origin of agro-pastoral village farming in the Near East is not regarded as relevant to the socio-economic developments in Europe, except as the original sources of a few cultigens and domesticates — emmer, wheat and possibly caprines — which were brought to Europe through exchange or even arrived independently by their own volition (Dennell 1985). Similar conflicting explanations are advanced to account for the transition to farming in temperate mainland Asia (cf. Dolukhanov, Chapter 9; Matyushin, Chapter 10) and in Japan (Akazawa 1981, 1982; Chapter 11, this volume).

I have argued in Chapter 1, and the succeeding contributions have shown, that this difference of view is based on misconceptions of earlier research and does not correspond to the variability evident in the data. It prevents us from seeing the essential similarity between two alternative pathways of economic development: one in the Near East, based on the domestication of a complementary range of cereals, legumes and social ungulates; the other in temperate Eurasia, based on a combination of broad-based and specialised strategies, the latter especially relating to aquatic resources.

Perhaps the most striking and at the same time the most common feature of all the contributions in this volume is the enormous regional variability which characterised the transition to farming. Even though this process occurred at a far slower rate than generally acknowledged, it varied a great deal from region to region. In the eastern Mediterranean, the

Balkans and Central Europe, the transition to farming was relatively rapid and involved the introduction of a complete or a near complete set of cultigens and domesticates; along the Atlantic rim of Europe and in Eastern Europe, it was staggered over several millennia. Similar differences can be observed in Central Asia and Japan (Dolukhanov Chapter 9; Matyushin, Chapter 10; Akazawa, Chapter 11). In some areas, farming was clearly adopted into the local mesolithic context; in others, the situation is more equivocal, with the introduction of new elements of material culture along with the cultigens and domesticates taken to indicate migration (Vencl, Chapter 4). These differences exist because the emergence of farming communities in the temperate zone was a function of several variables, which combined to accelerate in some regions (west Mediterranean littoral, for instance; Lewthwaite, Chapter 5) and to delay in others (Denmark or northeast Japan) the course of the transition. In this process, neither the condition of the local hunter-gatherer societies nor the dispersal of agro-pastoral village farming can be ignored.

The Near-Eastern Perspective

The colonisation model of the transition to farming provides, in a way, the simplest explanation for the process. The flaws associated with its application have already been discussed in Chapter 1. Regardless of these, the model gives us a conditional standard of the rate of farming colonisation, against which the actual spread of farming can be compared. Figure 5 shows the demic advance of the agricultural frontier across temperate Eurasia, the European mainland reaching saturation about 3000 bc. The actual spread of farming is shown in Figs. 6–8.

Comparing the actual rate and the rate of dispersal expected under colonisation, we can observe three phenomena. The actual rate of dispersal is clearly retarded in the North Atlantic coastal areas and in Eastern Europe. As shown in Chapter 6, the dispersal of farming comes to a halt in northern Germany by the middle of the fifth millennium bc and there is a gap of more than 1000 years before farming is adopted in Denmark and Scania. In the forest zone of Eastern Europe, instead of being adopted in 5000–4000 bc, as the model predicts, farming was adopted some 2000–3000 years later. In Central and southeastern Europe, the actual rate of dispersal resembles the modelled rate. As Fig. 6 shows, however, the pattern of dispersal is not uniform; rather, farming is first established in the best agricultural regions, while other areas, such as the Carpathians, the Dolomites or the Alpine region remain non-agricultural.

In the western Mediterranean, the dispersal of certain elements of farming, especially ovicaprid husbandry, appears to have taken place actually earlier than predicted by the colonisation model (Lewthwaite, Chapter 5). Farming also reached the Portuguese coast earlier (Zvelebil and Rowley-Conwy, Chapter 6). It would appear, then, that the westward diffusion of farming accross the Mediterranean occurred at a faster rate than would be expected through vigorous colonisation by farming populations.

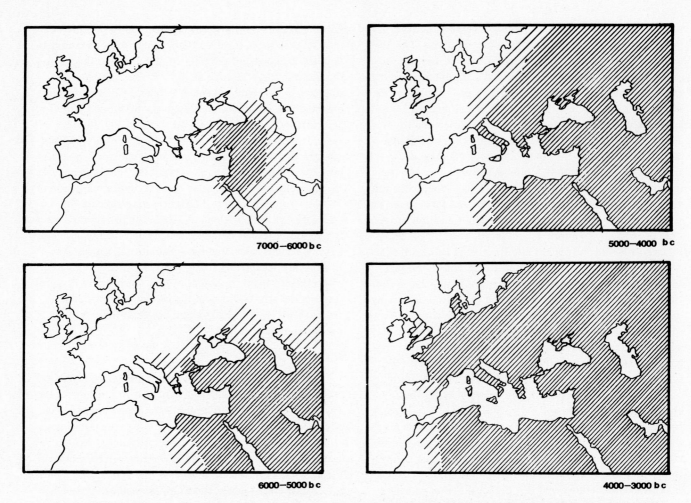

Fig. 5. 'Wave of advance' model of the colonisation of Europe. Predicted pattern of colonisation by advancing farming populations (after Ammerman and Cavalli-Sforza 1984, Fig. 7.6).

From these patterns it is clear that the transition to farming in Europe cannot be explained solely in terms of uniform advances by colonising populations. As Ammerman and Cavalli-Sforza (1984, p. 135) themselves admit, the correspondence between the predicted and the actual rate of dispersal, though highly suggestive, does not, in itself, prove migration. We are, therefore, dealing with two questions here: does the relative goodness of fit between the predicted and actual rate of dispersal in Central and southeastern Europe indicate colonisation? and how do we explain the different rates of agricultural dispersal in those areas, where the goodness of fit is poor?

Ammerman and Cavalli-Sforza (1984) seek additional support for their hypothesis in the genetic make-up of European populations, which, in their view, reflects the movement of people from western Asia into Europe. A similar argument, based on the differences in skeletal morphology of Stone Age populations, has been advanced by Vencl (Chapter 4). Neither of these two sets of data, however, offers unqualified support for the colonisation hypothesis.

Distribution of genetically controlled phenotypes, suggesting a diffusion from western *or central Asia*, even

though they appear convincing, could fit a number of prehistoric or historical migrations as effectively as the neolithic colonisation of Europe by farmers from western Asia. Thus the distribution of the genetic traits comprising the first principal component in Ammerman and Cavalli-Sforza's (1984, pp. 105—8) analysis could be explained by the more recent expansions such as those of the Turkish peoples during the growth of the Ottoman Empire. A number of archaeological horizons — if indeed they do indicate migrations — could explain the diffusion of traits comprising the second and third principal components, such as the Battle Axe/ Corded Ware complex in the case of the second, and the cultural complexes often taken to indicate Indo-european expansion in the case of the third component (Gimbutas 1970; Sulimirski 1970). Perhaps, more realistically, the diffusion of genetic traits from central Asia to Eastern and Central Europe, represented by the second and third components, could be seen as a result of several historical migrations, including the 'Scythians', Sarmatians, Huns, Avars and Mongols (Zvelebil 1980). The second principal component could also reflect the penetration of the Iberian peninsula by North African populations in the first millennium AD.

ARCTIC OCEAN

URAL MOUNTAINS

BLACK SEA

5000–4000 bc

Farming   Hunter-gatherers

Availability zone   0   1000   2000

km

Fig. 6. The actual dispersal of farming in Europe and Central Asia, 5000–4000 bc.

Differences in cranial and skeletal morphology between the mesolithic and neolithic populations, summarised by Vencl (Chapter 4), also pose a number of problems. The first is the small size of the sample, especially for the mesolithic/epipalaeolithic populations (Vencl, Chapter 4; Constandse-Westermann 1977). The second is the morphological variation in characteristics such as gracilisation, shape of cranium, dentition, and structure of the face, within the two groups, which, given a larger sample, might result in continual variation rather than in the division into two discrete populations (Živanović 1975; Constandse-Westermann 1977). Third, as data presented by Kozłowski and Kozłowski in Chapter 7 indicate, the re-emergence of 'epipalaeolithic' features during the later Neolithic cannot be fully explained by the reverse expansion of the remnant hunter-gatherer populations from Northern Europe (Vencl, Chapter 4).

Finally, the morphological differences observed between neolithic and mesolithic populations could conceivably result from a number of changes unrelated to neolithic colonisation such as changes in food procurement strategies (Frayer 1980) and in diet (Akazawa, Chapter 11; Armelagos 1981, y'Edynak 1978). A shift in nutrition from meat-based to cereal diet, for instance, could result in smaller dentition, smaller jaw size and altered structure of the face (y'Edynak 1978). Seen in this perspective, changes such as reduced body size, gracilisation, and leptodolichomorphy could be a result of a gradual shift to farming by the indigenous mesolithic population.

Other arguments voiced in support of the colonisation hypothesis include: (1) the direction of the dispersal of farming itself – from the east Mediterranean to the west and the north; (2) broad similarities in material culture between the neolithic farmers in the Near East and those of the Early

Fig. 7. The actual dispersal of farming in Europe and Central Asia, *c.* 3500 bc.

Neolithic in Europe, especially in ceramics and broad-bladed flint technology; and (3) the vastly greater population potential of farming communities (Vencl, Chapter 4). In opposition, Dennell (1983), Barker (1985) and others have argued that : (1) there is no evidence in the material culture for the colonist expansion westwards, merely for the diffusion of new traits; (2) there is a great deal of evidence for continuity with the preceding hunter-gatherers and for regional variation in material culture; (3) the distribution of wild progenitors of neolithic cultigens and domesticates extended across the Mediterranean, making local domestication possible; (4) there is no evidence for population pressure in the Near East at the time, and, in fact, very little evidence for early neolithic settlement in western Turkey, the presumed staging area for the colonisation of Europe; (5)

the demographic potential of the early neolithic farmers had been overestimated, while that of the hunter-gatherers was underestimated.

These arguments have to be seen in the context of other variables bearing upon the transition to farming. The search for early agricultural colonists from the Near East dominated the debate about agricultural transition in Europe to such an extent that it has obscured other factors involved in the process. These factors include the natural conditions and the role of the indigenous hunter-gatherers.

In terms of suitability for foraging and farming, various habitats of the temperate zone can be roughly divided into four types (Fig. 9). Part of the variation in the rate of transition to farming can be seen as a result of these different conditions. Areas settled first by farming populations were

Fig. 8. The actual dispersal of farming in Europe and Central Asia, *c.* 2000 bc.

precisely those which were poor in resources for hunter-gatherers but rich for farmers (see also Vencl, Chapter 4; Kozłowski and Kozłowski, Chapter 7). These areas include the plain of Thessaly, the Tavoliere, the loess areas of Central Europe, and the broad basins of large rivers, such as the Danube, Rhine or the Seine. River valleys and broad coastal plains, habitats favourable to both foragers and farmers, saw the introduction of farming next. Steep littoral zones, estuarine habitats, river gorges and lacustrine habitats, all of which were highly productive for foragers but relatively unproductive for farming, were the last to adopt farming during the initial period of transition. The delay in the agricultural settlement of these areas can be clearly observed throughout the temperate zone (Chapter 5–11). Finally, uplands and montane areas were placed under cultivation or animal husbandry only during the secondary expansion of farming in the Late Neolithic. This is,

of course, a simplified picture and explains only a part of the variation. But it serves to emphasise the regional nature of the transition and the *mosaic*, rather than 'wave of advance', pattern of its dispersal (Moddermann 1958; Kruk 1973).

Climate must have been another factor certain to influence the rate of transition. Two major points must be raised here: (1) with the dispersal northwards, farming was being introduced to progressively less favourable areas, and (2), after *c.* 3000 bc, farming was adopted in increasingly deteriorating climatic conditions. In Scandinavia and northeast Europe, the late adoption of farming meant that the influence of these two factors was combined and must have been at least partly responsible for further delay, and in some cases the reversal in the process of agricultural transition in these areas during the later third and the second millennia bc (Moberg 1966; Bergelund 1969; Welinder 1975; Zvelebil

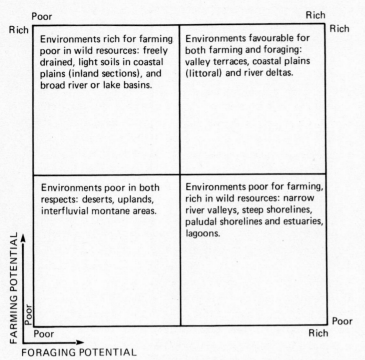

Fig. 9. Variation in temperate environments in terms of suitability for foraging and for farming.

1981). The important general point arising from the North-European data is that farming, as an alternative to other systems of subsistence, was of different value in different environments.

The delay in the adoption of farming could not be explained, however, solely by the climatic and edaphic conditions of the temperate zone. While it can account for some slowing down of the general process of transition, it cannot explain particular cases where the farming frontier remained stationary in ecologically uniform regions, such as the North-European Plain. In other places, such as the river valleys and terraces of the Ukraine and the southern Urals, farming remained an unexplored option in ecologically favourable areas. This variation can be explained only in terms of the socio-economic condition of the local hunter-gatherer groups.

The temperate Eurasian perspective

In a recent volume concerned with prehistoric farming in Europe, Barker (1985, p. 252) admits that 'the context of the abandonment of foraging for farming has rarely been discussed beyond a vague consensus that the benefits of farming must have eventually been obvious to the most obdurate mesolithic hunter'. Most of the contributors in the present volume have been considering the shift to farming from just the perspective which has been lacking, that of the mesolithic hunter-gatherers. The material presented can be summarised under the following headings:

Indigenous husbandry and agro-pastoral farming

We have to distinguish between two processes: (*a*) the intensive management of indigenous resources ('traditional

resources'; Dennell 1983) and (*b*) the adoption of agro-pastoral village farming, based on genetically domesticated cereals, legumes and livestock ('novel resources'; Dennell 1983). Within the context of the Mesolithic in the temperate zone, it is possible that the first process represents an early stage of indigenous domestication; yet, as Rowley-Conwy (Chapter 2) and Vencl (Chapter 4) point out, there is no clear evidence for local domestication actually occurring. As Rowley-Conwy (p. 27) noted, a degree of complexity could have been reached 'without the European Mesolithic having to emulate the Near Eastern'. As I have argued above, one reason why postglacial hunter-gatherers in the temperate zone followed a different course of development was because they specialised on a different range of resources, most of which were not suited for domestication. The use of cereals, legumes and ovicaprids, which in Dennell's (1983) and in Barker's (1985) view could represent incipient European agriculture, must be seen within the context of the intensive exploitation of other resources, such as red deer, wild pig, cattle, nut gathering, shellfish collection, waterfowling, sealing and fishing. In contrast, in the Near East, a more rapid orientation took place towards specialisation on a narrow range of cereals, legumes and ungulates. This does not mean that domestication did not occur in the temperate mesolithic context, merely that the implications were not the same. Even if the initial domestication of wild pig, cattle, caprines, einkorn, barley or legumes did take place in Europe, as Barker (1985) and Dennell (1983) suggest, there is no evidence that this process occurred together within one geographically discrete area, but, at best, individual genera were domesticated in different regions: i.e. ovicaprines in the Mediterranean, pig in the southern Ukraine, cereals and legumes in southeast Europe, cattle in the North-European Plain and the Central Balkans (Kozłowski and Kozłowski, Chapter 7). Further, there is no evidence of any of these possibly domesticated resources reaching positions of economic importance comparable to those in the Near East. Consequently, it can be argued that the European husbandry practices, whether considered to be domestication or not, remained integrated within the framework and the organisation of the mesolithic economy, which retained its broad spectrum yet specialised character. In this it constitutes a development which is parallel to, yet separate from, that in the Near East.

Compared to the temperate hunting and gathering, however, specialised and intensive, the agro-pastoral farming has two major advantages: it can be more productive and it can, as an integrated system, be adapted to a wider range of environmental conditions. As Dennell (1983, p. 167) pointed out, its productivity increases, especially if emmer and bread wheats, neither of which have progenitors in Europe, are added to the package. The adoption of the agro-pastoral system of farming was also likely to accelerate processes such as economic intensification or population growth, which had already begun to occur among the mesolithic hunter-gatherers, and to project them on to the scale which extended beyond the capacity of most – if not all – known hunting–gathering societies.

In the qualitative sense, then, the appearance of agro-pastoral village farming represents a continuation of the previous trends towards socio-economic complexity and a more intensive use of resources. It is quite likely that in some areas, such as southeast Europe (Dennell 1985), or the west Mediterranean (Lewthwaite, Chapter 5; Barker 1985), or, indeed, Japan (Akazawa, Chapter 11) the introduction of cereal-based farming merely replicated and expanded earlier patterns of resource use, based on intensive crop husbandry. In terms of the scale of these developments, however, agro-pastoral village farming opened a new dimension, a new range of possibilities in terms of population growth, food production and social differentiation. Surely it should be the emergence of this integrated system, rather than the appearance of isolated cases of domestication within an essentially hunting and gathering economy, that should mark the transition from mesolithic to neolithic society.

The transition to farming on a continental scale

The abandonment of foraging for farming took place earlier among mobile foragers with generalised resource-use strategies than among the more sedentary hunter-gatherers specialising in the use of aquatic resources.

To recapitulate, we have two traditions emerging in temperate and boreal Eurasia during the early Holocene (Clarke 1976). The first one is mainly confined to the interior areas with few migratory resources; there, hunting–gathering communities appear to be characterised by small sites, dispersed pattern of settlement, residential, rather than logistic mobility, dependence on ungulates rather than other food resources, simple social organisation and low population density (Vencl, Chapter 4; Kozłowski and Kozłowski, Chapter 7). It should never be forgotten, however, that these areas lack the conditions suitable for the preservation of organic materials, so our interpretations are based on a tiny fraction of the original material culture (Coles 1984).

In contrast, along the coastal and glaciated rim of Eurasia, along large river valleys and along the Central-Asian lakes, all habitats rich in aquatic resources, we can trace the development of storage-using, sedentary and specialised hunter-gatherers out of the more generalised patterns of mobility and resource use during the early postglacial period.

Despite the higher population density and therefore a higher likelihood of demographic stress among the more sedentary communities, the indications are that farming was adopted later among the more complex and sedentary than among the more mobile hunter-gatherers. This is made clear, for example, by Kozłowski and Kozłowski in Chapter 7. It is evidently the case along the west Atlantic coast of Europe and in southern Scandinavia (Zvelebil and Rowley-Conwy, Chapter 6), in the Ukraine (Dolukhanov, Chapter 8), in southern Urals and Central Asia (Dolukhanov, Chapter 9; Matyushin, Chapter 10) and in Japan (Akazawa, Chapter 11). The only exceptions are the coastal areas in peninsular Scandinavia and the northeast Baltic, where farming occurs earlier on the coast than in the interior: here, however, we are at the northern boundary of the temperate zone and the expansion of farming into the

interior would first have required its adaptation to the boreal, coniferous conditions: a process which did not occur until the first millennium AD (Zvelebil 1981, 1985).

This pattern can be explained by the greater productivity and resilience of the complex foraging system. On the one hand, storing, specialised and sedentary foraging societies were capable of supporting relatively high population densities and were probably able to absorb small-scale fluctuations in resources. On the other hand, this was achieved with technological and organisational investment in the foraging economy, which would have required an additional effort to change. It is significant that, in those coastal areas where the technological commitment to a marine economy was most advanced, such as northeast Japan, farming was adopted later than in adjacent regions, *despite* the higher population density and the sedentism of marine hunters (Akazawa, Chapter 11). In summary, the complex socio-economic nature of mesolithic societies produced its own dynamic equilibrium: the technological investment and economic potential of specialised foraging systems favoured the continuation of the old economy and its further development; social differentiation and latent population growth supplied the pressure for a steady increase in production and for an eventual shift to a more productive economy. In the end, the development of specialised resource-use strategies could delay, but not prevent, the adoption of a farming economy based on cereal cultivation and stock-keeping. The exception to this was the far north of Eurasia, where the indigenous systems of resource use continued to develop to the present day, through reindeer domestication and specialisation on marine resources.

Regional and local scales of transition

At a regional scale of resolution, the agricultural transition was a much slower process than hitherto acknowledged. We have distinguished three phases in this process: the availability, substitution and consolidation phases (Zvelebil and Rowley-Conwy 1984; Chapter 6, this volume; Zvelebil, Chapter 1). This scheme, emphasising the gradual nature of the transition, has been applied to coastal regions of Western and Northern Europe (Chapter 6), to Eastern Europe and to Central Asia (Dolukhanov, Chapters 8 and 9). With few significant exceptions, it was found to be compatible with the available evidence: in each region we can distinguish the availability phase, when farming was available nearby, but not adopted, the substitution phase, when cereal cultivation and stock-keeping replaced foraging as the principal means of subsistence; and the consolidation phase, when the role of farming was further expanded, in terms of space and intensity of production, while foraging lost its dietary significance (see Chapter 1, Fig. 3).

This model provides a descriptive framework for the interaction between foragers and farmers at the agricultural frontier and helps to evaluate the reaction of mesolithic communities to farming. The availability phase alone indicates that farming was not adopted automatically as a superior way of life, but only after a delay of varying length and after specific reasons had emerged for its adoption. In this light, the availability phase is the most crucial period for our under-standing of the transition. The existence of the availability phase also implies, though by no means proves, that the indigenous hunter-gatherers played a significant role in the dispersal of agriculture and animal husbandry. It is significant that the regional profiles where the availability phase was absent belonged to areas where there is clear evidence for colonisation: in middle Sweden (Welinder 1975; Spång et al. 1976), in Kopet Dagh, and in Tedjen and other oasis regions of Central Asia (Dolukhanov, Chapter 9).

The duration of substitution and consolidation phases must have been influenced by (1) the relative productive potentials of foraging and farming economies, (2) the risks involved in either one, and (3) the degree of integration which could have taken place, given the often conflicting demands placed by foraging and farming on time, space and labour resources. In Denmark, after a long availability phase, the transition to farming was rapid, and the substitution phase was short — a process no doubt enhanced by the suitability of Danish soils for cultivation — in southern Finland, east Baltic and northwest Russia, substitution and consolidation phases were particularly long and took the form of several integrated foraging–farming economies before the final shift to food production[2] (Zvelebil 1981, 1985; Dolukhanov 1979; Chapter 8, this volume).

The gradual transition model redefines the point where the Neolithic begins: since the substitution phase entails the actual transition to the agro-pastoral system of farming, the beginning of the Neolithic, if by the Neolithic we mean the development of such a system, occurs in the course of the substitution phase. At the same time, hunting and gathering continues to make an important contribution to the diet until the end of the substitution phase. In some regions, the advent of the Neolithic, as defined by the substitution phase, is delayed by several hundred years if compared to conventional interpretations (see Chapter 6, Fig. 7; Chapter 8, Fig. 4, Chapter 9, Fig. 4). The availability phase, on the other hand, would correspond in some areas, such as southeast Europe (Dennell 1983) or eastern Japan (Akazawa, Chapter 11) to a period of intensive management of indigenous 'traditional' resources.

Causes of the transition and the role of forager–farmer interactions
The adoption of farming by mesolithic communities took place in different socio-economic contexts, for reasons which were particular to individual situations. The common feature of the transition to farming was not the cause, but the objective: to increase the material well-being of the society or the individuals within it.

The range of case-studies, investigated in this volume, suggest several causes for the transition to farming. In Chapter 5, Lewthwaite makes a case for farming being selectively adopted in different parts of the western Mediterranean for different reasons: in Sardinia and Corsica, animal husbandry was adopted to fill in the gap created by the absence of indigenous ungulates; along the west Mediterranean littoral, pottery and caprines were adopted primarily as prestige items, in response to the demand created by the incipient social stratification and social competition. It was not until the end of the fifth millennium, some 1500–2000 years later, that the development of the cereal component resulted in the full agro-pastoral village way of life. Along the Atlantic margins of Europe, transition to farming also involved selective adoption of some elements of farming, designed at first to fit the existing foraging pattern, rather than to replace it (i.e. northern Spain, Brittany, western Netherlands). In some of these areas, the causes for the adoption of farming cannot as yet be elucidated, though the contact with the farming societies nearby must have played an important role (see below). In others, social competition in the case of Brittany (Bender 1985b) and the decline in the availability of local resources in Denmark and southern Finland have been advanced as explanations for the process of transition (Zvelebil and Rowley-Conwy, 1984; Chapter 6, this volume).

In Eastern Europe and along the northern fringes of Central Asia, the causes of the transition to farming also appear to be regionally variable. According to Dolukhanov (Chapter 8), the early neolithic Tripolye culture came into being through immigration; while in northwest Russia, social crisis, associated with the introduction of metal are held to be responsible for the eventual adoption of farming. In the southern Urals, Matyushin (Chapter 10) notes that periods of socio-economic innovation coincide with environmental stress, caused by desiccation. Transition to farming in this area, as well as in more southern regions of Central Asia (Dolukhanov, Chapter 9) are seen essentially as responses to environmental stress (see also Cohen 1981, 1985).

Akazawa, in Chapter 11, examines the pattern which has been emerging in other areas of the temperate zone: the transition to farming first occurred away from the main centres of hunter-gatherer settlement. Cereal farming (rice cultivation) was first adopted in southeast Japan, an area with a long tradition of intensive plant utilisation, but dispersed hunter-gatherer settlement; a situation which in some respects resembles the emergence of agro-pastoral farming in southeast Europe. In both areas, colonisation by farmers from outside the region — in Japan's case from China — is conventionally regarded as the most plausible explanation. Yet, as Dennell (1983) noted in the context of southeast Europe, these would be the societies most 'preadapted' to the development of plant husbandry. Even here, therefore, the replacement of a less productive form of plant utilisation — such as the harvesting of wild cereals, the tending of nut trees — by a more productive one (cereal cultivation) without outside immigration cannot be ruled out.

In contrast, the adoption of farming in northeast Japan took place after a delay of some 600 years in conditions similar to those which occurred in the southern Baltic some 3000 years earlier. Far from being preadapted for the transition to farming, maritime hunters of northeast Japan were in fact maladapted for the process, because the adoption of farming would interfere with their organisational and technological commitment to the exploitation of maritime resources. Akazawa's study implies that specialised hunter-fishers are in fact less flexible and more resistant to a shift to food production, and more likely to cope with problems of food supply within the framework of the existing economy.

One important process which has received less attention than it deserves is forager–farmer interactions. With few exceptions (Alexander 1978; Anderson 1981; Moore 1981; Dennell 1985), the transition to farming in temperate Eurasia has not been investigated from the perspective of forager–farmer contact. Yet, such studies as there are of the agricultural frontier (Zvelebil, Chapter 1) suggest that the existence of the frontier alone may encourage the transition to farming.

Dolukhanov (Chapter 8), Kozłowski and Kozłowski (Chapter 7), and Zvelebil and Rowley-Conwy (Chapter 6) stress the importance of forager–farmer contacts as a stimulus for the adoption of farming. Such contacts are evidenced by the presence of items, produced by farming communities (such as ceramics, polished axes, etc. and also cereals and domestic animals) and found on hunting–gathering sites on one hand, and by raw materials and objects originating in hunting–gathering territories and found on agricultural settlements on the other (e.g. Kozłowski and Kozłowski, Chapter 7. and Dolukhanov, Chapter 8). Not all of the items found in such contexts may be a result of trade or exchange across the agricultural frontier, some may not even indicate contact (the alternatives may be down-the-line trade, secondary re-use, movement of people rather than goods, local imitation manufacture), but even so, enough cases of probable contact can be gathered to be reasonably certain that the agricultural frontier in temperate Europe and Asia was 'open' and 'porous', rather than 'closed' (Dennell 1985; Zvelebil, Chapter 1, Fig. 1).

In a recent paper on forager–farmer interactions, Moore (1985, p. 94) has noted that 'the concept of *frontier*, when defined as a *mosaic*, suggests that the settlement, subsistence and social strategies of sedentary farmers and mobile hunter-gatherers may unintentionally interfere with each other and that this meddling can lead to rapid social transformation or cultural disintegration (of the latter)' [my second italics and parentheses]. Moore goes on to show that agricultural settlement limits the use of space and increases mobility costs for hunter-gatherers, and this not only interferes with hunter-gatherer subsistence activities but it also disrupts their mating and information networks, conflict resolution and other aspects of hunter-gatherer social life.[3] At the same time, the presence of farming settlement provides an opportunity to offset the increased costs of these activities by the development of exchange networks with farmers and by the recourse to farmers as mediators in conflict resolution. In

addition, Dennell (1985, p. 124) suggests that segments of hunter-gatherer society, especially the younger generation, would be drawn to emulate the farming way of life, since it possessed novel and exotic goods, objects which could easily be perceived as symbols of status. In this way, the agricultural groups in effect 'hijacked the mating and information networks of hunter-gatherers' (Dennell 1985, p. 125). Finally, Anderson (1981) has observed that trade between farming and foraging groups will accentuate the development of 'accumulation ideology' and contribute to the creation of 'prestige economy' (Watanabe 1983). In such situations, hunter-gatherers, without needing additional 'causes' for the transition to farming, would be drawn into the more intensive farming system, towards more permanent settlement along the agricultural frontier and towards the eventual adoption of agriculture. From what has been said above, it is clear that it would be more mobile hunter-gatherer groups which would be most at risk from exposure to the agricultural frontier.

In summary, then, one is forced to conclude that there is no single cause for the transition to farming. Several different factors can be seen as responsible for the transition to farming in different parts of the temperate zone. These may have included: an increase in population density, either through population growth or reduction in the size of hunter-gatherer territories; adverse environmental change and decline in local resources; social competition and a status-related desire for the acquisition of wealth; and forager–farmer interaction in the agricultural frontier zone. Some of these factors have been related to specific cases of transition in this volume, but in no instance can this be shown to have been the case to the exclusion of other, alternative explanations. In this aspect, we have not yet progressed from conjecture and hypothesis to explanation.

A conclusion

Having this in mind, this survey would nevertheless remain incomplete without at least an attempt at outlining those areas where farming, whether village-based or not, was introduced by colonisation and assimilation and those areas where it was adopted by indigenous hunter-gatherers. Figure 10 shows the areas where, all things considered, farming was most probably introduced through colonisation by immigrant farmers and assimilation of local hunter-gatherers on one hand, and areas where it was adopted by the local hunter-gatherers, initially at least, into their existing patterns of resource use. The colonisation model corresponds best to areas where the pattern of farming colonisation simulated by Ammerman and Cavalli-Sforza (1984) fits the actual rate of the spread, where there is no evidence for the availability phase, where the introduction of farming was rapid, and where it was introduced as a complete set of techniques and domesticates, as a package. Furthermore, it best fits those areas where farming rapidly replaced foraging (short substitution phase), where there is a break in settlement between the mesolithic

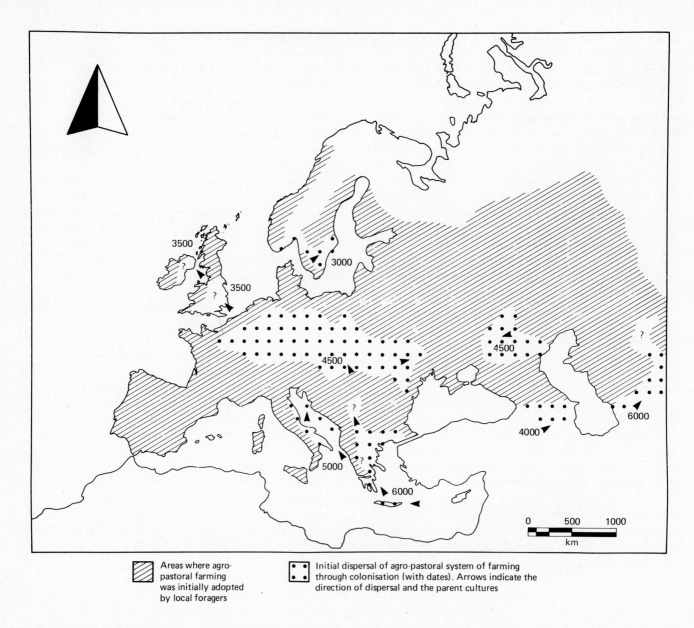

Fig. 10. Transition to farming as a colonisation process and as indigenous adoption. Dates are in years bc.

and neolithic sites, where the material culture of farming communities contrasts with that of the preceding hunter-gatherers and where it can be traced to a parent farming culture, and finally where there are no symbolic or ritual traces of ideology connected with hunting and gathering. Cultures which possess most or nearly all of the traits noted above include the early Greek and south Balkan Neolithic, the Tripolye culture, the Linear Pottery Ware (LBK), south Italian Impressed Wares, the Djeitun culture in Central Asia and the TRB culture in middle Sweden. At the same time it should be kept in mind that, in some of these areas such as southeast Europe, work on the Mesolithic has hardly begun. In those areas, such as Sweden or Central Europe, where extensive investigation has been carried out (cf. Kozłowski and Kozłowski, Chapter 7), it may be significant that, in almost

all these areas, mesolithic occupation appears to have been slight, and consisted of mobile, dispersed, generalised hunter-gatherer groups which could have been absorbed by the farming populations as a result of contact.

In contrast, the role of the indigenous populations appears to have been predominant in areas where the introduction of farming was too late (as in Eastern Europe) or too early (as in the western Mediterranean) to correspond to the expected rate. If we accept that these differences cannot be accounted for solely by geographical factors (seafaring accelerating the rate of spread in the Mediterranean, for instance, climatic factors delaying it in the north temperate zone), then the difference in the rate of dispersal *in both cases* probably reflects the receptivity of local hunter-gatherer to farming. Additional factors supporting this hypothesis include: selective and gradual, rather than complete and rapid, occurrence of farming; long availability phase and an extended transition from one form of economy to the other (long substitution phase); continuity in settlement; similarities in material culture between the neolithic and mesolithic communities; and retention of at least some aspects of hunter-gatherer symbolism and ritual into the Early Neolithic. Although not all of the cultures placed into the local adoption zone possess all the characteristics outlined above, most or nearly all are, in fact, present.

Not included in Fig. 10 are small-scale population shifts associated with secondary colonisation of less favourable environments, or situations with a mixed set of attributes, indicating neither of the two processes contrasted here. Despite this piecemeal and simplified picture, however, a pattern can be seen to emerge, which is far from the uniform,

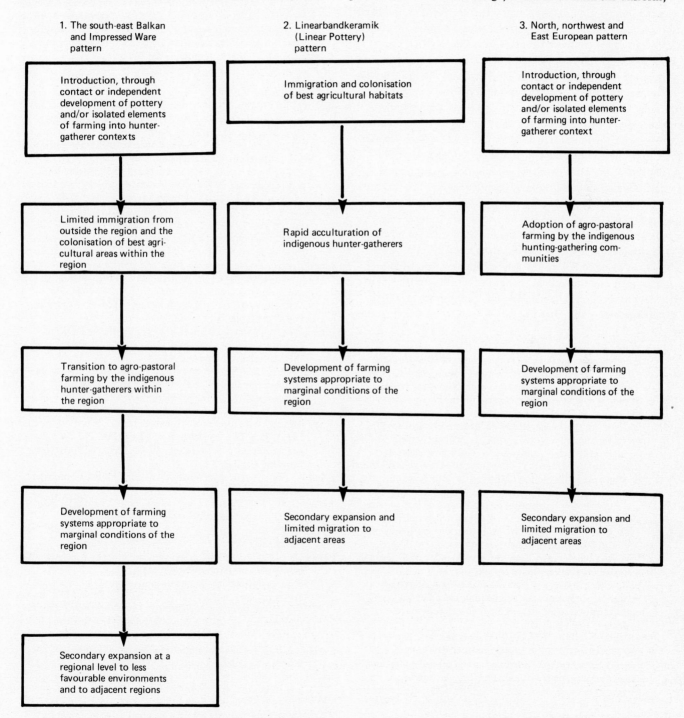

Fig. 11. Three different patterns of the development of agriculture in Europe.

unidirectional 'wave of advance' postulated by those favouring agricultural diffusion from the Near East. Rather, the dispersal of farming seemed to have occurred in outbursts of short duration, separated by periods of relatively stable frontiers. The actual role of farming populations in this process remains uncertain, as unequivocal evidence for actual colonisation remains elusive; but in those areas where a good case can be made for colonisation, it is best explained as a process of limited immigration on a regional scale (see Fig. 11), followed by the adoption of the agro-pastoral village farming by local hunter-gatherer communities. It is worth noting that there is far more evidence for population movements in Europe and temperate Asia during the Late Neolithic and the Bronze Age, reflecting presumably the increased productive capacity of farming systems adapted to local conditions, than there is at the beginning of the Neolithic. It would appear that, far from ending with the initial transition to farming, colonisation did not really begin until the end of the period. Seen from this perspective, the early neolithic colonisation, such as there was, loses much of its presumed significance.

These are preliminary patterns, and no doubt much of what is said here will be disputed and shown to have been inaccurate by subsequent discoveries. What we need now are case-studies oriented towards resolving the methodological problems associated with the agricultural transition and – as importantly – a theoretical framework which is sufficiently flexible to recognise the parallels and continuities between hunter-gatherers and farmers.

Notes

1 Despite frequent references to the process of intensification (Cohen 1977; Binford 1983; Price and Brown 1985) no objective measure of intensification has been developed. Intensification is not the same as increasing the range of resources used for food, or increasing the exploitation of any one particular resource, for these changes may be just opportunistic responses to the variation in resource availability, without actually involving an increase in labour input or in food procurement. It follows that intensification, often inferred on the basis of diversification or specialisation, is relative to the total range of resources available in the habitats (Zvelebil, 1986*b*).

In my view, intensification can be best defined in terms of increased labour investment (for a different view, see Ames 1985, p. 159, who equates intensification with overproduction). Although people can increase their labour input to *maintain* their food supply, extra labour investment will usually result in increased production. Defined in this way, intensification seems best assessed in terms of technological investment, settlement relocation, socio-economic organisation and other aspects of culture, converted into labour input as the most effective measure of intensification.

2 This was at least partly because cultigens and domesticates in these areas were at the ecological limits of their tolerance: farming was a high risk occupation, while specialised foraging in these areas was relatively productive. Edaphic conditions were uniformly poor and it was the availability of manure, rather than the quality of the soils, which was the limiting factor in the spread of farming. To increase the output of manure, animal husbandry had to be expanded, which in turn required an increase in the amount of fodder, by clearance, in the form of

slash and burn. This is why in Northern and Eastern Europe farming often begins with swiddening (produces fodder and short-term cereal harvest), continues with the development of animal husbandry (increases output of manure) and finally results in field cultivation. This process in itself, and the time needed for the development of cultigens and domesticates adapted to northern conditions, contributed to the length of the substitution and consolidation phases.

3 Seen in this perspective, it may be significant, for instance, that four out of the five individuals known to have been killed in the Mesolithic of Western Europe, date to the period after 4700 bc (Constandse-Westermann *et al.* 1984), a period when most of western Europe was located in the agricultural frontier zone (Chapter 12, Fig. 6; Chapter 6, Fig. 7).

References

Akazawa, T. (1981) 'Adaptation of prehistoric hunter-gatherers and their transition to agriculture in Japan', in S. Koyama and D. H. Thomas, eds., *Affluent Foragers*, pp. 213–60, Senri Ethnological Studies 9, National Museum of Ethnology, Osaka.

(1982) 'Cultural change in prehistoric Japan: receptivity to rice agriculture in the Japanese archipelago', in F. Wendorf and A. E. Close, eds., *Advances in World Archaeology*, pp. 151–212, Academic Press, New York and London.

Alexander, J. (1978) 'Frontier studies and the earliest farmers in Europe', in D. Green, C. Haselgrove and M. Spriggs, eds., *Social Organisation and Settlement*, pp. 13–29, BAR International Series 47, British Archaeological Reports, Oxford.

Ames, K. M. (1985) 'Hierarchies, stress and logistical strategies among hunter-gatherers in northwestern North America', in T. D. Price and J. A. Brown, eds., *Prehistoric Hunter-Gatherers. The Emergence of Cultural Complexity*, pp. 155–80, Academic Press, New York and London.

Ammerman, A. J. and Cavalli-Sforza, L. L. (1984) *The Neolithic Transition and the Genetics of Population in Europe,* Princeton University Press, Princeton, NJ.

Anderson, A. (1981) 'Economic change and the prehistoric fur trade in northern Sweden: the relevance of a Canadian model'. *Norwegian Archaeological Review* 14, 1–38.

Armelagos, G.J., Jacobs, K. H. and Martin, D. C. (1981) 'Death and demography in prehistoric Sudanese Nubia', in S. C. Humphreys and H. King, eds., *Mortality and Immortality. The Anthropology and Archaeology of Death*, pp. 33–8, Academic Press, New York and London.

Bahn, P. (1984) *Pyrenean Prehistory*, Aris and Phillips, Warminster, Wiltshire.

Barker, G. W. (1975) 'Early neolithic land use in Yugoslavia'. *Proceedings of the Prehistoric Society* 41, 85–104.

(1985) *Prehistoric Farming in Europe*, Cambridge University Press, Cambridge.

Bender, B. (1985*a*) 'Emergent tribal formations in the American midcontinent'. *American Antiquity* 50, 52–62.

(1985*b*) 'Prehistoric developments in the American midcontinent and in Brittany, northwest France', in D. Price and J. A. Brown, eds., *Prehistoric Hunter-Gatherers. The Emergence of Cultural Complexity*, pp. 21–51, Academic Press, New York and London.

Bergelund, B. E. (1969) 'Vegetation and human influence in south Scandinavia during prehistoric time'. *Oikos (suppl.)* 12, 9–28.

Binford, L. R. (1968) 'Post-pleistocene adaptations', in S. Binford and L. Binford, eds., *New Perspectives in Archaeology*, pp. 313–41, Aldine, Chicago.

(1983) *In Pursuit of the Past,* Thames and Hudson, London.

Bleed, P. (in press) 'The optimal design of hunting weapons: maintainability or reliability.' *American Antiquity*.

Braidwood, R. (1958) 'Near Eastern prehistory'. *Science* 127, 1419–30.

Childe, V. G. (1928) *The Most Ancient East: The Oriental Prelude to European Prehistory*, Kegan Paul, London.

 (1957) *The Dawn of European Civilisation*, Chaucer Press, Bungay, Suffolk.

Clark, G. A. (1983) 'The Asturian of Cantabria'. *Anthropological Papers of the University of Arizona*, University of Arizona Press, Tucson.

Clark, G. A. and Yi, S. (1983) 'Niche-width variation in Cantabrian archaeofaunas: a diachronic study', in J. Clutton-Brock and C. Grigson (eds.), *Animals and Archaeology*, vol. 1, *Hunters and Prey*, pp. 183–208, BAR International Series 163, British Archaeological Reports, Oxford.

Clark, J. G. D. (1980) *Mesolithic Prelude*, Edinburgh University Press, Edinburgh.

Clarke, D. (1976) 'Mesolithic Europe: the economic basis', in G. G. Sieveking, *et al.*, eds., *Problems in Economic and Social Anthropology*, pp. 449–81, Duckworth, London.

Cohen, M. N. (1977) *The Food Crisis in Prehistory*, Yale University Press, New Haven, Conn.

 (1981) 'Pacific coast foragers: affluent or over-crowded?' in S. Koyama and D. H. Thomas, eds., *Affluent Foragers*, pp. 275–95, Senri Ethnological Studies 9, National Museum of Ethnology, Osaka.

 (1985) 'Prehistoric hunter-gatherers: the meaning of social complexity', in T. D. Price and J. A. Brown, eds., *Prehistoric Hunter-Gatherers. The Emergence of Cultural Complexity*, pp. 99–114, Academic Press, Orlando, Fl. and London.

Coles, J. (1984) *The Archaeology of Wetlands*, Edinburgh University Press, Edinburgh.

Colinvaux, P. (1973) *Introduction to Ecology*, John Wiley, New York.

Constandse-Westermann, T. S. (1977) 'Mesolithic man in northwestern Europe: biological distances, genetic considerations'. *Journal of Human Evolution* 6, 195–209.

Constandse-Westermann, T. S., Newell, R. R. and Meiklejohn, C. (1984) 'Human Biological background of population dynamics in the western Europe Mesolithic'. *Human Palaeontology, Proceedings B* 87 (2), 139–223.

Dennell, R. (1983) *European Economic Prehistory*, Academic Press, London.

 (1985) 'The hunter-gatherer/agricultural frontier in prehistoric temperate Europe', in S. Green and S. M. Perlman, eds., *The Archaeology of Frontiers and Boundaries*, pp. 113–35, Academic Press, New York.

Dolukhanov, P. (1979) *Ecology and Economy in Neolithic Eastern Europe*, Duckworth, London.

Fitzhugh, W. (ed.) (1975) *Prehistoric Maritime Adaptations of the Circumpolar Zone*, Mouton, The Hague.

Flannery, K. V. (1969) 'Origins and ecological effects of early domestication in Iran and the Near East', in P. J. Ucko and G. W. Dimbleby, eds., *The Domestication and Exploitation of Plants and Animals*, pp. 73–100, Aldine, Chicago.

Frayer, D. W. (1980) 'Sexual dimorphism and cultural evolution in the Late Pleistocene and Holocene of Europe'. *Journal of Human Evolution* 9, 339–415.

Garrard, A. N. (1984) 'The selection of south-west Asian animal domesticates', in J. Clutton-Brock and C. Grigson, eds., *Animals and Archaeology*, vol. 3, *Early Herders and their Flocks*, pp. 117–32, BAR International Series 202, British Archaeological Reports, Oxford.

Geddes, D. S. (1985) 'Mesolithic domestic sheep in West Mediterranean Europe'. *Journal of Archaeological Science* 12, 25–48.

Gimbutas, M. (1970) 'Proto Indo-European culture: the Kurgan culture during the fifth, fourth and third millennia BC', in G. Cardona, H. M. Hoenigswald and A. Senn, eds., *Indo-European and Indo-Europeans*, pp. 155–196, University of Pennsylvania Press, Philadelphia.

Harris, D. (1977) 'Alternative pathways towards agriculture', in C. Reed, ed., *Origins of Agriculture*, pp. 179–235, Mouton, The Hague.

Hassan, F. A. (1981) *Demographic Archaeology*, Academic Press, New York and London.

Hayden, B. (1981) 'Research and development in the Stone Age: technological transitions among hunter-gatherers'. *Current Anthropology* 22, 519–48.

Henry, D. O. (1985) 'Preagricultural sedentism: the Natufian example', in T. D. Price and J. A. Brown, eds., *Prehistoric Hunter-Gatherers. The Emergence of Cultural Complexity*, pp. 365–84, Academic Press, Orlando, Fl. and London.

Jarman, M. (1972) 'European deer economies and the advent of the Neolithic', in E. Higgs, ed., *Papers in Economic Prehistory*, pp. 125–47. Cambridge University Press, Cambridge.

Jochim, M. A. (1976) *Hunter-gatherer Subsistence and Settlement*, Academic Press, London.

Koyama, S. and Thomas, D. H. (eds.) (1981) *Affluent Foragers*, Senri Ethnological Studies 9, National Museum of Ethnology, Osaka.

Kruk, J. (1973) *Studia Osadnicze nad Neolitem Wyżyn Lessowych*, Polska Akad. Nauk, Ins. Hist. Kult. Mat., Warsaw.

Lee, R. and De Vore, I. (eds.) (1968) *Man the Hunter*, Aldine, Chicago.

McCullough, D. R. (1970) 'Secondary production of birds and mammals', in E. D. Reiche, ed., *Temperate Forest Ecosystems. Ecological Studies*, vol. 1, pp. 107–30, Springer-Verlag, Berlin.

Mellars, P. A. (1976) 'Fire ecology, animal populations and man: a study of some ecological relationships in prehistory'. *Proceedings of the Prehistoric Society* 42, 15–46.

 (1985) 'The ecological basis of social complexity in the Upper Palaeolithic of southwestern France', in T. D. Price and J. A. Brown, eds., *Prehistoric Hunter-Gatherers. The Emergence of Cultural Complexity*, pp. 271–98, Academic Press, Orlando, Fl. and London.

Moberg, C. A. (1966) 'Spread of agriculture in the North European periphery'. *Science* 152, 315–19.

Modderman, P. J. R. (1958) 'Die Geographische Lage der bandkeramischen Siedlingen in der Niederlanden'. *Palaeohistoria* 6, 1–6.

Moore, J. A. (1981) 'The effects of information networks in hunter-gatherer societies', in B. Winterhalder and E. A. Smith, eds., *Hunter Gatherer Foraging Strategies*, pp. 194–217, University of Chicago Press, Chicago.

 (1985) 'Forager/farmer interactions: information, social organisation and the frontier', in S. W. Green and S. M. Perlman, eds., *The Archaeology of Frontiers and Boundaries*, pp. 93–112, Academic Press, New York.

Musil, R. (1970) 'Domestication of dog already in the Magdalenian?' *Anthropologie* 8 (1), 87–8.

Newell, R. (1984) 'On the Mesolithic contribution to the social evolution of Western European society', in J. Bintliff, ed., *Social Evolution*, pp. 69–82, University of Bradford, Bradford.

O'Shea, J. M. (1981) 'Coping with scarcity: exchange and social storage', in A. Sheridan and G. Bailey, eds., *Economic Archaeology. Towards an Integrated Approach*, pp. 167–83. BAR International Series S96, British Archaeological Reports, Oxford.

O'Shea, J. and Halstead, P. (eds.) (1987) *Bad Year Economics*, Cambridge University Press, Cambridge, in press.

O'Shea, J. M. and Zvelebil, M. (1984) 'Oleneostrovski Mogilnik: reconstructing the social and economic organisation of prehistoric foragers in Northern Russia'. *Journal of Anthropological Archaeology* 3, 1–40.

Perlman, S. (1980) 'An optimum diet model, coastal variability and hunter-gatherer behaviour', in M. B. Schiffer, ed., *Advances in Archaeological Method and Theory*, vol. 3, pp. 257–99, Academic Press, New York and London.

Phillipson, D. W. (1985) *African Archaeology*, Cambridge University Press, Cambridge.

Price, T. D. (1981) 'Complexity in "non-complex" societies', in S. van der Leeuw, ed., *Archaeological Approaches to the Study of Complexity*, pp. 55–97, Institut for Prae- en Protohistorie, Amsterdam.

    (1985) 'Affluent foragers of Mesolithic southern Scandinavia', in T. D. Price and J. A. Brown, eds., *Prehistoric Hunter-Gatherers. The Emergence of Cultural Complexity*, pp. 341–60, Academic Press, Orlando Fl. and London.

Price, T. D. and Brown, J. A. (1985) *Prehistoric Hunter-Gatherers. The Emergence of Cultural Complexity*, Academic Press, Orlando, Fl. and London.

Reed, C. A. (ed.) (1977) *Origins of Agriculture*. World Anthropology Series, Mouton, The Hague.

Rowley-Conwy, P. (1983) 'Sedentary hunters: the Ertebølle example', in G. Bailey, ed., *Hunter-Gatherer Economy in Prehistory*, pp. 111–26, Cambridge University Press, Cambridge.

Rowley-Conwy, P. and Zvelebil, M. (1987). 'Saving it for later . . . Storage and social differentiation among northern hunter-gatherers', in J. O'Shea and P. Halstead (eds.) *Bad Year Economics*, Cambridge University Press, Cambridge, in press.

Semenov, S. A. (1964) *Prehistoric Technology*, Adams and Dart, Bath.

Semenov, S. A. and Korobkova, G. F. (1983) *Tekhnologia Drevniikh Proizvodstv: Mezolit – Eneolit*, Nauka, Leningrad.

Sheehan, G. W. (1985) 'Whaling as an organizing focus in northwestern Alaskan Eskimo societies', in T. D. Price and J. A. Brown, eds., *Prehistoric Hunter–Gatherers. The Emergence of Cultural Complexity*, pp. 123–54, Academic Press, Orlando, Fl. and London.

Simmons, I. G. (1979) 'Late mesolithic societies and the environment of the uplands of England and Wales'. *Bulletin of the Institute of Archaeology* 16, 111–29.

Soffer, O. (1985) 'Patterns of intensification as seen from the Upper Palaeolithic of the Central Russian Plain', in T. D. Price and J. A. Brown, eds., *Prehistoric Hunter-Gatherers. The Emergence of Cultural Complexity*, pp. 235–70, Academic Press, Orlando, Fl. and London.

Spång, K., Welinder, S. and Wyszomirski, B. (1976) 'The introduction of the Neolithic Stone Age into the Baltic area'. *Dissertationes Archaeologicae Gandenses* 16, 235–70.

Sulimirski, T. (1970) *Prehistoric Russia*, Baker, London.

Suttles, W. (1960) 'Affinal ties, subsistence and prestige among coast Salish'. *American Anthropologist* 62, 296–305.

Testart, A' (1982a) *Les Chasseurs-Cueillers ou L'Origine des Inégalités*, Société d'Ethnographie, Paris.

    (1982b) 'The significance of food storage among hunter-gatherers: residence patterns, population densities and social inequalities'. *Current Anthropology* 23, 523–37.

Torrence, R. (1983) 'Time budgeting and hunter-gatherer technology', in G. Bailey, ed., *Hunter-Gatherer Economy in Prehistory*, pp. 11–23, Cambridge University Press, Cambridge.

Vankina, L. V. (1970) *Torfyanikovaya Stoyanka Sarnate*, 'Zinatne', Riga.

Watanabe, H. (1983) 'Occupational differentiation and social stratification: the case of Northern Pacific maritime food-gatherers'. *Current Anthropology* 24, 217–19.

Watt, K. E. F. (1973) *Principles of Environmental Science*, McGraw-Hill, New York.

Welinder, S. (1975) 'Agriculture, inland hunting, and sea hunting in the western and northern region of the Baltic, 6000–2000 BC', in W. Fitzhugh, ed., *Prehistoric Maritime Adaptations of the Circumpolar Zone*, pp. 21–39, Mouton, The Hague, Paris.

Winterhalder B. and Smith, E. A. (eds.) (1981) *Hunter-Gatherer Foraging Strategies*, Chicago University Press, Chicago.

Woodburn, J. (1982) 'Egalitarian societies' *Man* 17, 431–51.

Woodman, P. C. (1983) 'The Glencoy Project in perspective', in T. Reeves-Smyth and F. Hamond, eds., *Landscape Archaeology in Ireland*, pp. 25–35. BAR, British Series 116, British Archaeological Reports, Oxford.

    (1985) 'Mobility in the early Mesolithic of northwestern Europe: an alternative explanation', in T. D. Price and J. A. Brown, eds., *Prehistoric Hunter-Gatherers. The Emergence of Cultural Complexity*, pp. 325–40, Academic Press, Orlando, Fl. and London.

y'Edynak, G. (1978) 'Culture, diet and dental reduction in Mesolithic forager-fishers of Yugoslavia'. *Current Anthropology* 19, 616–17.

Živanović, S. (1975) 'A note on the anthropological characteristics of the Padina population'. *Zeitschrift für Morphologie und Anthropologie* 66, 161–75.

Zvelebil, M. (1980) 'Northern forest cultures and the arctic fringe', in A. Sherratt, ed., *Cambridge Encyclopedia of Archaeology*, pp. 320–4, Cambridge University Press, Cambridge.

    (1981) *From Forager to Farmer in the Boreal Zone*, BAR International series 115 (i and ii), British Archaeological Reports, Oxford.

    (1984) 'Clues to recent human evolution from specialised technologies?' *Nature* 307, 314–15.

    (1985) 'Iron Age transformations in north-east Europe', in C. Gamble and G. Barker, eds., *Beyond Domestication*, pp. 147–80, Academic Press, London.

    (1986a) 'Wetland settlement of Eastern Europe', in J. Coles and A. J. Lawson, eds., *European Wetlands in Prehistory*, Oxford University Press, Oxford, in press.

    (1986b) 'Economic intensification and postglacial hunter-gatherers in temperate Europe', in C. Bonsall, ed., *Proceedings of the 3rd International Symposium on the Mesolithic in Europe*, 1985, University of Edinburgh Press, Edinburgh, in press.

Zvelebil, M. and Rowley-Conwy, P. (1984) 'Transition to farming in northern Europe: a hunter-gatherer perspective'. *Norwegian Archaeological Review* 17, 104–28.

INDEX

Peer polity interaction and socio-political change
Edited by Colin Renfrew and John Cherry

Thirteen leading archaeologists have contributed to this forma-
tive study of the socio-political processes — notably imitation,
competition, warfare, and the exchange of material goods and
information — that can be observed within early complex
societies, particularly those just emerging into statehood. Their
common aim is to explain the remarkable formal similarities
that exist between institutions, ideologies and material remains
in a variety of cultures characterized by independent political
centres yet to be brought under the control of a single, unified
jurisdiction.

A major statement of the conceptual approach is followed
by ten case-studies from a wide variety of times and places,
including Minoan Crete, early historic Greece and Japan, the
classic Maya, the American Mid-West in the Hopewellian
period, early Bronze Age and early Iron Age Europe, and the
British Isles in the late Neolithic.

New Directions in Archaeology

Island societies
Archaeological approaches to evolution and transformation
Edited by Patrick Kirch

Concentrating their attention on the Pacific Islands, the contributors to this book show how the tightly focused social and
economic systems of islands offer archaeologists a series of
unique opportunities for tracking and explaining prehistoric
change. Over the last thirty years, excavation has revolutionized
Oceanic archaeology and, as the major problems of cultural
origins and island sequences have been resolved, archaeologists
have come increasingly to study social change and to integrate
newly acquired data on material culture with older ethnographic and ethnohistorical materials. The fascinating results
of this work, centring on the evolution of complex Oceanic
chiefdoms into something very much like classic 'archaic
states', are authoritatively surveyed here for the first time.

New Directions in Archaeology

Specialisation, exchange and complex societies
Edited by Elizabeth M. Brumfiel and Timothy Earle

This collaborative volume, the first comparative study of
specialised production in prehistoric societies, examines both
adaptionist and political approaches to specialization and
exchange using a worldwide perspective. What forms of
specialization and exchange promote social stratification,
political integration and institutional specialization? Can
increases in specialization always be linked to improved
subsistence strategies or are they more closely related to the
efforts of political elites to strengthen coalitions and establish
new institutions of control? Are valuables as important as subsistence goods in the developmental process?

These and other questions are examined in the contexts
of ten prehistoric societies, ranging from the incipient complexity of Mississippian chiefdoms through the more complex systems of West Africa, Hawaii and Bronze Age Europe,
to the agrarian states of Mesopotamia, Mesoamerica, Peru and
Yamato Japan. Each society is the subject of a separate study
by a scholar whose own research has provided new insights
into the interplay of specialization and exchange in the region
studied. An introductory overview by the editors develops the
more general implications of the essays that follow.

New Directions in Archaeology

Prehistoric farming in Europe
Graeme Barker

This book provides the first modern synthesis of our view of
prehistoric societies and our understanding of the processes
that allowed the change from hunting to farming. It draws on
data from waterlogged sites, analysis of small bone fragments,
environmental studies and social differences in settlements,
tools and weapons. Graeme Barker develops his argument
through analogies with the agricultural history of classical and
medieval Europe, and concludes that today's industrial farmers
can learn much from the successes and failures of early
European farming.

'His account is balanced, convincing and up to date. . . It is a
real achievement in its breadth of coverage and range of
reference.'   *The Times Higher Education Supplement*

'This is a volume which can be recommended without hesi-
tation to the student or interested layman as a "good buy".'
          Landscape History

New Studies in Archaeology

Production and exchange of stone tools
Prehistoric obsidian in the Aegean
Robin Torrence

The aim of this important study is to develop new methods
for reconstructing the processes of prehistoric exchange.
Recent archaeological work has concentrated on mapping
obsidian finds relative to source areas using trace-element
analysis and on investigating the effect of trade on particular
cultural groups. Dr Torrence, in contrast, draws extensively on
ethnographic analogy to develop a new approach which uses
differences in the level of efficiency for the acquisition of raw
materials and the productions of goods to infer the type of
exchange. Regional patterns of tool manufacture, specialist
craft production at central places and quarrying are analysed
in detail in the context of the prehistoric Aegean, and previous
ideas about the importance of trade in the growth of civiliz-
ations are re-assessed. The methodology developed will be
applicable to a wide range of artefact types and the book will
therefore be of value to archaeologists working in many different periods and places.

New Studies in Archaeology